APPROACHES TO WITTGENSTEIN

Approaches to Wittgenstein brings together for the first time many of the finest papers on Ludwig Wittgenstein, illuminating his philosophy by placing it in its biographical, cultural and historical context. Written by Brian McGuinness, well-known for both his biography of Wittgenstein and his work on Wittgenstein's philosophy, these papers represent fifty years of work on the most intriguing and fascinating of twentieth-century thinkers.

In the first section of the book, Brian McGuinness explains the close connection between Wittgenstein's life and work. He argues that Wittgenstein was deeply affected by his family, by his work as an architect, and by his experience of war and the powerlessness of his native Austria. The second section deals at length with Wittgenstein's famous *Tractatus Logico-Philosophicus*. McGuinness studies the book's origins and the 'picture' theory of meaning it presents, before going on to explore the central issues of solipsism, mysticism and the 'unsayable'. A third section considers the wider context of Wittgenstein's philosophy: his relation to the Vienna Circle, his philosophy of language and of mind, and his reactions to Freud and psychoanalysis. The final section is dedicated to Wittgenstein's highly individual methods of writing.

Of the twenty-four essays in this book, six are published here in English for the first time. *Approaches to Wittgenstein* will be essential reading for Wittgenstein scholars, and will also be appreciated by many with an interest in biography, history, philology and cultural studies.

Brian McGuinness was previously a Fellow of Queen's College, Oxford, and is currently Professor of Philosophy at the University of Siena in Italy. He is also Honorary Professor at the University of Graz in Austria. He has translated (with David Pears) Wittgenstein's *Tractatus Logico-Philosophicus* (1961) and *Prototractatus* (1971), both published by Routledge. He is the author of the acclaimed biography, *Wittgenstein, A Life: Young Ludwig 1889–1921*.

APPROACHES TO WITTGENSTEIN

Collected papers

Brian McGuinness

London and New York

First published 2002
by Routledge
11 New Fetter Lane, London EC4P 4EE

Simultaneously published in the USA and Canada
by Routledge
29 West 35th Street, New York, NY 10001

Routledge is an imprint of the Taylor & Francis Group

Typeset in Baskerville by Saxon Graphics Ltd, Derby
Printed and bound in Great Britain by Biddles Ltd, Guildford and
King's Lynn

British Library Cataloguing in Publication Data
A catalogue record for this book is available from the British
Library

Library of Congress Cataloging in Publication Data
Approaches to Wittgenstein: collected papers/Brian McGuinness.
p. cm.
Includes bibliographical references and index.
1. Wittgenstein, Ludwig, 1889–1951. I. McGuinness, Brian.

B3376.W564 A77 2001
192–dc21   2001049111

ISBN 0–415–03261–X

FOR GIOVANNA

CONTENTS

CONTENTS

PREFACE

The present collection requires some explanation if not justification. The papers here printed (alongside various editions and a volume of biography) result from a study, itself almost lifelong, of the life and work of Ludwig Wittgenstein. I did not want to leave them mouldering, as it were, in the obscurity, however undeserved, of the periodicals and languages where they first saw the light, for only a few have made their way into more widely known collections. Something was owed to the *lungo studio e il grand'amore*, the fascination that this philosopher had so long exercised on me, as on so many others. If the pieces were worth writing at all, they were worth putting together to give a general picture that might explain that fascination and perhaps to some extent justify the spending of so much time on the thought of another.

This last feature is more defensible in the sphere of philosophy than in most of the fields and disciplines into which learning is conventionally distributed, for it is a sphere in which the question why we are asking a certain question is almost as important as the question itself. Hence the evasiveness with which the practitioner is wont to meet the layman or child who asks to be told what philosophy is, a *Gretchenfrage* such as Faust faced when asked about religion. 'Don't ask' seems the only answer, in the sense that philosophical questions have to force themselves on one. Reflection on other matters or inside established disciplines leads to questions, which familiar methods do not suffice to answer. So it has been since Socrates, by whose time a number of sciences had been established, and so it was certainly viewed by the subject of these studies, who is famous for saying that the place of philosophy was above or below the natural sciences, not alongside them, and that its problems arose from a misunderstanding of the logic of our language. It was only twice that he gave a programmatic address at Cambridge, once on being appointed to his professorship and once to counter the effects of a paper given by Popper. On each occasion a quotation from Heinrich Hertz was central to his implicit definition of a philosophical problem: it would be one that resulted from our having associated too many ideas with a certain notion, and that was solved by unpicking them. There was (Hertz showed) no answer to the question, What is the definition of force? but once one had realized how the question came to be asked, steps could be taken to talk correctly about this subject matter.

Not only the activity of Wittgenstein and Hertz but the history of philosophy too is precisely the study of how and why certain questions arose and thus will be one particular form of the general activity of philosophy. Admittedly it was not the form that Wittgenstein's own thoughts took. He said that when he began to read an historical text – Hume was his example – he soon threw away the book and began to think about the problem for himself. Of course, what 'the problem' may be is itself a problem. He may have missed Hume's problem and found or invented another of his own. His friend Sraffa indicated this when he asked, about one of Wittgenstein's interlocutors, 'But has anybody ever actually made this confusion?'. Sraffa, whom Wittgenstein regarded as his severest critic, spent much of his time during the years of his closest association with the philosopher on the writing and rewriting of a devastating review of a paper by Hayek (who survived cheerfully enough). Sraffa's criticism and example may well explain much of the obsessional rewriting and revising that we observe in Wittgenstein's manuscripts.

This particular criticism may be countered by observing that when Wittgenstein was trying to get to the root of a way of thinking he was entitled to portray it in its crudest form. Many of the errors of reasoning in a Socratic dialogue are literary devices. The reader sees to his dismay or profit that what he thinks is after all not so dissimilar from the absurdity he reads. 'Strawson versus straw man', one of Russell's jibes, may not be a wholly useless form of argument (though it is by no means typical of Sir Peter Strawson).

One of the approaches to Wittgenstein from which this collection takes its title will be that of trying to think through the problems in his terms. Another, more indirect approach or at a higher level of historical awareness, if you will, is that of identifying the concerns of those who gave impetus to his thoughts, the 'influences' that he himself lists, and those also that he does not. In either type of influence we shall have occasion to see that he nearly always changed what he was given. He could not help rethinking a problem, trying to rise above the terms in which it was posed. This was his genius, if the word be permitted, but it was also his vanity. He criticized a near contemporary for not having his own problems (but dealing instead with Wittgenstein's). Thus another approach will be that of considering what sort of man this was for whom everything had to be new. We see him not as the product of but as conditioned by his family, its wealth, its culture, its fastidiousness, conditioned too by his time, its wars and depressions, the powerlessness of his native land, the experience of the émigré if not the exile. Finally thanks to the mass of his literary remains, we can follow the peripeties of the composition of his works: that constantly interrupted process also had an influence on his thought.

The essays are at various levels of difficulty, some frankly introductory, others following the texts, I hope faithfully rather than slavishly, and yet others catering to an interest in the intellectual background, while the final section presupposes a willingness to enter into the detail of manuscripts, versions and their stemmata. Once launched upon it is a fascinating subject, and I hope will here be found at least interesting on its own account, while it also gives an idea of what was involved in being a philosopher as far as Wittgenstein was concerned.

The variety of the papers reflects, dimly though it may be, the many-sidedness of their subject. It would be wrong to say of him, All human life is here. On the contrary, though there were many possibilities, there were equally many *Hemmungen*, complexes, which led to negation and sometimes to apparent contradiction, but they were *Hemmungen* grounded in human life, when lived with an intense desire for purity and perfection but with only human means of attaining them. The works too should be read with this in mind. A comparatively trivial example is the parallel between his struggle (inevitably self-frustrating) to be spontaneous and natural in human relations and the constant rephrasing of his philosophical writings in the search for a form of expression which should be incontestable.

So much to explain why the man and his work and life seem to me (and apparently to many others) worth exploration in depth. I allow myself these general remarks in a preface but nearly all the papers have more closely defined aims. I have not altered them much (except for the tacit and shamefaced correction of some gross errors) because they were written to throw light on the questions of their own time. To some extent they witness to the evolution of studies of this difficult thinker.

A rather personal account of how I myself came to those studies I have given in *Philosophical Investigations* (the periodical) of April 2001, where it will be seen how many debts I have incurred in how many countries, but in these pages too I must mention at least my chief mentors, first Balliol College, Oxford, that remarkable institution, in whose library I first picked up and read the *Tractatus*, then (also at Balliol) David Pears, with whom I first discussed it – learnt indeed what philosophical discussion was. There followed Gilbert Ryle, whose class on the book (then the only publication of Wittgenstein's available) introduced so many of us to the blend of historical and theoretical studies that with its strengths and weaknesses is characteristic of Oxford. Work on manuscripts and editions led into the exploration also of Wittgenstein's life: here I benefited by the encouragement and active assistance of Georg Henrik von Wright, not only successor of his teacher but chief prolonger of his work and memory. From the family I should mention John Stonborough, the true 'philosopher's nephew', who in innumerable letters and conversations enabled me to construct a picture, convincing to me at any rate, of life in that little world with its great privileges but exacting demands. My work took me often to Austria, where Rudolf Haller smoothed my path and helped me towards an understanding of another essential element in Wittgenstein's formation. Many other of my friends and colleagues have been laid under contribution, many librarians also, and former students or associates of Wittgenstein, from Cambridge or elsewhere.

Professionally I have worked closely and harmoniously with Joachim Schulte, one-time pupil and long-time colleague. In recent years I have been much assisted by collaboration with the Brenner Archiv of the University of Innsbruck thanks to Allan Janik. Monika Seekircher has tirelessly and even cheerfully answered my queries. The production of the present volume would have been impossible without the dedicated work of Anna Coda Nunziante, who resisted for me temptations to *Schlamperei*. For such as slipped through the net, I apologize.

The book was produced with the aid of research funds provided by the University of Siena. I am happy that it renews my long association with Routledge.

Brian McGuinness
Siena, June 2001

ACKNOWLEDGEMENTS

The papers collected in this volume originally appeared in the journals or collections here listed, though some have been reprinted or published in translation elsewhere.

Chapter 1, '"The lion speaks, and we don't understand." Wittgenstein after 100 years', in German as the title essay in *'Der Löwe spricht...und wir können ihn nicht verstehen'*. Proceedings of the Wittgenstein Centenary Conference at Frankfurt/M, Suhrkamp, Frankfurt, 1991.

Chapter 2, 'Philosophy and biography' in German as a part of the Vorwort to Ludwig Wittgenstein *Familienbriefe* (B. McGuinness, M.C. Ascher and O. Pfersmann eds), Hölder-Pichler-Tempsky, Vienna 1996.

Chapter 3, 'Asceticism and ornament' in German in the collection *Ornament und Askese im Zeitgeist des Wien der Jahrhundertwende* (A. Pfabigan ed.), Brandstätter, Vienna 1985.

Chapter 4, 'The idea of Jewishness' in German in the collection *Paul Engelmann (1891–1965): Architektur, Judentum, Wiener Moderne* (U. Schneider ed.), Folio Verlag, Vienna and Bolzano, 1999.

Chapter 5, 'It will be terrible afterwards, whoever wins' in the collection *Wittgenstein – towards a re-evaluation* (ed. R. Haller and J. Brandl), Hölder-Pichler-Tempsky, Vienna, 1990.

Chapter 6, 'The path to the *Tractatus*' in *Revista Portuguesa de Filosofia*, 38, 1982.

Chapter 7, 'Pictures and form' in the collection *Archivio di Filosofia*, 2–3, 1956.

Chapter 8, 'The supposed realism of the *Tractatus*' as 'The so-called realism of the *Tractatus*' in the collection *Perspectives on the Philosophy of Wittgenstein* (I. Block ed.), Blackwell, Oxford 1981.

Chapter 9, 'Language and reality' in *Teoria* 5, 1985.

Chapter 10, 'The *Grundgedanke* of the *Tractatus*' in the collection *Understanding Wittgenstein*, (ed. G. Vesey), Macmillan, London 1974.

Chapter 11, 'Philosophy of science' in *Revue Internationale de Philosophie*, 23, 1969.

Chapter 12, 'The value of science' (actually given as opening address at the 11th international Wittgenstein Symposium 1986) in the collection *Philosophy of Law, Politics, and Society*, (O. Weinberger *et al.* eds), Hölder-Pichler-Tempsky, Vienna 1988.

Chapter 13, 'Solipsism' in the collection *Wittgensteinian themes: essays in honour of David Pears* (W. Child and D. Charles eds), Oxford University Press, Oxford 2001.

Chapter 14, 'Mysticism' in *Philosophical Review* 75, 1966 (German translation in *Texte zum Tractatus*, Suhrkamp, Frankfurt 1989).

Chapter 15, 'The unsayable: a genetic account' (though here much expanded) in *Miscellanea Bulgarica* 13, Vienna, 1999.

Chapter 16, 'Wittgenstein and the Vienna Circle' in the special number of *Synthese*, 64/1985, on Moritz Schlick.

Chapter 17, 'Relations with and within the Circle' in German in the collection *Jour Fixe der Vernunft* (R. Haller and P. Kruntorad eds), Hölder-Pichler-Tempsky, Vienna 1991.

Chapter 18, 'Probability' in *Grazer Philosophische Studien* 16/17, 1982.

Chapter 19, 'Philosophy of language and philosophy of mind' in German in *Conceptus* 21, 1987.

Chapter 20, 'Freud and Wittgenstein' in *Wittgenstein and His Times*, Blackwell, Oxford 1981.

Chapter 21, '*On Certainty*: Comments on a paper by G.H. von Wright' in the collection *Problems in the Theory of Knowledge* (G.H. von Wright ed.), Nijhoff, The Hague, 1972.

Chapter 22, 'Bertrand Russell and the "Notes on Logic"' in *Revue Internationale de Philosophie*, 26, 1972.

Chapter 23, 'Some pre-*Tractatus* manuscripts' in *Wittgenstein in Focus – Im Brennpunkt Wittgenstein* (B. McGuinness and R. Haller eds), Rodopi, Amsterdam 1989 (also published as *Grazer Philosophische Studien* 33/34).

Chapter 24, 'Manuscripts and Works in the 1930s' in *Proceedings of the Lagopesole Workshop October 2000*, Pasquale Frascolla (ed.) Annali della Facoltà' di Lettere e Filosofia dell' Università' della Basilicata, Potenza, 2001.

In every case I am grateful to the editor or editors for permission to reprint the paper here.

ABBREVIATIONS

Manuscripts (MSS) and typescripts (TSS) are referred to under the numbers given in 'The Wittgenstein Papers' in von Wright 1982.

Briefe	*Briefe, Briefwechsel mit B. Russell etc.*
BüF	'Bemerkungen über Frazers *The Golden Bough*'
CL	*Cambridge Letters*
C&V	*Culture and Value*
Db	*Denkbewegungen, Tagebücher 1930–32*
FB	*Familienbriefe*
LCA	*Lectures and Conversations on Aesthetics*
LE	'Wittgenstein's Lecture on Ethics'
LF	'Logical form'
'LPA'	'Logisch-philosophische Abhandlung' (1921)
LPA	*Logisch-philosophische Abhandlung* (1989)
LH	*Ludwig Wittgenstein–Ludwig Hänsel: eine Freundschaft*
Nb	*Notebooks 1914–16*
NdM	'Notes dictated to G.E. Moore in Norway'
Nl	*Wittgenstein's Nachlass*
NL	'Notes on Logic'
OC	*On Certainty*
PhG	*Philosophical Grammar*
PhI	*Philosophical Investigations*
PhO	*Philosophical Occasions*
PhR	*Philosophical Remarks*
PT	*Prototractatus*
RoF	*Remarks on Frazer's* Golden Bough
TLP or *Tractatus*	*Tractatus Logico-Philosophicus*
WVC	*Ludwig Wittgenstein and the Vienna Circle*

Part I

THE MAN

1

'THE LION SPEAKS, AND WE DON'T UNDERSTAND'

Wittgenstein after 100 years

'Was der Gescheite weiß,' said Goethe, *'ist schwer zu wissen'*, – 'What a clever man knows is hard to know'; and there is truth as well as irony in this saying. Wittgenstein would be a very middling philosopher if he could be identified by his answers to a number of questions already posed for him. His merit is to have raised new questions himself. We know this in the history of philosophy – Socrates shocking the Athenians with the idea that it is better to do wrong deliberately, Plato explaining the good by generating the number series, Aristotle showing that the soul isn't in the body the way that a pilot is in a ship. None of these are questions that we can sensibly discuss as real issues: each at the time involved a change in paradigm, an escape from a restrictive framework (no longer our framework), that these great men made possible, and we learn much for all our thinking by following the processes, the hard work, that made the new conceptualization possible. And historically, of course, some of these advances led to whole new disciplines.

Wittgenstein reacted against two great idols of the early modern age – against metaphysics in his first book, against the ideal of progress to be achieved by natural science in his later writings. But it would be ridiculous to categorize him by these party-labels. *"Absage an die Metaphysik"! Als ob das was neues wäre!'* (' "Renunciation of metaphysics"! As if that were something new!'), he said to Waismann when the Vienna Circle manifesto was being planned. Not this slogan, but the work done by philosophers should be what they presented to the world. And his work – the *Tractatus* in this case – was a brilliant refutation of metaphysics by the use of its own methods. We must not think of him as akin to Kant – taking a different route to the same destination – because here it is the route itself that matters, not the form of words used at the end of it. Nor does his distrust of natural science put him in Heidegger's camp. He precisely does not think that there can be a superior science of ontology. The catalogue of misunderstandings could continue.

The important thing in Wittgenstein is usually not his position with regard to philosophical questions but his attempt to bring us not to ask

3

those questions at all. We speak – probably this is already an error – of the mind–body problem, of the problem of other minds, and so on, and are tempted to ask, Does Wittgenstein adopt a mentalistic or a behaviourist solution? And of course he is much nearer to the second of these: but it is misleading to say so, since he is not looking for a solution but is trying to get us not to accept the dichotomy between behaviour and the mental that creates the problems.

Wittgenstein's aim always was not to make cleverer moves than others within a given framework, but to change the framework which generated the problems. And not just that, but to give us the means to change frameworks for ourselves in other areas. Hence the puzzling nature of his works. In one passage he asks us to accept (he does not prove it) that if a lion could speak, we should not understand him. What a lion does and wants has nothing to do with language: language would not mesh into its life, to use another of his metaphors (of course, it may be possible to imagine circumstances which would alter the case). Now the point is, that often Wittgenstein too is so remote from what we are looking for, that we fail to understand him. Perhaps we lack a concept of what his life is about and how his philosophy meshes into it. We should not look in him for theories and for ingenious scepticism, as the bad habits of his profession led Saul Kripke to do. At every point Wittgenstein tries to put theory (as in his first book he put logic and science) in its proper place – and this can have good effects on theory as well as on practice. It is this that his method is suited to. He insists on extremely concrete and consequential thinking, on honesty to the phenomena, though he has great facility in handling abstractions. He avoids set positions as a basis for argument: everything must be up for reconsideration. He is a master in the invention and use of suggestive analogies (that of the lion, for example).

There have been many spin-offs of this method. In the foundations of mathematics, in linguistics, in social anthropology, in psychoanalysis, in psychology, in theology, in the foundations of the social sciences, and in new disciplines such as computing science and literary theory. He could have been – in spite of himself he was – an innovator in all of these fields. Think of the importance for the understanding of natural science and its history of the idea of revolutionary changes of paradigm, the brilliant idea of Thomas Kuhn, but inconceivable without Wittgenstein's work. Another development which has brought us closer to Wittgenstein's way of thinking is a perception of the limits (to some extent the disadvantages) of natural science as a motor of progress. Here Wittgenstein's own influence has counted, but there have also been at work other, in part obscure and irrational forces, contributing to a secular change in worldview such as he himself foresaw, though it is difficult to say to what extent he might have welcomed it.

And yet, even when there is this sympathy, do we really understand him? Rudolf Carnap used to describe the first impression made on him by Wittgenstein – a man informally dressed, without a tie, who immediately sat down on the floor to discuss something that surprised him. Carnap, serious, Germanic, a *Wandervogel* (member of one of the first Youth Movements, dissolved in 1933), thought he had found an ally and a friend. He was compelled to realize that any similarities between him and Wittgenstein were only superficial. The immediate occasion of the break between them was Wittgenstein's disapproval of an interest in parapsychology (the triviality of it all!), but this was only symptomatic of a fundamental divergence in value judgements, such as also emerged in Wittgenstein's relationship with Russell ('What would one not give for a little depth!').

And a similar misunderstanding was to underlie the adoption of Wittgenstein as a mascot by Berkeley students in the late 1960s: their printed T-shirts and departmental cats called Ludwig were an affirmation that his unconventionality was a step towards liberation and spontaneity in their sense: but he wanted freedom and spontaneity within quite strict limits and against a certain background. For, in fact, much that we have observed about Wittgenstein's philosophical method – the insistence on honesty about just what was at stake in any action, the rejection of received opinions as to fact or value – were features of his life too, or of what he wished his life to be. Like that of the ancient sceptics described by Sextus, his philosophy may be described as not a set of dogmas but a choice of life. At all events, in real life he was wont to set up for himself and for some circle in which he lived – family or friends – a programme of living in such a way that no issue was fudged and every departure from the highest standards in the few things that mattered was recognized as a failure and an occasion for improvement. This view of life as a task was far from making him an agreeable companion, but many accepted the challenge willingly. How it affected them later varied. 'He was a star in my life,' said one of his closest friends (a young girl when they were together) who thought all her life of the straightforward and unassuming behaviour that he insisted on. And yet, she had to go on to live her own life. When a chance to see her again came after an interval of war and many moves, he wrote, *'Wenn Du keine Dame mehr bist, würde ich Dich gerne wiedersehen'* ('If you're not still a lady, I'd be glad to see you'). She did not take this amiss, but it illustrates some of the difficulties of having to do with him. His sisters and aunts were ladies, surely, and he admired them. Everything turned on how a thing was done, and he was sometimes perhaps too quick to fear a falling-away.

In another case Wittgenstein discouraged a pupil (later a distinguished scholar) from work on philosophy: the point here though is that when this friend nonetheless returned to Cambridge, Wittgenstein felt (the friend too, I believe) that they no longer had anything to say to one another.

Others – schoolmasters, doctors, mathematicians, civil servants – stayed in touch with him and perhaps with one or two other members of their circle, still earnestly discussing what would be (or what would have been) best for one another.

The formation of such circles had much to do with the circumstances of Cambridge and the 1930s. It was a privileged life, and a life lived by young men or men who could still associate with the young, who still kept their youth. Surely Wittgenstein was such, but in this respect not specially exceptional for a don of his time. Nearly all (the young certainly) felt some guilt at the lot of the unemployed, and frequently their own prospects were far from clear. There were those to whom political solutions appealed, Cornford, Bell, Guest, and Hickman were the four Cambridge men killed in Spain – and three of them had been pupils, though critical, of Wittgenstein; while Skinner, the friend he had most influence over, attempted to volunteer. But Wittgenstein did not himself subscribe to a political programme. Religion appealed to others. In similar circles we find Thomas Merton, sent down from Cambridge, and Bede Griffiths in Oxford, both later to become monks: among Wittgenstein's friends there was Con Drury. Here again Wittgenstein had more sympathy than faith. His main contribution was to engage his friends or disciples in a moral enterprise characterized above all by the effort to see clearly and to be completely honest towards oneself and others. One disciple says:

> My own impression is that at some moment in his life – perhaps a moment of great difficulty and even despair – Wittgenstein may have made a resolution to live the rest of his life in a certain way and with a certain aim, and not to let himself be deflected by anything from this resolution. The aim might be described as that of doing his utmost to help others to think correctly about the important problems of life. To do this required that he should devote every bit of his time and energies with complete seriousness to the task and not allow himself to be distracted by lesser considerations of any nature.

This is a perceptive account: we need only add (what we see from his diaries) that Wittgenstein's task was just as much with his own self as with others. Of course, he will not always have lived up to his ideal, and, of course, there will often have been occasions when the ideal almost necessarily led to failures in spontaneity, in sympathy, in understanding. There was a danger (he saw it himself) of poring over the sick parts of the soul. Tolerance can perhaps hardly be mentioned.

Our theme however is not the rightness of Wittgenstein's ideals but the way he pursued them, for it is this that is essential to understanding his life and his work. What matters is not so much the particular ideals espoused (or in his work the particular ideas propounded) as the passion they called forth (a curious comment of Wittgenstein's on Soviet Russia in the early 1930s, 'The passion is an earnest of something'). The idea of dedicating everything to one main task and of that task's being to put one's own house in order, which includes recognizing one's own worthlessness, is bound to mean that political programmes, let alone a philosophy of morals, be set aside. A particular scandal is of course a different matter: one must attempt to put it right, but without theorizing, which (as he told Victor Gollancz) puts one 'on a wrong plane, on the plane of talk and inaction'. As for the relation of Wittgenstein's idea to religion – that room, as it were, into which he could not fully enter – this irked him all his life. With such preoccupations it was natural that in philosophy too his main aim was to see clearly and to avoid the evasions and confusions that we as men find attractive. But it would be this struggle each time that mattered, not the particular result. It would be no good if we rested on a happy formulation as a substitute for thought, any more than we can rely on the solution to an old moral problem in a new situation.

There is a parallel here from a quite other sphere: when Wittgenstein built a house for his sister, it was for her specifically that he built it (and so he always spoke of it). The woman friend already mentioned, who was there at the time, describes it very tellingly as an envelope for a certain form of life: the objects, persons, plants even, that were placed in it retained all their value. It was (in her figure) a perfectly proportioned jewel-case in which each of them found its place. He himself said it had required great understanding of a certain culture. And anyone who has seen it in something like its intended condition, with precious objects chastely displayed, will think that without them it has lost its soul.

Another feature which struck this friend (one of our best witnesses perhaps to the spirit that went into the house) was the contrast between the ugliness of its external aspect and the perfection, airiness, and harmony of the architecture of the interior – doors, windows, radiators and light bulbs so integrated as hardly to be seen as such.

Surely ugliness is too strong a word. Austerity might be a better one, but it is a particular kind of austerity: the wish to concentrate on the essential. It is important that the house should be luminous and adapted to a certain life, not that it should look such from the outside.

This brings us back to Wittgenstein's life, which we have been treating as a key to his work. There too we cannot avoid the word austerity, but, as with the house, it is an austerity which receives added meaning from a richness of background. He had experience of wealth and privilege. He had known famous old men (Brahms and all that was most eminent in

Vienna) and himself been cultivated by gilded young ones (the Cambridge Apostles before and between the wars). He had been an engineer, a soldier, an architect, a schoolmaster, hailed as the next great figure in philosophy, and yet also a gardener, a hospital technician, and briefly a factory worker. He had thought of being a monk, a psychiatrist, a doctor. He had tried his hand at sculpture and occasionally acted as a director of music. He knew Norway and Russia and he had seen the dissolution of Austria-Hungary. His personal life was far from empty: 'You think I'm just an old maid,' he said to one of his friends, 'but I say, Think again!' It was from a rich background and not from any lack of capacity that he chose to concentrate on a simple life with a perhaps unattainable moral aim and on his philosophical writing, lonely, often frustrating, and, as we now know, voluminous.

It may be asked whether this life was a success (we know that his last words were 'Tell them I've had a wonderful life') and here the answer is fortunately clear. The main point of such a life was to make clear the possibility of a certain ideal. By living it to the end in the way he did he showed us that that ideal could indeed be pursued. Of course a different man without those problems might have been happier but Wittgenstein showed how those problems could be met, and the modern interest in him shows that we have come to recognize his problems as those of our time.

His own writings, as much as anything that has been written about him, show the nature of that life. As he was fond of quoting: *Le style c'est l'homme même*', with emphasis on the last word. It is in the style that you see the real man. His work was to write, and the integrity that was his chief ideal means that his writings cannot belie him. There is variety in them: the *Tractatus* is in some measure oracular, deeply filled with meaning: the *Investigations* has startling philosophical jokes and it puts questions to the reader to involve him in a dialogue. Wittgenstein's letters to friends, fatherly sometimes, sometimes humorous, are always absolutely individual in their expression. The same is true even of letters of remonstrance, which his admirers might wish he had not written. The reader feels challenged by all Wittgenstein's writings, but it is an error to hope to reduce their message to a system. Better in the first place to feel their complexity, for in large part this complexity, the amount there is to be thought about in life – not excluding intellectual work – is their message. 'I'll teach you differences', as Wittgenstein used to say (a quotation from *King Lear*).

Just as communicating through language would not be a contribution to what a lion's life is about, so the development of a theory is not one of Wittgenstein's aims. We can indeed extract theories from his writings, but we understand him best – it is a truism – when we put ourselves into his frame of mind. There is the same sort of paradox in all his philosophy as is explicit in the *Tractatus*. All of it is meant to teach us that we should not look for a theoretical framework of justification for our practices and our sciences. They are best understood from inside: if we can bring ourselves to the fullest possible realization of each of them, then we shall have reached their essence. It will be seen that this renunciation of theory (strange aim for a philosopher!) is consilient with Wittgenstein's dislike of rhetoric in literature, his distaste also for any too emphatic interpretation of a musical work – even young Karajan failed to please him. Consilient too with what we may call his Protestantism, for that seems to have been the tone of the life of his family, despite the nominal Catholicism of his own branch and its strong admixture of Jewish ancestry. Not everyone will agree with these choices, but it is important to be alive to them when considering Wittgenstein. His is a negative philosophy in the sense of the deliberate renunciation, rather than the mere absence, of certain procedures. In life and in art his ideals lay in a form of restraint (though note that there had to be something to restrain – the 'wild beast tamed' that he felt was lacking in his house for his sister): philosophy too had to be a *docta ignorantia* or elected silence (the phrase from Hopkins used as an alternative title for Merton's book). Yet the final result (so far as Wittgenstein was successful) is not negative: consisting rather in a truer understanding of realities, an effective entry into them. This building too is modest and even repellent in its outward aspect but glorious within.

2

PHILOSOPHY AND
BIOGRAPHY

'Das Rätsel gibt es nicht', 'The riddle does not exist', said Wittgenstein in one of the more puzzling apophthegms in his *Tractatus* (6.5). The difficulty in philosophy is only that of looking at things from the right point of view, or to put it negatively that of avoiding *die falsche Fragestellung* (asking the wrong question). This may require a lot of work, but the result is the disappearance of difficulties. Perhaps his life too, which many have found *rätselhaft*, a riddle in itself, is in fact the answer to a different question from the ones we are inclined to ask. Our difficulties here are those of seeing what he wanted his life to be; only then can we judge how successful he was in it.

To take a question quite often rhetorically asked, but perhaps a *falsche Fragestellung* for all that: Did he see himself as Austrian or English? The answer may seem obvious, yet in both countries he stood out as a wilfully exceptional figure. His working and thinking language was German: it is fair to say that in English his letters (for example) are extremely telling, but perhaps not quite natural. *Die Schlichtheit*, the unaffectedness, of his German is missing. That is the quality he sought in his favourite authors, Keller, Hebel, Wilhelm Busch, Tolstoy (at any rate the Tolstoy of the folktales), above all Dostoevsky. In some of Tolstoy and of C.F. Meyer this topples over into the didactic or the faux-naif. On the other hand Wittgenstein's philosophical problems (not, as many suppose, self-generated) mostly came from Cambridge – from Russell, Ramsey, and Moore; a word from Sraffa would put him on a new track: *hinc lucem et pocula sacra*, as that university's motto has it. (Even the Vienna period 1927–9 was principally important for the contact with Brouwer, of whom Ramsey had already told him.) There was an austerity in the little world of the Cambridge of the 1930s that suited him. Ramsey can be taken as typical of it and now, from the 1920s on this type was preferred to seminal but flawed figures such as Kraus, Freud, and Russell.

Was Wittgenstein a positivist or an anti-positivist? Well, he refused to choose between physicalism and phenomenalism: false alternatives since both are equally possible. To be sure, he preferred the realists Hertz and

Boltzmann to the reductionist Mach, but he thought the question of the reality of the physical elements unimportant. Always he wanted to get behind, to get above the alternatives presented to him. This was his originality, which he defended so fiercely for his works. And defended in his life: for he would not let Vienna or Cambridge define him. As a boy he wanted to get as far away as possible, hence Linz, hence Berlin. Hence, later, Norway and Connemara. Hence (one may venture the thought) his renunciation of his inheritance: it would have confined him: 'You don't take a heavy rucksack to climb a mountain,' was how he explained it to a nephew.[1]

Two keys that have been tried and have broken in the lock may be briefly discussed. Wittgenstein himself used one – in the 1930s (significantly) he described his form of originality as a typically Jewish one, reproductive rather than creative. At the same time we know that he often, to his later shame, minimized his Jewish blood. There is a *scintilla* of truth in the remark about originality as applied to Wittgenstein himself: we have mentioned that his problems always came to him from elsewhere. Generalized to the Jewish race (if there is such a thing) the observation is puerile. But the more important point is that, *sub specie aeternitatis*, he was right to minimize his Jewishness. The tradition, the thought, the practices of no part of Jewry entered into his upbringing. Nor, to much extent, did Christianity. He sought complete honesty, complete emancipation and was fierce with priests (Russell reports) but at a certain point, following Tolstoy, he invented a religion for himself, and then, to be sure, on a New Testament basis. A deep concern with religion remained always with him but, as with so many of his generation, was most marked in and after the First World War. Socially, as well as religiously, he wanted to be like *Steinklopferhans* who had such a strong effect on him in *Die Kreuzelschreiber*,[2] *'kein Christ und kein Heid' und kein Türk'* ('not a Christian, nor a pagan, nor a Muslim either'). And it is simply not true that 'Jews' have more need than others to be emancipated, unless we are to take seriously the joke that they are like everybody else, only more so. Wittgenstein, whatever he was, was certainly 'more so'.

Another identity, this time foisted on Wittgenstein, is the homoerotic one. Whether such an identity exists at all, or at all times in the same form, is not the question here. The point is that it did not exist for Wittgenstein. He didn't see this as the problem. Sexuality and its powerful effect on life, fidelity, love loyalty, yes. But not the sex of the loved one.

---

1 *'Wenn du auf einen Berg gehst, nimmst du einen schweren Rucksack mit?'* Reported in *LH*, p. 290.
2 From Act II, scene i of the play by Anzengruber. For its effect on Wittgenstein see McGuinness, 1988, pp. 94, 114.

11

Surely enough has been published about his various confessions and the reproaches he heaped on himself to show this. The new notebook written in periods of isolation in Norway and now given to the world by the Koder family is painful reading in its dwelling on faults and shadows of fault, but has no hint of this particular source of guilt. (The suggestion that it was Wittgenstein's problem even though he didn't realize it, I shall consider later: in a subtle way it too involves a *falsche Fragestellung*.)

It is striking that these two, on the face of it, very different classifications are used to explain the same phenomena.[3] Peter Stern[4] relates how an Austrian writer said of Wittgenstein's talk about forms of life and everyday language, *'letzten Endes sind das doch nur jüdische Tüfteleien'* ('in the end it's just a lot of Jewish quibbling'), while, in my own reading, a prominent littérateur has described language games as a typically homosexual idea. There are two errors here: first an exceptional individual is regarded as an affront and has to be categorized; secondly the categories chosen are anything but homogeneous – they would 'explain' anything.

A better key to at least one of the locks on this enigma is to be found in a concept dear to Wittgenstein and not by accident: the concept of family resemblances. We understand him better if we do not try to find the intersection of classes that defines him, but a number of features occurring here and there, variously conjoined, among a whole group, and in the present case precisely among his family, in particular his brothers and sisters. It was a family that because of its wealth but also because of its self-confidence as a group was able to create its own world with its own support-system, its own values, its own *clientela*, in the old Roman sense – persons of every degree, artists, musicians, students, friends and associates of every kind were invited, protected, employed, subsidized, in a word absorbed. Wittgenstein brought his friends into it and they usually became the friends and protégés of everyone – Engelmann, Hänsel, Koder and others. He found friends there too, already half made, so to speak, and at least once a sweetheart. This is what he was – *kein Heid' und kein Türk*, so to speak, but a Wittgenstein. There he found, because he helped to create, the ethos of always doing the hard thing, the intolerance of anything perceived as moral weakness (strongest when a close relative was involved). 'The older generation,' another nephew told the present writer, 'didn't stop short of the other person's conscience.' Potential weakness might be recognized, but they were slow to think that

---

3 Yet the confusion is not uncommon: Charles Rosen has occasion to say, 'There is no specifically homosexual sensibility any more than there is a specific Jewish sensibility, two attractive fictions that Susan Sontag conflated in her well-known essay on camp', Rosen, 2000, p. 269.
4 Stern, 1989, pp. 30–1.

laying a person's faults clear would not be sufficient to make him amend them. Such were Margaret Stonborough's or, to use Ludwig's name for her, Gretl's '*Kopfwaschen*' (dressings down) to her brother Paul, and no doubt to many others. And at the end, when a person had to be broken with because he had done the easy thing – the comfortable, the self-interested, sometimes merely the obvious thing – there was a certain attitude of 'Naturally' or '*Der ist ein armer Kerl*' ('Poor devil').

A severe world then, with a sword over the gate, but an Eden none the less, marked by warmth and love and confidence and *Teilnahme* (feeling for the other), feeling for one another: these were the positive aspects of the candour that sometimes wounded. And all seemed, was made to seem, unforced and natural. (*Schlichtheit*, the willed simplicity we have mentioned, was once again the ideal.) It was a rarefied moral universe but much else as well and those taken into it were usually captivated immediately. How many became admirers, like Frank Ramsey, of Gretl; how many like Desmond Lee found on the *Hochreit* a hospitality reminiscent of Victorian times! In the same way a chance meeting with Wittgenstein on a train would convince Gilbert Pattisson that he had met an extraordinary man.

The moral basis of this universe was not distinct from the intellectual, the cultural, the artistic. Taste was not second to, but integral with the moral sense. Pictures, furniture, drawing, above all music were expressions of a single ideal. Drawing could be honest, pictures ethical, the piano could be played with due restraint, the furnishing of a house could be *wohltuend* (gratifying).

Intellectually strenuous also. Some rational occupation was required and conversation could be exacting. From childhood there had always been intellectual pursuits, psychological games, a simple code, theatricals (often self-composed), exchange of reading, passages marked for special attention. Most of these have left their traces in Wittgenstein's philosophical examples and his diary and in the family correspondence, not only on his side.

Descriptions of this world have been given by Menger in his memoirs,[5] and, long since, by Engelmann.[6] Marguerite Respinger describes for her grandchildren both the marvels she found in it and the demands it made on her – a fairy-tale setting of splendours and miseries, boxes at the opera, animated gatherings, jewels, recitals, buffets, with on the other hand good works among the hopeless poor of Vienna and serious walks with the compelling figure of our Wittgenstein, tweed-jacketed and open-necked whatever the occasion.[7]

5 Menger, 1994.
6 Engelmann, 1967.
7 Marguerite Sjögren, 1982.

Cecilia Sjögren relates the family's relation to music and the arts.[8] Wittgenstein's building of a house for Gretl (a joint project in many respects) has been analysed in detail by Paul Wijdeveld.[9] The structure of the *clientela* I have mentioned is illumined by the correspondence between members of the family and Ludwig Hänsel recently published.[10]

No doubt then that the Wittgenstein that came to Cambridge and his work could say with the hero,

> *Denn nicht komm' ich aus Nacht und Leiden,*
> *Aus Glanz und Wonne komm' ich her!*[11]

but like that hero he brought with him problems enough for his hosts and for himself. For he carried everywhere with him the preoccupations of that moral universe. His rejection of some features of it – the renunciation of his fortune, his wish at times not to be identified as member of a rich and powerful family (the secret of his name, as it were) – are in a sense also 'family resemblances', because they stemmed from his determination to make his own world and in particular to forge his own character. In a yet fuller sense than his father he was to be a 'self-made man'.[12] We see this in his determination to root out real or imagined defects of character – cowardice, laziness, a tendency to take refuge in lies. 'Cambridge is bad for many people because it is airless,' he told pupils or followers, 'but I produce my own oxygen.' He assembled his own court – like the *clientela* of his family – but the aim was more markedly a moral one: *'Ich bin ein Sammler von guten Menschen'*, he told one protégé, in which project he was sometimes successful.[13] A certain exclusiveness was an inevitable result: *secretosque pios, his dantem iura Catonem.*[14]

---

8 Cecilia Sjögren, 1989, pp. 98–117.

9 Wijdeveld, 1994.

10 *LH*. The editors have, surely misguidedly, stinted us, perhaps from motives of misplaced delicacy, of the replies by Hänsel (transcripts of which exist) to the severer letters of Wittgenstein. The friendship, the interaction, is precisely what is not shown. Hänsel's relations with the family, however, are exhaustively represented.

11 So Lohengrin in Act III when questioned about his origin: 'I come not from darkness and suffering, / I come from splendour and delight'.

12 Any reader of Karl Wittgenstein's essays will recognize this as his ideal, largely fulfilled; though for him too family connections and at times family investments (amply repaid) were the springboard.

13 'I collect good people,' though, as Gretl saw it: 'All Lucki's swans [were] geese'. But then finding swans was not the point. Perhaps the difference between brother and sister comes out here.

14 Vergil, *Aeneid* viii 670: 'Far apart were the good, with Cato giving them laws'.

This programme gives sense to his exclamation, 'Of course I want to be perfect!', gives sense also to the rules for the *minutiae* of life in his circle as well as to the agonizing over major decisions.[15] Here is the true *locus* outside philosophy for the construction of language-games, *Tätigkeiten* (activities), *Lebensformen* (forms of life), for the rejection of private language.

From such a programme paradoxes and failures were inseparable. An obvious one is that he often felt forced to retreat into isolation. More generally the insistence on *Schlichtheit* led almost inevitably to occasional artificiality, insincerity, exaggeration. Naturalness is the hardest of qualities to force. Thus he created for himself the figure of Wittgenstein the teetotaller, the old maid, the virgin, the shunner of great houses. It was redeemed of course by a measure of self-deprecation and by his obvious familiarity with the grander life that he had rejected. None the less there were some few who regarded him as 'another of those Cambridge charlatans, like F.R. Leavis', a judgement grossly unjust to both men, yet somehow in keeping with their lack of respect for forms.

Severity, as with himself, so with his disciples and friends, was not to be avoided. One pupil, after a particularly hard struggle, wrote, 'I'm tired of his going about laying down the moral law And yet there is a very great deal in him to love'.[16] Everyone realized that these aspects were indivisible. The earnestness was an essential part of his charm.

We have spoken of *falsche Fragestellungen* and a further two, at least, remain to be set aside. The fundamental one is perhaps the wish for an explanation, perhaps drawn from depth psychology. Here the error is particularly obvious if we ask, An explanation of what? We need to see what Wittgenstein's life was before we ask why he adopted it. The first explanation to be given is the internal one. We study his life because it shows us something we did not know before about what can be made of life itself. It is not something obvious or pathological, where the only interest is how it came about. We are not now to cure him nor is it of much interest how he would have behaved had he been a different person. Yet these absurdities are implicit in the attempt to apply posthumous psychoanalysis.

Still, it may be asked, what good came of it at last? Was he happy? This is perhaps the final *falsche Fragestellung*. There is not a standard happiness against which his life can be measured. He himself asked in his First World War Notebooks whether we have any more right to wish a person happiness than to wish him misfortune: the most we can say is *'Lebe glücklich!'* –

---

15 So, in his family, there were problems about how to celebrate Christmas and also how to react to the *Anschluß*.

16 See *CL*, p. 261.

Live happily! – which in context means something like, Live your life to the full![17] Happiness, on this view, is not something found in life but something put into it. Thus after the First World War it was his own life he was insisting on living. His last words also, 'Tell them I've had a wonderful life', are puzzling only if we ignore this conviction of his.

17 Entry for 29.7.1916 (*Nb*, p. 78)

Allgemein wird angenommen, daß es böse ist, dem Anderen Unglück zu wünschen. Kann das richtig sein? Kann es schlechter sein, als dem Anderen Glück zu wünschen?
Es scheint da sozusagen darauf anzukommen, wie man wünscht.
Man scheint nicht mehr sagen zu können als: Lebe glücklich!

It is generally assumed that it is evil to want someone else to be unfortunate. Can this be correct? Can it be worse than to want him to be fortunate?
Here everything seems to turn, so to speak, on how one wants.
It seems one can't say anything more than: Live happily!

3

ASCETICISM AND ORNAMENT

Asceticism and ornament[1] – it is hard to think of a man for whom this contrast is so important as for Wittgenstein (T.E. Lawrence is one of the few parallels). We know how fiercely Wittgenstein avoided the one and embraced the other. We have been told of the scrupulous simplicity of his later life, of his renunciation of his inheritance, of the small sums he needed for his own support. We know also that for him, as for his mentor Weininger, there was an obvious inner connection between logic, ethics, and aesthetics. Our task now is to tease out the unifying idea behind all this, if indeed it exists. Was there a single model exemplified in his life and thought or were there conflicting elements in his views as in his personality? Perhaps too there was no uniform idea throughout his life but rather changes, as there surely were in his circumstances and his occupations. Simplicity was always an essential for him: not so economy in the means used to achieve it. Was there, then, an essential change in his preferred model of life, leading perhaps to the voluntary choice of poverty? And were some elements in the supposed whole mere matters of taste? Wittgenstein used to say that his preference for simple food and furniture was exactly that, and by no means a merit of his.

To begin in the field of aesthetics: we can see from his earliest preserved letter how he undertook to explain the principles of painting to his sister Hermine. (A breathing example of the strong educative tendency of the Wittgensteins, for in fact she was the painter, not he.) He told her she should train herself on simple geometrical solids and display their relative situation and their shadows. An object should always be represented as a solid and not as a plane surface. So she should draw in the invisible sides as well. The same note is heard thirty years later, when he tells the daughter of his friend Haensel that she should draw

---

1 'Ornament und Askese', *Asceticism and ornament as seen by the Zeitgeist of Vienna at the turn of the century*' was the title of a symposium organized in Vienna in June 1985 by Dr. Alfred Pfabigan. This paper was first given there.

'*aufrichtig*', 'honestly'. And it is reminiscent of what the same sister, no philosopher, said even later, in her memoirs, about the collection of pictures made by her and Ludwig's father. Segantini, Rudolf von Alt and others were represented. A Goya which charmed the young Hermine was rejected because it would have been out of place – *es wäre herausge-fallen*. The daughter felt that all the pictures admitted were marked by *eine gewisse ernste Ruhe* – a certain calm seriousness, a stressing of the horizontal and vertical which she wanted to describe as 'ethical'.

We can see an approach to the ethical in the taste of Wittgenstein's early years (the period before the First World War). All his possessions had to be chaste and simple, *schlicht* would be the German word, but this by no means implied that expense was avoided. On the contrary he insisted on the best materials. Ornament was not excluded but was restricted to a minimum, so that it really achieved its effect, like the rare metaphor in a speech of Demosthenes that strikes the hearer like a sudden ray of light. So too Wittgenstein wanted it to be in his own written style.

Examples of this tendency are some of the books in Wittgenstein's library which Russell, by a friendly arrangement, purchased after the First World War when Wittgenstein needed to realize his possessions in English currency. The books most important for their owner were bound in the costliest manner. Especially lavish was the decoration on the spines and covers of a set of Leonardo da Vinci's notebooks. But the jewels of the collection were the works of Frege, two slim volumes in a Wiener Werkstätte binding of black morocco, coarse grained, with deeply recessed stamped titles (Wittgenstein's titles), spaced letters in thick gold leaf: '*Begriff der Zahl*' (*Concept of Number*) for *The Foundations of Arithmetic* and '*Formelsprache*' (literally, *Formula-Language*) for *Begriffsschrift* (*Conceptual Notation*). *Simplex munditiis*, so to speak.

This note of luxury was not recommended to his friend Eccles, but the same plainness and order. The two engineers discussed how Eccles's new house should be furnished and were agreed on the exclusion of ornament. Wittgenstein was, as usual, the critic and adviser: in July 1914 he wrote to Eccles,

> I can't see any drawing of a bed; or do you wish to take the one which the furniture manufacturers submitted? If so, do insist that they cut off all those beastly fancy ends. And why should the bed stand on rollers? You're not going to travel about with it in your house!? By all means [probably 'At all events' is meant] have the other things made after your design![2]

2 *Briefe*, p. 248.

In the same letter Wittgenstein pronounces 'splendid' the simple drawings for a wardrobe, a medicine chest, and a dressing table prepared by Eccles. His only suggestion for improvement was that the horizontal crosspiece on the doors of the wardrobe should be placed in the middle, so that the upper and lower panels would be of the same height, a more unconventional arrangement then than now. As for the decoration, Wittgenstein prevailed upon Eccles to plan a room with a royal blue carpet, black woodwork, and yellow walls. An uncompromising solution even in those last days of the arts and crafts movement.

He could give yet freer rein to his taste when it was a matter of furnishing a room for himself. These were the former rooms of his friend Moore, at the top of a tall neo-Gothic tower at the end of two narrow courts that stretch away from Trinity Gate on the opposite side of the street to the main college. Here was just the place for a quiet and private life, with a view towards the river over the town of Cambridge and away from the spires and courts of the University. Here Wittgenstein chose to live even later, as a Fellow, though he could have had much finer (to most tastes) and more comfortable rooms. There are many stories from the 1930s and 1940s of how the undergraduate noise around him and the lack of comforts (if a bathroom merits such a description) irked him. Yet they were his choice.[3] The Spartan aspect of the accommodation perhaps recommended it to his later moods, but he seems at all times to have liked neat and manageable quarters, and there is a kind of logic in a retiring man's preference for a tower: Wittgenstein was to seek one also during the First World War, regardless of the many steps up.

Pinsent in his diaries tells us how the search for furniture was conducted: Wittgenstein shouting, 'No! Beastly!' at ninety per cent of what the Cambridge shopman showed them. So the two went to London, where also Wittgenstein found unnecessary ornament in most of what they saw. Finally he decided to design most of the furniture for himself, 'Rather quaint but not bad,' Pinsent thought. The best materials were used and numerous modifications were carried out: in March 1913 we find him replacing the white marble top of a sideboard by one in black specially cut and polished in London. This is a very modern sort of simplicity and an expensive luxury.

It does not seem that the subordination of design to function, in the sense of intended use, would be an accurate description of Wittgenstein's tastes. These were connected, very typically for him,

---

3 The choice, too, of A.E. Housman, surely one of the most distinguished, though not the most agreeable, of the other fellows. He, however, had a bathroom (and would not share it with Wittgenstein). *Fallentis semita vitae* suited perhaps both poet and philosopher.

with his views on the value of abstract education. He used to say that mathematics would promote good taste, 'since good taste is genuine taste and therefore is furthered by whatever makes people think truth-fully'.[4] Speaking to Russell he emphasized construction as the decisive feature. A thing must be fully the thing it was; and life must go on around it in the way appropriate to that. Thus Eccles's bed, as we have just seen, was not to have rollers: it was to be a thing around which people moved. Similar features appeared later in Wittgenstein's archi-tectural work – for example the centrally or symmetrically placed light bulbs giving an even illumination, impersonal, not carefully adapted to some special need or preference of the user. For his Cambridge rooms in 1912, he chose porcelain beakers bought from a medical supplier or laboratory outfitter in London instead of cups, 'because they look so much nicer – but they are less convenient!', said Pinsent. His room had, though, one *Prunkstück* or showpiece, a large, almost square dining table, seating eight. It was made of peculiarly dark sombre mahogany with ornate carved Victorian legs. Conrad Russell recalls that his parents (into whose hands the table, along with the books already mentioned, came) used to discuss whether, on some special occasion, to dine on 'Wittgenstein'.

When Adolf Loos met Wittgenstein in 1914 and exclaimed, 'You are me!', it was surely an identity in taste that he detected: whether there was also one in style of thought is a question I shall return to. It was of architecture that the two immediately spoke, Wittgenstein characteristi-cally speaking with energy on the subject and profession of the older man. But he was at once accepted as an equal. Later, with Paul Engelmann, the pupil of Loos, he built the house that we have referred to: it echoes Loos's work in many features, for it is quite bare of orna-ment and it is exceptionally successful, at any rate in the lower storeys, in avoiding a division into floors: levels interlock and flow into one another. The stress on the vertical is not Loosian: the tall and narrow doors and windows, are reminiscent, rather, of Cambridge (where, certainly such features had impressed Margaret Stonborough, for whom the house was being built). They may also echo Wittgenstein's love of towers.

The house is of particular interest, because, though built nearly ten years after the First World War, it has much in common with the costly simplicity, almost the artificial artlessness, of Wittgenstein's pre-war taste. Note the high cost of the materials employed, the floors of

---

4 As reported by Bertrand Russell in a letter to Ottoline Morrell, 17 May 1912. See McGuinness, 1988, pp.131–132 which (as yet unpublished) I was drawing on here.

polished concrete, the metal fittings filed correct to the nearest millimetre, the ceiling raised by centimetres to achieve the correct proportions. Note also the fact that the house was planned to be and was in fact used as a frame for something else. It was a setting for art treasures, for a household and a style of life based on adherence to standards which no longer exist. So as a house it presupposed something else: it was never intended to be seen as an empty shell. In Bernhard Leitner's book about the house[5] there is a striking contrast between the photographs from the inhabited period and those from when the house stood empty. Chinese wallhangings, Klimt's portrait of Mrs Stonborough, classical statues, showcases for porcelain and glass, the coming and going of rich and poor, the professors, the gratin, the protégés, the dignified aunts, this is what the house had to harbour and embrace without itself obtruding.

It was in this sense that Hermine Wittgenstein in her memoirs could speak of it as *hausgewordene Logik*, logic turned into a house. There was something conveyed by the proportions and materials on which so much emphasis was laid. Talking about Loos's department store on the Michaelerplatz, 'the house without eyebrows', Karl Kraus said, 'What he's built for them there is an idea' ('*Er hat ihnen dort einen Gedanken hingebaut*'): and so it was also with Wittgenstein's house. But it was not an idea that could be put in words: what he aimed at was essentially an understatement. He sought to express the idea that precisely the absence of ornament allowed free play to the true nature of a house or a department store. This is not a purely negative constatation, but has its positive side, once it is understood that truth in art is, in the words of the *Tractatus*, something that gets shown. An ornament out of place is the attempt to say something that can only be shown. A house, a bed, or a handkerchief is a fine one, has beauty, solely in virtue of possessing the right proportions. Any attempt to add or introduce beauty by means of applied ornament is a fundamental misunderstanding and can only result in a marring of the harmony of the proportions.

This, then, is Wittgenstein's early aesthetic theory, completely of a piece with his early philosophy. But did he adhere to it throughout his life? And, whether he adhered to it or not, does it in fact fit his practice throughout his life? In answering this question I shall begin with a criticism of himself that Wittgenstein voices. For him style, the way something was put, was of enormous importance, and that not only in the artistic sphere. He said once, it wouldn't matter what a friend had done but rather how he talked about it. Similarly he used to insist on a careful

5   Leitner, 1973.

reading of the dictum, *Le style c'est l'homme même*. One should note the word '*même*': the thought is that the real man reveals himself in his style. The meaning of the words, the content, is something secondary, and so likewise is the brute action performed. Of course, it is an important philosophical observation that actions cannot be separated from the way in which they are judged by him who performs them. Still there are dangers, if a feeling for style becomes the supreme commandment. It is not to be thought of that this was a risk for Wittgenstein in the moral sphere, but in aesthetics he perhaps incurred it:

> In all great art [he writes] there is a wild beast – tamed. In Mendelssohn, for example, there is none. All great art has as its ground-bass the primitive drives of mankind. These are not the melody (as they are, perhaps, with Wagner) but they are what gives the melody its depth and power.
> This is the sense in which Mendelssohn can be called a 'reproductive' artist.
> In this sense too the house I built for Gretl is the product of an extremely sensitive ear, of good manners: it is the expression of a great understanding of a culture etc. But life, primitive, wild life with its tumultuous desires, is missing. One could also say, health is missing (Kierkegaard). (A hothouse plant.)[6]

In this quotation I have omitted all the signs of emphasis (single and double underlinings in the manuscript, italics and small capitals in the printed version). Wittgenstein's so frequent use of them distorts his text. His style, both in English and in German, is individual and clear enough without their adventitious aid. So their presence is a strange phenomenon. The editorial question is perhaps a separate one, with something to be said on both sides: the philological scruples of the inheritors of Wittgenstein's copyright are intelligible, but on the other hand the attempt to reproduce this form of emphasis in translation invites distortion.[7] Really all this difficulty arises from the excessive frequency of accidentals in his manuscripts and typescripts, and that is a problem relevant to our theme (no digression, therefore), to which I will return.

The content of the quotation suggests that Wittgenstein feared or felt that there was something missing in him too. Like Adrian Leverkühn in Thomas Mann's *Doctor Faustus*, 'he was obliged to disclaim for himself that robust naïveté which is one (and not the least) of an artist's requirements'. One is reminded of Roy Campbell's comment on some other South African writers:

---

6 *C&V*, pp. 37–8: my translation.
7 Anyone who has tried to translate Wittgenstein will admit as much.

You praise the firm restraint with which they write–
I'm with you there, of course;
They use the snaffle and the curb all right,
But where's the bloody horse?

Assume that things were really so. Assume that Wittgenstein really had no great artistic originality. Let us for the sake of argument allow that even the work on the house was only an improvement of Engelmann's conception.[8] Need that affect our judgement of him? Engelmann remained an admirer this side of idolatry and yet he comments that Wittgenstein never in his life wrote a poem and that never, or only once, did he, the great lover of music, invent a tune. The point of Engelmann's comment is that Wittgenstein was essentially a critic, a conductor, as it were, someone who could help others to improve, or to realize, their artistic creations. Such critical work, even if not the highest work of all, is invaluable.

Nor need we esteem Wittgenstein the man any the less for seeing him in this light. True he practised withdrawal, true he shunned anything that would complicate his life or disturb his equilibrium: his inherited wealth for a start. But life itself one cannot flee: passions spin the plot as much in the cloister as in the marketplace. Wittgenstein's temperament drove him to narrow the field within which he operated, to concentrate his attention on a number of objects manageable for him. But that was no negation of life. On the contrary, it is impossible to have the slightest doubt about the intensity of his affections and aversions or about the reality of his moral struggle with himself. Other criticisms may be justified, but hardly that of turning away from life.

A more serious question is the following: Does this reproach – that he was merely reproductive, merely a critic, merely an improver of other men's work – a reproach which he himself associates with those of lacking in life and of having an exaggerated feeling for style – does this reproach apply to Wittgenstein's proper work: do his philosophical thoughts incur it too? That was his own confession or fear and very relevant to the pair of concepts with which we started: when is ornament in place, and what is asceticism for?

In his writings, then, and his thoughts, was Wittgenstein merely reproductive, merely an improver? Was his philosophy bare asceticism without positive content to make it worth the effort and the abnegation? This

8   This was definitely not Engelmann's view: he insisted that everything good in the house came from Wittgenstein. However his sketchbooks (which seem to date from before Wittgenstein's involvement) much resemble the finished house.

difficult question must be resolved in any attempt to assign Wittgenstein a place in the history of ideas.

The notion of improvement reminds us of certain external features of his writings. Their production involved a constant refinement of expression, and an almost pathological insistence on finding the correct distribution of emphasis in a sentence. It is almost as if he regarded something as false as soon as it was written down. In a letter to Schlick, Waismann describes as follows the difficulties that he found when he attempted a collaboration with Wittgenstein:

> He has the marvellous gift of always seeing everything as if for the first time. But that only shows, in my opinion, how difficult any collaboration with him is, since he always follows the inspiration of the moment and demolishes what he has previously planned.

It is not surprising, therefore, that Wittgenstein was profoundly dissatisfied with the accounts of his work that others gave. From many examples I choose one in a planned preface (actually printed with *Philosophical Investigations*):

> I was obliged to learn that my results (which I had communicated in lectures, typescripts, and discussions), variously misunderstood, more or less mangled or watered down, were in circulation.

He goes on to explain that this was his reason for departing from a former resolve not to publish anything in his lifetime. So he writes. But we know that in fact he did not publish anything in his lifetime (of his work after 1930, that is). There can be no doubt that this arose from the fact that it did not admit of being brought to a conclusion. As he himself says:

> And this was, of course, connected with the very nature of the investigation. For this compels us to travel over a wide field of thought criss-cross in every direction.

Partly this is due to the negative aim of his work. It is intended to drive out the evil spirit from the reader as from his pupils. False philosophy must be exorcized. But that is an operation best performed *viva voce* and through personal contact. One false notion is driven out, and immediately the next false notion that threatens to take its place must be corrected. A book or an article freezes what ought really to be a living flow of ideas. It is legitimate to refer to Socrates' attack on writing in the *Phaedrus*, itself of course a written work.

All this, of course, in part accounts for the attraction of Wittgenstein's writing (just as the *Phaedrus* is one of Plato's literary masterpieces).

Wittgenstein cannot but write in a personal and tentative manner, which has its charm: the reader feels drawn into a dialogue. The upshot, however, is, for good reasons, not made easy to grasp or to formulate. Wittgenstein does not just say (though in some sense he clearly believes it) that philosophers have hitherto failed to describe the essence of thought, of language, and of the world. (He has his reasons for thinking that these three amount to the same thing.) The attempts of philosophers have been a failure, and could not have been otherwise. Yet when we see how they have failed, in what respects they do not cover what they are meant to, and what other partial points of view are possible, when all preconceptions, even the deepest, are put in question, and when we begin to sense the variety of possibilities in human life and thought, then we are being enabled to see something: something, in Wittgenstein's earlier terminology, gets shown.

Thus Wittgenstein's later work, as already the *Tractatus* did, in an indirect way, make manifest the limits of thought, language, and the world. That, of course, was Wittgenstein's claim in his letter to Ficker:

> My work consists of two parts: the one presented here plus all that I have not written. And it is precisely this second part that is the important one. My book draws limits to the ethical from the inside as it were and I am convinced that this is the only rigorous way of drawing those limits.

Just as the propositions of the *Tractatus* had done, so the language games in Wittgenstein's later writings show us what can be said and what cannot. They show us limits to human thought and to human life. Show, not state: any attempt to fix these thoughts within a philosophy is a misunderstanding. For similar reasons, Wittgenstein felt obliged to make arrangements at various times in his life, but in particular as his death drew near, to destroy collections of his writings and certainly all that touched on *das Unaussprechliche*, the inexpressible. What such collections contained we do not know, poems, perhaps, epigrams, telling and summary descriptions. Any idea that such *aperçus* really said everything that was needed would lead us astray. To be true to their purpose, they must be destroyed. This is the spirit, I think, that lies behind Wittgenstein's negations – his divesting himself of his inheritance, his refusal to publish, his ever renewed distrust of his own ideas. It was in his showing the possibility of such negation and in the way in which he performed it that we can find his form of assertion. In his case the asceticism is the ornament. Very typical of his way of thinking was his exclamation in a letter to Russell at the time of his father's death, 'Such a death was worth a whole life.' It reminds one of Henry Vaughan's poem:

25

Dear beauteous death! the jewel of the just!
Shining nowhere but in the dark.

It is as if Wittgenstein's whole life revolved round the mystery of abnegation. It was there naturally (typically in what is not said) that he found the key to the problems of expression and communication with which his name is professionally associated.

4

THE IDEA OF
JEWISHNESS

Wittgenstein in a confessional phase reproached himself bitterly for having minimized his Jewish ancestry. Yet he was right to minimize it, if a correct impression of his family and its influence on him was the aim. No one at the turn of the century would have thought of characterizing that large cousinhood as a Jewish family, as it is occasionally described today. Karl Menger, who knew them and was a particular friend of Wittgenstein's Aunt Clara, comments that in so far as there was any difference between Jewish and non-Jewish households, they seemed to belong rather to the former.[1]

They (Ludwig's parents and his uncles and aunts and their children after them) were Protestant or Catholic and married to Protestants or Catholics. Theirs was not a life with any Jewish dimension, or consciousness of their remote Jewish ancestry, a diminishing proportion in any case as the generations passed. Nor did they live among and consort with or feel especial affinity with other families with a Jewish element in their background. Such a possibility did not really exist in the Christian circles to which they did belong, since Jewishness as a family characteristic vanished on conversion and intermarriage: often only a name remained, on the male side.[2]

Ludwig himself came at the intersection of two such families, since Karl alone of that generation married one whose father had Jewish ancestors. The result still is that of Ludwig's three grandparents only one was herself demonstrably a member of the Jewish community, in as it happens Vienna, and her marriage – her marriage out, so to speak – was registered there as well as in Dresden, where it actually took place.[3]

---

1 Menger 1994, p. 74.
2 To all this discussion it is relevant that in Austria-Hungary registration for civic purposes was on a confessional basis. (Thus for instance it was a baptismal, not strictly a birth certificate that Wittgenstein presented to the Home Office when seeking naturalization in Great Britain.) In Austria therefore the term 'Jew' had a precise legal significance.
3 Whether as a result of a change in his first name or of his leaving the community or for some other reason, Wittgenstein's paternal grandfather could not be identified in any Jewish register in Korbach, when a search was made in 1938 in connection with the racial laws: this of course was anything but a disadvantage at the time.

She was a Figdor, from a family of bankers who had been financiers to court circles and later to the city of Vienna. Such families in fact were often the last to convert, if they did so at all: to belong to a supernational community was an advantage for them. But Fanny did convert, and when she went to Dresden to be married, she was also, the day before, baptized.

The story of the Wittgenstein family into which she married is an interesting, because so typical, one for the historian of what is sometimes called assimilation, though (borrowing a metaphor from Lewis Namier[4]) the evaporation of Jewishness might in this case be a more appropriate term. Their ancestors, not yet called Wittgenstein, had been Court Jews in Hesse since at least the mid-eighteenth Century. We can infer two lines, one signallized by the alternation Meyer Moses, Moses Meyer, the other Hirsch Meyer, Meyer Hirsch, going back to a Meyer born in the seventh century. Living in Laasphe, near the castle of one line of the Sayn-Wittgensteins, they were agents and factors to that family: one of them, Ahron Meyer Moses, our Hermann Christian's grandfather, leader of the community, must have been among the Laasphe Jews sent to England to collect the payment for mercenaries used in the Seven Years War. Probably it was the mediatization of the Sayn-Wittgensteins that brought the family to Korbach though the second line mentioned also spent some time in Gütersloh. About this time too, they all took the name Wittgenstein. Associated now with the Waldeck-Pyrmonts (for they were still known as Court Jews), they soon embarked on trade of their own.

The years 1815–48 into which Hermann Christian's youth fell were years of emancipation for the Jews throughout Germany, but in many regions, particularly in Hesse, this met with much resistance and nowhere more than in the little centre of Korbach. No doubt the town's decline as a trade centre was partly responsible for this. It was impossible for most Jews to assert their rights and difficult even for the Wittgensteins and Simons (the family of Hermann Christian's mother, Court Jews they too). Most members of the Wittgenstein connection went off, taking their business with them, some to Bielefeld, even more to Leipzig. And all became Christians. We know of only one, Jakob, son of a much older brother, who remained in the Jewish religion: he stayed on

---

4   Quoted from Namier in I. Berlin 1992, p. 34. Cf. also what Golo Mann says of his maternal grandfather in 'Ueber Antisemitismus' (1960, in Mann 1962, pp. 169–70): 'In seinem Fall wie in hunderttausend anderen, hat es kaum Sinn von Assimilierung zu sprechen, weil sie langst vollzogen war.' ('In his case, as in a hundred thousand others, it scarcely makes sense to talk of assimilation, since that had been accomplished long ago.')

in Korbach and fought through to civic equality, being elected to the Waldeck assembly in 1848.[5]

In centres such as Korbach conversion tended to mean exclusion from both of the local communities. Hermann Christian himself may have had difficulties with his line of the family perhaps on this very account[6] and went to join his cousins and uncles (in a wide sense) in Leipzig, the city of Felix Mendelssohn. When exactly he left the Jewish community and professed himself a Christian is not clear,[7] but he certainly had no regrets: 'We are glad to be out of the East!' he is reported to have said. By the time of his courtship and marriage he was already a prosperous wool merchant, mature, severe and of impressive culture.[8]

His own sub-branch of the Wittgenstein family, moving yet again, to Austria-Hungary, retained much of a family tradition of benefactions and support for worthy causes, no longer of course with the function of providing for needy and vagrant Jews arrived from the East (as had been the case in Korbach). That sort of community was left behind and they now found another one among the quietly prosperous Lutheran or Zwinglian burghers of their new country. Intermarriage was to bring in also Catholic elements: perhaps it is significant that there was some fluidity as to confessional adherence, which varied according to marriage and the convictions of the other party apparently without generating friction. Their friends and protégés and social lions might be of any stripe – Mendelssohn and Joachim, yes, but also Clara Schumann and Brahms: Hebbel and Bonitz – very often Germans, who, like themselves, found Austria congenial.[9]

5 Jakob's real prosperity however came after removal to Berlin. The account in the last two paragraphs is largely based on Bettelheim 1935 (which revolves round Jakob) and Medding 1951, pp. 348–50 and 402–3. I have also seen useful correspondence between the late W.W. Bartley and the late Thomas Stonborough.

6 In his will he speaks of difficult circumstances and being thrown back on his own resources at the beginning of his career: see Wittgenstein, Hermine 1944–9, p. 17 ('Ich habe unter anderen sorgenvollen Umständen meine Carrière begonnen; auf eigene Kraft angewiesen etc.') This may have to do with his father's death in 1822 and some disagreement with Jakob's father Simson, for no further contact with this, his own line of the family, is recorded.

7 The family tradition is no more precise than that he was *'stehend getauft'*, 'baptized standing' i.e. not in infancy.

8 See Laqueur 1996, p. 257, on assimilation as a perfectly natural process, 'Traditional Judaism had become irrelevant, certainly for the educated Jews. There was no Jewish culture outside religion, which put greater emphasis on ritual than on anything else.' The Old Orthodox of the day (the *Vormärz* or *Biedermeierzeit*) put the same thought in a different way, 'Vor allem emanzipiert die Emanzipation die Juden vom Judentum' ('The immediate effect of the emancipation of the Jews is to emancipate them from Jewishness'), see Toury 1965, pp. 65ff.

9 This account adds some details to that in McGuinness 1988, pp. 1–23; for references to the Wittgensteins of Korbach see 'Ein Bürgerrechtsstreit in Korbach' in Toury 1972, pp. 105–12, also Bettelheim 1935 and Medding 1951.

The existence of a number of Jewish ancestors was of little significance for most of the family. When Karl heard that his son Paul was studying their ancestry, he laughed, saying, 'As long as he doesn't find that one of them was hanged!' Only for very particular purposes did the non-'German' element in their ancestry create any hindrance, as in the case of a boyhood wish of Ludwig's to join a distinctively German gymnastic club.

The period of Ludwig's boyhood and youth is one regarding which it has become customary to stress the contribution of 'the Jews' to Viennese culture. There are severe limitations to such an approach. If Vienna itself and the concentration of science and culture there attracted many from outside and if for sociological reasons many of these had at divers periods been set loose from a Jewish background, this by no means implies any uniformity in their contribution and certainly not any Jewish colouring of the science and culture itself. How could it, indeed, saving the exceptional case – a Chagall, an Else Lasker-Schüler? As Max Liebermann said when Jewish origins were mentioned: But good heavens, what has that got to do with drawing? And just as for every Liebermann there was a Corinth, so, closer to our hero, for every Mach there was a Boltzmann, for every Kraus a Loos. Above all, the things said or produced, the cultural content, was generally above such classification. A Jewish element – there might be one: for Freud it has been claimed that there was one – would have to be proved in each case.

These are very general considerations and to a considerable degree obscured by the affections and passions of our own half of the century, but it is essential to have some objective basis for this sort of discussion. Ludwig at all events thought himself in 1914 completely German. He was aware, it is true, of the Jewish predominance in his ancestry. If he denied it (how flatly we cannot from his confessions absolutely know), this will at that time have been from a sense of its irrelevance. He was pained perhaps by a detail of descent which objectively meant nothing but might give others a wrong impression of him. He was, we might almost say, ashamed of being ashamed of it – an irrational reaction but perhaps shared with Hofmannsthal.[10] Wittgenstein's much later self-examination on the question of being Jewish is a different phenomenon to which we shall return. In youth he felt he was not a Jew, rightly, as I have tried to say. At his school the Jewish boys (defined, of course, confessionally) were a small minority and he notes some tension, not further specified, in his relation with them – 'with the Jews', not 'with the other Jews'.

10 Dr. Ritchie Robinson of Oxford kindly drew my attention to Rieckmann 1993.

It was at the outbreak of the First World War that Wittgenstein made his remark about feeling completely German. Whether this will have changed during the first two years of the war, as the differences between Germans and Austrians became clearer, is a matter for speculation: it may have gone either way. At all events, at the end of August 1916 he came, after perhaps his hardest-fought battles, to Olmütz and found himself for the first time in a Jewish circle – found himself *tout court*, we may say, since their thinking chimed so well with his own. The town was small and the intellectuals were mostly of Jewish origin, now perfect examples of assimilation but not mingling much with the few other German-speaking bourgeoisie. In Prossnitz, where many of their families originated, there was even a Jewish municipality, a remnant of the ghetto (Max Zweig came from there, and Stefan Zweig's family also, and the mother of Paul Engelmann). In Brünn, the city of Loos and of Gödel, there was still a German cultured class, alongside the emerging Czechs, for whom Janáček will serve as a symbol. Olmütz was a special case, betwixt and between one might say. Engelmann himself speaks of the cultural past still recognizable from its buildings, and indeed it had once been the capital of Moravia, with its own university (closed in 1858), and it was still home to a well-endowed metropolitan see, where the canons of the cathedral had the unique privilege of electing the archbishop rather than accepting the nomination of the emperor. (This circumstance may have put an edge on Franz Josef's tongue when they elected a worthy Mgr Kohen: *Ist er wenigstens getauft?*, 'I hope he's baptized', he is reputed to have said.) But Engelmann's account of the town (and Max Zweig's, too, of the gymnasium there) suggests that there was no lively intellectual life outside this group of sons and daughters of professional or merchant families that were at the height of their development and, as it happened, of Jewish descent, whereas the older German burgher families were like the town itself in decline.

To Olmütz then came Wittgenstein and after a summer of isolation and hostile relations with his comrades he found a circle that dedicated itself to things of the mind. Like his own family in happier days they spent their time making music, staging plays, and discussing books and poems. I have described elsewhere this circle and the effect Wittgenstein had on it, as others have also. Engelmann's memoir is a testimony to the profundity of that effect. Arrived in Vienna after completing his training in Olmütz Wittgenstein was to hear from Max Zweig that he had won from the latter the deepest respect of the heart.[11]

---

11 Letter of 27.12.1916, copy in the Brenner Archiv. Thus the warm but more measured account in Max Zweig 1992, written more than 75 years after the events, probably does less than justice to the original effect that Wittgenstein had on the circle.

The message he brought them is obviously too complex to express in a single formula, but its main effect was to confer an intellectual legitimacy upon their aspirations. The question of the part played by their Jewish ancestry in these is a rather artificial one, since the enthusiasms of youth appear in every part of our culture and are very similar in all of them. But perhaps that ancestry played some part indirectly: the main need they felt, the keystone missing for their devotion to culture and to good causes was a religion, so to speak a natural one. Many felt this need, but perhaps membership of an assimilated but not converted Jewry particularly predisposed these Olmützers to feel it. They certainly wanted something more than *Schöngeistigkeit* and *Schwärmerei* (say 'gushing aestheticism'). They were readers of Karl Kraus (Engelmann had been his assistant), they were or were preparing to be competent and serious practitioners in their own professions – architecture, music, drawing. They would look for standards in their intellectual life too.

Wittgenstein's earlier attitude to religion I have attempted to describe elsewhere.[12] His loss of faith was not due to a general lack of it in his family, which had many devout members, but perhaps to the mocking attitude of his father and the enlightenment of his advanced sister, Margaret Stonborough. Russell reports him as a fierce critic of organized religion, or at any rate of clerics. One such was told that he would do better to 'read some good book on some exact science and see what honest thought is'. Still Wittgenstein's interest in William James's *Varieties of Religious Experience* antedates the war as does (almost certainly) the performance of Anzengruber's *Kreuzelschreiber*, where the slogan *'Es kann dir nix g'schehen'* ('Nothing can happen to you') in its context of nature mysticism awoke echoes in him.

I will not repeat here how he came in the first year of the war to an intense living of the Tolstoyan gospels and a belief in the Spirit, only saying that all this is described in the coded or private part of his diaries.[13] But when Wittgenstein came to Olmütz he was at a crucial point in his reflections. Resuming his philosophical notes after the summer's battles (1 or 4 July 1916, misdated 11.6.16 in all editions[14]) he asks more directly than before,

12 McGuinness 1988, e.g. pp. 84, 111.
13 It will be recalled that in these early notebooks the code passages are entered separately on the versos and rapidly fall behind the philosophical notes on the rectos, as far as date is concerned. After 1929 Wittgenstein generally interspersed the two types of entry. (*Db* is an exception: it has remarks both in code and in clear, but none are philosophical. Conceivably but by no means necessarily, other such notebooks have been lost or were destroyed by Wittgenstein.)
14 This can even be seen in the photograph of the relevant passage now added to *Nb*.

Was weiß ich über Gott und den Zweck des Lebens?
(What do I know about God and the purpose of life?)

and then continues with reflections on God, prayer, good and evil, all themes that he had excluded from the chaste first version of the *Prototractatus* (a much more stratified text than we at first thought[15]), which really leaves unsaid all that is unsayable. That he was aware of this shift appears in the coded part of his diary, where he says, on 6 and 7 July 1916:

> *Habe viel über alles Mögliche nachgedacht. Kann aber merkwürdigerweise nicht die Verbindung mit meinen mathematischen Gedankenggängen herstellen.*
> *Aber die Verbindung wird hergestellt werden. Was sich nicht sagen läßt, läßt sich nicht sagen.*
> (Have thought a lot about everything possible. But, strangely enough, cannot establish the connection with my mathematical lines of thought.
> But the connection will be established. What cannot be said, *cannot* be said.)[16]

(where we have, probably, the first version of the concluding proposition of the *Tractatus*). Wittgenstein's position here may seem a self-contradictory one. If the religious realm is inexpressible, will it not be all the harder, indeed impossible, to connect it with 'mathematical lines of thought'?

This brings us, however, straight to the conversations that then took place in Olmütz. A main theme, indeed the main theme, of Engelmann's reminiscences is that Wittgenstein brought the others to see, by strict attention to the nature of science and mathematics, that the realm of religion was indeed inexpressible. And that not because it happens to be inexpressible, but because that is its very essence, just as an irrational number can have no rational expression nor can the velocity and position of a particle both be determined. The converse is even true: the inexpressible *is* the mystical: it is in seeing what cannot be expressed that we come near

---

15 I have dated the composition of this to the period from October 1915 (Wittgenstein tells Russell he is working on a treatise) to March 1916 (he goes off to the Front). Its content will have been the first 70 pages, in Wittgenstein's numbering, of MS 104. Wittgenstein probably brought a typescript based on this to Olmütz and may there have added in manuscript the passages from pp. 71–8 referred to below in the text. See also 'Some pre-*Tractatus* Manuscripts', Chapter 23 in the present volume and the prefaces to *PT*, 2nd edn, and *LPA*.

16 From MS 103. Publication of code passages is planned by the Brenner Archiv.

to the nature of the mystical. This body of thought has been characterized as negative theology, as man's urge to run up against the limits of language, and in various other ways. For Engelmann and Wittgenstein it entailed, in particular, a certain way of expressing what can be expressed which takes account of what cannot, and it was in such a light, we can see from their letters, that the two talked of poetry, as of other matters.

This jejune characterization is not intended to recommend their way of thinking. Quite the contrary: its main point is to indicate that the conclusions reached have sense only in the light of the route followed in reaching them.[17]

This was the lesson of Olmütz, this the corrective to the occasionally 'lukewarm atmosphere' of the Engelmann home.[18] But it is equally important to note that it was a lesson for Wittgenstein too. It was in these months that he added to his treatise two series of remarks, on the nature of science, and on the inexpressibility of ethics. These are to be found on pp. 71–8 of the *Prototractatus* manuscript but he continued to make considerable additions in the early months of 1917, shortly after his departure from Olmütz. These additions reflect the nature of his interaction with his friends there, Engelmann in particular. While his logical insights gave them an underpinning for their philosophy of life, he learnt from them how he could say something about his deepest convictions without running counter to those same insights. Hence in part his remark, reported by Engelmann, 'If I can't manage to bring forth a proposition, along comes Engelmann with his forceps and pulls it out of me!'[19]

But in all of this, what role was played by the 'Jewishness' of the Olmütz circle and by the Jewish ancestry of Wittgenstein? The common factor seems to have been the need for a self-made religion, the ethical equivalent of Christianity.[20] Here Tolstoy, too, played his part, and no doubt

17 Thus Wittgenstein's cousin, Lydia Oser, who said to Karl Menger (Menger 1994 pp. 83f), 'Is there really any merit in saying, 'Whereof one cannot speak thereof one must be silent'?' was in a sense right. The conclusion in isolation is banal. Ramsey's reported criticism 'What can't be said, can't be said, and it can't be whistled either', if genuine, is unwontedly superficial, not only because it too treats the upshot of the *Tractatus* as if it stood on its own, a procedure questionable even with the last line of a mathematical proof, but because it involves a *petitio principii*: indirect ways of making manifest may be possible, the *Tractatus* is itself meant as a way of making this itself manifest.

18 *'Lauwarme Atmosphäre'* – the phrase is Heinrich Groag's in a postcard of 1917 to Wittgenstein, original in the Brenner Archiv.

19 Engelmann 1967, p. 94.

20 Engelmann in particular was clearly influenced by Christianity: witness his quotations from the Fourth Gospel, his appeals to the Holy Spirit, and his certainty that the sayings of Christ in the Gospels cannot be of purely human origin. (References to Christianity, and to the relative incompleteness of the Jewish religion, are quite frequent in later, as in earlier, notes by Wittgenstein, but are sufficiently known to need not citing here.)

readings of the *Brenner* before the war, where there were translations of Kierkegaard and other writings of similar inspiration.[21] Finally, for all of them, the war was the great catalyst, making it imperative to come to terms with these questions. At all events, the Olmützers, objectively speaking, were looking for an alternative to a Jewishness that no longer meant anything to them, while Wittgenstein was making good the failure of his Christian upbringing to take root. Such in essence was the nature of Wittgenstein's first and only adventure into an environment that can in an intelligible sense be called Jewish.

Time was to bring its changes: most obviously when the plague of Nazi anti-semitism struck. Fritz Zweig emigrated. Max Zweig and Peter Eng had to abandon cosmopolitan Berlin, where perhaps they had never thought they were Jews. Eng committed suicide. Zweig began to write plays relating to the persecution and the resistance of the Jews. The success of one of these took him to Palestine, fortunately at exactly the time when the Germans occupied the Czech lands, where he had taken refuge from them. He spent the rest of his long life there, much of it in the company of Engelmann.[22]

Engelmann's own return to Judaism, or perhaps rather his turn to Zionism, came earlier. His correspondence with Wittgenstein and his notebooks from the years 1928 to 1932[23] have yet to be studied in depth, but it is at any rate clear that he was not content with the measure of success as an architect that was or might have been open to him, and certainly not with the relative comfort of the life he could live in Olmütz. He felt a strong call to live also, ideally it would have been entirely, for others, both by intervening in difficult or desperate cases and also by seeking to have an influence at the social level. At the same time (and to some extent for the same reason) he wanted to write, to carry further the work of his mentors: Kraus, Loos and Wittgenstein. It was natural to think of the new society that it was hoped to build in Palestine and to share the hopes of many of the early Zionists. And there, in 1933, he went. Who can say with what success? First of all, of course, it in fact ensured his survival in a decade of persecution. His life was both modest and full of idealism. He found some work in Tel Aviv as an architect, but could afford to live only in the poorest circumstances. He composed but did not publish a great deal of material, in some sense a seamless web,

21 The *Brenner* was an avowedly Christian periodical. Adolf Loos, who introduced Wittgenstein to Engelmann, was himself introduced to Wittgenstein by Ludwig von Ficker, the editor of the *Brenner*. To complete the circle, Wittgenstein came to Ficker through a favourable mention of him by Karl Kraus, also a Christian at this period.

22 See Max Zweig 1992.

23 Available in the Jewish National and University Library.

moving from logic, to psychology, to social organization inspired by ideals of the higher life, and (to complete the circle) to town planning and architecture. His practical activity issued from this thinking, since he was active in promoting cultural groups and discussions, which (as he explains in his writings) are the first step to creating the mentality required for his ideal state. Needless to say his was no religious Zionism. He happened to be a Jew so it was among Jews in Palestine that he sought to promote universal ideals. At one point he says that he feels for the welfare of Jewish workers in Palestine exactly as a Spaniard or a Swede would. He also envisages a government of Palestine by separate Arab and Jewish chambers. He himself says about his work that it was not so completely without effect as might be thought, and this must be respected, but there were elements reminiscent of his address to the Czech conscripts in the Mauritzkirche.[24] Here too he spoke only the language of a minority, and a distrusted minority at that.

In 1925, when Engelmann first broached the idea (not yet very concrete) of going to Palestine, Wittgenstein was half-inclined to go with him.[25] The idea of a new start, of a *tabula rasa*, no doubt appealed to him: we see this in his frequent impulses of flight, to Norway (more than once), to Russia, to Ireland (more than once): there was even talk of Brünn. By the time Engelmann actually went, Wittgenstein was principally in Cambridge and the two men seem hardly to have been in contact (though in 1937 Wittgenstein found a way to send one of his confessions to Engelmann).[26]

We leave here the sphere of Wittgenstein's actual contact with Jewish culture, though how 'Jewish' it was is, as we have seen, debatable, and turn to two different spheres: his thoughts about his own Jewishness at the beginning of the 1930s and the effect on him of racial discrimination in the late 1930s. That these themes need to be treated together, and in the same context as those touched on above, is evidence of the artificiality of the concept of Jewishness. We have here at least five different sets of phenomena or supposed phenomena, the religion, descent from persons professing it, the culture of assimilated Jews who still formed something of a community, the common genetic heritage of Jews (thought to exist) and (distinct from this) the supposition of such a heritage, typically the assumption by the anti-semitic that it existed and

---

24 At a *Feldmesse*, a Mass before they went off to the Front, he exhorted them, in the name of the Holy Ghost, to lay down their arms. Information from the late H. Groag.
25 Engelmann 1967, pp. 54–5.
26 We have a copy of Engelmann's reply among Wittgenstein's papers (and of Wittgenstein's reply to that in Engelmann 1967, pp. 58–9), but Engelmann seems to have tactfully suppressed the confession itself.

that it was an excrescence on European culture, with which we may class the mirror image of this assumption, which finds in Jewish consciousness the origins of the modern world-view. Of these five only the first and the last are reasonably clearly definable and certainly existed, though they are by no means identical or very closely related. Jewishness, '*das Judentum*', is surely one of those words of which Heinrich Hertz spoke in a favourite passage of Wittgenstein's

> We have accumulated around the terms 'force' and 'electricity' more relations than can be completely reconciled amongst themselves. It is not by finding out more and fresh relations that it [the question as to the nature of force and electricity] can be answered; but by removing the contradictions existing between those already known and thus [this?] perhaps by reducing their number.[27]

So far we have considered Wittgenstein's actual ancestry and the extent to which Jewish religion and culture entered (very indirectly, as it turned out) into his life. But in the early 1930s Wittgenstein, who had played down his ancestry to others, and who had made no reference to it previously in his private diaries, began, only for this period as far as I know, to think that his own work was marked by Jewishness. One passage will serve as an illustration:

> *Das jüdische 'Genie' ist nur ein Heiliger. Der größte jüdische Denker ist nur ein Talent. (Ich z.B.)*
> *Es ist, glaube ich, eine Wahrheit darin, wenn ich denke, daß ich eigentlich in meinem Denken nur reproduktiv bin. Ich glaube, ich habe nie eine Gedankenbewegung erfunden, sondern sie wurde mir immer von jemand anderem gegeben und ich habe sie nur sogleich zu meinem Klärungswerk aufgegriffen. So haben mich Boltzmann, Hertz, Schopenhauer, Frege, Russell, Kraus, Loos, Weininger, Spengler, Sraffa beeinflußt. Kann man als ein Beispiel jüdischer Reproduktivität Breuer und Freud heranziehen? ... ...*

---

27 Hertz 1899, p. 8. As a motto for *Philosophical Investigations* Wittgenstein originally thought of the passage from which this is taken, which he also used in both of the general talks he gave to the Cambridge University Moral Science Club, in 1939 (on taking up the Professorship) and in 1946 (his counterblast to Popper). (Minutes of the Society in Cambridge University Library.) For a lucid discussion of the concept of Jewishness, see Gombrich 1997. (I am grateful to the director Dr. Emil Brix for a copy of this pamphlet.)

Es ist dem jüdischen Geist typisch das Werk eines Andern besser zu verstehen als der es selbst versteht.

(Amongst Jews 'genius' is found only in the holy man. Even the greatest of Jewish thinkers is no more than talented. (Myself for instance.)

I think there is some truth in my idea that I really only think reproductively. I don't believe I have ever *invented* a line of thinking, I have always taken one over from someone else. I have simply straightaway seized on it with enthusiasm for my work of clarification. That is how Boltzmann, Hertz, Schopenhauer, Frege, Russell, Kraus, Loos, Weininger, Spengler, Sraffa have influenced me. Can one take the case of Breuer and Freud as an example of Jewish reproductiveness?...

It is typical of the Jewish mind to understand another's work better than the man himself does.)[28]

Even read with the caution we should bring to every self-assessment, the passage is fascinating, for the characterization of Wittgenstein's work and for his list of influences, but our main concern here is with the importance attached to Jewishness.[29] Wolfgang Kienzler has pointed out that the sense of such passages would not be materially altered if for 'Jews' we read 'philosophers'.[30] There is much in the idea that philosophy is of necessity a second-order activity, and perhaps Wittgenstein made this even clearer than before. Whether this excludes originality is more questionable – or perhaps the very idea of originality is questionable.[31] Moreover the idea that lack of originality should be associated with race, when differences within a race, whatever a race may be, are greater than differences between races is hard indeed to accept. At all events it suffices to read, for example, Mach's *Principles of the Theory of Heat*, not of course written with such as its theme, to see how the most original of scientists depended on their predecessors and how little room for chauvinism

---

28 *C&V*, p. 19. Note the order (clearly chronological) in which influences are listed: we can infer that Weininger became important to Wittgenstein *later* than his first meeting with Loos in July 1914, thus not as a result of a reading in boyhood or youth. See also note 30 below.

29 In a previous discussion, McGuinness 1988, p. 84, I dismissed this element out of hand, which earned me an accusation of 'positivism' in the *Philosophische Rundschau* (Bolz 1992). This may serve as an excuse for here arguing for what I think to be obvious.

30 Kienzler 1997, pp. 42–3.

31 A remark dating from 1939–40, *C&V*, p. 36, repeating the example of Freud and Breuer (but was not Breuer also 'Jewish'?), distinguishes between an originality 'of the soil' (Wittgenstein's own and Freud's) and an originality 'of the seed'. There, however, no reference is made to Jewishness.

there is in basic science. *All* contributions were necessary to get us as far as we have come. Of course a place and a period may, for reasons hard to divine, witness a surprising efflorescence: in England the Elizabethan poets are a striking example.

Yet Wittgenstein, for a while at least, subscribed both to the myth of genius, the absolutely original thinker, and to the idea that a national character was transmitted in the blood – the genes we would perhaps now say, with vague thoughts of selection, but on such matters Wittgenstein was happier with utterances which flew in the face of science (let alone of scientism). They corresponded better so to an emotional truth. One might almost say, alas, that he was thinking with the blood. Thus later in 1931 he writes:

> *Man hat manchmal gesagt, daß die Heimlichkeit und Versrecktheit der Juden durch die lange Verfolgung hervorgebracht worden sei. Das ist gewiß unwahr; dagegen ist es gewiß, daß sie, trotz dieser Verfolgung, nur darum noch existieren, weil sie die Neigung zu dieser Heimlichkeit haben.*
> (It has sometimes been said that the Jews' secretive and cunning nature is a result of their long persecution. That is certainly untrue: on the other hand it is certain that they continue to exist despite this persecution only because they have an inclination towards such secretiveness.)[32]

These characteristics do indeed belong to the *picture* of the Jew, as in Shylock's 'For sufferance is the badge of all our tribe'. No one today, with the example of the State of Israel before him, would choose this picture, or perhaps any single picture. But Wittgenstein accepted it and indeed spoke as if it corresponded to characteristics which had been in the Jewish race from the start and would remain so for ever.

At least he spoke in such a way for a while in 1931: later he discusses the same moral problems without the reference to Jewishness. But even so, why? Note that with this question we are engaged on a different enterprise from that so far undertaken. We are no longer talking about what Jews are really like (if there is such a thing), but solely about how Wittgenstein imagined them. We should surely also go on to ask, What conclusions for his life or thought did he draw from this picture? It will be seen I think that the answers to these two questions are closely connected.

We are speaking of a time when Hitler's ideas were in the air but not yet put into practice (which, of course, more clearly revealed their repulsive and self-stultifying nature but also their dangerous fascination), we are speaking of a time when Wittgenstein was reading, or at any rate

---

32 *C&V*, p. 22. Perhaps translate as 'furtive' rather than 'cunning'.

discussing with Moore, Weininger's *Sex and Character*.[33] It was also a time (but then, when was not?) in which he was questioning his own relation to the world. He spoke of himself as living in a more rarefied atmosphere than others, of his cowardliness, of his need to hide himself behind his words.[34] As always with Wittgenstein the direction of thought is from his own soul outwards. He accepts the picture of the Jew not because Jews are such, but because he thinks that he himself is. So he does not accept it on historical grounds, nor because he takes pleasure in preferring a folk belief to the lucubrations of the historian or the social scientist – though no doubt that did give him pleasure – but because it serves his purpose of self-examination. Something similar can be seen in his *Remarks on Frazer's Golden Bough*:[35] we understand a primitive rite when it makes us shudder, and in his remarks about religion, where believing in God is quite different from being convinced by a philosophical or historical argument.[36]

The upshot of such thought, then, the effect that it had on him, was precisely to provide themes for his self-criticism, though as we have said he contrived to continue this throughout his life without reverting often to this particular device. But in 1931, at any rate, Jewishness was a moral category, whose concrete manifestations are of secondary importance:[37] much more important is seriousness as Wittgenstein says (shortly after the main passages we have been discussing):

> *Das Judentum ist hochproblematisch, aber nicht gemütlich. Und wehe wenn ein Schreiber die gemütvolle Seite betont. Ich dachte an Freud, wenn er vom jüdischen Witz redet.*
> (Jewishness is deeply problematic but not cozy or warm-hearted. Woe betide the author who stresses the warm-hearted side. I was thinking of Freud when he talks about the Jewish joke.)[38]

33 See *CL*, p. 250. I have given some account of how Wittgenstein viewed this book in McGuinness 1988, pp. 40–3. However I suspect that when listing influences (text above) Wittgenstein was thinking of Weininger's other book *Ueber die letzten Dinge* (Weininger 1907). See note 25 above, also the parallels adduced in McGuinness 1988, pp. 40–1, further *FB*, p. 30 and 83, which suggest that the later book is what Hermine Wittgenstein refers to as 'Dein Weininger' in 1916.

34 In *Db*, pp. (ms) 72, 87, 97: compare, from *C&V*, p. 12, the idea that abstractness is a particularly Jewish characteristic. (Of course one might just as well say the opposite.)

35 *RoF*.

36 *C&V*, p. 32.

37 This is of a piece with Wittgenstein's remark to Moore, *CL*, p. 250, about Weininger 1906: 'It isn't necessary or rather not possible to agree with him but his greatness lies in that with which we disagree.' Similarly Jewishness, for Wittgenstein, is an interesting *idea*. See also Rush Rhees's discussion of Weininger in Rhees 1984, pp. 177–82.

38 *Db*, p. (ms) 141.

We too can enter into this discourse of Wittgenstein's. One is tempted to say, for example, that there is something in this last criticism of Freud. But such discourse will be anything but historical. We are saying rather that the emphasis on jokes, or to take a related example, the sentimentality, the *Schmaltz*, in this or that sketch or film does not represent Jewishness as we should wish it to be. For everyone can feel a fascination (the converse of that mentioned above) in this picture of an alternative smaller world in which all questions are resoluble, cut off, a secret garden. Whether this fascination is healthy is another question.

We return to history to round out our account. Objectively, but perhaps only objectively, Wittgenstein entered into a different relationship to Jewishness with the annexation of Austria, when his family (in some cases to their surprise) found themselves in differing degrees subject to the racial laws. Their story can be followed in letters exchanged at the time.[39] As others paid the emigration tax (*Reichsfluchtsteuer*) or used some similar device, so they were prepared to repatriate a part of their monies held abroad to purchase a racial status which permitted them to remain in Austria but in safety. Wittgenstein involved himself energetically in making these arrangements: like his sisters he fell out with the other brother, who chose the path of exile.[40] They made themselves what they had always thought they were, non-Jewish[41] and in their talk and discussions made the distinctions they had always made: for them a 'Jew' meant an *Ostjude*, a Jew from the East, with the corresponding appearance and manners.[42] At the same time the sisters in Vienna continued to consort with all former friends who were Jews or half-Jewish in the Nazi sense. To both categories they were most helpful, and Wittgenstein in England was involved in this too. But there is no trace – why should there be? one might ask – of solidarity with Jews as such. It had always been the family practice to help those in need (and to help in a direct and personal way). The race did not count.

So too Wittgenstein in England was active in helping individual refugees, many of whom were, of course, Jewish. His diaries are full of

---

39 *FB*, pp. 162ff (more details in Wittgenstein, Hermine 1944–9, pp. 154–80). It will be seen that there was something in the apparently naive remark about his sisters that Wittgenstein made to Drury, 'They are too much respected, no one would dare to touch them', see Rhees 1984, p. 139.

40 He was against giving so much to the Nazis, but to his brother and sisters this seemed a self-serving pretext. I have summarized in the text a process fraught with passion.

41 In February 1940 the *Reichsstelle für Sippenforschung* told the *Gauamt für Sippenforschung* in Vienna (these were the central and the local offices for genealogy, as it was called) that the declaration of Hermann Christian's German blood or *Deutschblütigkeit* went back to a decision of the Führer and Reichskanzler. Thus the family enjoyed a high degree of protection.

42 See e.g. *FB*, p. 166.

their addresses and he wrote letters to bring them to England, or to help them while there, he contributed to their upkeep, insisting that the source of the money not be revealed, all the things that one would hope or expect. But as one human being to another. And it was as a human being that he reacted to the revelations as the concentration camps were opened, Buchenwald was perhaps the first. 'Do you believe that?', he said to Peter Stern with horror and a sort of unbelief, although the truth was by now established, and, of course, because they did these things to human beings.[43]

In the end then Wittgenstein did not think of himself as Jewish, nor need we do so. The concept is an attractive, although or because a confused one. It is possible to think that it would have been well if all 'Jews' had felt solidarity, or to think that they now ought to do so – it is also possible to think the contradictory or even the opposite of these things. But in any case these are aspirations, not realities.[44]

43 'Die Erinnerung an jene Frage hat mich nie verlassen' ('The memory of that question has never left me') says Stern, in Stern 1989, p. 17. Anyone who remembers England at that date will confirm that the specificity of Jewish suffering under Hitler was not present to most minds, even in 1945. Similarly, earlier, the refugees seemed, as they indeed were, *Germans* driven away by their own government.

44 Having arrived so far I have the impression that the polemical part of what I have said has in essence been said before. I should mention in particular 'Wittgenstein's Judaism', a paper shown me by J.J. Ross of Tel Aviv University and (quoted by him) Lurie 1988. It seems always necessary to repeat it and yet by airing the topic one risks nourishing it. This is part of the fascination I speak of. Gombrich 1997 is more incisive about such considerations.

5

'IT WILL BE TERRIBLE AFTERWARDS, WHOEVER WINS'

One of the paradoxes of social observation, and of biography, is how often the most individual and original of men exhibit the same reaction in a crisis as the least learned and most conventional. In August 1914 (as we described in McGuinness 1988) Wittgenstein hastened to the colours and shared to the full the enthusiasm and devotion which swept over Austria just as it did over Germany and Great Britain. Not that he had precisely the same thoughts as all who felt that enthusiasm. He had little hope that Austria would win the war: hostilities against the English, 'the best race in the world', seemed to him doomed to failure, and he was depressed by the thought of the inevitable decline of the German race, with which he felt deeply identified. What he shared with others was thus not optimism or chauvinism – perhaps these were, in any case, not the fundamental phenomena: rather it was a fascination with the idea of a national task, something involving more than personal or selfish aims. I tried to show how the war came to him as a means of salvation: since it solved at a stroke the problems of what to do with his life: it promised to free him from the torments of a conscience surely too scrupulous, and thereby to make possible new work and new insights in philosophy. To some extent this proved true, though not quite in the form he expected. But it is interesting how, after all, though in a heightened form, his acceptance of the war as a relief from an enervating lack of direction in life resembles that of many of his contemporaries. Thomas Mann depicts the phenomenon in Hans Castorp, the anti-hero of his *Magic Mountain,* who only escapes that enchanted and unmanning height for the redemptive because all-demanding *Flachland,* the lowland, of the war.

How was it then in the Second World War? Wittgenstein was now middle-aged, and this time he was de facto engaged on the British side. But perhaps we should first note that at the time of the *Anschluß,* with his wish to do always the most difficult thing, he had even hesitated before taking that British nationality. The unattractive alternative was to accept the German nationality now imposed on all Austrians. Nonetheless he debated whether he ought to go back, to be with his family, and to accept, in fact, whatever happened in his own country. In this he may have been influenced by the attitude of his sisters. Two remained in Austria, a third, herself American by citizenship and so as yet able to come and go at will, abetted their plan to do so. Somehow, the sisters thought, they could live with the regime: they could obtain, perhaps, Yugoslav passports (here they laid themselves open to forgers) or otherwise evade the provisions of the Nuremberg laws. For they knew by now what ten years before they would never have thought of, that they would count as Jews, if not quite *pur sang*, as their uncle Louis used to boast sardonically, still Jewish as to three-quarters; for their father, alone of his generation, had married into a Jewish family. Their brother Paul, the pianist, emigrated rather than accept the restrictions of those laws. Was he, who still had the gait and some of the manners of an officer of the *Sechste Dragoner*, VIth Dragoons, to be prohibited from sitting on a park bench? He was for refusing all compromise with the German authorities and he betook himself with bag and baggage (and more important with his share of the Wittgenstein fortune) to America. He, to be sure, was an international figure, but the sisters felt they had no life outside the circle of their family and protégés and servants and charitable projects. *Our* Wittgenstein's idea of returning to Austria now seems a quixotic one – his life had not been centred there in the immediately preceding years and he would have had no function there. He could never have escaped. He would necessarily have been involved in whatever the Hitler regime engaged in. Most important of all he would not have been able to help his sisters to overcome their problem – indeed he would even have added to it. Some of these considerations were put before Wittgenstein by Sraffa in a letter of admirably dispassionate clarity (14.3.38, *CL* p. 290), and the idea was abandoned. Still, it was a strange impulse, of a piece with Wittgenstein's general tendency to expect, even to welcome, dark and terrible sides of human nature.

There was a practical side too, to Wittgenstein, which we see (along with something of his principles) in precisely this affair of the family's status under the Nuremberg laws. With great fire and energy he took part in discussions and negotiations between the family lawyers and the Reichsbank and the racial authorities. This involved him in visits to Austria and even to Berlin. The upshot was that, in return for the repatriation of a portion of the Wittgenstein holdings abroad, the sisters were acknowledged to be *Mischlinge ersten Grades* – only half-Jewish. (Their paternal grandfather, not clearly registered as Jewish, was allowed to count as an Aryan. Thus the still younger generation and the cousins issued from mixed marriages were *Mischlinge zweiten Grades*.) The outcome served to preserve them from the worst effects of the war and the developments of racial policy during it, and this will have been its justification for our Wittgenstein. He said to Drury that his sisters were too highly respected: no one would dare to harm them. He was in the end proved right, though they were in fact briefly imprisoned at the time of the fiasco over the Yugoslav passports. Still it is almost as if he underestimated Hitler. He also shows no trace of his brother's opposition in principle: indeed he talked as if it issued from some weakness of character that one had to excuse – *Paul ist ein armer Kerl* (Poor devil!) he commented. Our Wittgenstein always put first what was the personally right choice, especially when it was a difficult one: what was politically right came a long way after.

Not for one minute, of course, did he accept the politics of the Hitler regime. His sympathies in the 1930s (and, as we shall see, throughout the war) were with the Left. So were his associations: returned to Cambridge in 1929, he took up again with the Apostles, by now largely a left-wing group. He lodged with the leading left-wing economist who was their most active senior member (some now think him their spy master). Of four Cambridge men to die in the Spanish Civil War, three were, if not disciples, at least pupils or associates of Wittgenstein. His great friend, Skinner, also tried to enlist despite a game leg (and we may be sure he did it with Wittgenstein's approval). The Marxists, of course, criticized Wittgenstein's philosophy (confining themselves usually to that of the *Tractatus)* and he was critical of theirs – principally of its being a philosophy at all: but they had attended his classes and breathed his air. He, for his part, began (with Skinner) to study Russian. His teacher was Fania Pascal, she too wife of a Marxist and active in the British Soviet Friendship Society. Wittgenstein learnt the language well and had clearly retained a nostalgia for Russia formed in the First World War – a nostalgia for the Russia of Tolstoy perhaps, but it led him to visit the Russia of Stalin and even to think of settling there. The atmosphere of Stalinism contained something that attracted him: a total destruction of early twentieth-century social forms was required (he thought) if there was to be any improvement. *'Die Leidenschaft verspricht etwas'*, he said to Waismann: the passion that infused society there meant that some good could come from it. Again: Wittgenstein accepts the dark and terrible side of things. A Russian leader acts because he must: Lenin (here Wittgenstein repeated a cliché of the time) was like a man who seized the wheel from a drunk (Lenin's philosophy, of course, was piffle). Fania Pascal had the impression that the sufferings of so many in the Russia of the 1920s and 1930s were accepted by Wittgenstein as an accompaniment, relatively unimportant, of the affirmation of a new society. Misery there would have been anyway: now at least it was for a purpose. His attitude towards the Russia of Lenin and Stalin mirrors his dismay at the total unemployment and dejection of 1930s Jarrow (where Drury worked): the only solution, he said, is to get these people all running in the same direction. He seems to have thought that this had happened in Russia, and it is perhaps equally important for understanding his attitudes that he thought it would not happen in England.

When the Pascals moved to Birmingham they found Wittgenstein a frequent visitor: the Vice-Chancellor was a Cambridge friend (a former polar explorer) but Wittgenstein also belonged to a strongly left-wing circle there. He belonged not as one active politically but as a friend: yet for him that required a coincidence in approach to judgements of value. George Thomson and Nicholas Bachtin (brother of Michael) were his closest friends, the one a leading Marxist interpreter of antiquity, the other a former White Russian officer now a Communist, both also men of remarkable literary gifts. Birmingham University (one thinks also of E.H. Dodds and Louis MacNeice) was a centre of a literary culture that looked further afield than between-wars Cambridge. There and not in Trinity he found his friends. Though he did not applaud their ideology or their political activity when they went in for it, his sympathies lay with them and he shared their dislikes.

These attitudes did not dispose him to think well of the British government or of its attitude towards the European situation. He looked at a picture of them – 'a lot of wealthy old men' – and contrasted them (God forgive him!) with Stalin. Eventually it would be the Russians that would put an end to any European Empire of Hitler's. (The remarks this is based on were made before the fall of France. Perhaps, to correct any impression that Wittgenstein was a clear-sighted geopolitical prophet, I should point out that he was equally certain in March 1938 that Hitler had no motive to take over Austria and would not do so. Like his friends we have to learn to take many of his pronouncements seriously for their moral content, but not treat them as serious analyses of complex situations.)

Early in the war Wittgenstein was convinced that the British and French alone could not defeat Hitler (this time perhaps rightly). But he also felt (even before the war) that they did not really want to do so. He too was ashamed, he said to Fania Pascal, when he saw soldiers digging shallow trenches on a Cambridge green – a feeble simulation of preparation for war at the time of Munich. 'I am as much ashamed of what is happening as you are. But we must not talk of it.' Dante (Inf. III 51) puts almost the same words into Vergil's mouth: *Non ragioniam di lor, ma guarda e passa.* I have commented elsewhere on Wittgenstein's much deeper experience of defeat and the overthrow of whole societies, which cut him off from his Cambridge disciples. She, the Russian exile, shared this, but while she protested, he was simply confirmed in his pessimism. He reproved her again during the *drôle de guerre* for exclaiming, 'What are the government up to? Not a shot has been fired! There is no war!' This time he said, 'Some people feel disgusted because birds feed on grubs.' So it was only to be expected that the Allies would not fight against Hitler, their hearts were not in it – and, more than that, they were not (wealthy old men) really going to do anything. Here we have (that is to say, I think I find) a typical Wittgensteinian attitude. He could not withhold admiration from people who were businesslike, people who were capable *etwas durchzusetzen*, to get something done. Here his father came out in him. When Isaiah Berlin gave a talk in Cambridge, Wittgenstein said to him, 'Now come, I am a businessman, so are you: we can do business together.' In a different sphere, Stalin did not betray but saved the Russian revolution, because he was a man who could do something, set things moving, get everyone running the same way. Hitler too: a gangster, but one who knew exactly what he needed to do to get power and keep it. There was no question of his meaning what he said, of his being 'sincere' (a point that puzzled Drury) – 'Is a ballet dancer sincere?' Wittgenstein asked, with one of his telling parallels. Sincerity, meaning what one said, had no part in what Hitler was doing. Here we again see the ineffectualness (in Wittgenstein's view) of the British government over the whole period from 1938 to 1941. The Municheers thought one ought to give Hitler the benefit of the doubt: perhaps he did mean what he said. This was an example of failure to connect with reality. I guess, but cannot prove, that Wittgenstein attributed this to the fact that their real interest – those wealthy old men – was in the preservation of their privileged position. Failure to see was a moral failure – but (as with the birds) nothing else was to be expected of them. Now, in retrospect, certainly in the United Kingdom, 'appeasement' has become a key concept of practical politics: the need to avoid it was used to justify Suez and the Falklands campaign – I don't say wrongly, but I do need to point out that Wittgenstein's opposition to Munich wasn't an example of such thinking. He wouldn't have allowed that a better-run Foreign Office might have taken the right steps. *Realpolitik* was not in their power. Chamberlain's government wasn't in the same league as Hitler and Stalin.

Hitler, we have seen, he regarded as a gangster – someone who profits by others' observance of the rules of the European system: we shall return to the question of whether there was an underestimate here. Wittgenstein's view of Stalin was more complex. Stalin's power was owed to what was happening in Soviet society: a new conception of man, which placed a truer, a more human, value on manual work was being tried out. With all the suffering in the Soviet Union – even with all the lying involved in everyday life – there was still something being worked out, and this gave the whole society a strength which the Western democracies simply did not dispose of. Here (including the blind hope in Russia) we perhaps see the influence of, or in part the reason for, Wittgenstein's reading of Spengler, which is also echoed in many of his remarks about the decline of culture in his time and the inevitability of yet further decline.

Thus (as indicated in my opening remarks) Wittgenstein for a whole complex of reasons personal to himself arrived at a widely-shared view of the war and the events leading up to it. It was not, of course, the Government view, but, in practical respects, it was the view of the Left Wing and of the Party (as it liked to be called) in particular.

The practical consequence for Wittgenstein was that he remained in Cambridge carrying out the teaching duties of his new chair. Probably there was little else he could do. At the time of the fall of France it must even have seemed likely that he could be interned. After the fall of France, with the end of the *drôle de guerre,* it seemed to many that a new spirit was abroad in Great Britain. Wittgenstein himself commented to Drury:

> You have often heard me speak of my dislike of many features of English life. But now that England is in real danger, I realize how fond I am of her; how I would hate to see her destroyed. I have often said to myself that William the Conqueror got himself a very good bargain.
>
> (see Rhees 1984, p. 159)

Still it wasn't the Party view that the United Kingdom was now involved in a proper war. The Soviet Union, it will be remembered, was still a treaty partner – it can be said an ally – of Hitler's. But many, who perhaps didn't see things with quite that degree of realism, nonetheless thought that the war was being fought in the wrong way. There must be some other answer. The movement was summed up in the People's Convention of 1941. Their aims were by no stretch of the imagination modest: the living standards of the people were to be raised; adequate Air Raid Precautions and other means to protect the people were to be put in hand; emergency powers were to be used to take over the banks, land, transport, etc. in the interests of the people; trade union rights (theoretically abridged by the Defence of the Realm Act) were to be restored; national independence was to be given to India; friendship with the Soviet Union was to be established; finally there were to be both a people's government and a people's peace that got rid of the causes of war. It was supposed, or alleged, that such a proposal had only to be put squarely to the people of Germany in order to be accepted. The spirit of the conventioneers can be best illustrated by a quotation from Harry Adams's speech on 12 January:

> Because of our hatred of our ruling class and all that results from their greed and avarice at home and abroad, because we refuse to help them in their struggle for world supremacy against rival imperialisms, we are accused of assisting Hitler and Mussolini and their Fascist thugs. This is an abominable lie.

The points put to the People's Convention were enucleated (though in fact there was fair agreement even before that) at a series of other conventions, including a Students' Convention held at Cambridge in November 1940. This was supported by a number of senior members: mentioned first were the three professors Dent, Trend, and Wittgenstein; then other names follow – Mervyn Stockwood, Joseph Needham, and Dr. Raven, Master of Christ's, will be in different degrees familiar names (otherwise Dr. Raven is said to be easily identifiable in C.P. Snow's *roman-à-clef The Masters*). Among economists there were Maurice Dobb (referred to above as Wittgenstein's landlord) and Joan Robinson (she had forgotten the episode when I spoke to her – but then it was far from being the only skirmish she had engaged in since her youth). The Liberal Club denounced this Students' Convention: its sponsors were predominantly Communists and there would be an attempt to force through extremist proposals – and here it must be said that the convention can have had no other purpose. *Experto credite* how much fierce indignation was called forth by a meeting of such a kind in England in that year. The fact that there was then no very active front where Germans were being fought only increased the insistence on conformity. The reproaches can be imagined – the students were safe in Cambridge, their military service had been deferred, they were comparatively well-off (for the question of what we now call student grants also came up) and so on. Shortly afterwards Dr. Raven was defeated in the election for the Council of the Senate by 83 votes to 11. A meeting to be addressed by D.N. Pritt (a fellow traveller and one of the leading conventioneers) was banned by the University authorities and so on.

Perhaps it was precisely the indignation that led Wittgenstein to show some sympathy with the movement. We know that, as might be expected, he was a fierce critic of the intolerances that seem inseparable from war: he and Thouless composed a letter to *The Times* protesting when a sentence of imprisonment (it is hard to believe it) was passed on a young woman who gave cigarettes to a German prisoner of war. For some reason, whether less than wholeheartedness or tardy prudence, Wittgenstein did not join in the later Cambridge protests when the *Daily Worker* was suppressed (still in the context of the People's Convention), though Raven, Dent, Needham, and Joan Robinson did, and he will surely have been canvassed also. All the same, he would hardly have given his initial support if he felt really identified with the conduct of the war. The danger to his England having receded, dissatisfaction revived.

Such was Wittgenstein's attitude towards the war down to the summer of 1941, a mixture of personal prejudices (his dislike of the unreality and the pretences involved), of a gloomy view of the future of the West (a view whose intellectual credentials need discussion), and, finally, of some degree of faith in the spirit animating the Soviet system. How far the fatalistic element in his attitude was caused by his hopes that things would somehow turn out tolerably for his family in Austria, I cannot, on present evidence, say.

Certainly thoughts of them must have played some role. I should also emphasize that I have not spoken of his attitude towards war itself. Some say he hated it – Thouless for example – but on balance I am inclined to think he saw it as a testing-place for men, a background, an aid almost, in moral tasks. So it had been in 1914, and now he was making remarks like the following (to Drury): 'I wish you and I could have been together in an air raid. I would have liked that'; and speaking of the fascination of the sound of guns in a heavy bombardment. That sort of thing, but also a great number of instructions, sometimes simply kind and helpful, sometimes also morally earnest, to friends on enlisting or on going overseas. This attitude clearly changed in 1941 – the year of the invasion of Russia, certainly, but also that in which quite suddenly his great friend and companion Francis Skinner died of a medical complication. Thouless relates what a great grief this was to Wittgenstein and how it caused him to feel more than ever isolated. We can see some of the effect even in his pocket-diary and in the University notices. Though it was the beginning of October and of the academic year, Wittgenstein ceased to live in Cambridge continuously. His lectures were arranged for the weekends and he took a post at Guy's Hospital (introduced by his friend John Ryle, the medical professor, elder brother of the philosopher). 'A hospital porter' it is usually said, but we need not think of him moving patients about on trolleys. He was first Pharmacy Porter, transporting medicines and *materia medica*, no doubt, and then a Technical Assistant in the Pharmacy. We hear of his preparing the ointments with unusual care – no one else's were so smooth, – and devising new means of mixture. Thouless says that Wittgenstein first tried to be accepted by the RAMC (perhaps an echo here of Skinner's attempt to join the medical arm of the International Brigade in Spain) but was turned down as a former enemy alien (not strictly accurate, if that were the ground, but actually his age and health will hardly have recommended him). He gave Thouless no clear reason for the step he was contemplating, except that it was his wish to take on some sort of manual work, with no intellectual element – and we may conjecture that, as in the First World War, he wanted to share in the hardships of others. But note: only now. His private notebooks speak much of his inability for the last two years to do his real work (an unconscious effect, perhaps, of the war) but also of his especial loneliness now. Only unthinking manual work relieved either of these conditions.

Only now. Perhaps only now was it right from a national as well as from a personal point of view. At any rate there were many for whom the war began in earnest at this time. Not that Wittgenstein became any more optimistic. It can only have been at this time (probably after Pearl Harbour) that Wittgenstein made the remark I quote in my title,

> Things will be terrible when the war is over, whoever wins. Of course, very terrible if the Nazis won, but terribly slimy if the Allies win.

In a way this remark does more credit to Wittgenstein's judgement than some of the ones we have quoted. He saw the enormity of the Hitler regime as something one didn't need to insist on. It is a bit like Karl Kraus's *'Mir fällt zu Hitler nichts ein'* ('I can't think of anything to say about Hitler'), a phrase sometimes misunderstood. Kraus loved to convict out of a man's own mouth, but Hitler was too monstrous for such satire: Hitler *beim Wort genommen* would not come out as absurd or self-contradictory, but as dangerous. He was not playing the game of the liberal press, which can be shown to be insincere (echoes here of Wittgenstein's remark to Fania Pascal). Wittgenstein too didn't need to insist on that, but he could not repress a shudder at the war aims of the Allies, thinking that in fact a continuation of the old system by the worst possible means would result. (I myself think this prediction not wholly true, but of course it isn't wholly false either.)

Wittgenstein's war service, as we may call it, continued for a couple of years. The details are not our concern here, though it may be said that, like many who serve, he often found it, and the company it forced him to keep, disagreeable. Briefly, he moved from the pharmacy to assist a unit working on clinical shock (their main result, reversing the opinion of those days, was that *massive* blood transfusions were necessary: Wittgenstein was of use to them both technically and intellectually). Blitz victims failing – and also being less serviceable for research than industrial accidents and ectopic pregnancies – the group moved to Newcastle Royal Infirmary, taking Wittgenstein with them. At about this point he gave up his teaching, obtaining leave to do war work. In February 1944 Wittgenstein left his hospital post and went to Swansea, gripped, as it seems, by the need to work on what we now call *Philosophical Investigations*. Throughout the rest of the war he was preoccupied by his philosophical work.

Objectively viewed his contribution was a considerable one for a man of his age and his poor health; subjectively it is hard not to feel that the war years were ones in which he had for the time being lost his way. His intellectual reflection on the war (such as it was) is perhaps an index of the confused aims of those days. A more general survey of the intellectual scene in England during the war would show most philosophers rallying to the colours unquestioningly, with some relief even, usually finding employment in some branch of intelligence, dangerous or not as the case might be. They were often vaguely left-wing, sometimes distinctly secularist in their convictions. They returned from the war and took the universities back out of the hands of the theologians and idealists who had, somehow inevitably, predominated during the war – when indeed religion did somewhat revive. After the war then, for them, there was a new spirit abroad: it led to Linguistic Philosophy, Oxford Philosophy as it was often called, and the success of some related schools. In such developments Wittgenstein had no part. He neither shared their automatic patriotism, nor their reliance on brisk reasoning. When, in 1945, he wrote the preface printed at the front of *Philosophical Investigations* (it is not clear that it was ever intended for precisely that text), he said,

> It is not impossible that it should fall to the lot of this work, in its poverty and in the darkness of this time, to bring light into one brain or another – but of course it is not likely.

No trace here of the confidence that (at any rate in philosophy) went along with the doffing of khaki and the picking up of ration books. And for Wittgenstein, as has been pointed out, the darkness of our time did not mean the war. The war, one might say, was only an epiphenomenon of the break-up of a culture, which he had observed long before. So we do not find him addressing himself (perhaps it would be anachronistic to expect it) to what today *seem* to be inescapable and all-absorbing problems arising from that war – principally, of course, the Holocaust and nuclear armaments (the very terms did not exist then). At the same time, perhaps he was right to look for what makes such things possible, with what success we should have to consider some other time. He had after all once before lived through the last days of mankind.

Part II

THE *TRACTATUS*

6

THE PATH TO THE
TRACTATUS

Anyone who has read Ludwig Wittgenstein's *Tractatus* is struck, indeed is usually fascinated, by two apparently contradictory aspects of it. On the one hand it seems to confine all sensible talk to the propositions of natural science, and even puts the propositions of logic into the category of the senseless; on the other hand it itself embraces two extremely non-scientific positions – mysticism, for which it reserves an important place, and solipsism – the view according to which I alone exist and the world is, in Schopenhauer's phrase, my idea.

In the present article I want to discuss Wittgenstein's philosophical development up to the *Tractatus*, with a view to seeing how this apparently contradictory attitude came to be his, and where exactly he acquired or how he developd his views on thought and reality. He told his friend Drury that his first ideas in philosophy came to him extremely early. He also told his friends that in early youth he had been a passionate reader of Schopenhauer. This was a normal part of general culture at the time and Wittgenstein was a highly cultured young man. He was an engineering student at Berlin and later at Manchester with a large variety of ideas on aeronautics when, so his sister Hermine writes:

> He was suddenly seized by philosophy – by reflection on philosophical problems – so violently and so much against his will that he suffered severely from the twofold and conflicting inner vocation and seemed to himself to be torn in two. One of the transformations of which he was to go through so many times in his life had come over him and shook him to the depths of his being. He was engaged in writing a philosophical work and finally made up his mind to show the plan of the work to a Professor Frege in Jena, who had discussed similar questions. Ludwig in those days was constantly in a state of indescribable, almost pathological excitement, and I was very much afraid that Frege – whom I knew to be an old man – would not be able to muster the patience and understanding needed to go into the matter in a

way commensurate to its seriousness. Consequently I was very worried and anxious during Ludwig's journey to Frege. It went off much better however than I had expected. Frege encouraged Ludwig in his philosophical quest and advised him to go to Cambridge as a pupil of a Professor Russell, which Ludwig indeed did.[1]

Now, why did this happen? Why did the young engineer, who was passionately interested in the problems of life, in the question whether life had a meaning, in the difficulties of leading a decent life, why did he, not a mathematician even, turn to the driest works of an obscure professor of mathematics? What I shall say about this is mostly speculation derived from fragments of letters and other short writings dating from before the First World War and during the that, at the end of which his great work the *Tractatus* appeared. In discovering Frege – 'the great works of Frege' as he calls them – Wittgenstein was turning to a decisive figure in the history of philosophy. In saying that, however, I must at once add that Frege would not have had this decisive influence without a Wittgenstein to mediate it. For our present purposes, the essential point about Frege was his conception of the object of mathematics and logic. In the popular conception of his time among mathematicians and philosophers as well as among ordinary men, the world consisted on the one side of physical objects and on the other of our ideas. Mathematics and logic, however, as Frege saw, studied neither of these realms. There had to be also a third realm in which were housed concepts, propositions, numbers, and countless other categories of objects. These were not the products of our thinking but the objects of our thought and what Frege hoped to do was to recognize the eternal relations subsisting between them. Take the notion of a proposition and its truth: a proposition here means that which is thought, not the thinking of it. If such a proposition is true it is so quite independently of whether anyone ever judges it to be true. That Brutus killed Caesar is an eternal object eternally true. But the recognition that there are eternal objects in a third realm is especially necessary if we are to understand the nature of the laws of thought so called, the laws of logic or of truth itself as Frege called them.

> By logical laws I do not mean psychological laws of taking something to be true but laws of truth itself. If it is true that I am writing this in my study on the 13th of July 1893 while the wind howls outside, then it is true even should all men later hold it to

---

1 Hermine Wittgenstein 1944–8, p. 107.

be false. And if being true is in this way independent of being recognized to be true, then also the laws of truth are not psychological laws but are boundary stones set in an eternal soil: our thinking can indeed wash over them but it cannot displace them.[2]

Frege thought that logic and arithmetic, Russell thought that all of pure mathematics, gave an account of eternal relations holding between objects which did not affect the senses. The existence of these objects and the holding of these relations could not be thought of as depending on the representations of a knowing subject.

Now Schopenhauer, and Kant before him, had not thought exactly of such a dependence. They had held that logic was a priori inasmuch as it contained the form of thought and they supposed that its laws were to be discovered simply by reflection on the exercise of the understanding. It was not at all apparent to sceptical critics of Schopenhauer and Kant why these laws of thought were valid or what force they had as laws. Boltzmann, for example, a physicist much respected by Wittgenstein, said:

> These laws of thoughts can be called a priori because many thousand years of experience by the species have made them innate in the individual, but it seems to be nothing but a logical howler on Kant's part when he proceeds to infer that they are infallible in all cases.[3]

Against such views Frege and Russell seemed to oppose the picture of a crystalline world of eternal objects eternally possessing those properties and relations that the truths of logic and mathematics ascribed to them. It was not just the form of thought that was embodied in these truths but the form of reality itself. They had discovered amid the uncertainty and the relativity of human thinking, amid the contingency of the physical world, something whose existence and nature was absolute. Small wonder that under the influence of this conceptual realism of Frege's, Wittgenstein gave up the Schopenhauerian idealism of his early youth. But just as he was to retain this idealism in a modified form, so he could not accept that realism without modifying it too. His first point of attack was the fundamental logical concepts – the logical constants which Russell at this time thought of as eternal objects like Frege's numbers. Wittgenstein questioned not only the composition of the list of logical constants but the ontological status assigned to any that had to be retained. The first philosophical remark of his that has been preserved is in a letter to Russell of 22 June 1912:

2   Frege 1962, p. XVI.
3   Boltzmann 1974, p. 195.

Logic is still in the melting-pot, but one thing gets more and more obvious to me: the propositions of logic contain only apparent variables and whatever may turn out to be the proper explanation of apparent variables, its consequence must be that there are no logical constants.

Logic must turn out to be a totally different kind than any other science.[4]

This was vehement dissent indeed – and dissent from the very feature of the doctrines of Russell and Frege that at first attracted him. But it was entirely in their spirit – or at any rate in Frege's – to see logic as totally different from all other sciences. Wittgenstein used logic to reveal or to point to the transcendental features of the world, but denied logic the status of a substantive science of one category of objects. The development of his thought on these questions can be traced by reading in order the notes on logic on 1913, the notes dictated to Moore in 1914, and what remains of the wartime *Notebooks*. I shall not attempt to trace it here in detail. All that we need to grasp is that Wittgenstein began by trying to account for the special status of logic and ended by producing a revolution in philosophy. He saw that a logic which was the science of a special set of objects would have no higher claim to hold absolutely than any other science, and he saw it as a mere evasion of a difficulty to allege, as Russell did, that truths about these objects had a self-evidence for us which other truths did not have. To his great surprise Frege too was guilty of this evasion. Wittgenstein seized upon the truth perceived by Frege and Russell that logic was not the study of thought and exploited their idea that it was the study of the form of thought or the form of reality. In concrete terms this meant that logical truths were not truths about anything whatsoever: they possessed a characteristic which he was the first to isolate and to name: they were all, so he thought, tautologies. They were empty of content. They were by-products not of other truths but of the possibility of expressing other truths. For technical reasons Wittgenstein's identification of the common feature of all logical truths with tautology was to prove a will-of-the-wisp, though it is extremely important that he formulated so clearly the desirability, if it were possible, of finding such a common characteristic. But of even greater importance was the light which Wittgenstein threw upon the purpose of philosophy itself. He was clear that logic was the basis of philosophy and he therefore applied to philosophy what he believed to be true of logic. After the appearance of his work philosophy was to become – or people were to see that philosophy already was – the study, not of what was known or could

---

4 *CL*, p. 14.

be known, but of what could be the case. This meant that the philosopher had to study not people's psychology, not what they were capable of thinking or knowing; not even their language, not what they were capable of saying or putting into words; but what was capable of being true. Frege's study of the laws of truth itself was seen by Wittgenstein to be nothing but the study of what could be true, the study of the proposition, as he called it. In a very wide sense this can be called the philosophy of language, but the emphasis must fall on the word philosophy. Wittgenstein was not interested in our actual language or in the conditions under which it came into being but in the principles of symbolism as such. It was these, his theory of symbolism, that he explained to Frege on their meeting in December 1912. By a symbolism Wittgenstein understood essentially a vehicle for truth and falsity: this was perhaps a limitation in his point of view, which he corrected in his later writings. Wittgenstein was delighted when he discovered, or rather when he thought that he had discovered, a theory of symbolism provided a simple decision procedure for the whole of logic. He wrote to Russell in November 1913,

> Now listen! – I will first talk about those logical propositions which are or might be contained in the first eight chapters of *Principia Mathematica*. That they all follow from one primitive proposition is clear enough because one symbolic rule is sufficient to recognize each of them as true or false.[5]

The details of his method of deciding whether a given proposition was logical or not do not concern us here: those who are interested will find the method described in Proposition 6.1203 of the *Tractatus*. As it happens the *Tractatus* also contains another, perhaps simpler, decision procedure for the proposition or calculus – the method of truth tables – and it is probable that Wittgenstein had discovered this too before November 1913.[6] Both methods were devices for showing that logical truth was something implicit in any method of symbolizing whatsoever and was therefore of a totally different kind from the truth of ordinary propositions.

Wittgenstein wanted to deal with all the problems of philosophy by a proper theory of symbolism:

> The word 'philosophy' ought always to designate something over or under, but not beside, the natural sciences. Philosophy gives no pictures of reality, and can neither confirm or confute scientific investigation. It consists of logic and metaphysics, the former is its

---

5   *CL*, p. 52.
6   Reasons for thinking that he discovered it approximately a year earlier are given in McGuinness 1988, pp. 160f.

basis A correct explanation of the logical propositions must give them a unique position as against all other propositions.[7]

These were Wittgenstein's words in September 1913. In April 1914 he said to Moore:

Logical so-called propositions show the logical properties of language and therefore of the universe, but say nothing.[8]

I hope it will now be clear that already before the First World War Wittgenstein, starting from the need to account for the peculiar position of logic among other sciences, had reached a totally new view of philosophy. Its task was to show or mirror the properties of the universe. It was to do that by showing or mirroring the properties of any symbolism, of any language, whatsoever. The words 'show' and 'mirror' were ones of extreme importance to Wittgenstein because, in his view, philosophy did not consist of true propositions in the ordinary sense at all. At best we might reckon as part of philosophy the so-called propositions, the tautologies, of logic. But the greater part of philosophy would consist in the attempt to make readers, or better still hearers, see what was shown by their quite ordinary propositions, be they true or false. In this way they would obtain a true view of the world. To be sure, part of giving them this true view of the world consisted in making them see that metaphysical questions about the good, the beautiful, the self-identity of objects, and about whether relations were internal or external, were meaningless. This meant that a constructive and systematic philosophy was an impossibility. But the main lesson of the *Tractatus* was a positive one for all that. It showed that the failure of a scientific type of philosophy to provide an answer to the problems of life was not, as it might seem to be, a disappointment. That answer was to be found, not in some new fact, but in some new way of looking at the world, of seeing what the world showed. Before the First World War the implications of Wittgenstein's work for philosophy were perhaps not so clear to him. It was halfway through the war before he wrote in his *Notebooks* 'My work has broadened out from the foundations of mathematics to the essence of the world.'[9]

Nonetheless it is also part of his intellectual history that a correct instinct led him from the technical difficulty of providing a foundation for mathematics to an acceptable solution for those problems – in the widest sense religious problems – that had exercised him since youth. It has been the purpose of this paper to sketch the path he followed.

7 *Nb*, p. 106.
8 *Nb*, p. 107.
9 *Nb*, p. 79 (my translation).

7

PICTURES AND
FORM

Wittgenstein's *Tractatus* is a series of propositions numbered in such a way as to indicate their respective importance within the whole and their logical dependence upon one another.[1] That a system of numeration so troublesome for an author to devise will give many useful indications to the interpreter, is a truth that has only to be stated to be acknowledged. It may fairly be assumed, for example, that the propositions beginning with the number 6 represent what he regarded as the chief results of his enquiry: this assumption is confirmed by the frequent echoes to be found in these propositions of what Wittgenstein said in the *Vorwort*.

The structure of the 6's is roughly as follows:[2] in 6 itself the general form of a proposition is announced. By this is meant the form that any expression which is to be a proposition must have: the 4's and 5's have been largely devoted to showing that this form will be identical with the form that any truth-function must have (4's) and to showing what form it is that any truth-function must have (5's). It is then shown, in the 6.1's, that the propositions of logic are tautologies, which say nothing and have no content. In the 6.2's it is shown that the propositions of mathematics are likewise pseudo-propositions: the essential thing here is that mathematics is a *part* of logic, as Wittgenstein says twice (6.2, 6.234). In the 6.3's Wittgenstein deals with the apparent a-priority of at least some parts of natural science. His conclusion here is in accord with Einstein's dictum about Geometry: some propositions of 'science' are necessarily true, in the sense that they are necessary consequences of our choice of a partic-

---

1   *Tractatus Logico-Philosophicus*, by Ludwig Wittgenstein, London, Kegan Paul, 1922: in this article KP (Italian translation: by G.C.M. Colombo, S.J., Milan, Fratelli Bocca 1954: in this article CFB). I am indebted to Fr. Colombo for the suggestion that I should write this article and for frequent discussions: in this latter point I am also indebted to my colleague in Oxford, Mr D.F. Pears. Wittgenstein explains his system of numeration in a footnote printed on KP, p. 30, CFB, p. 164.
2   By 'the n's' I shall mean those propositions that begin with the number n.

ular method of describing the world: but these say nothing about the world. There will be other propositions in science that do say something about the world (6.3431) but these will not be necessarily true and are the only 'scientific' propositions properly so called.[3] The 6.4's and 6.5's discuss those questions to which natural science doesn't even seem to give an answer. Ethics is clearly one field of such questions, and Wittgenstein claims that there are *no* ethical propositions. On other matters, such as the freedom of the will, the 'meaning' of life and 'the riddle' (perhaps this is the felt contingency of the world) there can be no questions, because there are no propositions that would be their answers. Finally Wittgenstein recommends philosophical analysis (to borrow a later term) as a cure, and mystical feeling as a substitute, for metaphysics. The book closes with the often-quoted warning not to try to put the data of this feeling into words (7): *Wovon man nicht sprechen kann, darüber muß man schweigen* (What we cannot speak about we must needs leave in silence.)[4]

3 This remark seems to me to follow not only from 6.34 but also from the requirement of consistency with 4.111 from which it may be inferred that propositions, which have content and are not a priori are coextensive with natural science. However it may well be felt that there is a lack of clarity in the 6.3's concerning the existence within what we normally call natural science of a distinction between a priori pseudo-propositions and real, non-a priori propositions, and a complete absence of any indication how to assign a given proposition to one or other of these two classes. It may be questioned whether any very precise indications could be given.

4 The sequence of the last four propositions is interesting and may briefly be commented on here. 6.522 alludes again to 'the mystical' which is however something inexpressible. 6.53 describes 'the correct method' of philosophizing – that is, philosophical analysis resulting in the demonstration of the meaninglessness of metaphysical propositions. 6.54 is another well-known proposition in which he describes his own propositions as nonsensical, and compares them to a ladder which one who has climbed it must throw away. A consideration of the context illuminates both 6.54 and 7: Wittgenstein is reproaching himself for not following the only strictly correct philosophical method. Instead of saying things like, 'What is mystical is not what the world is *like*, but that there *is* a world', he ought to have confined himself to the demonstration of the senselessness of metaphysical propositions – the attempt to *say* anything about what is mystical – and to the silent practice of mysticism. Thus he does not wish others to produce 'propositions' like his but to engage in a quite different activity. It is in virtue of this fact – that they lead to something quite different from themselves – that his propositions resemble a ladder. Remarks such as that logic is a mirror image of the world (6.13) or that the existence of the world is mysterious (6.44) do not themselves convey a correct view of the world, since such a view will not consist in holding any propositions, but they may help others to attain such a view – provided those others see what is wrong with these propositions themselves (this, I think, is part of the force of *'überwinden'* in 6.54). These propositions (for it is to such that 6.54 principally applies, in my view) are right in what they deny – that logic is a theory, or that the nature of the world is mysterious – but wrong in what they seem to assert. Even construed as denials, they ought more properly to be put in the form of demonstrations that certain 'propositions' about logic or the world are senseless, for when there is a 'subject' about which nothing can be said, one

The assessment of what is 'important' in the *Tractatus* will vary with judgement, interest and taste: about what the author regarded as his conclusions, he himself has left us in no doubt: they can be seen from the foregoing summary. He has examined the 'propositions' of logic, mathematics, natural science, and traditional philosophy (principally metaphysics and ethics), and he has shown that of all of them only the non-a-priori parts of natural science have a claim to the title of 'proposition', the others are either contentless like those of logic, or nonsensical like those of metaphysics.[5]

This sketch of Wittgenstein's conclusions contains, of course, nothing new; but the consideration of them within the sequence of thought of the 6's and of the terms in which Wittgenstein actually puts them brings out two aspects to which I should like to draw attention. First is the way in which all these conclusions are announced as conclusions about the features of certain propositions or pseudo-propositions. This, of course, is not a property peculiar to the 6's, since throughout the *Tractatus* '*Satz*' is by far the most common technical term. It is not the terms used in them, we might say, but the sorts of combinations of terms of which they

---

ought *not* to *say* that nothing can be said about it, *but* one ought to say *nothing* about it and make others do likewise.

It will be clear that at the end of the *Tractatus* Wittgenstein is not saying that he has reached no results, for results, though unimportant ones, are what he lays claim to in the *Vorwort*: rather he is concerned lest his method shall have seemed to give a new handhold to metaphysical reflection about the world and about logic: it has been his principal aim to remove the temptation to such speculation, but in doing so he has attempted to do justice if not to the truth, at least to the legitimate feeling that underlay this temptation. It is by this generosity that he has incurred the danger against which he here attempts to guard.

5 The distinction between a 'proposition' that says nothing but is without content and even senseless (*sinnlos*), and one that is nonsensical (*unsinnig*), comes out very clearly not only from the well-known passage (4.461–4.4611) where tautologies and contradictions (!) are said to belong to the former but not to the latter class, but also from 5.5303: 'Roughly speaking, to say of *two* things that they are identical is nonsense, and to say of *one* thing that it is identical with itself says nothing.' It is true that the particular example of an *Unsinn* given here raises some difficulties, since it implies that, where a and b are two things, '$a = b$' is not a contradiction (otherwise, by 4.4611, it would not be an *Unsinn*); but if so, it should seem that '$a = a$' is not a tautology (a result that would also follow from the truth that a tautology is a particular kind of truth-function). If, however, '$a = a$' is not a tautology, why should not it too be an *Unsinn*? It is a weak defence to say that in a language properly adapted to the expression of thought (that is how I interpret '*Begriffsschrift*') the sign of equality would disappear. In my view Wittgenstein ought to have said that this sign did lead to sense when put between expressions one of which was a description, but would always lead to *Unsinn* when placed between names. This raises the question of whether it is possible for one thing to have two names. None of this, however, affects the truth that Wittgenstein here draws a distinction between '*nichtssagend* ' and '*unsinnig*'.

consist that characterize logic, mathematics and metaphysics, just as the world is the totality of facts, not the totality of things (1.1). Carnap suggested (1937, p. 303) that, in the formal mode of speech, this sentence would run: 'Science is a system of sentences, not of words.'[6]

That all the conclusions are expressed as conclusions about propositions is chiefly interesting here because of its connection with the second aspect of those conclusions that I have in mind, an aspect which brings us directly to the particular subject of this paper: namely that all of them are thought either to follow from or to be comments on the discovery of the general form of a proposition. The central parts of the 6's are intended to show that the propositions of logic, mathematics and the a priori parts of natural science are *not* results of the application of the operation of simultaneous negation to elementary propositions (or are in certain cases self-cancelling results). The 6.4's start with the consideration that since what is good or bad is the existence of a state of affairs, an ethical proposition, if there were such a thing, would be the assertion of a proposition (compounded exclusively of elementary propositions) about the interior of the world (so to speak) plus an assertion *that* the truth of this assertion was a good or bad thing. As such it would involve the formation of a proposition out of elementary propositions by the use of operations other than of simultaneous negation. But the general form of a proposition does not permit this: ergo. Thus to think of something as good (if 'think' is the right word) is not to assert anything about a state of affairs, but to have a distinct feeling about a state of affairs. Suppose a

---

6   6.53 says, it is true, that in a metaphysical proposition there are certain signs to which no meaning (*Bedeutung*) has been given, but it may fairly be assumed that Wittgenstein has in mind words which in certain uses do have *Bedeutung*, but which are used in metaphysical propositions in a way in which they have none. His own favourite example of such a word is '*identisch*': the reason why 'Socrates is identical' is nonsense, he says (5.4733, cf. 5.473), is that we have given no meaning to the word 'identical' as a *property-word* (the word '*Eigenschaftswort*' is *gesperrt* [spaced for emphasis] in the text, which helps to make our point).

Further support for the view that metaphysics is characterized not by the use of meaningless words but by the use of meaningful words in nonsensical combinations comes from 3.323–3.324 where it is pointed out that our vernacular language gives rise to the confusions of which philosophy is full by, for example, allowing 'identical' to look like a word for a property. Also from 4.003 where it is said that most of the questions raised and the propositions asserted by philosophers are rooted in misunderstandings of the logic of our language. It seems to me clear that the introduction of meaningless names would not naturally be the result of such misunderstandings, and that the example given of an extremely obviously nonsensical question (whether the good is more or less identical than the beautiful) is nonsensical because of the way the words are used rather than because of the words that are used. At any rate, the parallel, with the nonsense-example 'Socrates is identical', suggests that what is wrong here is the misuse of 'identical'.

certain state of affairs which seems good to one man and bad to another: for each it will have the same *structure*, but the dimensions of it will seem larger to the one than to the other: thus the happy man's world will be (or could be) of exactly the same structure as that of the unhappy man, but it will have, as it were, larger dimensions.[7] The structure of the world is expressible in language, these 'dimensions' are not. The 6.5's chiefly deal with what are felt to be questions, even though we cannot think of any propositions that would be their answers.

Enough will have been said to make clear the importance of 'the general form of a proposition' in the sequence of Wittgenstein's thought as he has presented it to us. Briefly the difficulties with which this confronts us are the following: in the first part of the *Tractatus*, notably in the 3's and early 4's, we seem to be told that the essence of a proposition is to be a picture, while in the later parts we are told that its essence is to be a truth-function, that is to say a result of applying the operation of

---

7   This is the best sense that I can at the moment see for 6.43. It might seem more consistent with 5.6–5.62 to understand talk about 'the limits of the world' in 6.43 in such a way that by altering the limits of the world was meant altering the objects named and the elementary propositions possible within a man's own private language ('that language which I alone understand', as some think the translation should read at 5.62, see below 'Solipsism', Chapter 13 in the present volume). In that case, the happy man (the man who thinks things good) would see more (or less or different) things than the unhappy man. There might be enough agreement between their private languages to permit the sort of communication we now have (this is a problem that will in any case arise for Wittgenstein, given the superficial meaning of the 5.6's), but the analysis of a given proposition in the public language into the elementary propositions of each man's private language will be different. Thus a change *of* a man's world, as opposed to a change *in* it, would be a change of the objects that constituted the form of his world, and thus a change of the analysis in his language of some propositions of the public language: a change of 'the limits of his world' (5.6). On this view, if men could see the world in the same way they could all see that it was good (or bad).

There are two difficulties for this interpretation: first 2.022–2023, from which it appears that all possible worlds have their objects (and thus, in one sense, their limits 5.5561) in common. Against this must be set 5.123, which speaks (presumably allegorically) of the *creation* of objects by God, and seems to envisage the possibility of his including or omitting certain objects from creation. It may be thought that the objects that form the limits of a man's world, also limit the worlds that he can at that time think of as possible. It is conceivable that he should change, but he cannot conceive *how* he might. This would be of a piece with the inexpressibility of an ethical viewpoint. The second difficulty is that in 6.43 Wittgenstein speaks of the world's waxing or waning *as a whole* (my italics). It seems to me that this last phrase is more suited to my interpretation (where it is, as it were, the dimensions of every single fact that change) than to the mere adding, subtracting or change of some, not necessarily all, objects.

In either case it is to be noted that living the good and living the bad life are matters of *viewpoint*. This, I think, is also the lesson of 5.621–5.63. 'The world and life are one. I am my world.'

simultaneous negation to elementary propositions. The 'picture theory' requires further elaboration, and the truth-function account of what it is to be a proposition seems to involve circularity by presupposing a prior understanding of what it is to be an elementary proposition. But a more serious difficulty is that the two accounts seem to be quite separate things, and, if this is so, cannot both be adequate accounts of what it is to be a proposition.[8]

That a proposition is a picture is first absolutely asserted in the 4's, at 4.01–4.012 and 4.021: unless it were a picture it could not assert anything (4.03) nor be true or false (4.06). Thereafter, apart from passing references at 4.462 and 5.156, the notion of the proposition as a picture disappears from the *Tractatus*. It has of course been previously implied, most clearly at 3.42 and 3–3.1, but also by the almost exact parallelism between the 2.1's, which discuss pictures, and the 3.1's to 3.4's, which discuss propositions. Russell in his introduction to the *Tractatus* (KP, p. 8, CFB, p. 136) says that Wittgenstein is concerned with 'the question: what relation must one fact (such as a sentence) have to another in order to be *capable* of being a symbol for that other. In order that a certain sentence should assert a certain fact there must, however the language may be constructed, be something in common between the structure of the sentence and the structure of the fact. This is perhaps the most fundamental thesis of Mr Wittgenstein's theory.' Wittgenstein himself puts this at 4.03, by saying that the essential connection that a proposition must have with a state of affairs, in order to communicate that state of affairs to us, is that it must be its logical picture. The particular aspects of being a picture that are stressed in the 4.0's are: being such that signs within the proposition deputize for (*vertreten*) objects (4.0312) and being logically articulated and composite (*logisch gegliedert, zusammengesetzt*: 4.032). There must be composition within the proposition, and composition of such a kind that a mere list of the names occurring within it is not sufficient to characterize it, rather each of them has a different role within the proposition, though all of them have the role of deputizing for objects.[9] In fact the notion of deputizing for an object is inseparable from that of playing a particular role in a proposition or

---

8 The existence and importance of this problem were first, to my knowledge, pointed out and many directions for its solution (on which I have drawn freely) given by Miss G.E.M. Anscombe in lectures at Oxford (later published as Anscombe 1959).

9 We may here draw attention to a passage to which we must return: 3.14–3.142, of which 2.14–2.141 is a parallel. It is by being articulated that a proposition is a fact, *the* fact that its elements, the words, are related to one another (*sich zu einander verhalten*) in the way they are. And it is by being a fact that a proposition is distinguished from the set of names occurring in it.

picture.[10] It seems then that the essence of a proposition includes the deputizing for objects of its names and that this in turn involves that the proposition is articulated or composite in a way that a set of names is not. It is not my intention here to try to give all the reasons which may have led Wittgenstein to such conclusions, but it may be worth pointing out that one important premise is the possibility of understanding a proposition or putting together a picture without knowing whether it is a true proposition or picture (4.021, 4.03).[11]

These passages show, it seems to me, that what it is for a sign to be a deputy for an object is to be understood in terms of what it is for a fact to represent another fact and not conversely. Ramsey in his review of the *Tractatus* (Ramsey 1931) maintained the opposite view, citing 5.542 (where Wittgenstein speaks of 'a coordination of facts by means of a co-ordination of their objects') as a proof that Wittgenstein regarded 'deputizing' as the more intelligible notion, and 'representing' as explicable in terms of it.

That the proposition or picture should consist of elements which deputize for objects, and that it should be compounded out of these elements in a quite definite way (so that a different composition would result in a different proposition), these are necessary conditions for the proposition to assert any fact, but more is required if it is to assert *the* fact that it does assert. It must be composed of elements that deputize for the objects whose combination is that fact; and those elements must have the same relation to one another as the objects have in the fact.[12] This requirement, which is brought out very clearly in the 2's and 3's, is the requirement of an identity of form (2.17) between the picture and the pictured. It will be clear that, since our interest is in the general form of a proposition, any remarks about the form of a proposition are important for us.

We meet the form of a fact in 2.033, of a picture in 2.15 (*die Form der Abbildung*) and of a proposition in 3.312 and 3.315. The first two have much in common but leave certain obscurities, which with the help of the third, which is somewhat different, we may be able to resolve.

---

10 I think this is why Wittgenstein says: 'The elements of a picture are, *in the picture*, deputies for objects' (2.13) and 'A name is a deputy, *in a proposition*, for an object' (3.22, my italics in both cases). In any case 3.3 and 3.314 explicitly say that a name and an expression respectively have meaning only in the context (*Zusammenhang*) of a proposition.

11 I suspect that the same premise is used in the proof of atomism. 2.0212 runs: It would then be impossible (sc. if there were no objects) to *essay* a depiction of the world. (This is a possible translation of '*entwerfen*', and the only one that fits the context, in my opinion.)

12 It is sometimes suggested that an atomic fact is uniquely determined by the objects that occur in it: cf. Colombo, CFB, p. 40. It seems to me that in this case a class of names would be sufficient to assert a fact, contrary to 3.142.

Both for facts and for pictures the notion of form is introduced *via* the notion of structure. The structure of a fact or picture is the way in which its elements hang together (2.032, 2.15 ... *Dieser Zusammenhang* ...): The form is the possibility of the structure (2.033, 2.15). It is first of all necessary to see that two facts or pictures are of different structure (or are different structures) if their objects (or elements) are arranged in the same way, but are different objects; in such a case however they will have the same *form*. Thus a fact and its picture may have the same form (must have, indeed), but cannot have the same structure.[13] Each fact that we are aware of has its own structure: that *these* objects stand in *this* arrangement constitutes *this* structure. The structure of the fact that John loves Mary is the fact that John stands in the relation of loving to Mary. It will be obvious from this example that to assert the existence of the structure is nothing other than to assert the fact, and it will also seem that to say that a fact has a certain structure is to say nothing beyond what one has already said in asserting the fact. It does not seem to me, however, that this triviality is an objection to my interpretation of '*Struktur*'. Wittgenstein says of *Form* that the logical form of reality cannot be represented in or expressed by a proposition, but is exhibited or shown by a proposition (4.12's passim, 6.124). A rough paraphrase of this for our purpose would be: the logical form of a proposition and of the fact that it states is perceived *eo ipso* by anyone who understands the proposition: but since, in order to understand any proposition P_n about a proposition p, you must already understand p, therefore the proposition P_k ascribing a certain logical form to p is bound to be otiose. It is evident that the same will hold of propositions about the structure of a proposition: indeed we find Wittgenstein using the fact that a proposition shows its own *structure* as a sort of illustration of the fact that it *shows* (rather than represents) the logical form of reality. 'Thus a proposition '*fa*' shows that in its sense the

---

13 This interpretation of '*Struktur*' was suggested by Ramsey in his review on the grounds that it could be seen from the structure of propositions when one followed from the other (5.13, cf. 5.2, s.22). Also 4.1211 says that the structure of two propositions shows when they contradict one another: if contradiction could be seen from the *forms* of propositions, then p would be the contradictory of not-q. However 5.131 says that if one proposition follows from another, this is expressed by relations in which their forms stand to one another.

I can reconcile this with Ramsey's view (which I follow) about the contrast between '*Struktur*' and '*Form*', only by saying that if one proposition follows from another, then there must be *at least* a relation between their forms – though there must be more as well. When one proposition follows from another, there will always be between the forms of the two a relation much closer than that between p and not-not-q. But, however close the formal relations between two propositions, it is always possible that, because of some difference in the objects named (a difference of structure, not of form), they should be logically independent of one another.

object *a* occurs' 4.1211. The occurrence of the particular object *a* is surely
a feature of structure rather than of form.[14] Although it touches a more
general question than we are here concerned with, the reader may wish
to consider the suggestion that we feel a need to speak of structure and
form only because our everyday speech disguises our thoughts (4.002),
fails to make obvious the structure of our thoughts and of the facts that
we state, though *implicitly* (*stillschweigend* 4.002) we do grasp those structures. Thus when we speak of the structure of the fact that John loves
Mary, as if this were something different from the fact that John loves
Mary, we are really thinking of a translation of the statement that John
loves Mary into a more explicit language, one obeying logical grammar
(*eine Zeichensprache, die der logischen Grammatik ... gehorcht* 3.325).

How, then, are we to understand the statement that the form of a
picture or fact is the possibility of its structure? My view will be conveyed
by the following analogy: suppose a system within which three or more of
the letters *a, b, c* and *d* in immediate succession (repetitions being allowed),
immediately preceded by the sign (') and immediately followed by the sign
('), constitute a well-formed formula. Within such a system '*aba*' and '*aca*'
will be structures, and they can be said to be of the form
'*a a*', on the grounds that they are possible ways of turning '*a a*' into a well-
formed formula. We may wish to say instead that they are of the form '*a
( ) a*' or '*axa*', a suitable role, that of a variable, having been ascribed to the
letter *x* or the signs ( ). Alternatively, on similar grounds, we may wish to
say that they are of the forms '*xyx*' or '*xyz*' or finally '... *xyz* ...' The last
alternative is of course equivalent to saying that they are well-formed
formulae. But probably, if we had to choose which of all the possible
candidates was the form of these structures, we should say that '*xyz*' was.

The application of the analogy will be obvious: that John loves Mary is
(let us suppose) a fact, so it is a structure.[15] It is of the form 'that *x* loves
y' or of the form 'that *x* loves but is not identical with *y*' or of the form
'that *x* stands in a relation to *y*' or of the form 'that something is true of
an ordered couple of objects' or of the form 'that something is true of one
or more objects'.[16] Of course *all* facts are of the last of these forms. The

---

14 It is perhaps worth saying that I cannot use 4.122 to prove my point, since the structures he there speaks of are those of complex facts (*Tatsachen*) and he speaks as if the
structure of a complex fact is something that corresponds to the *formal properties* of an
atomic fact.

15 The last paragraph but one will make clear how saying that it *is* a structure is identical
with saying that it *has* a structure.

16 We cannot say, however, that it is of the form 'that someone loves someone else' or of the
form 'that one thing stands in a relation to another' for these are themselves facts, or
could conceivably be so. Just as '*a a*' is not a well-formed formula in my analogy, so in
the *Tractatus* the form of a fact is not itself a fact. Otherwise it could itself be asserted by
a statement, contrary to the 4.12's.

fact or the structure that John loves Mary can be said to be of each or all of these forms, for each of them defines a range of facts and states of affairs that may or may not hold, such that one fact or state of affairs among these, one possible instantiation of each of these forms, is: that John loves Mary. If we had to say which of all these was *the* form of the fact John loves Mary, we should probably say that 'that x stands in a relation to y' (with a stipulation that we wished to indicate that range of facts which resulted if identical substitutions for x and y were excluded) was *the* form. For the stipulation, cf. the 5.53's.

To avoid difficulties arising from the particular example and irrelevant to the general case, let us say that the form *par préférence* of the fact that aRb (where 'a', 'R' and 'b' designate constants, though Wittgenstein would not put it in this way) is '$\phi\,(x, y)$'.[17]

At first sight it may seem that a slightly different account has to be given of the form of a picture, as this is described in the 2.1's. 2.15–2.151 seem to mean the following: the structure of a picture (namely the fact that its elements are related to one another in a definite way: which fact, by 2.14, is identical with the picture itself) sets forth (*stellt vor*) that things are related to one another in this way: the picture's form of depiction (by which Wittgenstein means: that it is possible for the elements to stand in this relation to one another) is at the same time the possibility that objects should stand in this relation to one another. 2.151 may seem puzzling, but it should be evident that if form is the possibility of structure (2.033, 2.15) and if picture and fact are to have their form in common (2.17, 2.2, etc.), then to say that the one structure is possible will be to say also that the other is. Thus the structure or the fact that the part of the picture

---

17 For the use of 'ϕ' as opposed to 'R' in the indication of forms, cf. 3.333, 4.24.

There is evidence in pre-*Tractatus* MSS, to which I shall return, that Wittgenstein at one time spoke of two kinds of indefinable symbol, Names and Forms, understanding by the latter symbols for relations and properties. If we followed this way of speaking we could say that the fact that aRb was of the form 'xRy' rather than '$\phi\,(x, y)$'. But we have already seen that there are many different, because more or less general, 'forms' of a particular fact. It might well be that 'xRy' was a form of the fact that aRb but not the form in the sense in which Wittgenstein was speaking of a unique form at 2.033.

'x loves y' has a good claim to be *the* form of the fact that John loves Mary, but this is because since 'loves' is not an indefinable it confers logical (by which I mean inferential) properties on any proposition in which it occurs – e.g. whatever x and y may be, if x loves y, then x does not hate y. It cannot be for this sort of reason that Wittgenstein thought of *indefinable* relational symbols as 'forms'.

One reason for regarding 'R' in 'aRb' as a form but not 'a' or 'b', where all designate constants, is that, unlike a name, the symbol for a particular relation determines how many and what type of other symbols there must be in an elementary proposition. Thus knowing that the symbol for a particular relation occurs in a proposition tells us more about the form of that proposition, than knowing that a particular name does so.

which deputizes for *a* (let us call this part: '*a*') stands in a certain relation to '*b*' sets forth the structure or the state of affairs that *aRb*. Further, if it is possible for '*a*' to stand in a certain relation to '*b*', then it is possible that *aRb*, and conversely.[18]

In reality, 2.15–2.151 agree very well with my previous account of the form of a fact. Since a picture is a fact (2.141) it has a certain form, say 'that *x* is to the left of *y*' or 'that *x* stands in a relation to *y*', and since there are just as many elements in the picture as there are objects in the fact it represents,[19] this form will also be that of the fact. And this is indeed the case, for the fact that *a* is to the left of *b* has the form 'that *x* is to the left of *y*' or 'that *x* stands in a relation to *y*'. Both fact and picture are possible instantiations of this form.

We can also explain why Wittgenstein speaks of 'the form of depiction' of a picture, rather than simply of its form. The reason is that a picture may have many alternative 'forms' some of which may be irrelevant to its rôle as a fact that depicts. For example, a picture showing forth that *aRb* might contain as a deputy for *a*, a complex pattern of strokes, *A*1, *A*2, ... *An* in that order, whereas *a* was a simple and indefinable object. Let us call *A*1, *A*2 ... *An* in that order: '*a*'. Clearly one way of giving the structure of the picture will be 'that *A*1, *A*2, *An* in that order have a certain relation to '*b*'', the corresponding form being: 'that *x*1, *x* 2, ... *xn* in that order have a relation to *y*'. Another way of giving its structure and form will be: 'that '*a*' has a certain relation to '*b*'', and 'that *x* has a relation to

---

18 For further propositions where Wittgenstein says or implies that the existence of a picture guarantees the possibility of the state of affairs represented, see 2.203, 3.02, 3.4.

The particular way in which I have described the setting forth of a state of affairs by a picture is derived from 3.1432, a proposition which occurs more than once in pre-*Tractatus* MSS (see *NL*, pp. 96, 106, *NdM*, p. 109). On the analogy of that proposition it should seem that there will not be an element of the picture which deputizes for *R*. '*a*' and '*b*' are elements of the picture and deputize for *a* and *b*. That '*a*' has a certain relation to '*b*' sets forth that *a* has a certain relation to *b*, but there is no object *R* and no picture-element '*R*'. See discussion below and note 17 above.

The further question arises and must be discussed, whether '*a*' stands to '*b*' in the *same* relation that *a* is said to stand in towards *b*. 3.1432 appears to go against, and (on a certain interpretation of the German word '*so*') 2.15 seems to support, this view. Even if the elements of the picture and of the fact stood in the same relation to one another (as would be the case if the fact that '*a*' was to the left of '*b*' set forth that *a* was to the left of *b*), the structure of the picture would be distinct from that of the fact, since the elements of the two are different.

19 This is the first feature of pictures that Wittgenstein mentions, at 2.13, and therefore, by implication, a very significant one. He stresses it again, of course, e.g. at 4.0312. I think that whatever may be true of the propositions and pictures that we are used to, it can be shown that the thoughts (cf. the 3's) which they express must possess the same multiplicity as the facts they state or represent. For one suggestion about the premises that may have led Wittgenstein to his view cf. note 11 and the text to it.

y', respectively. Now, though both structures and both forms in a sense belong to the picture, it is clearly in virtue of the latter pair that it is called a picture of the fact that *aRb* (where *a* and *b* are indefinables): being of the latter form is a necessary and sufficient condition for it to be a possible picture of, a possible way of depicting, the fact that *aRb*. So this is the form of depiction of the picture. A picture as a fact has many forms, its form of depiction is that form which includes all and only (or at any rate only) what the picture has in common with the fact it represents. We shall automatically arrive at this form if we recognize into what elements the picture *qua* the picture that it is must be divided.[20] Conversely we can say that *the* form of a fact (we were seeking previously a criterion for *the* form) is the least that a fact must, or the most that it can, have in common with a fact which is to depict it.

The alternative in this last suggestion will help us to show that there is a range of generality or specificity within the form of depiction itself. A picture which represents that *a* is to the left of *b* by putting '*a*' to the left of '*b*' has as its form of depiction 'that *x* is to the left of *y*' and is a spatial picture (2.171), and has spatial form (2.18) in common with reality. On the other hand, a picture which represents that *a* loves *b* by putting '*a*' to the left of '*b*' has as its form of depiction 'that *x* stands in a relation to *y*' and is a logical picture, having logical form in common with reality (cf. the 2.18's). It will be clear that a spatial form of depiction is one kind of, and thus presupposes, a logical form of depiction (2.182). It should seem that generally in a spatial picture or model there will be grounds for saying that the relation in which the elements of the picture stand to one another is the same as the relation in which the objects in the fact which it shows forth stand to one another, while in a logical non-spatial picture this is not so. This will perhaps explain the discrepancy, remarked in note 18 above, between 3.1432 where Wittgenstein is speaking of propositions, i.e. logical pictures, and 2.15 where he may have principally spatial pictures in mind.

There is one difficulty, alluded to in notes 17 and 18, above, that must be mentioned here. In some unpublished writings prior in date to the *Tractatus*,[21] Wittgenstein spoke of symbols for properties and relations as *forms*, in contrast to the symbols for objects, which were *names*. Some may

---

20 This is one reason why the depicting relation, constituted by the coordination of the elements of the picture with things, belongs to the picture (2.153–2.1514). To recognize what picture it is, we must know what count as its elements when it is regarded as a picture, and what these elements stand for.

21 The MSS in question are: *NL*, listed by Colombo in his Bibliography (*CFB*, p. 316), and *NdM*. I have been enabled to consult the latter through the kindness of Miss G.E.M. Anscombe, one of Wittgenstein's literary executors. (Note added in 1964): Versions of these notes have now been published in *Nb*. See e.g. *NL*, p. 106 (earlier p. 98), *NdM*, p. 111.

see the persistence of that terminology in 2.0251: 'Space, time and colour (colouredness) are forms of objects', though I find that proposition obscure. Certainly, such symbols are not thought to be names: I think this is clear from 3.1432 (see note 17 above, p. 146) and 4.24 (where 'f' and 'ϕ' are functions of names, not themselves names). This latter proposition occurs precisely in a context in which Wittgenstein asserts that an elementary proposition is a complex or concatenation of names. We must assume that, e.g., 'R' in 'aRb' is not itself a name but that its occurrence between them is (part of) the way in which the names 'a' and 'b' are connected to form the proposition: there is thus no object corresponding to 'R'.[22] We have explained how this way of speaking may be accommodated in our account of form: a particular relation may be called a characteristic of the structure or of the form of a fact: when a picture shows forth a fact by putting its elements into the *same* relation as the objects in the fact, then we may say that that particular relation is a characteristic of the form of depiction of that picture. Otherwise the form of depiction of a picture in which the elements stand in a particular two-termed relation will be 'that x has a relation to y'. The *Tractatus*, however, raises a new problem, for it seems to imply that not all predicates of n places are of the same logical form, whereas we have assumed the contradictory of this. The implication arises from the talk about the form of an object 2.0141, and 2.0233 (cf. 2.0121 and 2.0131). If two objects have different logical forms, then there are states of affairs in which the one can figure and the other cannot, in the way that a colour can be bright and a weight cannot. So we might think that there would be on the one hand objects which could have with one another only certain two-place relations, and on the other hand two-place relations which could hold only between certain ranges of objects. Thus the form of depiction of a picture showing forth that aRb would be either 'that x has a relation to y' or 'that x' has a relation to y''' or ... different styles of variable being used according to the different types of object and relation involved in the state of affairs pictured. We should have different types of the same multiplicity, or on the same level, and a ramified theory of types. Words like 'object' would be typically ambiguous.

22 It has been thought that 4.123 affords proof that properties also are objects. But Wittgenstein expressly points out there that the word 'object' is improperly used there. That he does so does not however prove our point, since the impropriety may be due to the fact that a certain blue colour is a complex with logical properties (that give rise to inferences), rather than to the fact that it is a property. The temptation to think of properties and relations as objects arises from Wittgenstein's talk about the proposition as a concatenation of names; it is hard to see how 'fa' could be so described unless 'f' too were a name. However at 4.24 Wittgenstein seems to rule this out, so he must be thinking that 'fa' is the limiting case of a concatenation of names.

At the very least it must be said that Wittgenstein overlooks or neglects this. All his examples of type-differences, of differences of logical form, are of the order of the difference between n-placed predicates and $n + 1$-placed predicates,[23] or between propositions, facts and things. He says, at 3.331 (cf. 3.333), that the *whole* 'Theory of Types' is contained in the observation that a propositional sign cannot be its own argument. Confusions arise (3.323) because what is really a relational word looks like a property-word (cf. 5.4733): he never mentions that ordinary language does not distinguish between *property*-words of different type, though this, one would imagine, would be a more abundant source of confusions. His example of a conceivable special form of elementary proposition is one containing a sign for a twenty-seven-place relation (5.5541).

In view of this silence, and this preference for a certain kind of example, I am tempted to conclude that Wittgenstein did not recognize difference of type or logical form within objects properly so-called, properties, or n-placed relations. His main interest, as in the 4.04's, was in multiplicity. The proposition which seems to suggest a contrary view need not necessarily do so: 'Two objects of the same logical form are distinguished from one another (if we ignore their external properties) only in that they are different 2.0233'. This is a general remark asserting that distinguishability demands a) external properties or b) difference of logical form: there is no absolute implication that objects ever do differ in logical form from one another.[24]

This will give us a true 'logical atomism' with no two particulars differing in type, no difference of type, for example, between mental and physical particulars: neutral monism.

We may now turn to the description of the form of a proposition in the 3.31's, which suggested and now confirms our account of the form of a fact or picture. He is speaking of what he calls an expression or symbol. This is something that characterizes (3.31) and presupposes (3.311) the form of a number of propositions. It is exhibited or

---

23 In *NdM*, p. 107 *et al*, things, properties and relations are called 'types'; at *Tractatus* 5.5351 they are called 'prototypes' (*Urbilder*).

24 It seems to me that some support is given to this view by the consideration that it makes the form of one object give us knowledge of all states of affairs that are possible (cf. 2.01.–2.0141). That in turn makes it easier to understand how one proposition 'gives us' the whole of logical space, 3.42. If there was a type of object whose form was unknown to us, then (it should seem) we could very well understand a single proposition, or very many propositions, and yet be unaware of many of the possibilities and impossibilities that make up logical space.

It may be thought, however, that the 5.55's go against this point. My view also depends upon finding a satisfactory interpretation of 2.0251.

presented by the general form of a class of propositions (3.312), that is to say by a propositional variable (3.313). We are told in 3.315 how such a variable may be constructed: we are to put a variable in place of some constituent part of the proposition, e.g. 'aRx' for 'aRb'. By so doing we shall have determined a class of propositions: all those that assert that a has the relation R to a thing. But of course what propositions belong to this class will depend on the meaning we attach to 'a' and 'R'. We can of course put variables in the place of any sign to which we have arbitrarily assigned a meaning: thus we should obtain the expression or symbol 'xRy', and finally, when all such signs have been replaced, we obtain the expression '$\phi(x, y)$', which characterizes the class of all two-termed relational propositions. This, Wittgenstein tells us, corresponds to or, as he might have said, presents to us, a logical form, a logical prototype (*Urbild*). What class of propositions this symbol determines does not depend on any arbitrary assignment of meaning.[25] It would be idle to pretend that the selection of a particular typographical sign, such as '$\phi(x, y)$', for a variable was non-arbitrary: I have introduced it into my account of 3.315 purely for expository convenience. It is by our arbitrary convention that this sign designates the class of two-termed relational propositions: what is not arbitrary is that any propositional sign which expresses such a proposition (or in other words: which states that one object has a relation to another) will consist in the fact that one name is put in a relation to another. *Any* way of putting one name into relation with another *could* (by an arbitrary convention) express this same proposition: and nothing save such a fact or what was recognized as being linguistically equivalent to such a fact could express that proposition. Further, any object whatever could be a name (3.3411), therefore the general form of this class of propositions (3.312) is 'that x has a relation to y' which we choose to express by the variable: '$\phi(x, y)$'.

Thus the fact that aRb is depicted by the fact that something deputizing for a (whether an element of a picture or, less generally, a name in a propositional sign) stands in a certain relation to some-thing deputizing for b. Fact, picture, proposition and thought have the same form 'that x stands in a relation to y'. The existence of the picture or proposition guarantees the possibility of the fact – it shows that there can be facts of this form by *being* a fact of this form.

---

25 This interpretation demands that the sign 'R' in the propositional sign 'aRb' shall have a meaning (*Bedeutung*). It might therefore be argued that 'R' must be a name and R an object, contrary to my conclusions above. 3.314 however implies that expressions other than names have *Bedeutung*. Likewise at 3.333 Wittgenstein speaks of the *Bedeutung* of functions, while at 4.24 he distinguishes functions from names.

It might be thought that I have erred, or even that Wittgenstein erred, against the principle that a picture cannot depict its form of depiction (2.172–2.174) and that we cannot represent the logical form of a proposition of a fact by a proposition (4.12–4.121). However the full subtlety of his position is brought out by the fact that I have not erred in this way. I have not explained what the logical form of any-thing is, I have merely produced other things of the same logical form, thus presupposing that the logical form of the fact I began with and the logical form of the facts I produced were equally easy to grasp. To say that 'John loves Mary' is of the form '$\phi (x, y)$' is merely to say that we could have used any of the following signs to assert that John loves Mary: 'aRb', 'bRa', 'ab', 'ba', '$aRSb$' … and in general any sign consisting in the fact that one object is put into relation with another. If, however, we used a sign of which this was not true, then we should be said to be asserting that John loved Mary only if we were prepared to adopt instead some sign of which it was true.[26]

The general form of a class of propositions (3.311–3.312), for the expression of which we are given instructions in 3.315, is obviously something more specific than the general form of a proposition. Nor can we reach an expression for the latter by further conversion of symbols with arbitrarily assigned meaning into variables, since '$\phi (x, y)$' is already a completely variable expression. Nor can we hope to give a priori a list of all the special forms of propositions (5.554, 5.555), that is to say of all the classes of propositions, that there are: we cannot say a priori that we shall need or that we shall not need a sign for a twenty-seven-termed relation – experience will decide (5.5541). It remains for us to determine what can be seen to be necessarily true of every proposition from the examples of the form of a proposition that have already been given, or are implicit, in the *Tractatus*.

Two closely interconnected features of a proposition are of overriding importance here: First that a proposition is a fact and has the form of a fact, second that a proposition is composite (*zusammengesetzt* 3.1431, 4.032, 5.5261; *gegliedert* 4.032; *artikuliert* 3.141, 3.251): a propositional sign consists not in a set of names (3.142) but in some fact about certain names.[27] All propositions, then, will have the form: 'that such and such is the case' or in other words 'that such and such is true of such and such

---

26 For the importance of 'possible ways of symbolizing' cf. 3.3421. The last sentence of this paragraph requires more explication and argument than can be given here.

27 Facts, as opposed to objects, must be composite: what is a fact is that something is true of some objects. But why should what asserts a fact be composite? Clearly it will be so, if every proposition contains (or must be translatable into something containing) words whose function is to stand for objects without implying, by their occurrence in the proposition, any fact about those objects. Thus if in a fully analysed proposition there must be names that deputize for objects (*das Prinzip der Vertretung* 4.0312), then every proposition must be composite (4.032).

objects'. Now these are precisely the accounts of the general form of the proposition that are given at 4.5 and 5.47 respectively, only that the intervening argument allows further conclusions to be drawn, which are then stated, without a repetition of the premises, in the early 6's.

The chief point made in the 4.1's to 4.5's is that every fact is either an atomic fact (*Sachverhalt*) or consists in the existence or non-existence of certain atomic facts.[28]

Thus every proposition either asserts that an atomic fact exists, in which case it is an elementary proposition,[29] or it is equivalent to the assertion or denial of some set of elementary propositions. Obviously the former alternative is a limiting case of the latter, so we can describe the general case by saying that every proposition is some truth-function of elementary propositions (5).

If an atomic fact were defined as a fact that does not consist in the existence or non-existence of other facts, the above argument would be logically impeccable. Wittgenstein however assumes that an atomic fact so defined will at the same time be a combination of objects (2.01), or in other words that an elementary proposition will consist of names in immediate combination (4.221). It might well be thought that there must indeed be elementary propositions in this sense, but that there are propositions compounded out of these in such a way that they are not merely truth-functions of elementary propositions. Wittgenstein does not allow this possibility: as he says at 5.54, in discussing the general form of a proposition he has assumed that propositions occur in other propositions only as bases of truth-operations. All cases of intensional inoccurrence,

---

Whenever the occurrence of a word in a proposition implies a certain fact about an object, we can replace that proposition by another one in which that fact is explicitly stated, in a way which Russell in his article 'On Denoting' (*Mind*, 1905, reprinted in Russell 1956) was the first to point out. Application of this method wherever possible will produce fully-analysed propositions containing names (3.24).

It can also be seen that such an analysis must be possible if we are capable of forming propositions which are essentially connected with the states of affairs they inform us of and thus are capable of communicating 'a new sense with old words' (4.027–4.03). In other words analysis of all propositions into elementary propositions must be possible if we can understand a proposition without knowing whether it or any other proposition is true. (2.0211, cf. note 11, and the text to it.)

Wittgenstein appears to have thought it obvious that this condition was fulfilled. It could easily be maintained however (to mention but one counter-example) that no ethical proposition could be understood without prior knowledge of several matters of fact.

Finally it must be noted that the assertion at the head of this note, that facts are composite and objects simple, is itself thought to be established by these considerations about sense and understanding.

28 Cf. 2.06: The existence and non-existence of atomic facts is reality.

29 This term is introduced at 4.21.

such as the propositions that someone knows a certain proposition to be true, or that such and such a state of affairs is bad and ought to be remedied, are ruled out in advance: it is hard not to find this exclusion somewhat arbitrary.[30] It may be argued on epistemological grounds that there must be elementary propositions; it cannot be argued on logical grounds that all propositions are truth-functions of them. This assertion seems rather to be an arbitrary definition or a metaphysical thesis.

It is these conclusions that give content to the assertion at 4.5 that the general form of a proposition is expressed by the variable (4.53): '*Es verhält sich so und so*' – which we must translate 'Such and such combinations (sc. of objects) hold'.[31] i.e. every proposition asserts or denies some combinations of objects, or in other words the existence or non-existence of some atomic facts. Thus every proposition is a truth-function of elementary propositions. At the same time every proposition, since it is a fact, will itself consist in certain combinations of objects: '*Es verhält sich so und so*' is a form of which a proposition and the fact it states are two different possible specifications.[32]

30 Wittgenstein gives some justification for the exclusion of former example at 5.542, claiming that '*A* says *p*' is of the form ' '*p*' says *p*', so that we are dealing not with the coordination of a fact and an object, but with the coordination of two facts via the coordination of their objects. This seems to mean that we are saying (1) that a conformation of a certain kind is occurring in the man's mind (cf. '*Gegenstände des Gedankens*', at 3.2. Perhaps Wittgenstein is thinking of the words of the proposition going through the man's mind). (2) that this conformation says that ... The chief objection to this account is that in order for the words or whatever it may be in the man's mind to project the possible state of affairs he has to 'think the sense of the proposition' cf. 3.11. I do not say this is a refutation of Wittgenstein, but it points to a serious lacuna in his argument.

31 Colombo's '*Le cose stanno così e così*' makes this point (CFB, p. 219). 'Such and such is the case' in KP obscures it. Wittgenstein thinks it worthwhile to *explain* (2) that what is the case is the existence of atomic facts (*Sachverhalte*) and *ein Sachverhalt = daß sich die Sachen (Dinge Gegenstände) so und so zu einander verhalten*. Cf. the frequent use of *sich verhalten* to describe the role of objects in an atomic fact: 2.031, 2.14, 2.15–2.151, 3.14, see also 5.5423.

I do not wish to imply that for Wittgenstein all propositions were ultimately relational, though it would have given greater simplicity to his theories if this were so: Carnap (1967) developed many of Wittgenstein's theses in a manner which did involve this assumption. Wittgenstein explicitly rejected it in *NL* (see note 21) and seems still to do so at 5.553. 2.01, etc., when taken in conjunction with 4.24 imply the doctrine, however odd it may sound, that a proposition such as '*fa*' asserts a '*sich verhalten*' or '*Verbindung*' of the object *a*.

32 We do not however generally represent the fact that certain objects do not stand in a certain relation by the fact that certain signs do not stand in a certain relation. Instead we use a sign of negation. This may seem to be a difference in form between a complex proposition and the fact that it states.

Cf., however, 5.512 where Wittgenstein says that the general rule for forming the negation of a proposition 'mirrors negation'. I take this to mean that in virtue of this general rule there can be said to be an identity of form even between a negative proposition and the fact it asserts.

By 5.47, where the next reference occurs, this description of propositional form in general can be carried further, since Wittgenstein is in a position to show that all truth-functions of elementary propositions can be arrived at by the application of one fundamental truth-operation (see the 5.5's). The operation in question is the joint negation of a set of propositions: any alternation, conjunction, implication, equivalence or negation of elementary propositions can be represented as a joint negation. He further holds that anyone who is capable of asserting a proposition is thereby capable of asserting, and also of denying, a set of propositions. Thus, if you grasp any one proposition, you thereby grasp all the possible ways in which complex propositions can be constructed out of elementary propositions.[33] Since all propositions are truth-functions of elementary propositions, the general form of propositions can be given by describing the operation which produces any truth-function.

Now this is precisely the programme announced at 5.47 and the result produced at 6. We have seen that proposition and fact alike are essentially composite (*zusammengesetzt*), a fact does not consist of a set of objects, nor a proposition of a set of names – each consists in something's holding of some objects or names. Thus when a man apprehends such composition, he apprehends that something holds or is true of some objects, and this (in the terminology of 4.24) is the apprehension that a function is satisfied by certain arguments. But the apprehension that any proposition is true implies the capacity to conceive that it should be false, and indeed to conceive that all of any set of propositions are false, which in turn involves the capacity to construct any truth-function whatever of propositions. Thus ability to employ the fundamental logic operation is a necessary condition of the apprehension of any form of composition. It is at the same time a sufficient condition – that is to say, if a man can negate elementary propositions, he can obviously frame any truth-function whatsoever.

These considerations make 5.47 comprehensible: 'Where composition is to be found, argument and function are to be found also, and where these are, all the logical constants are implicit. – You might say: the sole logical constant is what all propositions, by their nature, have in common with one another. This, however, is the general form of a proposition.' It is also clear how, at 6 and 6.001, Wittgenstein is able to regard a description of this logical operation as a sufficient characterization of the general form of the proposition. It is significant that the first point about this that

33 To take simple examples: '*p*' itself is the negation of the negation of '*p*', '*p* = *q*' is the joint negation of '*p*' and the negation of '*q*'.

  Space compels me to present in a rough and undocumented fashion what I take to be Wittgenstein's argument here.

he chooses to stress is that it gives us the only way in which one proposition can be formed from another (6.002).

We are thus brought back to our starting point in the 6's and our first aim has been achieved – namely to show the unity of Wittgenstein's account of a proposition and its form throughout the *Tractatus*. This was part of the general work of exegesis, which, particularly for this book, has to precede criticism. For that reason we have often delayed over particular propositions on our way. At the end however it may be possible to draw some general conclusions.

The following seem to be the most questionable among the premises that led Wittgenstein to the wholesale devaluation of ranges of propositions that we find in the 6's.

1   That there are elementary propositions in which names deputize for objects. More explicitly this is the thesis that all propositions which presuppose a fact can be so reformulated as to state that fact rather than to presuppose it. (Some indication of Wittgenstein's reasons for this view are given in my notes 11 and 27 above.)

2   That the objects referred to in such propositions are of one type. More explicitly: that the occurrence of apparent type-differences between objects referred to in a pair of propositions shows that at least one of those propositions is not fully analysed. (I have argued that Wittgenstein did hold this view in note 24, and the text to it.)

3   That the truth or falsehood of any complex proposition is wholly determined by that of the elementary propositions occurring in its analysis. (This is what I have called the rejection of intensional inoccurrence, and I have argued, in note 30 above and the text to it that Wittgenstein gives no good reason for it.)

Even if these premises be rejected, there is one lesson, which seems to me of great epistemological importance, to be drawn from what we have seen of Wittgenstein's account of propositions. I mean his insistence on the truth that having a thought, seeing a picture or entertaining a proposition is not merely a means towards the apprehension of a fact, but is itself the apprehension of a fact. There could be no process by which people were taught to apprehend a fact, since all instruction takes place through the presentation of facts to the pupil. Likewise there can be no true explanation of our ability to apprehend a fact: we must regard it simply as an inexplicable human capacity (perhaps a way of thinking similar to this is discernible at 4.002). The considerations thus vaguely indicated seem, or seemed to Wittgenstein to suggest that in our ability to apprehend a fact we have a sort of a priori knowledge, which there is no way of expressing. In our awareness of the essence of a proposition we are aware of the essence of a fact and thus of the essence of the world

(5.4711). Further, in our knowledge of any fact there is implicit all our a priori knowledge of logical truth (5.47, cf. 3.42), and Wittgenstein certainly thinks that logic shows us or mirrors for us something about the world (5.511, 6.12, 6.124, 6.13).

I have suggested above that the rejection of ethical propositions seems arbitrary, if all that supports it is the fragmentary argument against intensional inoccurrence that Wittgenstein gives. But perhaps its true basis is the inexpressible metaphysic constituted by our intuition (if I may use the word) of what it is to be a fact: ethical 'facts' do not measure up to its standards. If this is so, then it seems likely that Wittgenstein will prove guilty of circularity in the following way: his metaphysic of silence is supported by the logical and epistemological doctrines which precede the 6's, but these themselves depend at their crucial points on that metaphysics. I leave this suggestion to be explored on another occasion.

8

THE SUPPOSED REALISM OF
THE *TRACTATUS*

On the face of it we have in Wittgenstein's *Tractatus* the classic statement of a realist semantics. In his picture theory an explanation is given of how propositions have sense, i.e. are true or false, which immediately invokes ontological categories. He tells us:

> The possibility of propositions is based on the principle that objects have signs as their representatives.
>
> (4.0312)

and further,

> One name stands for one thing, another for another thing, and they are combined with one another. In this way the whole group – like a tableau vivant – presents a state of affairs.
>
> (4.0311)
> A proposition or a picture is the fact that its elements are combined in a certain way: it says something because those elements are correlated with objects in the world.
>
>   These correlations are, as it were, the feelers of the picture's elements, with which the picture touches reality.
>
> (2.1515)

In a proposition, in the ideal case, the elements are of course names. Their meaning (*Bedeutung*) is identical with the objects they stand for (*vertreten*). There is no trace here, for these names, of the distinction that Wittgenstein was later to draw between *Träger* (bearer) and *Bedeutung*, according to which one could say that Herr Schmidt was the *Träger* of the name Schmidt, but not, I think, that he was its *Bedeutung*.

We are naturally inclined to attribute to Wittgenstein, therefore, a theory on the following lines. Propositions have sense, i.e. are either true or false, because the following is a conceivable series of events for every one of them: first, a set of names or simple signs (that is to say signs no parts of which function as signs) is correlated with a set of objects by ostensive definition. Second, some of these names are put into a relation which is possible for them. It happens that any relation which is possible for the names is possible also for the objects with which the names have been correlated. The fact that the names stand in the relation in question will then be a proposition to the effect that the objects also stand in that relation. Now, one of two states of affairs holds, either the objects are so related or they are not. Whichever of these two is the fact must be compared with the proposition, and if it corresponds, the proposition will be true. However, it will be seen that it can only be either true or false. Thus given that every proposition could in theory be constructed in the way described, it will be seen that every proposition will be either true or false and what its being true or false consists in. It is this that a semantic theory should establish for us.

Now many features of this account are not in Wittgenstein at all. He does not mention ostensive definition – he was to say later that its nature was unclear to him at the time of the *Tractatus*. Nor does he talk as if names just happened to permit of precisely those combinations that were possible for the objects they represented, as it were by some lucky power of our minds. This Hertz seems to suggest when he says:

> We make for ourselves inner pictures or symbols of outer objects, and we make them in such a way that the consequences of the pictures that are necessary for our thought are also at the same time pictures of the consequences that are naturally necessary for the objects depicted. In order that this requirement should be capable of being fulfilled, there must be certain correspondences already in existence between nature and our mind.[1]

Wittgenstein took much of his notion of picturing from Hertz, but not, so far as I can see, this part. Ostensive definitions and a coincidence in the capacity to form relations are introduced into Wittgenstein's account only by interpretation, and should be viewed critically.

What he certainly seems to assume, and what this account of his views is right in presupposing, is a magazine of objects which form, in one sense, the realm of *Bedeutung*. The objects assumed are simple in a much stricter sense than that given above for the simplicity of signs, and one consequence of their simplicity is that they are common to all possible worlds. They form the substance of the world or the form of the world. They are what is unalterable and persistent (*bestehend*), while the configuration of

---

1   Hertz 1894, p. 1. English translation supplied by the author.

objects, the states of affairs, are what varies from one possible world to another. These configurations of objects, these states of affairs, give objects what material or external properties they have. Naturally, there is only one set of configurations that is actually realized, and this is what we call reality or the world. The internal properties of objects are their possibilities of combination with one another, and the possession of these properties is necessary, not a mere matter of fact.

What is meant by assuming a magazine of objects of this kind? Clearly not that something exists which might not exist. All unrealized possibilities are simply dispositions of objects different from that which actually obtains. To put the same matter in another way, all questions of existence are questions about what configurations of objects actually obtain. Thus we might say that all existence is a matter of fact, a matter of what is in the world. This corresponds to an early statement in the *Tractatus*: The world is a totality of facts, not of things. (1.1)

This seems to yield a moderately complicated ontology: the world or reality consists of facts, that is to say in the *Bestehen* (in one sense), the obtaining, of states of affairs. States of affairs themselves, on the other hand, are combinations of objects, which *bestehen* or exist (subsist) in another sense. Existence as normally spoken of is equivalent to the *Bestehen* in the first sense of a certain state of affairs. Professor Black suggests that this ontology was suggested to Wittgenstein by his views about language.[2]

Now, to be sure, the attraction of the opening pages of the *Tractatus* is that they seem to derive substantial and metaphysical results like those long hoped for from philosophy, all on the basis of some quite natural assumptions about propositions being true or false. However, I agree with Mr Rhees[3] that it is important not to be misled by these opening pages. It was not Wittgenstein's intention to base a metaphysics upon logic or the nature of our language. He was not saying that there is something by which our grammar is determined, and therefore he did not try to infer features of the world from our language. It may seem, indeed, that he argues that propositions with sense are possible only because some more primitive operations are possible – notably the correlation of names with objects, and it may seem that he goes on to argue that these more primitive operations are possible only because the world possesses certain characteristics. However, it will be clear on reflection that such arguments would be the sort of metaphysics that he condemns.

2   Black 1964, p. 8.
3   Rhees 1970, pp. 24f.

How then are we to account for the ontological parts of the *Tractatus*? This is a larger form of our earlier question, what is it for objects to subsist (*bestehen*) as this is understood in the *Tractatus*? Still more generally the question might take the form, what is Wittgenstein doing in the *Tractatus*? I have so far been saying merely what he is *not* doing. Some interpretation is clearly needed. The answer here is that he is doing logic and basing philosophy on it. He thinks and says that philosophy is not a science alongside the others, but is something over or beneath them. Yet occasionally he speaks of philosophy or logic as if it were a science with its own range of data or facts. Thus, for example, in the middle of 2.0121 he says: 'Logic deals with every possibility and all possibilities are its facts'.

I want to say that there we have a transferred and strictly illegitimate use of the word 'fact', and that similarly the whole ontology is a transferred and illegitimate use of words like *bestehen*. It is a kind of ontological myth that he wants to give us to show us the nature of language. As is well-known, one of the chief results of the view of language so attained is the rejection of all such myths.

I say that Wittgenstein is doing logic and basing philosophy on it. It is important to see what this means. When Russell wrote to him with some questions about the *Tractatus*, then a mere typescript newly arrived in England, Wittgenstein wrote:

> I'm afraid you haven't got hold of my main contention to which the whole business of logical propositions is only a corollary. The main point is the theory of what can be expressed (*gesagt*) by propositions – i.e. by language – (and which comes to the same thing what can be *thought*) and what cannot be expressed by propositions, but only shown (*gezeigt*); which, I believe, is the cardinal problem of philosophy.[4]

Philosophy, it will be remembered, is thought of as a critique of language – it is the activity of making clear the limits of language, which are identical with the limits of thought. It is a pointing to, or an attempt to make clear, something that cannot be stated directly, since it is not one half of a contradiction, not one of two mutually exclusive alternatives. What philosophy tries to make clear is not sayable, but it is shown by ordinary propositions that can be true or false. Conversely, a mistaken philosophy will be the attempt to say these things. Logic comes in, in the first place, because it was Wittgenstein's starting-point: its propositions were the first

4   *CL*, p. 124.

that he discovered to say nothing but to show something – to show: '...
the formal – logical – properties of language and the world' (6.12).

He wants to bring out in the *Tractatus* that philosophy and logic have
to do not with a special realm of objects but with the necessary features
of language – that is to say of any language whatsoever. This happens
most clearly in the case of logic. The propositions of logic, the tautologies,
are by various devices shown to be inevitable offshoots or by-products of
the activity of saying anything true or false. As such they show us something about what it is to say something true or false.

It is in order to reach this result that Wittgenstein must say what it is
for a proposition to be true or false in the ordinary way, and in the
course of doing that he gives the semantic theory we described at the
beginning. There can be propositions which are always true or always
false – i.e. tautologies and contradictions, because there are propositions
which may be true and may be false, and this is so because it is possible
for a proposition to exist which *may* be false, but which, if not false, is
true. I will not argue that connection here. For our present purposes –
which is the derivation of objects – I wish to take it as a premise.
Wittgenstein's thought is that in order for there to be propositions that
may be either true or false, but must be one of the two, there will have
to be a possibility of expressing those propositions by means of signs
which of themselves will serve to express a proposition independently of
what is the case. A state of affairs cannot be designated independently of
whether it exists or not unless signs can be used whose significance
could be given and understood and determined without reference to
the obtaining or non-obtaining of that state of affairs. This can be done
only if, in order to say that a state of affairs exists, it would be possible
to produce a complex of signs. A simple sign could be correlated with a
state of affairs only by revealing or assuming the existence of the state of
affairs. It follows that in order to make a statement which would have
sense, i.e. be either true or false, whatever the case in the world was, it
would be necessary to suppose that in principle that statement could be
made by the use of signs which could function in a proposition whatever
the case in the world was.

Now Wittgenstein believed (and I think there are good grounds for
thinking him correct, though it is not my purpose to argue it here) that
we could make statements knowing them to be either true or false whatever the case in the world was. He therefore thought that we were
committed to the possibility of those propositions being expressed in such
a form that all the constituent signs used could function in that particular
combination whatever the case in the world was. They would therefore
(those supposedly possible signs) be possible constituents in propositions
or possible contributors to producing a true or false proposition, regardless of what was the case in the world. He did not necessarily suppose us

to have produced signs with these characteristics, as our actual signs may depend for their meaning on all sorts of accidental circumstances, but he thought us committed to the possibility of rephrasing all that we want to say with the use of such signs alone.

Such signs, I believe, were Wittgenstein's names, and you will notice that in sketching an argument for their possibility I have made no reference to the complexity of a state of affairs or to the fact that 'objects' figure in a state of affairs. Wittgenstein does indeed mention that states of affairs are combinations of objects and introduces objects themselves into his *Tractatus* before he says anything about the necessity for a proposition to be articulated and to consist of simple signs, but I believe that the order of his exposition reverses the order of his thinking.

It will be evident to those who have read Professor Tugendhat's article on Frege in *Analysis* (Tugendhat 1970) or Mr Dummett's criticisms of it in his book on *Frege*,[5] that I am suggesting an interpretation of Wittgenstein rather like Tugendhat's of Frege. An object in the *Tractatus* which is the reference of a name or simple sign can be viewed as simply the truth-value potential of a certain expression. The semantic role of the supposedly possible simple sign or name is that of being combined with other simple signs or names to produce a proposition having a truth-value. Any sign which in the same combinations will produce exactly the same truth-values is the same sign or has the same reference. Another parallel with the view I am advocating is the conclusion reached by Miss Ishiguro in her article on 'Use and Reference of Names'[6] when she says that *Bedeutung* is an intentional notion in the *Tractatus*. In her view the existence of objects adds no extra content to the logical theory.

I shall have occasion shortly to disagree with some points she makes, but one powerful argument she uses I can adopt. She points to Wittgenstein's repeated use of the Fregean slogan – 'only in the context of a proposition does a name have a reference' – and interprets this as meaning that reference cannot be determined independently of how we settle or understand sense. To understand the reference of a name is to know something about the truth-conditions of some propositions. By this Miss Ishiguro does not merely mean (like Miss Anscombe in her *Introduction*) that there is no point in attaching a reference to a name unless you are going to go on to use that name in a proposition. She means, rather, that it is a fundamental idea of the *Tractatus* that there is no securing of reference prior to occurrence in a proposition. To show this she points out, quite correctly, that objects as spoken of in the *Tractatus* cannot be identified by a definite description or picked out by

---

5 Dummett 1973, pp. 199–203.
6 Ishiguro 1969, pp. 20–50.

pointing, since their *Bestehen* (existence or subsistence) is supposed to be independent of what is the case. (She goes on to give an account of how reference can be secured – an account of Wittgenstein's notion of *Erläuterung* (elucidation) – with which I disagree.) The chief result of Miss Ishiguro's discussions – and a result that I think valid in any case – is that we ought not to contrast the *Tractatus* with its notion of *Bedeutung* and the *Philosophical Investigations* with its notion that the meaning is the use. Use determines reference in the *Tractatus* also – though to be sure it is only 'use for the purpose of saying something true or false', since other forms of use are not there considered.

Now, can Tugendhat's account of *Bedeutung* (whether true or false of Frege) be applied to Wittgenstein's *Tractatus*? To see this I will consider some objections brought by Dummett against Tugendhat considered as an interpreter of Frege, and see whether they would hold against Tugendhat considered as an interpreter of Wittgenstein. First, however, I will indicate one point – curiously enough a linguistic point about German – in respect of which Tugendhat does not fit Wittgenstein. Tugendhat says that the rendering of *Bedeutung* by 'reference', 'denotation' and 'nominatum' suggests, what is false, that Frege meant by the *Bedeutung* of an expression the object which the expression names. Now I believe it is very clear in Wittgenstein's *Tractatus* that the *Bedeutung* of a name is meant to be identical with the object named. Indeed translating '*Bedeutung*' as 'meaning', for which I am partly responsible, could be criticized on this ground alone. At the same time it is true that in the long run I wish to explain the object as an entity definable in terms of semantic equivalence.

I will discuss Dummett's criticisms of Tugendhat because disposing of the minor ones throws some light on what Wittgenstein is doing, as opposed to Frege, while the major one raises the whole issue of this paper. The minor criticisms are first that the identification of *Bedeutung* with truth-value potential (that is to say with the semantic role alone) does not at first sight allow us to distinguish between intentional and extensional contexts, or between contexts in which the name is used to refer to its indirect reference (its sense) and those in which it is used to refer to its real reference (its bearer). '... there would be a natural presumption', Dummett says, 'in favour of a uniform semantic treatment for all contexts'.[7] That is, however, precisely what Wittgenstein wants, and he does indeed allow no distinction between intentional and extensional contexts. The reason for this can be seen by considering another form of Dummett's objection to Tugendhat. (It will be remembered that we are

7   *op. cit.*, p. 401.

here by no means criticizing Dummett's argument in itself, but only as applied to a supposed interpretation of Wittgenstein.) The second minor objection is that if reference is defined solely in terms of semantic role, or if having the same reference (*Bedeutung*) is defined in terms of inter-changeability in all contexts without change of truth-value, then the use of an expression without a reference would be its use in a sentence which failed to say anything at all and failed to perform a linguistic act. What we wish to be able to say, however, is that there may perfectly well be intelli-gible utterances of sentences containing expressions which lack a bearer. These will differ (on Dummett's and Frege's view) from other sentences all of whose expressions of the same kind have bearers, in that the others will be and they will not be either true or false. The conception of refer-ence as semantic role pays no attention to whether there is a bearer or not and does not allow us to call these sentences devoid of truth-value. This last is most easily done by identifying the reference with the bearer and saying that an expression may lack reference but still have sense. In virtue of its sense, a sentence in which it occurs is intelligible; in virtue of its lack of reference (bearer), a sentence in which it occurs lacks truth-value.

This may be a reason for saying that Tugendhat's account will not fit Frege, but it serves here to bring out that Wittgenstein, like Tugendhat, rejects the notion that names have both a reference and a sense. He does indeed think that the use of a name without reference results in saying nothing whatsoever. The only case parallel to those mentioned by Dummett that Wittgenstein mentions is the sentence about a *complex* that does not exist. Such a sentence does not indeed become nonsense, but simply false (3.24). As Wittgenstein said to Russell early in the develop-ment of the thoughts published in the *Tractatus*:

> Your theory of descriptions is quite certainly right, even though the objects are quite other than you imagined.[8]

The fact is that the objects he has in mind are quite different from any Russell talked of, for the same reason that the notion of 'bearer' is an odd one when applied to his names. It is inconceivable that anything which can function as a name at all should lack a bearer, just because its bearer is given with its semantic role. All that can go wrong with a name is that it may be used, or an attempt may be made to use it, otherwise than in its proper semantic role. The examples that Wittgenstein gives of this are the nonsensical propositions, 'Socrates Plato'[9] and 'Socrates is identical'.[10]

8 *CL*, pp. 56ff.
9 *NdM*, p. 115.
10 *Tractatus*, 5.4733.

They only show the sort of thing that might go wrong: 'Socrates' and 'Plato' are not real names in Wittgenstein's sense, they might lack bearers. (The case about 'identical' is more complicated than we need discuss here.) Miss Ishiguro gives a good example of the sort of name that could not lack a bearer: 'Let *a* be the centre of a circle ...' In the discussion that follows, the question whether *a* exists cannot be raised. That is the sort of impossibility Wittgenstein has in mind. Of course it is true, as regards the actual example, that it may be part of an activity parasitic upon the identification of drawn figures and marked points on a sheet of paper. We have to consider what it would be like for names of this sort to form the whole substructure of language.

This brings us to the main difference between Frege in Dummett's account and Tugendhat's interpretation of Frege. Frege, Dummett says, surely with some justice, took the relation of name and bearer as the prototype of a semantic role. He assumed 'that the semantic role of every expression which is a semantically significant unit can always be construed as consisting in its relation to something in the real world'.[11] This amounts to saying that Frege makes use in his account of how our sentences have sense and reference of a number of intuitive pre-systematic notions, among them that of the relation of a name to a bearer. This comes, Dummett says, from our practice of ostension, 'from our possession, in the use of a demonstrative accompanied by a pointing gesture, of another means than the employment of a name (the text has: as a name) for picking out a concrete object'.[12] Dummett points out, surely correctly, that the notion of reference supplies us with a definite and readily acceptable picture of the semantical roles of the simplest types of expressions just because it is associated with this fundamental practice of identifying an object as the bearer of a name, and also with a fundamental practice of ostensive predication – of applying predicates to objects picked out ostensively. Now we have already seen that Wittgenstein wishes to assume no such fundamental practice, and we have claimed that he talks in the language of reference and bearer because of its attractiveness, but does not rely on the network of assumptions that make it so attractive. What we have to ask therefore is what contribution *Wittgenstein's* notion of reference makes in clarifying both what it is for us to utter sentences which are either true or false and how it is we come to do so.

We have already seen that every proposition we utter is true or false whatever is the case in the world. This demands that every proposition be capable of a full analysis in just one form, whether or not such analysis has ever been reached. If we imagine the totality of all propositions,

11 Cf. Dummett 1973, p. 405.
12 *op. cit.*, p. 406.

true and false, in their fully articulated form (which form we know to be possible in principle), then we know that every element in this articulation has meaning in the sense that it contributes to the truth-value (whatever it is) of any proposition in which it occurs. However, this is all we are saying when we say that objects form the substance of the world. Understanding those elements or becoming acquainted with those objects (the two processes are identical) does not demand any experience of what is the case, since by definition the proposition is fully analysed and hence the objects have *Bestehen* (existence or subsistence) independently of what is the case. How then do we understand a proposition? What does it require? It is interesting that the question never appears in quite this form in Wittgenstein. I believe there is a good reason for this. It is not a *feat*, not an achievement, to understand a proposition. To have in the mind a conformation or structure corresponding to that of a possible state of affairs is to understand a proposition. It will be seen at once that this amounts to saying that there is no proposition to be understood *until* there is an understanding of a proposition. Thus the question is transferred to that of how we come to understand a propositional sign. How do we think a sense into a set of words? Wittgenstein tells us:

> We use the perceptible sign of a proposition (spoken or written, etc.) as a projection of a possible situation.
> Thinking the sense of the proposition is the method of projection.
> (3.11)[13]

Thinking the sense into the proposition is nothing other than so using the words of the sentence that their logical behaviour is that of the desired proposition. Or, to look at the matter in another way, whatever logical properties we give to the words we use will determine which proposition (if any) it is that we assert by means of them. Thus we must not think of the realm of reference as a mysterious, infinitely extended magazine of things, as if they were concrete objects, with which we might or might not be lucky enough in a full life to have acquaintance by, so to speak, coming across them in a street. There is already contained in language and thought the possibility of all objects that are possible. All logical forms are logically possible within language, within thought. No separate investigation or exploration of 'reality' is conceivable.

When I say we can do anything we like with language, I mean the triviality that whatever we do with the elements of language or thought will

---

13 This translation differs in the last line from the rendering in the translation of the *Tractatus* (Pears and McGuinness 1971), which was justly criticized by Rush Rhees. Cf. Rhees 1970, p. 39.

have the logical consequences that it actually has. However, there is of course also the question how I learn a language, an existing language, a particular language. On this issue we have a much discussed pronouncement by Wittgenstein:

> The meanings of primitive signs can be explained by means of elucidations. Elucidations are propositions that contain the primitive signs. So they can only be understood if the meanings of those signs are already known.
>
> (3.263)

Miss Ishiguro thinks that elucidations will be propositions in which the internal properties that objects possess are ascribed to them. I do not believe it is necessary to assume this. The internal properties of an object are its possibilities of combination with other objects, and these properties are shown by any ordinary proposition about that object, be it true or false. I conclude that Wittgenstein is pointing out that teaching can be earned out only by means of complete propositions or complete thoughts. The learner has to grasp these as a whole, and, when he has done that, he will have an understanding of the primitive signs contained in that proposition. I am not reverting here to the use of ostensive definitions. Propositions used in teaching meaning need not be true or concerned with the immediate environment, any more than we can claim these properties for '*Balbus aedificat murum*'.

However, whether I am right and elucidations are quite ordinary propositions, or Miss Ishiguro is right and they are more like logical propositions, the reader may wish to ask me or her: How do I know *which* object is meant by a particular sign, or *which* fact or state of affairs is stated by a particular proposition used in teaching? Surely there can be more than one object with the same logical form? With questions like this, we are in constant danger of supposing that there is some particular mental act of meaning or intending a particular thing which has to be explained. However, if I suppose two objects of the same logical form and call them 'a' and 'b', and if I suppose that 'a' has one set of material properties and 'b' another, there is really no sense to the question whether perhaps in reality 'b' has the set of properties I have assigned to 'a', and conversely. Miss Ishiguro puts this well by saying that names are in effect dummy names and can be interchanged (within the same logical form) if one does so consistently. To some extent, therefore, the question which object is meant is empty of content. In so far as it does make sense it must mean, How do I indicate to myself or to others, that I mean just the F that has G? To this question the answer is clearly that to mean this I must say it, or in other words my statement must have the appropriate overt or concealed logical multiplicity.

Perhaps Wittgenstein's fundamental point about semantics can be put by saying that only structure can represent (*darstellen*). 'Only facts can express a sense, a set of names cannot' (3.142).

The problem of language is the problem of the false proposition. The false proposition is possible only because it is possible for us to form a structure which will serve to express just that situation which (in saying that the proposition is false) we are supposing not to exist, and no other. It need not, and we need not judge whether it can, do this in virtue of its visible or audible form alone. However, the use of the elements of the structure must be such that only the situation in question could correspond to it. This I take to be one of the main points in the picture theory of propositional meaning. It rests on a certain insight which is compatible with some aspects of what Dummett calls realism. For Wittgenstein, as for Frege,

> ... a sentence is determined as true under certain conditions, which conditions are derivable from the way in which the sentence is constructed out of its constituent words.[14]

However, the processes of explaining the truth-conditions of a proposition and of determining the truth-value of a proposition cannot be broken down into any simpler operations than that of grasping or expressing the proposition. All these operations possess the same multiplicity. Wittgenstein was to urge this point as a justification of his picture theory in the early 1930s, and it obviously also underlies the development from the *Tractatus* to the dictum that the sense of a proposition is the method of its verification.

However, if, after all, objects are required by Wittgenstein's theory of language, then why should we not call him a realist in respect of them? The answer is that Wittgenstein's objects are not concrete objects which may sensibly be said to exist or not. Nor are they properties of concrete objects, since that makes the self-contradictory assumption that there is something simpler than the simplest thing that can be referred to. Miss Ishiguro makes them 'like' instantiations of simple properties, and that is certainly the model that Wittgenstein himself used in the *Philosophical Investigations*. Relative to the language there described those instantiations are simple, but it is easily seen that an example of an absolutely simple object cannot be given. We cannot grasp anything other than a concatenation of objects.

14 Cf. Dummett 1973, p. 194.

The answer to the question about realism then, is: Wittgenstein does indeed subscribe to the view Dummett attributes to Frege:

> ... the thoughts we express are true or false objectively, in virtue of how things stand in the real world – the realm of reference – and independently of whether we know them to be true or false (of whether we exist or can think at all);[15]

however, from Wittgenstein's point of view the words 'the realm of reference' are a misnomer here. I have previously called it a myth, but I might equally call it rhetoric, to say as Dummett does:

> ... we do actually succeed in speaking about the actual objects, in the real world, which are the referents of the names we use, and not about any intermediate surrogates for or representations of them.[16]

Certainly, our propositions in the last analysis are not about the workings of our own minds: what Wittgenstein is trying to convey is a point of view according to which what they are about is not in the world any more than it is in thought or in language. Objects are the form of all these realms, and our acquaintance with objects (our contact with them, to borrow the metaphor of Aristotle's *hoion thinganein*) is not an experience or knowledge of something over against which we stand. Thus it is not properly experience or knowledge at all. Objects are *eti epekeina tes ousias* (beyond being, Plato's phrase this time), and it is therefore misleading to regard Wittgenstein as a realist in respect of them. His position is one, as indeed he tells us, from which realism, idealism and solipsism can all be seen as one. That remark, however, deserves a separate investigation.

15 *op. cit.*, p. 198.
16 *op. cit.*, p. 196.

9

LANGUAGE AND REALITY

The propositions of the *Tractatus* (*TLP*) are meant to give illumination by being recognized as nonsensical, yet many expositors devote their labours to clarifying and rendering more plausible the myth that the work embodies. They fail to make the necessary leap to the destruction of that myth by its own absurdity. I have argued this elsewhere for the ontology of objects that form the framework of the world.[1] The work looks as if it gives a theory of language – a semantical theory of how propositions can be true or false – which rests on that ontology. But in fact it cannot, on its own principles, give for language or for the truth and falsity of propositions any account that rests on describable features of the world. Such an account would be metaphysical and the work itself is a subtle form of the rejection of metaphysics.

The positive aim of *TLP* is that of explaining philosophy and logic (and hence other forms of discourse also) by means of features necessarily belonging to any language. These logical features can be demonstrated or exhibited, but not described or accounted for. That is why the main point of the work (as Wittgenstein himself said)[2] is the theory of what can be expressed by propositions and what cannot be expressed but only shown. Rhees was right to say that Wittgenstein is not inferring something about reality from the nature of logic:[3] there is nothing by which our grammar is determined. In particular we cannot give, and Wittgenstein does not give, an account of language by building it up from simpler pre-existing elements. Thus the presupposed objects, existing eternally and setting limits to what we can say, turn out to be really a feature of our thought and language – but a feature that eludes our powers of expression.

---

1 See 'The supposed realism of the *Tractatus*', Chapter 8 in the present volume.
2 Letter to Russell of 19 August 1919 *CL*, p. 124.
3 Rhees 1970, pp. 24–5.

It is not too difficult to connect this anti-realism as regards 'objects' with various slogans of Wittgenstein's: that the world consists of facts not things (*TLP* 1); and that realism, idealism, and solipsism coincide (*Nb* 15 October 1916, see also 2 September 1916 and *TLP* 5.64). On the other hand remarks about the 'existence' of objects are interpretable as part of the 'myth' of *TLP*, the story that is told us so as to reveal its own untenability.

What, then, particularly recommends *this* interpretation (a methodological question) and, if this is a correct interpretation, what recommends it as a way of looking at the world? It is necessary to show that it is on the whole consistent with *TLP* (since some inconsistency in a work of this nature cannot be excluded), and, if *TLP* is, as it seems to be, an important and suggestive work, that the interpretation proposed has an application of some philosophical value. I use the word 'suggestive' deliberately, because a striking feature of *TLP* is the reader's suspicion that behind its sentences there is a body of thought that does not quite get expressed. Of course this is exactly what is claimed by the book, so the style is right for the message.

First the question whether this position is consistent with, and the only one consistent with, most of *TLP*. On the negative side, I have argued that *TLP* does not rest understanding of propositions on a process of ostensive definition. It does not suppose that the elementary propositions in which use is made of certain names are connected with reality by the correlation of those names with objects independently identifiable. This is because the notion of independent identification of objects in the *TLP* sense is an incoherent one. Only in a proposition does a name have meaning, so that there cannot be a pre-propositional act of giving meaning to a name by, for example, pointing to an object. This can be put in another way, also in terms of the *TLP* system, by saying that the situation of pointing to an object and giving it a name (possible enough in a macroscopic world) cannot be applied to the objects of *TLP* because that situation demands the existence of an object as a matter of fact, whereas the objects of *TLP* exist independently of what is the case in the world. One of the main points of the book is to insist that the 'experience' necessary to understand language (the experience that there is a world) is quite different from the experience of what there is in the world (*TLP* 5.552). The former is not an experience of facts whereas confrontation with a concrete object is an experience of fact. The former is rather, as Aristotle said about the relation of intellect to his simples, a sort of contact. The reader may think that Wittgenstein is wrong to call both these things experiences if his point is to warn us against identifying them. If this be a mistake, it is interesting that Aristotle also makes it; but in Wittgenstein's case it is surely part of his ironical treatment of himself and his readers. He commits or flirts with mistakes in *TLP* in order to teach us not to do so. I hope in the end to show convincingly that this is not an unfair trick. The apparent objection – that Wittgenstein after all says things that are not meant to be sayable – can be dismissed, because the point is that he not only accepts, but wants us to see from his own saying of it, that what he says is unsayable.

This rejection on a priori grounds of the ostensive definition of names of objects brings with it another point that should be made clearer. It is not the case that we think sense into propositions by mentally associating the words (and implicitly the elementary names that occur if the proposition is fully analysed) with objects. Such mental association would be another form of the ostensive definition just rejected. But there is another and more general Wittgensteinian reason for excluding such a solution of the problem of giving reference to names and for accepting Rhees's reading (and retranslation) of 3.11:[4] Thinking the sense of the proposition is identical with the method of projection.

The meaning is that the use of the proposition is what gives meaning to its names, not some additional act of mental dubbing or intending. This is, I think, a fundamental point in understanding *TLP*. The picture theory is meant as an account or model of what it is for propositions to have sense and names meaning. If you describe how 'pictures' can be constructed and then say that their elements acquire reference and they themselves acquire truth-value in virtue of an *act of meaning* or *intending*, you will have done nothing. It would be like the peasants to whom the working of the steam-locomotive was carefully explained, who then asked, But where does the horse go? The point is that the picture theory and the account of language associated with it is meant to be an *account* of mental phenomena: we do not need mental power – the power of *thinking* — as well, unless the account is a complete failure. We shall see this shortly in Wittgenstein's account of knowledge and belief in *TLP* 5.541 ff. In general you cannot explain what pictures are by introducing human agency. Rather you explain human agency by the notion of picturing. It is not man that makes pictures so to speak, but pictures that make a man.[5]

This is all meant to exclude a certain type of answer to the question, How is reference secured? Not by ostensive definition, not by the mental act of associating a word with a thing. Words *are* learnt, of course, and are learnt from their occurrence in ordinary propositions. These are the elucidations (*Erläuterungen*) of 3.263 as I argued in Chapter 8 above. But it is not as if we learned an (elementary) proposition of the form '*a* is

4 *op. cit.*, p. 39.
5 This line of thought is very well expressed in Warren Goldfarb's seminar notes (unpublished as far as I know) where he discusses Hacker 1972.

between *b* and *c*' and *then* asked, *Which* objects *are a, b* and *c*? What we learn much rather (implicitly for the most part) is how to understand propositions of the form 'if *a* is the centre of a circle and *b* and *c* end-points of a chord then the angle [...]'. In *such* a sentence, as Hidè Ishiguro[6] has well pointed out, you *could* not ask, But which points *are a, b,* and *c*?

The learner of language is confronted with a whole language in use, consisting of propositional facts or pictures. Each of these is of a complexity which, he eventually realizes, can only have one meaning, can only indicate or affirm one state of affairs. Here we come to one of Wittgenstein's most subtle but, I think, most consequential and rigorous distinctions between showing and saying. A proposition *shows* its sense, shows how things stand if it is true, and it says that they do so stand (*TLP* 4.022). The thought here is that while the complexity, the organization of the proposition, fully understood, adequately indicates what state of affairs is concerned, there is the further function of sense which must be added to the proposition or rather understood in it. Here (i.e. in my remarks) sense means something like direction: we have to understand which way the proposition is to be taken. Is it to say that *p* or that not-*p*? Or, more accurately, it must be determined what or which is the *p* that it here states and which the not-*p*. Later in these interesting propositions numbered 4.0, which contain his account of truth and his criticism of Frege, Wittgenstein points out that from the point of view of complexity (multiplicity) alone *p* and not-*p* are equivalent. *p* and not-*p* can say the same thing, so that what they *show* is the same thing (*TLP* 4.0621). They have opposite senses, but which sense is which is indicated by use.

If I am not wrong, this gives us the clue to Wittgenstein's way of approaching the question raised above. I asked how reference is secured in general and as a first move denied that it commenced with the conferring of reference upon simple signs by a procedure equivalent to ostensive definition. Reference is a function of fact-stating, not vice versa. Thus the question is how truth-conditions are conferred upon sentences i.e. how in learning a language a speaker comes to associate the requisite truth-condition with each sentence. This is very relevant to the general topic of realism, for reasons which will be familiar to any reader of Michael Dummett. Wittgenstein in *TLP* obviously thinks that the sense of a proposition is given by its truth-conditions and that every proposition is either true or false. This seems to Dummett to be possible only in a realistic framework such as that of Frege, which involves both a cluster of views about reference (realism about objects) and a realism about facts

6 Ishiguro 1969.

implicit in the acceptance of bivalence. To every proposition p, whether we know it or not, there will correspond either the fact that p or the fact that not-p. In his *Notes on Logic* Wittgenstein seems to put a point like this by saying that every proposition has a meaning which is the fact which actually corresponds to it (*Nb*, p. 94). In Chapter 8 above I argued for, and I hope to have reinforced here, the view that realism with respect to objects is not compatible with *TLP* but that leaves me (1) with the question of how truth-conditions are conferred upon sentences, (2) (depending on the answer to this) with a residual realism with regard to facts.

Now it might seem natural to say that *TLP* is realistic with regard to facts – it starts after all with the statement that the world consists of facts. In that case truth-conditions could be learnt or conferred by associating the utterance of a sentence with the appropriate fact. There are two flaws in this: (1) as I have already indicated, while the complexity of the sentence may suffice to indicate which area of fact is to be consulted, it will not itself indicate whether the sentence is to be understood as asserting or denying that fact. (2) How is the comparison of proposition with reality to be carried out? What is the pre-linguistic act of grasping a fact? This might seem to be an easier thing to understand if we had such a thing as acquaintance with the constituent objects. The process might then be described as looking at the objects named and seeing the relation in which they stand. But (if I am right about *TLP*) Wittgenstein has cut himself off from this way of viewing the situation.

Perhaps this is healthy – we know (now) how little is said by an account of truth which defines a proposition as true when the objects referred to have the relation ascribed to them. But certainly our remarks are in the spirit of *TLP*. The grasping of a fact in order to compare a picture with it must itself be a picture 'in the mind'.

Here it is necessary to examine Wittgenstein's account, first of what it is to believe or grasp something, and then of what it is to know something. These are chiefly given, in his usual compressed form, at *TLP* 5.541ff, as part of his discussion and correction of 'modern theory of knowledge'.

'A believes that/thinks/says p' is actually of the form: '"p" says p'. I expand and interpret this by supposing that in appropriate cases it will be of the form: '"p" believes that p'. In all such expressions, the second 'p' is an utterance in the language of the speaker (usually not A), who is not reflecting upon his own language or describing it but using it as a form of language in general (what Wittgenstein calls 'the only language he understands'). The speaker does not correlate the imagined fact that p with a subject, A, but only with an occurrence, a fact, a thought. This fact belongs to a series connected also in other ways, which series is called 'A'. Thus the supposed 'subject' or 'soul', A, is actually composite out of thoughts, and hence is complex, and hence not really a soul. (Such is

Wittgenstein's criticism of the 'superficial psychology of the present day' at *TLP* 5.5421.)[7]

'A says/believes *p*' thus becomes:

'There is a conformation to the effect that *p*'

or: 'This conformation [such and such a conformation] is to the effect
    that [is to be understood as being to the effect that] p'

i.e. 'It is a fact that "*p*" [the proposition] and what this means/says/ believes is that *p*'.

This is a possible statement only if '*p*' can be mapped onto the state of affairs in question.

What constitutes a saying as a belief? Or perhaps the question could equally be, What constitutes a saying as a mere saying and not the expression of a belief? Wittgenstein does not tell us but it is possible to infer the general lines of his answer and *TLP*. We shall have filled in a missing stretch of the graph.

First, it looks as if he here uses 'belief' as equivalent to 'judgement', so that 'A believes *p*' here means 'A arrives at (or: assents to) the judgement that *p*'. The actual difference of meaning is probably unimportant for our present purposes. Whether a mental or physical utterance, then, expresses a belief or an idle fancy will depend upon the nature of the series to which it belongs. Constant asseveration and a certain range of contexts will stamp the belief, quite other contexts the entertaining of an hypothesis.

By analogy 'A knows that *p*' will essentially mean '"*p*" knows that *p*'. We are bound to ask: How can '*p*' know anything? How can '*p*' be a knowing or cognition that *p*, a piece of knowledge? Once again we are dealing with a rather restricted, and from an idiomatic point of view artificial, sense of the word 'know', in which 'A knows that *p*' means something near to 'A correctly forms (or: assents to) the judgement that *p*' or 'A recognizes that *p*'. Let us assume (as with belief) that these related notions are interdefinable, and concentrate on the case of the occurrent cognition of or that *p* by A, i.e., as it seemed, by '*p*'.

'*p*' can be a knowing that *p* only if the occurrence of '*p*' guarantees that *p*. This is clear from *TLP* 5.1362. I cannot know anything that lies in the future because (here we must fill in a step) I can only know something now present which will cause what lies in the future. But causality is not an inner or logical necessity, so that my knowledge cannot extend to the future, since the logical necessity required for knowledge will be lacking. It is important to note that the logical necessity required for knowledge is not a necessity internal to the content of knowledge. Wittgenstein explic-

---

7 This interpretation of *TLP* on belief is in accordance with Russell's account, see
  Appendix C to the second edition of *Principia Mathematica*.

itly points out in this very context that if p (so written, without quotation marks) is a tautology, 'A knows that p' is senseless. When there is nothing to be known, the knowing of it cannot guarantee it. No, the necessity in question extends from the cognition, from 'p' itself, to the fact that p.

The 'theory of knowledge' of *TLP* – the implicit analysis of terms such as 'belief' and 'knowledge' – thus leads us to the view that if there is any knowledge at all it will reside in or depend on propositions known in the act of being formulated. That there is taken to be some knowledge seems clear: it would be excessively odd to rule out knowledge of the future if knowledge of the present were also excluded. Thus we may fairly say that *TLP* presupposes the existence of observation sentences, what Wittgenstein later called '*Aussagen*' ('statements'), as opposed to '*Hypothesen*' ('hypotheses').[8] It is not to our purpose here to inquire at length whether these were thought by Wittgenstein to be physicalistic or concerned with sense-data, but *TLP* 6.3751 rather suggests the former alternative, or at any rate an indifference between the alternatives. Perhaps the two were thought to coincide on fuller analysis.

The application of these doctrines, or in so far as they are true these insights, to our main problem, that of the securing of reference, is clear. A proposition itself tells us – more correctly, it shows – what fact it refers to (i.e. what fact it states or misstates). There is not a separate act of correlation with that fact but there is the act of acquiring that language, i.e. of using pictures as they are used in the language. In limiting cases the use in the language will be that of being taken to be certainly true or certainly false – here I do not mean taken to be tautological or contradictory, but taken to be obvious once stated. The important thing is that this 'being taken in such and such a way' is something that manifests itself inside language. The *use* of language shows that something is taken as a true elementary proposition, in that the other things that are then unhesitatingly said reflect its being so taken. Put mentalistically this means that we base inferences on it.[9]

Thus what a proposition means and whether it is true depends (a) on its multiplicity (which is the only feature that will tell us what sort of thing it is about – the only feature that allows a redescription of the subject matter) and (b) on the relation that it has to the propositions that are or would be unhesitatingly accepted as true in the language. Note again that acceptance *means* something much like frequent occurrence in appropriate contexts.

But if that is true, facts fall out of the account. There are *verification*

---

8 *PhR*, pp. 282ff.
9 Compare and contrast Wittgenstein's analysis of the role of mathematical 'propositions' – we use them to get from one proposition not belonging to mathematics to another such (*TLP* 6.211).

procedures, which correspond to the analysis of a given proposition into elementary propositions, and these may result in verification, falsification, or more frequently probabilification. In many cases we shall not know whether a proposition is true or false. Language is, however, such that we talk *as if* each such proposition *is* either true or false. That is because we cannot exclude from the use of language the situation in which that proposition would be conclusively verified or falsified. It may happen or it might have happened. That is a possibility contained in language or (what is the same thing) in thought. *The system* allows for it.

Wittgenstein's remarks about facts are then merely a way of asserting the principle of bivalence, *for which no ground can be given*. The ontological or realist myth of *TLP* is apparently an attempt to give such a ground but it suffers from the *Selbstaufhebung* — the self-cancelling character – of the whole of *TLP*. We are meant to give up such talk as a result of the talk itself. That is, in a way, healthy and good – but extremely frustrating. We feel that talk about what is required in the world generally by truth, what the nature of reality is and so on is philosophy. Read any work of Michael Dummett's. Above all read *TLP* – but *TLP* is a way of saying that it cannot be done.

It would be bold to claim that *TLP* is right. It is not *clear* that the principle of bivalence is compatible in the way Wittgenstein requires with his implicit verificationism. But the work is at any rate an important stimulus to *try* to get a way of treating logical or methodological questions which shall be free of metaphysics.

Wittgenstein's method has its own temptations – not only in that it allows itself to use or feign to use a whole metaphysics in the task of getting rid of metaphysics. This sort of *Abschreckungsmethode*, a deterrence by example, is perhaps legitimate. But when we end up having strictly thought through everything then (according to my earlier quotation from Wittgenstein) we see that realism coincides with idealism (even with solipsism though I have not done justice to this last element here). Now we can easily get the idea that we are studying a vast system, one system, which is common to the world, to language, and to thought, and which forces us to talk in certain ways. I have myself above used vocabulary reminiscent of such a view. In doing so we seem to be tracing the lineaments of some cosmic countenance. Of course, you can say (and one sees traces of this in Wittgenstein) that what we thus reveal or discover is not a constraint on us, that we are discovering, rather, the nature of our own inquiry (this would be another consequence of the self-cancelling character of philosophy). But is not philosophy too a human activity, a human need that shows us something about ourselves? All of this has its echoes in the later work of Wittgenstein and shows how protean the metaphysical urge is. Perhaps we are to draw a lesson from that too.

10

THE *GRUNDGEDANKE* OF THE *TRACTATUS*

I take as my text proposition 4.0312 of the *Tractatus*:

> The possibility of propositions is based on the principle that objects have signs as their representatives.
>
> My fundamental idea (*Grundgedanke*) is that the 'logical constants' are not representatives; that there can be no representatives of the logic of facts.

Practically the same words occur (with two additional sentences) in Wittgenstein's *Notebooks* for 25 December 1914, where Miss Anscombe translates them:

> The possibility of the proposition is, of course, founded on the principle of signs as going proxy for objects.
>
> Thus in the proposition something has something else as its proxy. But there is also the common cement.
>
> My fundamental thought is that the logical constants are not proxies. That the logic of the fact cannot have anything as its proxy.

If this is the fundamental idea or fundamental thought of Wittgenstein's early philosophy or even just of the *Tractatus*, it would be presumptuous to attempt to bring out all its implications in a single paper. I will set myself two more modest tasks: first, the historical one, of showing that this was the first or one of the first philosophical insights that Wittgenstein had and of sketching the historical background against which, and the set of problems from which, it arose; as a second task I shall set myself the exegetical one of indicating roughly how fundamental it is to the *Tractatus* and how wide its implications were, or seemed to Wittgenstein to be.

The idea that I am primarily considering is the one that the so-called logical constants do not represent, in the sense of stand for or go proxy for,

103

objects of any kind. The details of the way in which other words do go proxy for objects came later in his thought. Taking the narrower thesis, then, we find it foreshadowed in the very first philosophical remark of Wittgenstein's that has been preserved. In a letter to Russell of 22 June 1912 he wrote:

> Logic is still in the melting-pot but one thing gets more and more obvious to me: The propositions of logic contain ONLY APPARENT variables and whatever may turn out to be the proper explanation of apparent variables, its consequence must be that there are NO logical constants.
>
> Logic must turn out to be of a *totally* different kind than any other science.[1]

It is clear from many other passages in the pre-war letters and Notes that Wittgenstein regarded the occurrence of real variables among the primitive propositions of *Principia Mathematica* – 'the old logic' as he rather condescendingly called it – as a blemish: to take one example, he says that the true form of the Law of the Excluded Middle is not p v $\sim p$ but $(p)p$ v $\sim p$, giving as his reason that the former contains the nonsensical function p v $\sim p$ while the latter only contains the perfectly sensible function p v $\sim q$. He would want then to rewrite all logical laws as completely general propositions, and to explain generality (the quantifiers, if you prefer) in a way that did not involve the existence of logical objects. But was there any more direct connection between the idea that real variables might be necessary and the idea that there were logical constants?

I think there was one: any statement involving real variables would be a statement about the form of a proposition, treated as an object. In 'Notes on Logic'[2] Wittgenstein takes the trouble to assert that there are no such things as the forms of propositions.

The supposed logical constants, then, whose existence Wittgenstein was concerned to deny were not only the supposed references of words like 'and', 'or', 'not', etc.; nor these together with the supposed referents of the words 'some', 'all' and 'is identical with' – though these (truth functions, generality, and identity) did in time become the three ranges of so-called logical constants that he thought he had to deal with. Originally the notion covered much more: all the forms of propositions – the general notion of predicate, the general notion of dual relation, triple relation, and any other forms there might be of whatever complexity and level had been supposed to be logical objects, and Wittgenstein was denying them that status.

1 *CL*, pp. 14f.
2 *Nb*, p. 99.

Supposed by whom and why? Clearly, in Wittgenstein's view, by Frege and Russell: he says as much at *Tractatus*, 5.4. Now as to Frege it is clear that he did think there were mathematical objects, for example the natural numbers. It is also clear that Wittgenstein was fascinated by this belief of Frege's (from the account reported by Geach of Wittgenstein's last conversation with Frege).[3] But it is doubtful whether, in criticizing Frege in the *Tractatus*, he can have had only those in mind. For one thing, it is not in the context of numbers but in that of truth-functions that he expresses his dissent from Frege. It must be remembered that when Wittgenstein says 'There are no logical constants or logical objects', he does not mean: but there may perfectly well be logical functions or logical concepts. Indeed this is just what he goes on to deny. In Wittgenstein's view, truth-functions must not be assimilated to ordinary or material functions. Yet this is just what Frege does and on Frege's own principles, these functions must have a reference just as much as any other function. Similarly for the function of identity and for the higher-level functions which correspond to our quantifiers. Now, I will not say anything here regarding Frege's doctrine as to the reference of functions in general. I believe that Wittgenstein in fact learned from it (as may appear shortly). In any case he is not criticizing that in general, but its application to logical notions. It was partly this application that led Frege to his view that besides the real or actual physical world and the subjective world of our ideas, there existed a third world, inhabited by thoughts (in Frege's sense) and numbers and countless other things (in the widest sense) to which the attribute 'objective but not actual' could be applied. It is clearly of this world that Frege is speaking when he scoffs at those who take the laws of logic to be mere laws of thought and when he insists instead that they are laws of truth – *Grenzsteine in einem ewigen Grunde befestigt*, boundary stones fixed in an eternal soil.

In this deeply felt passage Frege does not go far enough to show how totally different logic is from any other science; but he does go some way. Moreover he does not sin against the other commandment that Wittgenstein has in mind. Precisely because of his view about the meaning of functions and their unsaturatedness, he does not think that they can have meaning in a proposition unless their gaps are filled. He too would not allow real variables to occur in the propositions of logic.

It is Russell, much more than Frege, that Wittgenstein is criticizing in his denial of logical constants, and to see why, we need to look briefly at the position both in the foundations of mathematics and in the philosophy of logic as it presented itself in 1912 and 1913 when Russell and

---

3   In Anscombe and Geach 1961, p. 130.

Wittgenstein had their discussions. Despite the great technical achievements of *Principia Mathematica*, it was clear that the reduction of mathematics to logic still rested on axioms (such as that of reducibility) which were not at all obviously logical. Indeed Russell himself offered the justification that they at any rate led to the desired results and to none that were not desired. Again, as to the general status of logic, there was considerable confusion. The a priori was explained in *The Problems of Philosophy* essentially as that which was more self-evident, i.e. which recommended itself more strongly to the human mind, than other apparently self-evident propositions.

It was not a situation to be tolerated, and Russell set himself to write a book on *Theory of Knowledge*, originally intended to deal with Acquaintance, Atomic Propositional Thought, and Molecular Propositional Thought. The third part never got written and the second part and one-third of the first part were not published in the author's lifetime.[4] What did appear (although the publication was delayed) was the first six chapters, in the *Monist* for 1914 and 1915 (the first three are reprinted in *Logic and Knowledge*). With these six chapters we shall not concern ourselves here, but the last three chapters, and particularly the last chapter of Part I and the whole of Part II, are directly relevant to our theme. Russell discusses the acquaintance involved in our knowledge of relations. He uses all the terminology familiar to readers of the early Wittgenstein: atomic and molecular complexes, the atomic ones consisting of two kinds of constituents, the objects related and the relation relating them. He assumes that we have acquaintance with the relation relating two terms (as it were with another object alongside them) and has his old difficulty with what then it is to know or think that the relation actually does relate the two objects in the desired sense or direction. The next chapter is concerned with our acquaintance (if any) with predicates and raises what he calls the logical problem whether there are complexes with only two constituents: on the whole he thinks that experience is in favour of this, although formally speaking colour predicates could be replaced by the relation of colour-similarity to a certain given example of the shade in question. (Perhaps this is Russell's theory of manufactured relations referred to in *Notes on Logic*, *Nb*, p. 103.)

This is only to show that we are in the general realm of Wittgenstein's discussions and to set the scene for the next chapter, which deals with 'logical data' or 'the basis of acquaintance that must underlie our knowledge of logic'. Russell is not certain in what sense this acquaintance is a dual relation, but is clear that there must be some logical experience which

---

4 Posthumously published as Russell 1984.

enables us to understand terms like 'particulars', 'universals', 'relations', 'dual complexes', and 'predicates'. The 'logical constants' involved in such experience are really concerned with pure *form*, Russell says, and are attained by carrying abstraction to the utmost. For example, to understand the proposition 'Socrates precedes Plato' we must have acquaintance not only with Socrates and Plato and 'precedes' but also with the form of the complex xRy, in which none of x, R, or y is itself a constant. Similarly, where non-atomic complexes are concerned, we must be acquainted with the logical objects associated with words such as *or*, *not*, *all*, and *some*. Russell admits that it is very difficult to detect in introspection these objects, or our acquaintance with them, but he regards the logical argument from our understanding of these notions to the existence of such objects and of our acquaintance with them as outweighing this difficulty.

The general idea of this passage is not new. It is a fuller statement of what is contained in the Preface to the first edition of *Principles of Mathematics*, where Russell said:

> The discussion of indefinables – which forms the chief part of philosophical logic – is the endeavour to see clearly, and to make others see clearly, the entities concerned, in order that the mind may have that kind of acquaintance with them which it has with redness or the taste of a pineapple. Where, as in the present case, the indefinables are obtained primarily as the necessary residue in a process of analysis, it is often easier to know that there must be such entities than actually to perceive them; there is a process analogous to that which resulted in the discovery of Neptune, with the difference that the final stage – the search with a mental telescope for the entity that has been inferred – is often the most difficult part of the undertaking. In the case of classes, I must confess, I have failed to perceive any concept fulfilling the conditions requisite for the notion of class. And the contradiction discussed in Chapter X proves that something is amiss, but what this is I have hitherto failed to discover.

Nonetheless, though the *Principles* presuppose such a view of the nature of logic, it is fair to say that the book does not develop it or argue for it, whereas such was evidently part of the aim of the then unpublished *Theory of Knowledge*, and would clearly have had to be pursued yet further in the projected but unwritten third part on Molecular Propositional Thought.

Moreover, for our present purposes, it is fairly clear that it is with the problems and in the terminology of *Theory of Knowledge* that Wittgenstein and Russell were wrestling at this time. Part II, for example, clearly contains the analysis of judgement that Wittgenstein criticized in summer 1913, a criticism that left Russell, on his own admission, paralysed. To mention some themes more relevant to our main subject, Part II discusses propositions and says that the fundamental characteristic that distinguishes them from other objects of acquaintance is their being true or false. Conversely, truth and falsity are described as being *properties* of beliefs, propositions, etc., such that a proposition is true when there is a complex consisting of its objects, otherwise false. (Russell recognizes that this requires modification to allow for the difference between the truth of *aRb* and that of *bRa*.) Finally, when he proceeds beyond belief to knowledge, Russell says that all knowledge must rest on self-evidence, and the self-evidence of a judgement consists in the fact that at the time of making it the person who makes it perceives its correspondence with some *complex*, whether this be a complex given in sensation or one given in our acquaintance with the meanings of words.

Before turning to the consequences of these views and to Wittgenstein's reactions to them, I shall mention one further historical fact: we know from Russell's correspondence with Lady Ottoline Morrell that it was Wittgenstein's criticisms of this book that led Russell to put it (for the most part) aside and only return to this sort of philosophical writing in *Our Knowledge of the External World*, where, on page 208 of the first edition (Chicago and London, 1914), he withdraws some of the characteristic position described above, saying:

> If the theory that classes are merely symbolic is accepted, it follows that numbers are not actual entities, but that propositions in which numbers verbally occur have not really any constituents corresponding to numbers, but only a certain logical form which is not a part of propositions having this form. This is in fact the case with all the apparent objects of logic and mathematics. Such words as *or, not, if there is, identity, greater, plus, nothing, everything, function*, and so on, are not names of definite objects, like 'John' or 'Jones,' but are words which require a context in order to have meaning. All of them are formal, that is to say, their occurrence indicates a certain form of proposition, not a certain constituent. 'Logical constants,' in short, are not entities; the words expressing them are not names, and cannot significantly be made into logical subjects except when it is the words themselves, as opposed to their meanings, that are being discussed.[5] This fact has a very important bearing on all logic and philosophy, since it shows how they differ from the special sciences. But the ques-

---

5 Here Russell has a footnote, 'In the above remarks I am making use of unpublished work by my friend Ludwig Wittgenstein'.

tions raised are so large and so difficult that it is impossible to pursue them further on this occasion.

Where then did Russell's 1913 account leave logic, given that it was already in difficulties with axioms such as that of reducibility and infinity? On Wittgenstein's view, it left logic no better off than any other science. It seemed to be an account of what was true of a particular set of objects. Moreover it was an account of what was *accidentally* true of them; all the *necessity*, what he was later to call the hardness of the logical 'must', had gone out of logic. We have seen that, as regarded *Principia Mathematica*, there was much truth, which Russell could acknowledge, in this criticism.

In the early letters to Russell, Wittgenstein attempts to eliminate all talk about forms of propositions and about logical constants. First he formulates them all as *copulae* – predicational, relational, or finally truth-functional (though that term was not yet used). Logical forms and logical objects generally arose (or were thought to come into being) when all material components had been thought away by abstraction and only the cement that formerly held them together was left: and this, of course, is, in the typical case, the copula. It then occurred to him that if you could understand the way in which the copula functioned in an atomic proposition (Russell's term – Wittgenstein later used 'elementary proposition', which meant something else for Russell) – if you could understand this, then all the problems would be solved. We have an echo of this, for it remained his view, in the *Tractatus* remark (I syncopate it slightly) that in an elementary proposition all the logical constants are present (5.47). The next move in 1912–13 occurred, significantly, after a visit to Frege:

> I now think that qualities, relations (like love), etc. are all copulae! That means I for instance analyse a subject-predicate proposition, say, 'Socrates is human' into 'Socrates' and 'something is human', (which I think is not complex). The reason for this is a very fundamental one: I think that there cannot be different Types of things! etc. etc.
>
> (Letter to Russell, January 1913)[6]

The thought here is one clearly derived from Frege. In a properly constructed language the names of objects and the signs for concepts are such that you cannot construct the nonsensical statement 'mortality is Socrates'. 'Socrates' fits into 'something is human', but 'something is

6 *CL*, p. 24.

human' does not fit into 'Socrates', and in this respect the properly constructed signs (and our own signs when properly understood) exactly match that for which they stand.

From this time on Wittgenstein's efforts were mainly devoted to his theory of the bipolarity – the necessary truth-or-falsity of atomic propositions, from which feature he hoped to derive the truth-functions, generality, and identity. But before turning to that aspect, I want to emphasize the importance which this Fregean doctrine retained for Wittgenstein, which can be seen precisely in the quotations with which I opened.

Signs go proxy for objects precisely because when properly constructed – or, what comes to the same thing, properly understood – they cannot be combined in ways which are impossible for the objects. This guarantees that every possible proposition is well-constructed; that no nonsensical proposition can be formulated; and consequently that no theory of types is necessary. In the passage we have quoted from *Notebooks*, 25 December 1914, Wittgenstein says that this is what makes propositions possible. Thus Socrates is the sort of thing that can be human, and being human is the sort of property that Socrates can have. For our part we can say that Socrates is human because the expression 'Socrates' has been given a meaning for the context '... is human' and the expression '... is human' has been given a meaning for the context 'Socrates is human'. These two trivialities are the same triviality: they are an attempt to say what is shown by the sense of 'Socrates is a man', namely – to attempt the impossible again – that the same relation of possible argument for a function (and conversely possible function for an argument) holds between Socrates and what it is to be a man and between the linguistic units 'Socrates' and '... is human'. This common relation – in the general case that of function and argument – is, I suppose, the common cement that Wittgenstein talks about in the *Notebooks* passage. It surely is the pictorial form that picture and fact have in common in the *Tractatus* (2.17). But, to stay within the *Notebooks* terminology, if we try to put in some proxy for the logic of the fact in question, assuming for simplicity's sake that Socrates *is* human, we find it impossible. We try it, for example, by saying 'Socrates has the *property* of humanity', but this still has the same common cement as before – 'Socrates' is a possible argument of the function '... has the property of humanity'.

Notice the historical fact which this exposition of the *Notebooks* passage brings out: in his denial that logical constants can have proxies, Wittgenstein is still thinking in the first place of attempts to grasp or isolate or describe the form of a proposition – precisely, in fact, of those logical notions with which Russell in *Theory of Knowledge* said that we had acquaintance.

It is clear enough – or at any rate as clear as I can make it – that Wittgenstein thought that the forms of elementary propositions were given to us by mere acquaintance with the objects composing them, by mere understanding of the names composing them. (I may say in passing that I take it that the names and the objects, by the time of the *Tractatus* at any rate, were alike simple in the sense of containing no parts that were names or objects. In this sense something like '... is human' might be a name, and stand for an object.) But how did he extend this doctrine that logical words did not stand for anything to words such as 'and', 'or', 'some', 'all', and 'is identical with'? We have seen already *why* he wanted to do so: logic must not be the science of a particular set of objects. Its difference from all other sciences must consist in everything logical's being non-contingently and obviously true of any objects whatsoever. We find the conclusion he wants to reach enunciated most clearly at *Tractatus*, 5.47:

> Wherever there is compositeness, argument and function are present, and where these are present, we already have all the logical constants.

But *how* did he get to this conclusion? What was the route by which he reached it? It seems to me very interesting as a fact in his philosophical biography that he already felt this in the summer of 1912, when he wrote to Russell saying:

> I believe that our problems can be traced down to the atomic propositions. This you will see if you try to explain precisely in what way the Copula in such a proposition has meaning.
>
> I cannot explain it and I think that as soon as an exact answer to this question is given the problem of 'v' and the apparent variable will be brought very near to their solution if not solved. I now think about 'Socrates is human'. (Good old Socrates!)[7]

Not that he didn't try out blind alleys of many kinds in the course, for example, of writing his *Notebooks*, but the general direction of his thought remains the same throughout. Events like the picture theory's occurring to him were not, I suspect, as crucial as they have been thought. That theory was principally a way of putting more clearly something he had already grasped.

Clearly, even if I saw the whole development of this theme in Wittgenstein's early writings, it would diverge from our present theme to expound it here; but in any case there is in this respect a tantalizing gap. We have very little to show us what Wittgenstein thought was the connection

---

7   *CL*, p. 20.

between his Fregean way of explaining, or explaining away, the copula and what he called (in 1913–14) 'the bipolarity business'. For it was in this latter that the seeds of those views that flowered in the picture theory lay hidden. The bipolarity business was Wittgenstein's theory of how propositions had sense and how they differed from names. The view is perhaps most fully expressed in the fourth MS of the original version of *Notes on Logic*.[8]

The idea, roughly, is this: whereas a name has meaning by referring to an object, there is no object or complex for which the proposition 'p' is a name. What there is, is either the fact that p or the fact that $\sim p$. Whichever of these is a fact is the meaning both of 'p' and of '$\sim p$'. So to understand 'p', we must know both what is the case if it is true and what is the case if it is false. We understand 'p' as soon as we understand its constituents and forms (this was Wittgenstein's terminology at the time).

This understanding via constituents and forms comes about in the following way: suppose we have the proposition aRb: we must know what object 'a' stands for, and what object 'b' stands for. We must also know how the form of the proposition – in this case 'xRy' – symbolizes (Russell's or Costello's text here erroneously and indeed meaninglessly says 'how it is symbolized'): here I will insert Wittgenstein's crucial paragraph:

> But the form of a proposition symbolizes in the following way: Let us consider symbols of the form 'xRy'; to these correspond primarily pairs of objects, of which one has the name 'x', the other the name 'y'. The x's and y's stand in various relations to each other, among others the relation R holds between some, but not between others. I now determine the sense of 'xRy' by laying down: when the facts behave in regard to 'xRy' so that the meaning of 'x' stands in the relation R to the meaning of 'y', then I say they they [the facts] are 'of like sense' [*gleichsinnig*] with the proposition 'xRy'; otherwise, 'of opposite sense' [*entgegengesetzt*]; I correlate the facts to the symbol 'xRy' by thus dividing them into those of like sense and those of opposite sense. To this correlation corresponds the correlation of name and meaning. Both are psychological. Thus I understand the form 'xRy' when I know that it discriminates the behaviour of x and y according as these stand in the relation R or not. In this way I extract from all possible relations the relation R as, by a name, I extract its meaning from among all possible things.
>
> (*Nb*, pp. 98–9 or p. 104 in the second edition where, as here, the errors are removed.)

---

8   *Nb*, pp. 103ff. in the second edition. For versions of *NL* see below 'Bertrand Russell and "Notes on Logic" ', Chapter 22 in the present collection.

Wittgenstein, of course, later abolished this distinction between 'forms' and 'constituents' in propositions, but we shall not deal with the point for a moment. The essential thing is that in the process of giving meaning to the components (forms and constituents) of the propositions, we have given the proposition a sense. We have made it *say* that things are so and not not-so: we have discriminated possible facts into two classes and indicated which class we prefer. Wittgenstein expresses this by saying that the proposition has two poles '*a*' and '*b*' and that one of these is, somehow or other (I shall not discuss that question) designated as the preferred pole. If we, then, write the proposition in the form '*a-p-b*', it is obviously, once it has been stated, possible to use this proposition to express the opposite sense to that originally intended. This is the operation of negation and is symbolized by attaching a further '*a*' and '*b*' in the opposite direction, yielding '*b-a-p-b-a*'. By a further extension – again luminously simple once it has been explained – it is possible to take a pair or any number of propositions and to produce any desired *ab*-function, or in effect truth-function, of the original proposition. An important case, of course, is that of Sheffer's stroke, which (in the VEL-form, as opposed to that used in the *Tractatus*) is represented as:

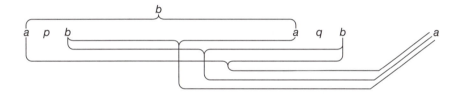

Now, about these *ab*-functions, Wittgenstein says, on the next page of the fourth MS (*Nb*, p. 101, p. 105 in the corrected edition):

> The *ab*-functions use the discrimination of facts, which their arguments bring forth, in order to generate new discriminations.

In other words: the truth-functions do not *introduce* new discriminations of facts, new material functions, but merely operate with the discriminations already introduced when the components of propositions were given a meaning. I will not here discuss how Wittgenstein thought he could eliminate identity as a possible independent logical constant – that came after the *Notes on Logic* – or how he thought he could show that generality also did not introduce some new element not already given with the components of propositions. Those are important questions, but the chief thing Wittgenstein is saying is already clear: that nothing is introduced by the logical constants, which is not present in the atomic proposition.

The general consequences of this for the propositions of logic is familiar to all readers of the *Tractatus*. It may be put in something nearer the terminology of *Notes on Logic* by saying that supposing logical propositions to be ones in which only the logical constants occur essentially, then nothing is being said about anything in them: no components – constituents or forms – occur in them essentially. They are used merely to show (for example) that two apparently different discriminations of facts into two classes (with a preference for one class) are really only one discrimination of facts into two classes (with preference for that same class).

Before considering how this is not only one of the original ideas from which the *Tractatus* arose, but also an idea that underlies its most important conclusions, I will mention briefly the change which took place between *Notes on Logic* and the *Tractatus*: namely the abandonment of the notion that the components of propositions could be divided into constituents (names of individuals, apparently) and forms. Wittgenstein, anticipating much in his later philosophy, came to see – or to think – that naming also was not such a self-explanatory process as he had originally supposed. A name in his former sense also carried with it a conception of the form of proposition into which it would fit. Thus these names did not differ in principle from any other components of the proposition, all of which carry with them some principle for the discrimination of facts. All therefore come to be called names. I do not myself think that this was an error, but I see that it can be argued that proper names (as we use the term) do not dictate the form of the proposition – or the place at which they must occur in the proposition – in quite the way that other terms do; and I further see that this would raise the question whether, in that case, Wittgenstein envisaged the occurrence of anything at all like our proper names in a fully analysed proposition. The answer to this depends on how like is like. It is at any rate a question better left to a separate inquiry.

I will end with a few words on the importance of this idea that the logical constants do not represent. This idea hangs together with the notion that our terms are given meaning and our propositions sense only by a process of discriminating facts into two classes. From this conception it follows that anything else we may do with language can only serve to bring out features of the discrimination of facts already effected. Whatever we do will not belong to the realm of sense and reference and truth but only to that of showing. As is well known, it is not only logic that is transcendental according to Wittgenstein but ethics, and hence aesthetics, too. We know, that, according to him, a poem – for example the one by Uhland quoted in his correspondence with Engelmann[9] – can *show*

---

9 *Briefe*, p. 78.

something by its way of *saying* something perfectly simple. We know also, from his letters to Ficker,[10] that the main point of the *Tractatus* (at any rate as he viewed it in 1919) was to demonstrate what could not be said. Not only the limits of philosophy, but also the nature of ethics and the mystical, were reached by considering how and whether the logical constants had meaning. It is not clear *when* the depth of the implications of this question became apparent to Wittgenstein. Perhaps the connection between logic and life first became apparent to him (it certainly became *more* apparent to him) during the war. Towards the end of the *Notebooks* (*Nb*, p. 79) he says, in a passage, I think, mistranslated by Miss Anscombe: 'My work has broadened out from the foundations of mathematics to the essence of the world' (My translation).

On the other hand we have Russell's anecdote, which is perhaps more than just a good joke, about a pre-war evening when Wittgenstein was pacing about his room and Russell asked him: 'Wittgenstein, are you thinking about logic, or about your sins?' – to which Wittgenstein replied 'Both!'

10 *Briefe*, p. 96.

11

PHILOSOPHY OF
SCIENCE

The *Tractatus* was clearly much influenced by writings on the philosophy of science, notably by those of Hertz. Indeed Wittgenstein is said to have thought that Hertz's name ought to have been added to those of Frege and Russell as one of the 'begetters' of the book. To be sure, such anecdotes do not prove very much: he also spoke of Paul Ernst, a figure now little known outside German-speaking lands, as a name that ought to have been mentioned, obviously with reference to that author's '*Nachwort*' to the Grimms' tales (Ernst 1910). Hertz thought that our minds were capable of making pictures or representations of reality and in such a way that the possible variations or alterations of the elements in the representation faithfully mirrored all the different possibilities for the physical system in question. Wittgenstein generalized this and took it not merely for an account of how natural science was possible for us but for something much more general, an account of how thought and language were possible. This was one respect in which the human race could not err: we can indeed say false things, but they are at any rate false. We can often not be sure that they are true; we can always be sure that they are either true or false. This insight – the realization that there was a framework within which the world was contained, the knowledge of which framework was logic, that logic, in this sense, was the possession of us all (rather like Descartes' 'good sense'), the simple and the learned alike, seemed to Wittgenstein of great importance, though I cannot discuss all the reasons for that importance here.

At the same time, *latet anguis in herba*: there were some dangers. Not all the features of our language were pictorial in the ways we are apt to take them to be. Here perhaps the debt to Paul Ernst came in: the forms of our language can mislead us (the thought is too common in the *Tractatus* to require quotation) rather in the way that primitive men drew conclusions that we now think false from the pictorial way in which they spoke of natural phenomena and human relations. It is a tension that remained throughout Wittgenstein's thinking – I mean for all his philosophical life: on the one hand, the primitive man is right to think as he does, the

116

picture is meant to be taken as a picture and followed up, the human body, as Wittgenstein said in a well-known passage, *is* the best picture of the human soul. On the other hand, the theories of the philosophers are useless because they take some elements in the pictoriality of language, some pictures, too seriously. But who is the primitive man and who is the philosopher? No doubt there is an answer to this question, but for the moment, and dealing with the *Tractatus* only, I will say no more than that it is not, as some have supposed, an easy task, nor does the end of the *Tractatus* say that it is an easy task, to discover when we have given no meaning to one of the signs that we use. It is a difficult and tortuous task to find out what has misled us, or, if you prefer, what has misled the philosopher, and it is to this task, in my opinion, that Wittgenstein devoted much of the rest of his thinking. I am not saying that there was no change from the *Tractatus*: there was some change, if only because in the *Tractatus* he sometimes spoke as if the essential pictorial element in our language (which of course would be the test of misunderstandings) was something to which we could in principle break through. It was there at any rate as an ideal: but later he spoke as if the generation and removal of misunderstandings would be an endless task.

Wittgenstein, then, extended Hertz's account of science in order to say that in our grasp of the essential pictoriality of language we have a trivial but important variety of infallible knowledge. (I have briefly indicated above the limits of that grasp and of that knowledge, points that Wittgenstein did not make clear in the *Tractatus*.) But it remains to ask what infallibility he thought the scientist to possess: how far did he accept Hertz's picture theory for the area it was designed for? I shall proceed by a fairly straightforward analysis of the relevant texts in the *Tractatus*, but since these texts are so familiar (and indeed I shall not expound them, so to speak), I can mention at once another and converse problem that arises from those texts: why did he not apply, or perhaps to what extent did he apply, the striking image of the net or network that he uses there of science to all the propositions of language, or to language as a whole.

Philosophy of science is discussed almost nowhere save in the 6.3's and this placing at once indicates what Wittgenstein wishes to establish, namely that the various types of propositions found in science can be accounted for without supposing that there are propositions which are *neither* propositions with sense (i.e. pictorial propositions) *nor* propositions without sense (i.e. tautologies or contradictions). Compare the 6.1's, which show that logical propositions are propositions without sense, the 6.2's, which show that mathematical propositions are not propositions at all, and 6.4's and 6.5's, which show that ethical, aesthetical, and metaphysical propositions are also (though for very different reasons) not propositions at all.

Roughly speaking, the answer about scientific propositions is twofold, according as we direct our attention to general Principles of Nature (such as the Principle of Induction itself, the Law of Causality, or the Principle of Least Effort) or to particular application of these that enable us to predict actual events or the results of experiments.

To deal with the Principles of Nature first: they are clearly not tautologies or contradictions but there are two ways detectable in the *Tractatus* in which they can be viewed indirectly as a priori. The first is this: it is obvious a priori that there can be particular laws connecting phenomena or physical events or measurements, laws that conform to these Principles. Such particular laws (be they true or false) will be propositions with sense (i.e. pictorial propositions) and, in addition to what they say, will manifest the possibility of propositions of that particular form. The Principles, however, at any rate when viewed in this light, *say* nothing but merely *manifest* the possibility of propositions having the form of such particular laws. The second and more complicated way in which the Principles can be viewed as a priori is this: we may in fact adopt them and make them part of our network for describing the world. This corresponds in Wittgenstein's analogy to making up our network of squares, triangles, or hexagons as the case may be. Note that we are not committed to using a uniform network: we might have both triangles and hexagons. Wittgenstein's pupil Watson, in *On Understanding Physics*, has shown how physicists do in fact use quite different patterns for laws covering different areas or required for different purposes. We adopt the Principles, then, a priori, but of course to apply them to the world as it actually is, we have to discover laws of the appropriate form (i.e. of the form dictated by the Principles) that will fit the facts. Depending on the Principles we have chosen it will be more or less difficult and circumstantial to find these laws. More or fewer exceptions and interfering factors will have to be allowed for. In the analogy (though we ought not to let this govern our interpretation too minutely) this corresponds to a coarser or finer mesh. On the whole a coarser mesh is preferable, though Wittgenstein does not say this.

One difficulty that arises here (pointed out by Professor Black in his *Companion*, 1964, pp. 344f, 364f.) concerns the Principle of Induction itself. This is hardly a Principle in the sense in which the others are. It does not dictate (or signalize a preference for) any particular form of law. Every scientific law, every hypothesis is an inductive one. Now it is certainly a psychological fact (6.3631) that we feel it necessary to adopt scientific principles and to erect scientific laws corresponding to them. But the Principle of Induction itself does not express this psychological fact: it merely expresses our determination to continue to form hypotheses. It shows something about our scientific language and thus would seem to be a priori in the senses described above. But at 6.31

Wittgenstein describes it as obviously a proposition with sense. One way out would be to say that *all* Principles are really propositions with sense, but that they are treated as a priori inside the activity of science. But the objection to this is that the Principles are too abstractly stated to be true or false. *Some* law of the kind in question can always be found. Perhaps the point Wittgenstein is making is that the Law of Induction is not a law at all (which would have to be true or false) but a Principle (as indeed he says, more or less, about the 'Law' of Causality at 6.32). When it *is* used as a law, as, for example, to predict that the sun will rise tomorrow, it is a proposition with sense and its truth is in no way guaranteed.

I am inclined to think, however, that the true explanation is another one. The Law of Induction is not a true scientific Principle and differs from all that are truly such in a certain respect. It consists in assuming a certain framework and a certain degree of fineness (i.e. a certain way of employing that framework) and then asserting that that particular network at that particular degree of fineness will inevitably fit the future. Obviously it is far from certain that it will fit it as well as it has fitted it. If this be so, then induction will not be the method of science, which is much more subtle and much less liable to outright refutation. I think we should all agree with this, and it has an important consequence for Wittgenstein: it was this crude view of what underlay science which had the result (by no means necessary on Wittgenstein's own view of science) that the success of science demanded that the world should be of a certain sort and should contain causal regularities and objective necessities. The beauty of science is that it can fit any world whatsoever.

Another difficulty raised by Professor Black (p. 349) is that given a certain form of network (say squares) and a certain pattern of black and white, it might be the case that no matter how fine we made the mesh each square was exactly half black and half white. To translate this back from the analogy (to which, as I have said, we should not be too attached) this would mean that a certain system of mechanics or physics might continually prove unsatisfactory. Now [in 2001] this seems to me to be incompatible with determinacy of sense. At the level of elementary propositions we should have reached a stage where every point was either black or white and a more or less complicated mapping of black point would be theoretically possible. But it is more important to say that *of course* one system of mechanics might be very unsatisfactory, in which case another would no doubt be chosen, but even if (which I doubt) the system of mechanics in question were in principle incapable of being more right than wrong, we could never know it to be so, because at each stage it would always be possible for us to try a further refinement of the mesh. In practice, however, we should no doubt try another system.

To turn now to the second category of scientific propositions, the actual laws: the general answer about their status will be clear from what has

119

been said: they are propositions with sense, pictorial propositions, being truth-functions (admittedly generalized ones) of elementary propositions. That is how physics manages to talk about objects in the world (6.3431). Often Wittgenstein talks about describing the world completely and on this way of looking at it the ideal of science would be to reach generalizations, which were true without exception. Only at one point in 6.341 does Wittgenstein speak of approximating *as closely as we wish* to a description of the world – as if in science we might be content with a certain looseness of fit.

I hope I have said enough to show that in my opinion Wittgenstein's philosophy of science need not involve any departure from his picture theory of propositions. I turn now to consider why he identifies the totality of true propositions with the totality of natural science. It is true enough that any truth-function of elementary propositions that was true would be derivable from a complete and unified description of the world, which is the ideal of natural science. But it seems almost sleight of hand to say that elementary propositions are themselves limiting cases of truth-functions of elementary propositions. Even if we take into account Wittgenstein's later distinction between *Hypothesen* and *Aussagen* ('hypotheses' and 'statements', *WVC*, p. 99 *et al.*), it remains a redefinition of natural science to include in it all true descriptions of the world. This redefinition was motivated by the desire to find a single category into which to place all descriptive (or, in Wittgenstein's term, pictorial) propositions. It is thus further evidence that all the propositions of natural science were pictorial propositions.

I turn lastly to an interesting thesis of Professor Stenius's (Stenius 1960, pp. 84ff.), which he, perhaps surprisingly, does not relate to Wittgenstein's account of the philosophy of science. He says that the statement that the world consists of facts not things means that different analyses of the world into distinct facts are possible and that these will generally entail different frameworks for the world, different sets of objects to figure in it. This amounts to the suggestion that Wittgenstein's account of science applies to language as a whole. There would be no fixed set of objects, no one and only complete analysis of a proposition, except in relation to a prior and more or less arbitrary choice of language. This view derives some historical support from the fact that Wittgenstein's pictorial theory of language is largely derived from Hertz's pictorial theory of science. It seems to me in fact ruled out that Wittgenstein held the view at the time of writing the *Tractatus*: he later accused himself of holding at that time that analysis might in time discover what elementary propositions there were and hence what objects there were, which in turn implies that there is one definite set of elementary propositions and of objects. Also he thought for some time that there was a phenomenological language and a set of *Aussagen* (statements) which, so to speak, imposed itself on us. But it is of considerable interest to consider whether Stenius's view is a possible development of the *Tractatus* and whether it is in fact reflected in Wittgenstein's later philosophy.

That Wittgenstein did not at the time of writing the *Tractatus* hold a view like that suggested by Professor Stenius can, I think, be demonstrated not only by his later comments and by general probability but also by two passages in the book itself which have a certain significance when read together. I mean the simile used in the account of truth at 4.063 and the remarks made about logic in 5.511. The text at 4.063 implies that the actual state of affairs in the world, the state of reality, the sum of all obtaining states of affairs (*Sachverhalte*) is something determinate like the question whether for a given point on a piece of paper it is black or white. Now whether this actually is a determinate question I should not like to say, but I think it certain that Wittgenstein took it to be so at the time. In 5.511 he implies that logic provides us with an infinitely fine network which completely and exactly covers the world, inasmuch as there is no point in the world (here thought of as a surface – that is why 4.063 is more useful for our purposes than the many passages which speak in a similar sense of logical *space*), no point in the world, then, which does not have its corresponding point in language. For every point's being black or white there is a corresponding proposition to the effect that that state of affairs obtains (or alternatively, of course, that it does not). The very image of the network is here used (I mean in 5.511) to say that the network of logic is infinitely fine – that is to say that there are no possibilities with which the logic of our language does not already deal. It is true that Professor Stenius might say that these pictures deal only with facts or states of affairs, not with objects. But objects are clearly only a function of the states of affairs in which they figure (the facts in which they *can* figure). If a language (to talk in Professor Stenius's way) has the multiplicity requisite to deal with all possible states of affairs, then it has the possibility of referring to all the objects that it is necessary to refer to *and hence* to all the objects that it is possible to refer to (3.328).

It seems to me quite clear that Wittgenstein meant that while many different scientific networks were possible, only one logical one was. Thus Hertz's scientist was infallible, in the sense described at the beginning of this paper, only within an arbitrarily or at any rate not necessarily chosen network: what he said was necessarily true only because it was true of the network, not of that which the network described. But the logician, that is to say Everyman with his logical insight, says something or knows or has an inkling of something, which he cannot alter by choosing another point of view.

That said, it is necessary to consider what truth there could be in Professor Stenius's conjecture. The first possibility (and in some ways the most interesting) is one that, as I hope to have shown, completely traverses the position of the *Tractatus*: namely that all language is in the position of a scientific theory or framework as these are described in the *Tractatus*. The actual facts, the bare facts, the whole realm of what the Germans call *Sachverhalt* – the incontestable – may not exist. It is not necessary for our purposes to consider the full Platonic position according to which *no* fact about the world is completely a fact. It is enough to consider that many things about the past, even the present, certainly the future, about numbers, sizes, shapes, colours of things (and of course about numbers themselves) are as a matter of fact indeterminate. In the *Tractatus* Wittgenstein always talks as if everything could be viewed *sub specie aeternitatis*, that is to say, as if there were in principle such a view, let us call it God's view. Now: why do we suppose that there is such a view? why do we suppose that there is a true account (to take the simplest example) of what happened at an accident? Because there is a God? Well, it is surely wrong to bring God in in this way. It is like Berkeley's use of him to explain how objects could continue to exist when no one was seeing them, or like saying that God must know the full expansion of π. God knows the truth, to be sure: but only in the sense that if we can be sure that something (or other) is the truth then we can be sure that God knows it. This rather vague and vaporous position, which has obvious connections with intuitionism and other philosophical positions is worth mentioning here, because it is so opposite to the position taken by Wittgenstein in 4.063 and so many other propositions of the *Tractatus* and also because it has some relation to Wittgenstein's later thought, particularly about mathematics. But I cannot see (perhaps through lack of vision – and that is partly why I mention it) that it has any tendency to show that there could be different basic frameworks for describing the world.

A second possibility, which I will describe more briefly still, is that there might be different sets of objects and different elementary propositions implicit in the languages of distinct individuals. For my part I do not think that the *Tractatus* is a book written to suggest that each man has a private view of the world, except in the ethical sense, to which I will come shortly. I think this for a slightly paradoxical reason: namely that the book seems to me itself intensely private. It is largely about how one man can think and frame propositions. Briefly I think that the implication of 5.62 is that whatever anyone else says that I do not understand does not count as language. All the same, something like this second possibility appears in the later thought of Wittgenstein, which allows for the possibility that different groups (one cannot say different individuals) might have languages so different that a member of one could understand the language of the other group only by being introduced to and in a sense being converted to all their practices. To this extent, Professor Stenius is supported by the later writings, except that a main theme in them is that language is not a framework for the description of reality.

The third possibility for the truth of Professor Stenius's conjecture probably never occurred to him and perhaps deserves little discussion, but nonetheless some. It is the following: perhaps when a man becomes happy or unhappy (if indeed Wittgenstein allows this possibility) the facts and objects of his world become different. There are really no grounds for such a supposition. Wittgenstein's whole ethical position rests on the statement that the facts all belong to the task set, not to the solution of the task. It was naive of Engelmann to suppose that one solution might be to change the facts, precisely because the whole emphasis is, in a certain sense, on acceptance. Of course one does something, but its ethical value does not depend at all on its being successful. The sort of change there is in the world when a man becomes happy or unhappy is described in the *Notebooks* 1914–16 as its coming to have or ceasing to have a sense (*Nb*, p. 73, though the translator prefers 'meaning' for '*Sinn*'). This brings me back to my main theme: language and science (according to the *Tractatus*) have this in common, that each is the application of a mesh (be it as coarse as possible and arbitrary or infinitely fine and necessary) for the description of reality. Both alike could be opposed to other activities and other dimensions: it was the point of the *Tractatus* not to glorify either of them but to signallize those differences.

12

THE VALUE OF
SCIENCE

Wittgenstein did more than contribute to the philosophy of science: his
early work was one of the influences – and an important one – that made
its foundation possible. He also did less than contribute, not only by
ignoring the special philosophical problems of science in his later thinking, but also by the implicit and explicit denial of a central or paradig-
matic role for science in our thought and life. Those who sought
enlightenment from it, or who looked on it as the instrument or motor
of progress, incurred his bitterest polemics. Now, fifty, sixty, or seventy
years on, science has proved even more influential than could have been
foreseen. To learn today from Wittgenstein's attitudes, we need to alter
them – to mollify or to intensify or more probably to refocus them. I shall
limit myself to the humbler task of reminding you what Wittgenstein
conceived science to be, and of suggesting how this conception affected
his valuation of it.

Note first, though, that Wittgenstein was in general opposed to the
division of philosophy into a number of areas, each with its main problems, which time and hard work would perhaps overcome. (I argue this
as much from his practice as from his professions.) Epistemology he was
particularly against, in so far as it incorporates the idea of the need to
find foundations on which all our convictions – construed as claims to
knowledge – rest. We act and live and interact in a great multiplicity of
ways: our avowals and constatations are not antecedent, temporally or
logically, to this life of ours: they are part of it and depend on it as much
as it on them. Considerations like this are collected in *On Certainty*, not,
be it noted, a *work* of Wittgenstein's but a selection by editors from his last
writings. Wittgenstein, in general, did not write *works* (this was part of his
hostility to the divisions of philosophy) but reflected promiscuously on a
number of topics. Each area illuminates the others – hence the constant
reordering of his remarks. This last practice does not show that there
exists an ideal order towards which he was striving, but rather that no
order is the correct one. The consequences of this for the editing of his
literary remains I must leave for another occasion: they have yet to be

drawn and are philologically and philosophically fascinating. Here it will be enough to say that it is very significant that Wittgenstein hardly ever brought any of his voluminous writings to completion. It sometimes seems that their incompleteness, their unpublished character, the need always to move on to a fresh consideration of the matters touched on, *is* their message. (This contributed, I believe, to Waismann's difficulties over collaboration and to Carnap's over priority.)

These prefatory remarks have their relevance (I hope) also for those who are not primarily interested in Wittgenstein, those perhaps who have the urge to ask, What *is* his contribution? His is not a philosophy of contributions but of conversion. In his aims he has much in common with the disturbing and apocalyptic authors whom he admired, Hamann, for example, Kierkegaard, Nietzsche, and more remotely St. Augustine and Plato. This is not immediately obvious, because, unlike most of these, Wittgenstein concerns himself with something like traditional philosophical argument, presented dialectically. The nearest parallels are some of the Socratic dialogues. In a well-composed dialogue, as in a drama, the point is not, or not chiefly, that one party is right, but that from a welter of partial views and false analogies which have generated conflict, contradiction, or difficulty, a new and higher point of view emerges, from which there are no doubt problems to be faced, but not the ones we were originally bogged down in. (Plato, incidentally, makes the point, which we have already seen in connection with Wittgenstein's literary remains, that this process is a live one, not really susceptible of being frozen into a book.) Now clearly it would be a tremendous enlightenment and release if we could transcend problems in this way – factitious ones like scepticism about the external world or ones with deeper social and psychological roots like the demand for a foundation for morality – but the cure is never an easy one. A palmary example of this is the notion of an inner object or private language, where Wittgenstein, in my opinion, has given us all the materials for a solution, with considerable repercussions for our whole picture of man, but, for that very reason, the issue and his own thought is still discussed in the very terms he sought to transcend. It is an irony that he is represented as a sceptic and a shame (in my view) that problems about brains in vats are still regularly posed. I incline to the view that all this is due to our reluctance to abandon intellectual luggage, and in this respect Wittgenstein does demand a lot of us – perhaps that we should give up philosophy of language and philosophy of science in the form that we know them.

To turn now to Wittgenstein's original attitude towards science (using the term to mean natural science): that attitude was formed at a period when Russell wrote his *Scientific Method in Philosophy* (Russell 1914d), a phrase which also occurs as part of the title of *Our Knowledge of the External World*. The idea was that by using the new grasp of logical form given by advances in logic such as those of Russell and Whitehead, philosophical problems could be resolved or rendered soluble, being rewritten as theses (sometimes self-evident or self-contradictory) of science itself. It was in this spirit that the young Wittgenstein gave his first paper at the Moral Sciences Club (it lasted four minutes, if the minute-book may be relied on), maintaining that philosophy consists of all those propositions that are common to all the sciences. When worked out, in the *Tractatus*, Wittgenstein's position is subtler than that, but still one that gives enormous importance to science. Science has a central position: it alone fulfils the real function of language. In comparison logic and mathematics, mere aids to description, are devalued. This (if valid) was a radical simplification of our grasp of the world. The position of Frege and Bolzano, whose follower in many ways Wittgenstein was, consisted in stressing the fact or supposed fact that our knowledge was not confined to the material world, or to the material world together with that of the psyche, but embraced a third realm, the realm of consequence, of number, of conceptual truth generally. This realm Wittgenstein purported to abolish by demonstrating the triviality of logic and mathematics: they were merely techniques for getting from one statement that mattered (i.e. a statement of natural science) to another such statement. Philosophical statements were even less useful. Employing a measure of interpretation and reformulation I might say that they attempted to state as principles or truths something whose opposite was inconceivable, something, therefore, which itself was strictly inconceivable – something, say, of the order of 'There is only one number One'. Propositions like this seem to express a truth, until, on reflection, we see that they embody and perpetuate the confusion they seek to remove. How valid this account of logic and mathematics is, and how consistent Wittgenstein's own (philosophical) account of philosophy is, I will not discuss here. I will only point out that the *Tractatus* view of the elucidatory function of philosophy is thoroughly compatible with the absence of philosophical theses – contributions, as I have called them – in Wittgenstein's later philosophy. This account of mathematics and logic can be seen as a determined attempt to keep their status and hence their methods distinct from those of natural science. This aim still has considerable relevance in our own time.

My point in the present discussion is that the *Tractatus* account of language and thought is a scientific one, and that in two senses. The function of language is seen as the utterance of true or false sentences, attempts at description, and, since description *is* science, the utterance of scientific propositions. Conversely, the features of language that make it capable of fulfilling this function are read off from a scientific model. Hertz's and Boltzmann's accounts of what is required of an adequate physical theory are used as an account of what is implicit in all language. Language must proceed by constructing models of reality, and these will presuppose a division of reality into elements (typically point-masses). All possible states of reality are simply different arrangements of such elements. The internal economy – figuratively speaking the consequences – of one state of reality will be fully contained, as consequences, in the model or description of that state. Hertz constates that there is this agreement between our minds and reality (he is thinking of physical truth), Wittgenstein is concerned to show (he is thinking of meaning) that anything else is inconceivable. This means, of course, that he is not arguing from the nature of language to that of the world: language, thought, and the world are one system as far as their necessary features are concerned and these necessary features he is attempting to demonstrate.

I have said that *all* description is science, but clearly the term science is normally used for the more systematic forms of description. The *Tractatus* allows for this. To simplify description, general hypotheses are introduced, and to further this simplicity, a general form that all hypotheses should follow is introduced – say a general law of causality or the stipulation that all laws be mechanical in form. All such stipulations are equally justified (or equally unjustified, if you prefer), but some are intrinsically simpler than others, while some (not necessarily other than and not necessarily the same as the foregoing) are extrinsically simpler, in that they require a smaller number of subsidiary hypotheses in order to fit the phenomena equally well. Wittgenstein does not say how a system should be chosen, but clearly his view is a variant of the conventionalism not uncommon in his day. For his purposes (which are those of showing the limits of natural science, of language, or, in a paradoxical sense, of philosophy) the main point is that general principles like the law of causality or the principle of least action are not insights into the nature of reality, but are present a priori in our language as logically possible forms of description that we may opt for (I shall return to this point).

We begin to arrive at the negative side of the *Tractatus* account of science. All plain truth-telling discourse is part of science and no attempt should be made to utter truths not belonging to science. So far we have much that could be, and indeed was, used as a programme for logical positivism. But Wittgenstein wrote his *Tractatus* as much against science as in defence of it. He insists (not with special originality) that while science describes everything it explains nothing. One might ask – Mach does and Wittgenstein means us to – What then would explanation be like? For Mach explanation would be the removal of hidden contradictions in our perception of the facts – and in this sense, of course, explanations can be given. For Wittgenstein the demand for a complete explanation is itself a confusion: there must remain the brute givenness of the facts – symbolized by our ancestors' ascription of responsibility for them to God or Fate. This is the same thought (I believe) as that which he expresses by saying that even if all scientific questions were answered our real problems would not be touched. The real point of isolating so clearly the nature of science turns out to be that any attempt at a scientific approach to human problems – moral, social, religious, or existential – involves a misconception of those problems. The same would apply to a social science or a social philosophy. This is a part of Wittgenstein's legacy that has been much contested, and that fact itself shows, I think, that he is not just drawing formally correct conclusions within his own system when he says that the facts only contribute to the problem not to its solution. It is, perhaps, a further point that problems in ethics, for example, are not to be dealt with *like* ones in science, using hypotheses, generalizations, thought-experiments, etc. It may, in fact, be wrong to talk about problems at all. There is no special *intellectual* difficulty. But here I perhaps go too far into speculation in my effort to show that Wittgenstein was not contributing to an ongoing philosophical discussion, but trying to convert us to a new and not totally congenial approach to intellectual problems.

Science, at all events, was not the key, nor were its problems the main ones we had to face. It is natural therefore, that they do not bulk large in Wittgenstein's later writings, apart from some discussions of hypotheses, of induction, and of probability in the early 1930s. I ought to say, however, that I base these observations principally on the published writings, which of course form a selection, perhaps a selection made by editors who have already reached the view I describe. One reaction to my account of Wittgenstein's earlier views on science (an account which I am pretty sure is substantially correct) would be to investigate more thoroughly than I have been able to what he said in his later teaching and writing (published as yet or unpublished) about natural science. For this purpose, as for others that I have mentioned, we badly need the easier access to his papers that has now [2001] become possible with the Oxford-Bergen edition of the manuscripts and typescripts. It is now also possible to approximate to a thematic index, extending at least to proper names and quotations, signalized or unsignalized.

A certain use of science which suggests itself and which Wittgenstein occasionally seems to recognize I will mention shortly, but the main tendency of his philosophy as his life proceeded was to shun the scientific paradigm and to direct our attention to thought about human possibilities. *Lebensform*, the form of life, is the key concept and on grounds of principle I agree with Newton Garver that this usually means the general form of human life rather than the various specifications that are possible. Wittgenstein's, then, is a philosophy of *gnothi seauton*. Gompertz has given excellent philological grounds to show that this does not mean, as Socrates is said to have thought, Know your own individual character, but, Know what it is to be human. This, of course, was Pope's interpretation.

128

Know then thyself, presume not God to scan:
The proper study of mankind is Man.

The methods of such studies are various. We find them described in Wittgenstein's discussion of Frazer's *Golden Bough*. We find them exemplified in the method of constructing language games, i.e. of imagining how men might behave. There are limits to the possibility of such behaviour, but like the limits of language and the world in the *Tractatus*, they are not brute matters of fact, which we could imagine to be other than they are. At most we can show the incoherence of attempts to describe life beyond such limits. Wittgenstein's attack on the notion of an inner object (a private language) is one example of this.

Much of Wittgenstein's philosophy, then, is rightly described as a natural history, not of what man has done, but of what he might do. Psychoanalysis is one form of such exploration – a possible restructuring of the problems and of the approach to life and understanding of life of those concerned. Wittgenstein did not view it as a scientific exploration, because it did not fit the Helmholtzian pattern of the testing of hypotheses by experiment. The occasional (and dubious) reconstructions by the analyst are trivial: the main criterion of analytic success is the patient's acceptance of a new way of thinking.

Now the reader may long have thought that in all of this Wittgenstein takes too narrow a view of science as an activity. I have no doubt that there is room for a Wittgensteinian critique of Wittgenstein's own paradigm or reconstruction of science. Much more attention needs to be paid to the practice of the scientific community and to its aims and choices. Such considerations, happily, feature in recent writings on the philosophy of science. I will not dwell on them here, for one reason mainly: that they do not affect or neutralize Wittgenstein's doubts about the value of scientific method as applied to human or philosophical problems Certainly there is an ethos in the scientific world, but I think he would feel that always the solution looked for is not appropriate for the problems of life – the thrust is all towards *esprit de géométrie*, rather than *esprit de finesse*. But this lesson too has been learnt, I think, or is slowly being appreciated, at least when it is a question of reconciling a technical solution with a human environment.

What I will briefly and finally dwell on is a limitation in Wittgenstein's account of science, not unusual for its time, which too much sharpens the distinction between the scientific mode of thinking and all others. Wittgenstein gives (this is clear in the *Tractatus*) a static account of the logic of science. Constatations are constatations: hypotheses are (mere) hypotheses: principles are embodiments of the general form in which hypotheses might be cast. As such, principles are simply a selection from the totality (surveyable in theory) of the possible forms of general propositions. Little attention is paid to the dynamics of science itself, to the question how and why a set of principles comes to be adopted and what sort of revision it is liable to. Wittgenstein's emphasis is all on the equal logical admissibility of scores of theories. Now, as Einstein says, the task of the scientist is not merely to be prolific of theories, but to discern the nature of physical reality that theory must capture. We can see this particularly clearly in the account Mach gives in his *Principles of the Theory of Heat* (1986). It is all very well to say (as Wittgenstein does say) that we vaguely know in advance that there must be a law of least action, but no importance attaches to such presentiments, if they indeed existed. What was needed was to find a way of conceiving of heat that would free us from hidden contradictions and inconsistencies in the pre-existing conceptions of it – as a stuff, as a quantity, as a form of motion – and this is possible only for one who is both a great theorist and capable of restructuring in thought a large body of data hitherto confusingly described. Carnot, Thomson, Clausius, and J.R. Mayer were such men: their work would have been inconceivable except as the result of interaction with a large body of phenomena and a large body of scientific reflexion, as Mach pointed out.

There is no reason why Wittgenstein should not have seen this for himself. True he was somewhat dismissive of Mach, but the scientists he refers to – Clerk Maxwell, Hertz, and Boltzmann – were of the type described. The true paradox is that the method described by Mach is Wittgenstein's own in philosophy: it is precisely what I described at the beginning – the effort to get away from confused and conflicting views about a mass of material to a higher point of view encapsulated in new concepts. It is not that Darwin and Einstein tell us something about the nature of reality as a whole, but that their ability to make conceptual advances can be a model to us. Wittgenstein does occasionally use scientific discoveries as examples of the sort of conceptual conversion necessary in philosophy. Such passages, and indeed all references to conversion or change of paradigm, we ought to collect and set against his hostility to the misuse of science. For not only can the idea of a paradigm be traced back to his writings but (partly for that very reason) he himself was a changer of paradigms.

13

SOLIPSISM

The question is that of the place of discussions of solipsism in the *Tractatus* and preparatory writings and also whether these have in this respect any relation to the work of the 1930s. In *The False Prison* volume I (1987) David Pears (to simplify drastically) regards solipsism as a theory refuted in the early work by showing that the supposed subject does not exist and rendered totally harmless in later discussion by showing that the supposed private objects of such a subject cannot exist either. One difficulty with this account is that in the earlier work Wittgenstein does not refute but affirms solipsism. At best it might be argued that he rejects a false solipsism in favour of what is, in his view, the only true form of it, but there is in fact little sign that he was much concerned by or about any theory of solipsism that would involve the notion of privacy.

If we ask what Wittgenstein meant by 'solipsism', it was not, to judge by what he mentions, the view that the individual finds himself in the Cartesian situation of not knowing whether there is anything outside his own thoughts, in particular not whether there are other minds. This was not in fact the way solipsism was viewed when he came to philosophy. We may take one of Mach's formulations as an example:

> If I now call the sum of my mental aspect, sensations included, my ego in the widest sense (in contrast with the restricted ego), then in this sense I could say that my ego contains the world (as sensation and idea). Still we must not overlook that this conception does not exclude others equally legitimate. This solipsist position seems to abolish the world as independent, blurring the contrast between it and the ego. The boundary nevertheless remains, only it no longer runs round the restricted ego, but through the extended one, that is through 'consciousness'. Indeed we could not have derived the solipsist position without observing the boundary and the analogy between my own and

others' ego. Those who say we cannot go beyond the ego therefore mean the extended ego, which already contains a recognition of the world and other minds.[1]

Analogies to Wittgenstein's position can indeed be seen in this, yet I do
not think even this was his starting point, for he does not start from a self-
centred position. In 1912 we find him dismissive of Russell's struggles to
escape from solipsism by finding, in immediate experience or in self-
evident principles, grounds for a belief in matter.

> I argued about Matter with him [Russell wrote to Lady Ottoline
> Morrell]. He thinks it is a trivial problem. He admits that if there
> is no Matter then no one exists but himself, but he says that
> doesn't hurt, since physics and astronomy and all the other
> sciences could still be interpreted so as to be true.[2]

These are considerations arising from epistemological solipsism, as G.
Gabriel has called it[3] and there is no indication that they bulked large in
Wittgenstein's earlier intellectual history. It seems much more the case
that he finds the world self-evident and the self a mystery and so comes to
it at the end of his trajectory.[4] No, the *Tractatus* is written and his thoughts
prior to it were formed under the influences he mentions in a celebrated
list:[5] first of all – for the list seems to be chronological – Boltzmann and
Hertz, the opponents of Mach. And indeed the book he later wrote presents an attack on philosophy very similar in its conclusions to Boltzmann's
and is based on a picture of the world modelled on Hertz's mechanics, a
world, that is, thought of as consisting of arrangements of objects (which
may be highly theoretical ones – like Hertz's point-masses). For this reason

---

1 Mach 1976, pp. 6f. (trsl. P. Foulkes).
2 Letter of 23 April 1912, quoted with a brief discussion in McGuinness 1988, pp. 105ff.
  He had more doubts about this in January 1913, when he wrote to Russell (who had
  been reading Mach):
     I am very interested in your views on matter, although I cannot imagine your way of
  moving from sense data forward. (*CL*, p. 25).
3 See Gabriel 1998 and also Gabriel 1991, pp. 89–108.
4 When he says (15 October 1916 *ad fin.*) 'The way I have gone is this: idealism singles
  man out from the world as unique, solipsism singles me alone out, and at last I see that
  I too belong to the outside world ...' he must be describing his thought of recent
  months, for the remark certainly does not correspond with the course followed in the
  abundant notes and drafts that we possess from earlier years.
5 From a diary entry of 1931 (see *C&V*) after the two mentioned come: Schopenhauer (!),
  Frege, Russell, Kraus, Loos (these two not discussed here), Weininger, Spengler and
  Sraffa (the last two evidently after both the War and the *Tractatus*).

Wittgenstein was indignant when it was thought that the physicalism of Carnap and Neurath in the 1930s was something new. It will be remembered how he deals with the incompatibility of red and green at *Tractatus* 6.3751 – it is explained by the physicalist formulation (*'die physikalische Ausdrucksweise'*), in which the assignment of the two colours would be a logical impossibility. He assumes that such a reformulation is always possible. This implies of course that a non-physicalist formulation, presumably a sense-datum-based language, would also be possible (and we have indeed seen this from his discussion of the problem with Russell before the war). This complementarity anticipates that of Carnap's *Der logische Aufbau der Welt*,[6] and, more important, it is an example of Wittgenstein's tendency always to transcend a problem. He attempts, *modo suo*, to dissolve it by moving to a higher level. In the present case there are ontological implications not always clearly recognized. Useless to ask whether the ultimate components are sense data or point masses: useless, because there is not anything that they *are*.

But Wittgenstein also follows another tradition that may broadly be called realist, that of Frege and the early Russell, both of whom are mentioned in his list of influences. This brings him near the conceptual realism of Moore at the turn of the century (who was surely Russell's inspirer) and of early phenomenology – Meinong and Reinach, of whom there are more than echoes in Wittgenstein's book. To the specific linguistic turn that he gave to phenomenology we shall return. Of course the views of Boltzmann on mathematics (that its laws were those which evolution had taught us were best for pursuing natural science) were quite the opposite of Frege's position, but Wittgenstein, following Frege and Russell in many things, corrected the two of them (corrected, as he called it, 'the old logic') by showing that the truths of logic and mathematics were empty of content. He may thus be seen attempting to transcend the difference between Frege and Boltzmann.

In the list of influences we also find the name of Schopenhauer, which must give us pause. If Boltzmann was his first idol, how does Wittgenstein still contrive to value the thinker who seemed to Boltzmann to represent philosophy at its most sterile and ridiculous? Once again the answer lies in Wittgenstein's wish to transcend the old philosophy. He uses Schopenhauer's terms, or ones like them, to make philosophical moves that confirm Boltzmann's hostility to philosophy.

This is evident from the first proposition of the *Tractatus*, which is an echo of Schopenhauer's, but at the same time a seeming denial of it. The

6 Berlin 1928, see Carnap 1967.

world is not my idea but is all that is the case (*sc.* regardless of what is known or thought to be the case). This contrast remains, even if there is also a contrast with the idea that the world consists of objects. Later in the book we realize that Wittgenstein none the less wants to accommodate Schopenhauer's insight within his own: 'The world is my world' is the point of reconciliation between the two.

It is here, in this formula, that we come to what solipsism meant for Wittgenstein. To be sure Schopenhauer did not himself describe his position as solipsism. That characterization of it is due to Weininger, another in Wittgenstein's list of influences, as has been well pointed out by G. Gabriel in the articles referred to above. This may be seen particularly in the posthumous collection *Ueber die letzten Dinge*,[7] where it is said, for example, that the philosopher who accepts that the world is his idea accepts everything in it and identifies himself with it. Any shrinking from solipsism in this sense indicates, Weininger says, incapacity to give a value to existence as such. The evident parallelism with Wittgenstein's views not only on solipsism but on ethics we will return to after considering the philosophical justification provided in the *Tractatus* and *Prototractatus*, thus bringing our methodology closer to that of Pears: so far we have been considering the matter almost exclusively from the standpoint of the history of ideas, but from that position it is important to note that the apparent influence of Weininger (or, if you will, Wittgenstein's finding a kindred spirit in Weininger) is an intrusion into Wittgenstein's logical notebooks precisely in the middle of the war.[8] This corresponds with the chronological place of Weininger in the list of influences: he is mentioned after Loos (whom Wittgenstein met in July 1914) and before Spengler (whose influence must be sought after the war and in Wittgenstein's later thought). Indirectly we have indications that Wittgenstein was interested precisely in Weininger's posthumous book at just this period.[9]

Naturally enough, therefore, the basic propositions about solipsism are all added in the *Prototractatus* manuscript after page 50 when the main lines of '*Der Satz*', as the work was originally to be entitled, had been established.This, and the fact that most of the propositions on the topic are added at a much later stage in the preparation of the manuscript, corresponds to the dates of the related entries in the *Notebooks*, which are described above. Peter Hacker was right, as a matter of history, to see

---

7   Echoes of that work in Wittgenstein are indicated in McGuinness 1988, pp. 40f.
8   The theme is first broached on 23 May 1915 but chiefly discussed after June 1916.
9   His sister Hermine, in a letter of 18 November 1916, says that 'Dein Weininger' has been for her in some measure a substitute for Wittgenstein himself, and there is reason to suppose she is referring to this book. See Wittgenstein *FB*, pp. 83 and 102.

them as an afterthought.[10] No doubt Wittgenstein felt attracted by Schopenhauer's ideas at an earlier stage, but it is only now that he is able to incorporate them in his logical investigations. He says at this very point (on 23.5.15) that he has long been aware of the possibility of writing a book, 'The sort of world I found myself in', as if he is now returning to an old theme.

As to the place he chose for these considerations in the work he was composing, Wittgenstein at first meant to insert them in the discussion (5.33 ff in *Prototractatus*, becoming 5.53 ff in *Tractatus*) of pseudo-propositions, those connected with identity and statements such as 'p is a proposition' being typical examples, but in the *Tractatus* they are, after their gradual expansion, moved to a section of their own, the 5.6's. Originally the point was that to say the world is my world has as little real content as saying that a thing is identical with itself. It could be paraphrased by saying meaninglessly – 'The *world* we describe is the world *we* describe.' (We shall shortly see Wittgenstein himself using distribution of emphasis to make a point.) It is as if he reacts to the tendency he finds in Mach and Russell by saying to them, Look, you're not saying anything different from what the realist or physicalist (Hertz or Boltzmann) wants to say. No insight is being conveyed when the solipsists say, 'The world is what I experience (or could experience)', unless one goes on to say with Wittgenstein, 'But I am nothing', and then one conveys both a logical lesson (as here) and (in the diary and *Notebooks*) a moral lesson, which we have yet to consider.

The logical lesson is that just as there is no a priori science of identity or of the nature of a proposition (two of his examples in this context), so there is not an a priori experience of the world's relation to the subject, no a priori order of the world.[11] Thus Wittgenstein takes a further step in the rejection of the a priori, and hence of philosophy itself, which was his heritage from Boltzmann, and yet at the same time is able to do justice

---

10 In Hacker 1972, pp. 60–85. Hacker there criticized my 1966 assimilation of the moral and logical features of 'solipsism', but I hope would now be more sympathetic to the lateral thinking necessary for understanding Wittgenstein, who indeed introduces these features concurrently.

It will not have escaped attention that in this paper I take the view that Wittgenstein's method of composition, the construction of a jigsaw of *aperçus* extracted from his notebooks, requires a methodology of interpretation that takes into account the context, the original context, and the known facts of Wittgenstein's life and reading. The surface argument of the final outcome must of course be followed, but with due awareness that the need to fit a new remark into a framework already determined before the thought occurred to him may have had Procrustean effects. Thus a remark may often carry implications not particularly in place in its final context. This might be summarized by saying that Wittgenstein thought intuitively, not discursively.

11 *Nb*, 12 August 1916, cf. *TLP* 5.634.

to the hidden stream, with its origin in Schopenhauer and Tolstoy, that has all along accompanied his devotion to logic. In 1914 this stream runs through the versos of his *Notebooks* and is veiled in the code reserved for family and private remarks, now, after 1916, it is to be found among the philosophical remarks on the recto and in clear.

Just as Wittgenstein's ontology is a reflection of language so his solipsism arises from language, in the sense that every person, and the author in particular, can envisage the world only in so far as he is a speaker of language, in which the world can be described. I say 'of language' rather than 'of a language' to emphasize Wittgenstein's idea that there is only one language. He often speaks as if this were so and he affirms it explicitly in his *Notebooks* (29.5.15) and this reflects the assumption that all natural languages are different realizations of the one system. Thus he says that man is capable of constructing languages in which every sense can be expressed.[12] This uniqueness of language implies that there is one and only one set of possibilities for the world, but it also means that there is no higher language, no metalanguage, to use a later term, for talking about language, and hence for talking about sets of possibilities.[13] This creates for Wittgenstein the difficulty that none the less he himself writes (what seem to be) propositions: this, which we may call the Problem of the Ladder, is well known but is not our immediate concern here.

And the speaker of language is unique also, in the sense that language is essentially the world, the totality of possibilities, as seen from a point of view,[14] but of course from a point of view that is entirely impersonal. Language (the central theme of the *Tractatus*) has as precondition a subject (which Wittgenstein calls the metaphysical subject). But just as the limits of language, or, to speak absurdly, what lies beyond them – the possibilities that are inexpressible –, just as these cannot themselves be described or stated, so too the subject cannot be expressed.

It is necessary to consider here the much-discussed proposition (*Tractatus* 5.62 para 3): 'That the world is my world gets shown in the fact that the limits of language (of language which *alone* I understand) mean the limits of *my* world (*die Grenzen der Sprache [der Sprache die allein ich verstehe] die Grenzen meiner Welt bedeuten*).' This translation, which I now prefer, differs from that favoured by, for example, Hintikka[15] and Stenius,[16] who said that the meaning clearly was 'the only language that

---

12 *TLP* 4.002.
13 He thus anticipates the suggestion made by Russell in the Introduction to the *Tractatus*, but rejects it for reasons other than those imputed to him by Russell.
14 This corresponds to Plato's saying that thought is the dialogue of the soul with itself, a constant theme of Wittgenstein's writings.
15 Hintikka 1958.
16 Stenius 1960, pp. 221f.

I understand', whereas Miss Anscombe in her *Introduction* (still in print) proposes, or rather revives, the translation 'the language that only I understand'.[17] But there is in fact no question of different languages, one of which is understood only by me. Wittgenstein speaks of the limits of *'der* Sprache', to use the emphasis of the *Prototractatus* manuscript, i.e. of the limits of language as such, which he contrasts in an obvious stylistic device with 'die Grenzen *meiner* Welt' (the limits of *my* world). To bridge the gap between the one and only language and a world, which is mine, he inserts the epexegetical observation that language (*sc.* language as such) is the only thing that I understand, i.e. that something not expressible in language would not be a possibility. It is very important that the parenthesis is epexegetical of the phrase *'der* Sprache': it says something previously unmentioned which is true of language as such: this surely cannot be that I alone understand it. The marks of emphasis in the *Prototractatus* show that Wittgenstein means something like this: the limits of the world are those of the one and only language and this language is by definition something that the speaker or thinker, in this case myself, can understand and hence these limits are also those of my language.

As has been pointed out before there is a philological fact that supports this interpretation. The first edition of the Ramsey-Ogden translation actually had 'the limits of the language (the language that I alone understand)' but Wittgenstein asked Ramsey to have this corrected to 'the language (*the* language which I understand)', and this was in fact done in later printings of that translation. While this new translation clearly excludes the Anscombe interpretation, it is not itself particularly clear. Perhaps we have to allow for some unawareness of differences between the use of the article in German and in English: the first 'the' is unnecessary and confusing because there is no prior implication of a plurality of languages of which one in particular is being spoken.[18] But some insensitiveness to idiom would be natural enough for Wittgenstein who had been ten years away from England at the time of the correction, and indeed we find traces of such in his letters. The limits of language (hence those of what is possible, hence of the world) must be the limits of a language, of the very language, that I myself understand.[19] This corresponds fairly well with the translation that seemed correct to Pears and myself in 1959.

---

17 Anscombe 1959.

18 True 'the language' might indicate something semi-familiar, such as 'the language that we all speak' or 'the language in question', but then the explanation '*the* language etc.' becomes hard to understand.

19 Thus the translation 'the only language that I understand' makes the right point, though I do not think it is exactly what Wittgenstein originally said, if the distinction is not too refined.

I think that the Anscombe reading not only is not Wittgenstein's (as the correction shows and the distribution of emphasis in the *Prototractatus*, just described) but also could not be. For how would privacy help the argument? It even hinders it: if we imagined everyone with his own language, there would be worlds that I had no access to, whereas in truth all possibilities are implicit in language, which is the same for all and the only medium of understanding. It is the last point here that Wittgenstein wants to make: there are no possibilities other than those guaranteed as such, permitted to be such, by language, and since anyone can envisage everything language allows (and cannot envisage anything else), everyone has the same relation to the whole world.

You may say, Why then call it my world? Because it follows from the above that everyone is, and I in particular am, a measure of the world. We define its possibilities by being a completely neutral point of view. We are dual with it, as language is and for the same reason. It is for this reason that Wittgenstein exclaims, It is true: Man is the microcosm (*Nb*, 12 October 1916).

Not the privacy of language but its availability or transparency to a speaker is at issue. The point is that language has to have a centre and when I speak or think I am that centre. I alone – but the same would be true of anyone else. When I speak or think it is the World Soul, *die Weltseele*, speaking, but so it is whosoever speaks.

The *Weltseele* is mentioned in this context in the *Notebooks*, which indicates a way in which content can be given – and undoubtedly was given by Wittgenstein – to his 'solipsism'. So far from being a doctrine which leaves us separated from others – 'Yes, in the sea of life enisled /.../ We mortal millions live *alone*' as Matthew Arnold put it (in *To Marguerite*) – it is a doctrine that seeks to bring us all together, for we can all participate in *die Weltseele* and should do so, should deny our individuality and refuse to attach importance to 'our own' concerns. This is the Tolstoyan message of the last pages of the *Notebooks* and the first pages of his code diary, where holding fast to the Spirit, *der Geist*, is the only way he can hope to behave decently. It is entirely consistent, of course, with the nature mysticism of this period, which I (and others) have described elsewhere. There are two forms of interiorization implicit here, two forms of response to the precept of Wittgenstein's Angelus Silesius: *Mensch werde wesentlich!* Man should seek his true nature.[20] By going into the soul we find the true

20 'Become essential, Man! When the world fails at last,/Accident falls away, but Essence, that stands fast'. In a way this is the same as the original meaning of the Delphic 'Know thyself': man should know that he is not a god. Socrates' interpretation, suggesting an examination of conscience, is an anachronism and (more to the point) not the same as what Wittgenstein is here saying.

nature of the world and by retreating into the soul (making ourselves independent of fate) we attain the purpose of life, though the actual self vanishes in both cases.[21] Of course there is a temptation here to two forms of exaggeration – an indifference to the advance of science on the one hand and a quietist refusal to attempt to alter facts on the other, and Wittgenstein has been accused of both of these. As to the former attitude, Wittgenstein's attitude was highly nuanced but certainly affected by a fierce preference for an engineer's practice over a physicist's theories, while the latter indeed was almost imposed on an Austrian officer in 1918. On a philosophical level, however, such evaluation is unjust simply because the twin attitudes described or presented are not on the level of facts at all.

The problem of privacy certainly dominates later. It seems to have arisen in discussions with Ramsey and members of the Vienna Circle in 1929 and 1930. Slightly later there was his hostility to the idea of physicalism as a panacea, so that his own followers – Schlick and Waismann principally – were dubbed 'die Ich-Gruppe' ('the Self Group', or here perhaps better, 'the Ego Group') by Neurath. And the development of the theme (regarding which for the most part I would gratefully follow David Pears) will have owed much to the problems discussed in Cambridge, with Ramsey in the first place. Curiously enough – this by way of a concluding note – Wittgenstein, who was dismissive of others (Ryle for example) for not producing their own problems, was himself above all a reactive philosopher. But it is human to see one's own qualities in others, *imputat se quisque*, and in any case *his* reactions were often ingenious and original above the norm, including (as the richness of discussion shows) those to this very complex of problems called 'solipsism'.

---

21 *Hence* it is that 'consciousness of the uniqueness of my life is the origin of religion, science and art' (*Nb*, 1 August 1916).

14

MYSTICISM

It is not certain that Wittgenstein had read Russell's essay, 'Mysticism and Logic', when he composed the *Tractatus*. That essay was published in July 1914,[1] and Wittgenstein's last visit to England before the war seems to have been in October 1913. If he did read it in 1914, he seems to have put it out of his mind for a good while, since 'mystical' themes hardly appear in his *Notebooks* until 6 May 1916, when propositions 6.371–6.372 of the *Tractatus* are first propounded.[2] The particular notebook in which they occur was begun in mid-April after a silence – perhaps explicable by his work on the first version of his *Abhandlung*[3] – covering ten months. It contains only a handful of entries prior to the 'mystical' ones, and once they have appeared they dominate the notebook. Thus, as far as our information goes, the latest in date of the pre-*Tractatus* passages which foreshadow the *Tractatus* are those which foreshadow its mystical sections – though, of course, there are large parts of the *Tractatus* for which no pre-*Tractatus* parallels have been preserved, notably the 6.1's and 6.2's (except in later sections of the *Prototractatus*, as later discovered and now described in Chapter 22 of the present collection). When mystical themes are discussed in the *Notebooks*, not much use is made of the term 'mystical' itself and, on the other hand, there is a good deal of terminology drawn from Schopenhauer and a number of fairly obvious allusions to him. Thus, both negatively and positively, the style of the mystical passages differs from Russell's.

For all that, there is a considerable coincidence between the presuppositions and results of the *Tractatus* and those of Russell's essay. Russell describes metaphysics as an attempt to conceive the world as a whole by

---

1 Russell 1914a. Reprinted in Russell 1918, pp. 1–32.
2 *Nb*, p. 72, pars. 8–10. An exception is the anticipation of *Tractatus* 6.52 which occurs in the notes for 25 May 1915 (*Nb*, p. 51, par. 3). That passage is more reminiscent of Tolstoy than of Russell (cf. Tolstoy 1940, especially pp. 23–4).
3 See Chapter 23 below.

means of thought: in this, metaphysics unites two tendencies in man's mind, the mystical and the scientific. The mystical tendency manifests itself in certain moods and feelings, in which one has a sense of certainty and revelation. This certainty does not easily lend itself to expression in words, unless it be by way of paradox; but four things chiefly characterize the beliefs, if such they may be called, of the mystic: first, there is typically a belief in an insight into reality, an insight which is superior to and quite different from sense and reason, an insight common to the mystic and the poet but far clearer in the former; second, the mystic believes that reality is one, containing no opposition or division; third, he holds or feels that time is unreal; and fourth, he thinks that evil is mere appearance, or perhaps that good and evil are both illusory (in any case, his ethic involves an acceptance of the world). As regards all four of these beliefs, Russell maintains that mysticism is mistaken but that there is some value in the feelings of the mystic, which may inspire not only the artist but even the scientist. Metaphysics, however, being the attempt to express these feelings in the form of a creed, Russell implicitly rejects.

The kinship of much of this with the end of the *Tractatus* will be clear enough.[4] Wittgenstein too holds that there is no such thing as metaphysical doctrine; there is a feeling which may be called *das Mystische*, an inexpressible feeling, to have had which is to have solved the problem of life: those who have had it feel that they know something, but cannot put it into words (*Tractatus* 6.522). This felt 'insight' was the first mark of Russell's mystic: the second was the mystic's conviction of the unity and indivisibility of reality, which is surely parallel with Wittgenstein's description of mysticism as 'viewing or feeling the world as a limited whole' (6.45). The third mark was timelessness, as parallels for which in the *Tractatus* we have both the view of the world *sub specie aeterni* (Russell too quotes Spinoza in this connection) and the eternal life, which, according to Wittgenstein, belongs to the man who lives in the present (6.45, 6.4311). Finally, as a parallel to the fourth mark, we have Wittgenstein's account of good and evil, in which he denies that they are in the world. Rather, they attach to the subject; they consist in an attitude of the will toward the world – acceptance in the case of the happy man, for whom the world is good, while the unhappy man finds the world inharmonious: he has a bad conscience and is therefore in disagreement with the world (6.4's passim). Thus all four marks of Russell's mystic are in the *Tractatus*

4 In the present paper I shall concern myself chiefly with the mysticism of the *Tractatus* and though I shall draw upon the *Notebooks* often enough it will only be for the better illumination of *Tractatus* passages: some themes are omitted altogether in the *Tractatus*, while in some other cases two opposing points of view are represented in the *Notebooks*, only one of which survives into the *Tractatus*.

at least implicitly and there is the same evaluation of metaphysics. I think we may assume that if these four marks are indeed all marks of a single phenomenon (whether 'mysticism' be its true name or not) then they were so conceived by Wittgenstein. But I have to establish that they do form such a unity by presenting Wittgenstein's thought on all these matters as a single, intelligible whole. That will be my first task, and I can derive some encouragement as I embark on it from the fact that these different themes, though not all associated with mysticism in the *Tractatus*, are closely interwoven in the *Notebooks*. Indeed, Wittgenstein's mysticism there embraces not only the four themes from Russell's mysticism that I have already touched on – the powerlessness of the will, the nature of ethics, the immortality that timelessness confers, and the vanishing of the problem of life – but also that peculiar form of solipsism which, in the *Tractatus*, is outlined in 5.62–5.63. (The other mystical passages, of course, occur between 6.371 and the end of the work.) Can there be a single 'mystical' *Weltanschauung* which will consist in living in the present, which will involve a grasp of the sense of the world, which will see the world as a good world and as a limited whole, which will accept the world, and which will, at the same time, see the world as my world? If the last element is included in 'mysticism', then we can find a passage in the *Notebooks* where Wittgenstein, like Russell, sees mysticism as the inspiration even of the scientist: for he there says that it is only from the consciousness of the uniqueness of my life that religion, *science*, and art arise (*Nb*, p. 79, par. 2, my emphasis).

Our first question then is whether Wittgenstein is entitled to have (supposing for the moment that he does have) a single doctrine of mysticism embracing all these elements. To the extent that we find him justified, we shall go on to discuss that mysticism in order to discover how far it is entitled to the name and what relation it bears to other forms of 'mysticism'.

The historical question I raised at the beginning is relevant to the question about the appropriateness of the term 'mysticism'. Does Wittgenstein's mysticism in the *Tractatus* go beyond what he and Russell had already thought: was there during the war a further 'mystical' experience which played its part in the production of the *Tractatus*? Certainly the impression that any reader gets when he compares the *Tractatus* with the pre-war writings is that the latter are much less intense, much less mystifying, much less enigmatic. To a certain extent this is because Wittgenstein had found his own style of writing and thinking: the same differences appear between the *Notes on Logic* (1913) and the *Notes Dictated to G.E. Moore* (1914),[5] the latter being much more characteristic

---

5   Printed in *Nb*, pp. 93–106 and 107–1 18.

of their author and less like Russell, who seems to have had great difficulty in understanding them.[6] This is perhaps a point at which the history of Wittgenstein's thoughts necessarily involves us in that of his life: did he, as has been asserted,[7] have a mystical experience of some sort during the war, perhaps after reading Tolstoy? It is undeniable (and Wittgenstein himself asserted in letters) that the war very radically changed his attitude toward life,[8] but it may well have been his general experiences during it that led to such changes as there were in his philosophical outlook: it would be rash to *infer* that there were mystical experiences among them. That Wittgenstein read and was deeply influenced by some of Tolstoy's ethical and religious writings during the war is well attested, however, and there are echoes of those writings in the *Tractatus*.[9] There are also clear allusions in the texts to Schopenhauer, as mentioned already,[10] and one to Dostoevsky (*Nb*, p. 73, par. 19), and one, signallized by the editors, to Schiller (*ibid.*, p. 86, par. 7). Wittgenstein's mysticism, as will be clearer later, was of a quite different kind from Schopenhauer's. The investigation of sources, however, will not go far toward settling the question whether there was an actual mystical experience. I shall return to that question later after discussing whether what is spoken of *could* represent a mystical experience.

Even if there are additional elements in Wittgenstein's mysticism, the parallels with Russell's essay remain striking. A somewhat similar anticipation of the conclusion of the *Tractatus* (though not of its arguments) occurs in the essay, 'Scientific Method in Philosophy', which was also published in 1914:[11] it speaks of extruding the idea of the universe

---

6 This is apparent from unpublished letters to Russell written in 1915 and 1919, *CL*, pp. 100f., 115.

7 Urmson 1960, p. 408. I have been unable to discover the precise grounds for the statement there made.

8 See von Wright 1958, pp. 9–10. In a letter to Keynes of 4 July 1924 (*CL*, p. 206) Wittgenstein is very emphatic in saying that he has become quite a different person in the eleven years since they last met. (I have drawn on these letters at a number of points and must express my indebtedness to the executors of the late Lord Keynes and to the Librarian of King's College, Cambridge, for their courtesy and help.)

9 See von Wright, *loc.cit.* For echoes of Tolstoy see note 2 above and compare 6.4311 with 'The Gospel in Brief' (p. 118, secs. 9 and 10, in Tolstoy 1940) and 6.4312 with 'A Confession' (*ibid*, p. 48, par. 4). In an unpublished letter of 1912 Wittgenstein speaks with much enthusiasm of *Hadji Murád*, which he has just read. That work is, of course, one of Tolstoy's most successful attempts to convey his ethical ideas in artistic form.

10 Allusions to Schopenhauer are frequent in the last part of *Nb* and he is mentioned at p. 79, par. 12. For a comparison of Schopenhauer with Wittgenstein, see Gardiner 1963, especially pp. 275ff.

11 Reprinted in Russell 1918, pp. 97–124, but published in 1914 and apparently referred to by Wittgenstein in May 1915 (*Nb*, p. 44, par. 13).

(perhaps what Wittgenstein would call 'the world as a limited whole') and that of good and evil from scientific philosophy. Russell there takes the view, however, that the actual task of scientific philosophy is to catalogue the logical forms that make up the world: a view repudiated by Wittgenstein in the 5.55's. The extrusion of the universe and of good and evil is very reminiscent of 6.4–6.5, which no doubt represent Wittgenstein's own development of themes that were common ground between him and Russell before the war.[12] A yet closer parallel is the otherwise rather surprising remark at 4.1122 about the lack of any special relation between Darwinism and philosophy, which should be compared with *Mysticism and Logic* (pp. 105ff.) and *Our Knowledge of the External World* (pp. 11ff.).

Important though it is to notice these parallels between the *Tractatus* and Russell's works, there is one big difference between the two men, a difference affecting precisely this question of mysticism. Russell took for granted that philosophy itself was not inexpressible in the way that mysticism was. We can see Wittgenstein's reaction to this in a letter written from prison camp to Russell. Russell had described the theory of types as a theory of correct symbolism: 'a symbol must have the same structure as its meaning'. 'That's exactly what one can't say,' replies Wittgenstein. 'You cannot prescribe to a symbol what it may be used to express' (*Nb*, p. 129, par. 5). In Wittgenstein's view, the logical properties of the world also were shown or manifested: they too could not be expressed. It was true that tautologies might be used to show those properties, but really they were shown equally well by all propositions; the chief difference was that logical propositions had no other function than to make them manifest.[13] Naturally, therefore, Wittgenstein says some things about logic which are very similar to what he says about ethics and the mystical. What is mystical is not how things are in the world, but that the world exists (6.44): similarly, to understand logic we need a certain 'experience' not of how the world is (not of *how* things stand in the world) but of the

12 See also Russell 1914b, especially pp. 18, 28, 46. Though Wittgenstein may not have seen this work (he was asking Keynes, probably vainly, for a recently published book of Russell's in early 1915), he contributed some of the ideas in it (see p. vii) and must have known the rest. His own interests at that time were logical rather than mystical (*ibid*.; see also Russell 1951, which describes Wittgenstein's mysticism as a change which took place 'during or perhaps just before the first war', i.e., after his virtual collaboration with Russell).

13 No doubt Wittgenstein would have admitted that, in the case of some 'logical properties', there are no proposition-like entities, such as tautologies, which express them in so far as they can be expressed: e.g. the property of being a function. That something is a function does indeed get shown, but not by a 'logical proposition' whose sole function is to show it. On this point see Black 1964, pp. 199–201.

existence of something (5.552). Both ethics (6.421) and logic (6.13) are said to be transcendental: or, as he says in the *Notebooks* (p. 77, par. 7), both of them are 'conditions of the world'(*Bedingungen der Welt*).

This difference from Russell will also serve as a good starting-point for our projected inquiry whether all the themes that I have been calling mystical can indeed be viewed as belonging to a single realm of experience or quasi-experience. It seems at first blush very improbable that there should be a single quasi-experiential ground for logic, ethics, mysticism, and solipsism – not to mention aesthetics and the conviction of one's own immortality. At best, we should expect that these would represent different stages of a single kind of experience. We might suppose this experience to be merely implicit in the case of logic and at its height in the case of seeing what the meaning of life is. It may be well to say that at this stage in our inquiry we can make no special objection to Wittgenstein's thinking that mystical experience was involved in so common a thing as mastery of the logic of our language. Even if we suppose that mystical experiences properly so called are not universal, we are not at the moment discussing whether the experience of which Wittgenstein speaks, if it exists at all, is properly called 'mystical' but are considering simply whether there is any single experience embracing all these elements.

Let us concentrate, then, on the experience that is presupposed by logic: the experience that something *is*. This cannot be knowledge of the truth of an existential proposition, since whether or not a given function is satisfied by no objects or by one or more objects is a matter of how things are in the world. It must, then, be an experience of the existence of objects whose existence is not a matter of experience in the ordinary sense: it must consist, that is, in acquaintance with simple objects and with their possibilities of combination. Not that the logician must be able to list the objects which figure in the facts that he knows and in the possibilities that he can envisage. In order to do logic he must be able to answer the question 'What?,' but the answer he must be able to give is not a catalogue of the objects that there are (in a peculiar sense of '*Es gibt*') but simply the answer that there are objects. Wittgenstein in fact held that we did not know what objects there were (5.55) or what the composition of elementary propositions was. To be sure, this is something shown or displayed by our language, but we have not grasped it in the way that we can grasp the *general* form of a fact (which is of course identical with the general form of a proposition). Our grasp of logic can give us implicitly all possible forms of elementary propositions and of molecular propositions: it will not tell us what application these forms will have or which of them will be found as elementary propositions. Experience, too, is incapable of telling us what elementary propositions there are: this is only natural, since every experience is bound to be the experience that some possibility is realized. To know what elementary propositions there are would be to know exhaustively what possibilities our language possessed or, in more technical terms, to know the full analysis of our propositions. All we can know in advance is that they have a full analysis, that there is some limit to the possibilities of language: otherwise nothing would have a determinate sense (3.23).

It is true that there are traces in the *Tractatus* of the view that one of the tasks of logic was to discover the analysis of the propositions of science. In his 1929 article, 'Logical Form', Wittgenstein indicates that this is necessary in order to substitute a clear symbolism for the 'unprecise one' that we have: 'We can only arrive at a correct analysis by, what might be called, the logical investigation of the phenomena themselves, i.e. in a certain sense *a posteriori*, and not by conjecturing about *a priori* possibilities'.[14] This is to bring into logic something which, according to the *Tractatus*, belongs to the application of logic (5.557), hence perhaps the tentative air with which the investigation is called logical; but the *Tractatus* itself, as I am conceding, is not quite single-minded on this point: 4.112 seems to ascribe to philosophy not only the task of setting limits to what can be thought but also that of elucidating (presumably by correct analysis) the propositions of science. At 4.1211, when Wittgenstein wants to illustrate his statement that propositions show or display the logical form of reality, he does so by saying that the proposition '*fa*' shows that the object *a* occurs in its sense. This tendency in the *Tractatus* he was later to condemn, for in conversation with Schlick and Waismann in December 1931, he said:

> Much more dangerous [than dogmatism] is another error which also pervades my whole book – the notion that there are questions the answers to which will be discovered at some later date. [I recognised that we cannot make a priori assumptions about the forms of elementary propositions] but I thought nonetheless that it would at some later time be possible to give a list of the elementary propositions. Only in recent years[15] have I freed myself from this error. At the time, I wrote in the manuscript of my book, though it wasn't printed in the *Tractatus*, 'The solutions of philosophical questions must never come as a surprise. In philosophy nothing can be discovered.'[16] However, I myself did not yet understand this sufficiently clearly and made the very mistake that it attacks.[17]

14 *LF*, p. 163.
15 He must mean the years since the composition of 'Logical Form' in 1929.
16 Wittgenstein does make a similar remark with regard to *logic* at *Tractatus* 6.1251, cf. also 6.1261, but to assert it of philosophy in general would presumably have been more sweeping.
17 Taken from notes made by Waismann, now published as *WVC*, where see p. 182.

Quite clearly, however, this tendency is not prevalent, indeed not even present, in those parts of the *Tractatus* in which Wittgenstein alludes to the 'experience' necessary for logic. That experience will not find expression in lists of objects and possible states of affairs but, if put into words at all, can be identified only as the experience that there are objects and states of affairs: as Wittgenstein says at 6.124, 'Logical propositions presuppose that names have meaning and elementary propositions sense and that is their connection with the world'. The knowledge that there must be elementary propositions (which knowledge we can now fairly equate with the experience necessary for logic) is said by Wittgenstein, reasonably enough, to be possessed by everyone who understands propositions in their unanalysed form (5.5562).

What is it, then, to have this experience? Nothing special, you might say, since everyone who can handle the logic of any propositions whatsoever must have it. When one says, 'must have it', one does not, of course, imply that it is a single experience or revelation preceding all others: rather, it is something implicit in all of a man's thought. The experience, then, has the same object as the mystical feeling (the term 'feeling' here is perhaps more literally used than the term 'experience'): the same object, since both are an attitude toward the existence of the world. I am here assuming that there is no difference between 'that something is', which is the experience presupposed by logic, and 'that there is a world' which is what is mystical.[18] That something is means that there are objects; that there are objects means that there are possibilities each of which must either be realized or not; that there are such possibilities means that there is a world. Conversely what the mystic finds striking is *not* that there is the particular world there is – for he is not interested in *how* the world is – but that there is *a* world – namely, that some possibilities or other (no matter which) are realized – which is no more than to say there is a set of possibilities some of which (but no determinate set of which) must be realized, which is no more than to say that there are objects. The only difference between the ordinary man and the mystic is that the latter is not content to accept this existence and to operate within it; he is filled with wonder at the thought of it – perhaps more, too, but that at any rate. Is there any bridge that can be built between these two, any way in which the ordinary man shares the experience or, more properly speaking, the feeling of the mystic? I think that such a bridge is to be found in the ordinary man's

18 For Wittgenstein's recognition that there is no difference between the two, see 5.5521, where 'if this [the former] were not so' is equated with 'if there were no world'. It is important to bear in mind that, in Wittgenstein's sense of the word 'object', the objects that exist are the set of all possible objects and not a proper subset thereof. To know that there are any objects, in this sense, is to know that there is a unique set of objects. (The terms 'exist', 'set', and 'possible' are, therefore, wrongly used here.)

ethical attitude toward the world, which attitude Wittgenstein somehow equates with a man's happiness or unhappiness. We shall come to that shortly; but there is also a less direct route from the ordinary man's position to that of the mystic, a route exemplified by the *Tractatus* itself. There is, of course, a great difference between taking the general nature of reality for granted and wondering at it; but there is not so much difference between wonder and the reflection and description to which the general nature of reality is subjected in that work. Logic is there spoken of as if it were a science, having for its realm or province super-facts, which could not be otherwise: logic deals with every possibility and all possibilities are its facts (2.0121). What logic studies is spoken of as if it were the true reality: objects are what is unalterable and subsistent, their configuration is what is changing and unstable (2.0271). Constantly he talks about totalities – the totality of objects (5.5561), the totality of existing states of affairs (2.04), the totality of true propositions (4.11) – and he speaks of a single proposition as having a force that reaches through the whole of logical space (3.42); this seems to me like the 'view of the world as a limited whole' which we are told that the mystic has: the reflective logician reaches it by concentration on the essential features of reality. Finally, just as the discoveries of the mystic cannot be put into words and yet are in a sense the answer to the problem of life – an answer which consists in the vanishing of the problem – so also the propositions of the *Tractatus* ought not to have been spoken and yet are in a sense a definitive answer to the problems of philosophy, an answer which consists in the understanding that the problems ought never to have been propounded. In logic a correct apprehension of the general form of a proposition, which is also the general form of reality, leads to contentment with what can be said; in mysticism the right feeling about the existence of the world (which is the same as to say: about the ultimate nature of reality) leads to an acceptance of the sort of world that there is, so that we cease to ask what the purpose of life or of the world is. In the pseudo-propositions of the *Tractatus* we see how things really are and are intellectually satisfied, though we cannot explain why; in the quasi-experience of mysticism we experience what the point of everything is, though we cannot afterward put it into words.

The thoughts of the reflective logician are then part, though only part, of what is involved in mysticism: something of the remainder we have already indicated. The content of mysticism – that toward which the feeling is directed – is the existence of the world. In the *Notebooks* he calls this '*das kunstlerische Wunder*'.[19] What is the *Wunder*? What question does it raise? Not apparently a question of origin or cause. An origin or cause that was

19 *Nb*, p. 86, par. 5. 'Aesthetically the miracle is that the world exists. That what exists does exist' in Miss Anscombe's translation. A possible paraphrase would be that it is a *tour de force* that the world exists: the world (any world) is a miracle of construction.

outside the world might give sense to the world and might answer the felt question; but Wittgenstein seems to think that any origin or cause would in fact be inside the world and would hence form not a solution but rather part of the problem to be solved. To put it more in his own terms: he holds that if the value of the world resided in the fact that, say, it had been created for a purpose by God, then its creation for a purpose would be one of the facts which there were in the world. Moreover (he appears to think), if it were a mere matter of fact that God had created it, there would still be room for a question why this matter of fact was a matter of fact. It is clear that in this way we reach a demand for an explanation (in a certain sense) of the world that will derive the sense of the world, the reason why there is a world, from some necessary features of all possible worlds. I am not here defending the rationality of these questions, nor of course does Wittgenstein do so: his chief point is that they are not proper questions. A question 'why?' is asked which refuses to be satisfied with any statement of fact and which must therefore find its answer, if anywhere, in the necessary general features of reality, which are precisely what is presupposed in logic.

By mysticism, Wittgenstein does not mean merely the attitude of mind in which a man asks these questions, but rather that attitude of mind in which he finds a certain answer to them. The mystic grasps the world as a whole and sees that, or rather feels that, it is a system with a definite character (just as the philosopher is inclined to talk as if logic were a special sphere of facts). At this point it is a bit difficult to follow Wittgenstein: it seems possible that there are two answers that the mystic may find, only one of which is final: he may find that the sense of life becomes clear to him, or he may remain a prey to doubt whether life has any sense. The former, certainly, is the case of the happy man: for him life is no longer problematic, he no longer needs to have any purpose except to live (*Nb*, p. 73, par. 20); that is to say, he is in agreement with the world (*ibid*, p. 75, par. 4). The unhappy man (to judge by the *Notebooks*) may be one who understands the question whether life and the world have sense, but is unable to find a sense for them. If this is correct, it would be possible, according to Wittgenstein, to have not only the yea-saying mysticism that his texts usually suggest, but also a pessimistic mysticism like that of Schopenhauer. Perhaps the same man could have experiences of both types.

It remains to trace the connection between this 'mysticism' with its evaluation of the world and ethics in its more usual sense. The connection is, of course, implicit in Wittgenstein's view that the will is an attitude toward the world. He describes it as entirely accidental if things happen to fall in with my wishes (6.374): that is, if I have a wish, then whether anything happens which coincides with that wish is quite out of my control. What is in my control, however, is to make my wishes coincide with what will in any case happen, which they will do only if I am resigned to and prepared to accept whatever happens (*Nb*, p. 73, par. 12). If I do that, I accept the world, I see the point of it, I am doing the will of God (he says in *Nb*, p. 75, par. 5), and I shall be happy. This is what it is to be a man of good will.[20] While the man of good will accepts whatever may be the case, knowing that it cannot be meaningless or hostile, the man of bad will, of bad conscience, is at odds with some particular actual feature of the world. He identifies himself with some accidental feature of the world, usually with the life of a particular person (himself) whose death he dreads (*ibid.*, p. 75, par. 6). His feeling of the meaninglessness of life may even go so far as to lead to a longing for death. In Schopenhauer this took the form of pessimism, of a desire for non-existence (though Schopenhauer condemned suicide),[21] while Tolstoy's depression recounted in William James's chapter on the sick soul often tempted him to commit suicide.[22] At the end of the *Notebooks* (p. 91, pars. 10–14) Wittgenstein says that suicide is the elementary sin, and I think his thought is that it is the ultimate form of non-acceptance of whatever happens.

The man of good will lives in a different world from that of the man of bad conscience: but the difference is not a describable one, not a difference in facts. In the *Tractatus* Wittgenstein says that the world must, so to speak, wax and wane as a whole for them (6.43): in the *Notebooks* he had explained that waxing was the addition of a sense or meaning, waning its subtraction (p. 73, par. 17). Clearly this will be the 'ethical reward or punishment' which Wittgenstein postulates at 6.422: the attitude of mind which constitutes being a man of bad will or bad conscience itself consists in not being able to see the sense of the world, in the feeling that the world is a restrictive and hostile place (see *Nb*, p. 78, pars. 9, 11, 13–15).

Two other aspects of Wittgenstein's mysticism, which appear in the *Tractatus*, but whose relation to the mystical feeling is not very well brought out there, have already been mentioned. They are his solipsism and his reference to the man who lives in the present. The *Notebooks* make clear that both the realization that the world is my world (pp. 82, par. 9; 85) and the ability to 'live in the present' (p. 74, par. 20) are essential parts of happiness. The insight which Wittgenstein expresses by the words 'I am my world' is in part a refusal to identify oneself with one part

---

20 *Tractatus* 6.43 is perhaps concerned with being a man of good or bad will. 'Good or bad acts of will' (the version first chosen by Mr. Pears and myself) precludes this and in a later impression we have put 'the good or bad exercise of the will'. C.K. Ogden had 'good or bad willing'. In *Nb* (p. 73 e, par. 15), Miss Anscombe has 'good or evil willing'; in that context the reference probably is to individual acts of will.

21 See, e.g. Schhopenhauer 1833, pp. 488–520, and 1892, pp. 41ff.

22 James 1902, pp. 153ff. Tolstoy, *op. cit.*, pp. 17ff. Fear of death was the chief motive that led Tolstoy to want to kill himself.

of the world rather than another (pp. 82, pars. 8–9; 84, pars. 2, 9). One who has this insight does not identify himself with the physiological or psychological peculiarities and life of a particular individual human being. The higher or metaphysical self feels itself identical with the whole world (p. 80, pars. 11–12), and its happiness is the goodness – the expansion – of the whole world. Naturally, fear or hope are remote from such a self (from the self with such an insight), since it has no particular concern with the future of any individual. The present is enough for it, and any present is good enough, since all momentary states of the world (together with the thoughts of past and future that are present in each of them) are merely different actualizations of a set of possibilities, all of which are good. It is not the future, or death, that poses the problem to this higher self, nor will immortality in the usual sense solve the problem. That self will not die, and its problem is posed by the existence of anything, not by the limited temporal duration of some complex objects. I think it is fairly obvious that Wittgenstein quite justly speaks of 'timelessness' (6.4311) with regard to such an attitude of mind. Where there is neither fear nor hope, there is no real concept of past and future. It is only the empirical self that is attached to a particular position in space and time: for the metaphysical self, space and time are ingredients of the world it contemplates and accepts.

Two brief epexegetical notes: lest it be thought that in the *Tractatus* Wittgenstein has retained his solipsism but ceased to believe in its ethical and mystical relevance, I would point out that in his account of mysticism and ethics Wittgenstein uses the premise enunciated in the 5.6's that life is the world.[23] This is equivalent to what is expressed by saying 'I am my world' which, as we have seen, means in part that nothing *in* the world is particularly important or unimportant. The second note is to draw attention once again to a certain ambiguity about the wicked man: it is not perfectly clear whether he is one who fails to identify himself with the world, or one who identifies himself with the world but finds the world bad or meaningless: I think the former, since it is obvious in the *Notebooks* that Wittgenstein thinks the wicked man has failed to attain the state of living in the present. The wicked man may reach a mystical state only in the sense that he can be tormented by the question what the meaning of life is, but he can never reach the resolution, namely the realization that there is no question, since this involves an acceptance of whatever is the case, as such, which is impossible for a man whose conscience is bad since,

---

23 That premise is required for 6.431: 'so too at death the world does not alter but comes to an end'.

unlike the unjustly mocked Margaret Fuller, he must needs be at odds with the universe.

This leads to our summing up on the question whether these various aspects of the *Tractatus* are concerned with a single feeling or experience or realm of experience. It is obvious enough that Wittgenstein's good man and bad man can both exist in a more or less sophisticated form: the unsophisticated will simply enjoy the benefits, or labour under the disadvantages, of his good or bad conscience; the sophisticated will feel that he has or lacks the answer to the problem of life. (In the former case he will, of course, be realizing implicitly or explicitly that there is no problem.) Now, whether the sophisticated man differs from the unsophisticated in that he has an extra feeling – the mystical feeling – is impossible to answer in Wittgenstein's own terms, since for him there cannot be anything but feeling in this matter. We cannot say that the sophisticated have an understanding of what the unsophisticated can only feel. There can only be feeling in any case. I am inclined to say that the difference between the sophisticated and the unsophisticated is unimportant for Wittgenstein; he would probably say that the mystical feeling was equally present and effective in each of them.

I hope our conspectus of *Tractatus* mysticism will have shown that all the different elements mentioned belong to a single realm of experience. To have experience of the world at all, to know any facts, we must grasp the general nature of reality which logic is an attempt to exhibit: this is the logical experience, so to speak, which is common to all men. But it occurs in different men in a different form, since we are able not only to grasp the general nature of reality but to accept or reject it. To accept it is to detach oneself from all particular parts of the actual world; to reject it is to set one's heart on particular possibilities – to be distressed, for example, by what happens to a particular human being, to render oneself liable to fear and hope, particularly the fear of death.

If I can assume that this is accepted on the evidence of the general account of his mysticism that I have given, we can turn to the second question: is Wittgenstein talking about a genuine mystical experience, or is he misusing the term? First, is he ascribing a mystical experience to everyone who can do logic and is happy (possibly also to those who are unhappy)? Here my remarks about the sophisticated and unsophisticated are in point: for Wittgenstein there is no difference between having thoughts about good and bad and having a mystical experience that involves them. We think of the mystic as distinguished by having direct knowledge or acquaintance: *ou monon mathôn alla kai pathôn ta theia*. On his account no such distinction is possible. Since this paper is not intended to attack directly the whole question whether this account of ethics, aesthetics, and metaphysics is correct, perhaps we should consider a more limited question: granted that Wittgenstein is saying that all talk about ethics and the sense of life is identical with the attempt to express a certain experience, let us waive the question whether all such talk is identical with such an attempt and ask whether the experience that Wittgenstein has in mind is a genuine mystical one. In other words, is there a genuine mystical experience with which Wittgenstein is (mistakenly or not) identifying the whole of ethics, aesthetics, and metaphysics? If we decide that it is a genuine mystical experience, the question will still remain whether that experience was actually had by Wittgenstein or was known to him only from the writings of others.

When I say a genuine mystical experience, I do not of course mean a genuine theistic mystical experience. True, there are references to God in the *Notebooks* and even in the *Tractatus* but clearly to a God who is identical with Nature: *Deus, sive Natura*.[24] At best Wittgenstein allows a form of pantheism: in the spirit of Whitehead's remark about Unitarianism, he might be said to hold that if there is any God, then the world is God. Most definitions of mysticism refer to it as a union: in Wittgenstein's case (that is to say, in the case described – whether experienced or not – by Wittgenstein) the union will be a union with the world, with Nature, particularly well expressed by such phrases as 'I am my world – the world and life are one'. Abundant examples of this feeling are given, for example, in James 1902 (pp. 382–98).[25] Here is an account of cosmic consciousness which James gets from R.M. Bucke, a Canadian psychiatrist:

> The prime characteristic of cosmic consciousness is a consciousness of the cosmos, that is, of the life and order of the universe. Along with the consciousness of the cosmos there occurs an intellectual enlightenment which alone would place an individual on a new plane of existence – would make him almost a member of a new species. To this is added a state of moral exaltation, an indescribable feeling of elevation, elation, and joyousness, and a quickening of the moral sense which is fully as striking and more important than is the enhanced intellectual power. With these come what may be called a sense of immortality, a consciousness of eternal life, not a conviction that he shall have this but the consciousness that he has it already (James 1902, p. 398)

24 I do not wish to quarrel with Mr. E. Zemach's contention that Wittgenstein means God to be identical with the world in one sense and not identical with it in another (Zemach 1964). God is not to be identified with what is contingently the case. I am, of course, very much in agreement with Zemach's thesis that the mystical is an integral part of the *Tractatus*.

25 In the unpublished part of the letter to Russell, dated 22 June 1912, Wittgenstein says that he is reading James's book whenever he can and that it is doing him a lot of good, since it is helping him to get rid of *Sorge* (in the sense in which Goethe used the word in the second part of *Faust*). Probably groundless anxiety or *Angst* is meant.

This is, of course, classificatory material rather than a protocol report of experience, but it will serve our present purpose well enough, since it indicates a number of the Wittgensteinian elements to be found in nature mysticism. I say 'nature mysticism' but, of course, there is no indication by James that this is at all different from other forms of mysticism. The distinction of the various forms of mysticism is one to which those who have themselves had experience only of nature mysticism are much opposed, but many people have drawn the necessary distinctions, most notably in recent times Professor Zaehner. Here is his characterization of nature mysticism:

> Certain states usually referred to as mystical are also characteristic of lunacy, whether criminal or otherwise. There seem to be three principal modes of these states: (1) an intense communion with Nature in which subject and objects seem identical. ... (2) the abdication of the ego to another centre, the 'self' of Jungian psychology: '*Je est un autre*', '*On me pense*' (Rimbaud) etc. (3) a return to a state of innocence and the consequent sense that the subject of the experience has passed beyond good and evil. To these must be added (4) the complete certainty that the soul is immortal and that death is therefore at least irrelevant and at most a ludicrous impossibility.[26]

Zaehner argues that the fourth element is different from the other three 'because it represents not a diffusion or uncontrolled expansion of the personality but the organization of the completed psyche under the central control of the self', but I think it will not be really misleading to regard it here as a further development of nature mysticism and to contrast it, as indeed Zaehner does, both with Christian mysticism, which involves union with God by love, and also with the sort of mysticism in which the subject experiences his own soul as being the absolute and does not experience the phenomenal world at all. It is apparently some form of this last that Schopenhauer recommended, and Russell has some of its features in mind when he says that it is an essential part of mysticism to regard the phenomenal world as unreal. For Wittgenstein's mystic,[27] as for Aldous Huxley under

---

26 Zaehner 1957, pp. 101–2.

27 Despite the many echoes of Schopenhauer in Wittgenstein, we have more than once seen that he differs in some essential points from the philosopher whom he had read and admired as a boy. To borrow a metaphor from *Tractatus* 6.54, Wittgenstein has transcended Schopenhauer. In this he resembles Tolstoy (1940, pp. 33 and 38ff.) and the Tolstoyan figure of Levin (Tolstoy 1949, Pt. VIII, p. 404).

mescalin,[28] the phenomenal world is very far from unreal: indeed it is a kind of dwelling on its reality or *Istigkeit* that is the most important part of the mystical experience.

Zaehner's characterization of nature mysticism is (quite properly) highly conceptualized and many of the instances he actually quotes and discusses come much closer to Wittgenstein's words. To take just Huxley, we find him talking, much as Wittgenstein does, about the miracle of naked existence – neither agreeable nor disagreeable, it just *is*[29] – and Zaehner (p. 6) quotes Meister Eckhart's view that the mystic lives in an eternal Now as a parallel for Huxley's remark, 'My actual experience had been, was still, of an indefinite duration or alternatively of a perpetual present made up of one continually changing apocalypse'. Even more striking on eternity is Richard Jefferies:

> Realizing that spirit, recognizing my own inner consciousness, the psyche, so clearly, I cannot understand time. It is eternity now. I am in the midst of it. It is about me in the sunshine; I am in it as a butterfly floats in the light-laden air. Nothing has to come: it is now. Now is eternity; now is the immortal life. Here this moment, by this tumulus, on earth, now; I exist in it.[30]

To grasp the world as a whole, to identify oneself with it, and to feel as if one has passed outside space and time so that death is no longer an important problem: these, which we have seen to be marks of the experience referred to by Wittgenstein, are recurring themes in the accounts of mystical experience quoted by James and requoted by Zaehner:

> Individuality itself seemed to dissolve and fade away into boundless being and this not a confused state but the clearest, the surest of the surest, utterly beyond words where death was an almost laughable impossibility – the loss of personality if it so were seeming no extinction but the only true life. I am ashamed of my feeble description. Have I not said the state is utterly beyond words?[31]
>
> Thought pierces the great enigma. ... one feels one's self great as the universe and calm as a god.[32]

---

28 Huxley 1954. Professor Zaehner's book originated as a counterblast to Huxley's.

29 *Op. cit.*, p. 12 (quoted by Zaehner, p. 4).

30 Jefferies 1912, p. 30 (quoted by Zaehner, p. 47).

31 Tennyson, quoted by James (1902), p. 384 (Zaehner, p. 37).

32 Amiel, quoted by James, p. 394 (Zaehner, p. 37)

> To return from the solitude of individuation into the consciousness of unity with all that is; to kneel down as one that passes away and to rise up as one imperishable.[33]

More distinctive of Wittgenstein is the emphasis on the ethical character of this experience, though I would see this as continuous with the joy and certainty felt by the nature mystics already quoted. Perhaps most interesting in this connection (and with this I will end my quotations from Zaehner) is the Muslim mystical treatise by Abu'l Qâsim al-Qushayrî. He describes two states of soul: expansion (*basT*) and contraction (*qabD*), which are the equivalent in the mystic of hope and fear in the ordinary man. The difference is that the mystic does not refer these states to the future but feels them for the present: this is the nearest approach in mystical writings that I have seen to Wittgenstein's happiness and unhappiness; and there is an obvious, though not an exact, parallel to his idea of the world's waxing or waning as a whole.

> The subject experiencing either fear or hope has his mind fixed on the future; whereas those who experience expansion and contraction are presently and actually the prisoner of an overwhelming obsession (inspiration or mood) ... the expanded man experiences an expansion great enough to contain all creation and there is practically nothing that will cause him fear. Nothing affects him, in whatever state he may be. ... One of the proximate causes of contraction is that the mind is attacked by an obsession, the cause of which is the presentiment of damnation and a mysterious intuition that such punishment is deserved.

Note that this is the cause or occasion of contraction; the mood itself does not refer, as its cause does, to the future. 'The only remedy for this condition is complete submission to the will of God until the mood passes' (*ibid.*, pp. 85–6).

Qushayrî contrasts even the expanded state with true mysticism, which leads to union with God. The experiences described are of course similar to those of mania and depression. In all these states there is usually a departure from ordinary moral consciousness, which may be annihilated or felt to be irrelevant, as in Huxley, or turned into new channels, as in a manic-depressive described by Zaehner (p. 89) who felt compelled to give large sums away to prostitutes and in Qushayrî's contracted man who felt his guilt so deeply.

---

33 Malwida von Meysenbug, quoted by James (1902), p. 394 (Zaehner, p. 37).

The *Notebooks*, in passages already quoted, refer to guilt and sin and misery. In his own life and particularly during the years which saw the composition and publication of the *Tractatus*, Wittgenstein constantly struggled to live up to his own high standards, to be *'anständig'* ('decent'), as he put it. It would be paradoxical indeed if his account of mysticism in the *Tractatus* were meant to imply that in the expanded mystical state all distinctions between good and evil vanished, that the happy man was exempt from all law and might do whatever he would, even the most atrocious crimes, without affecting his happiness. Yet theoretically this might appear to be its implication. If what happens is indifferent, my actions too are indifferent and whatever I try to do will be equally acceptable – will be part of the problem set (6.4321), to which a correct attitude of acceptance will be the solution.

I believe this to be largely a mistake. It is like confusing St. Augustine's *Ama Deum et fac quod vis* with Rabelais's *Fay ce que vouldras*. True, a man for whom all facts are indifferent will be equally content with anything he may will, but it is not true that such a man can will anything whatsoever. To promote his own happiness at the cost of another's, for example, would not be a possible motive for him. Conversely, if a man can have such a motive, he will *eo ipso* be unable to view the matter *sub specie aeternitatis*. What is true in the supposed implication is that Wittgenstein's happy man will have no room for ethical maxims and precepts which proscribe a form of action as such. Ethical criticism of an action without regard to its motive will be meaningless for him.[34] (It is, of course, common ground that the happy man must be indifferent to the success or failure of his efforts.)

If I am right in the main body of what I have said, there is a common enough mystical state which has little to do with religion, as that term is normally understood, but which agrees with the feelings described by Wittgenstein. It remains to answer the question whether Wittgenstein had mystical experiences of this kind. This question is easier to answer since the publication of his 'Lecture on Ethics', where he describes three experiences which he has had and which seem to him to have absolute value.[35] First is what he calls his experience *par excellence*[36] in which he wonders at the existence of the world. Second is the experience of feeling

---

34 Dr. Rhees's description (1965, p. 22) of Wittgenstein's unwillingness (in 1942) to discuss the case of Brutus and Caesar because he could not imagine what went on in Brutus' mind is an example of the sort of attitude I am referring to here.

35 *LE* p. 1–11.

36 Anscombe (1959, p. 170) quotes an intrinsically less probable text: 'my experience for excellence,' from the typescript (TS207) that she had made from MS139a, but the latter (and the newly discovered MS139b, discussed in Chapter 24) have 'par excelence' (sic).

absolutely safe: 'nothing can injure me whatever happens'. Third is the experience of feeling guilty, about which he says very little.

There can be little doubt, I think, that the first and third of these were in his mind when he wrote the *Notebooks* and the *Tractatus*. Whether the first is always to be called a mystical experience is perhaps a matter of choice: sometimes, certainly, such experiences are mystical. By any standard, however, the experience of guilt is only exceptionally mystical in character, though perhaps Wittgenstein's reference to *Sorge* (see note 25) indicates that his was one of the exceptional cases. My own conjecture is that Wittgenstein in the *Tractatus* would not have associated ethics and the existence of the world with mysticism, unless the first and third of the experiences later described in his lecture had been felt by him with a degree of intensity beyond the normal, so that he was compelled to recognize their kinship with the experiences he had read of in James.

The experience of feeling absolutely safe is perhaps the most clearly mystical of the three mentioned in the lecture but it is less obvious that Wittgenstein had it in mind in the *Tractatus*. The chief reason for thinking that he did so is that the happy man of the *Notebooks* and the *Tractatus* would need to have the attitude of one with this experience. He would have to feel perfectly content, completely free from fear and anxiety, in the face of *aller Not dieser Welt* (*Nb*, p. 81; 'all the misery of this world'). To be indifferent to the facts, to live without fear or hope (*ibid.*, pp. 74, pars. 17–18; 76, par. 13) involves feeling safe whatever happens.

It happens that we have some indirect evidence (though without any reliable indication of date) that Wittgenstein did have a mystical experience of this kind, in that he is reported to have experienced a kind of religious awakening thanks to a performance of Anzengruber's *Die Kreuzelschreiber*.[37] Undoubtedly this will have been associated with the scene in which one character describes the 'special revelation' or '*afflatus*' (*extraige Offenbarung, Eingebung*) that he has had: previously his life had been one of unalleviated misery but one day when he had thrown himself, at the point of death as he thought, into the long grass in the sunshine, he came to himself again in the evening to find that his pain had gone, to be visited with unreasoning happiness as if the earlier sunshine had entered into his body, and to feel as if he were being spoken to: 'Nothing can happen to you! The worst sufferings count for nothing once they're over. Whether you're six feet under the grass or know that you've got to face it

---

37 Heller 1959, p. 42. The passage in the play that I refer to occurs in Act III, scene 1: I am indebted to Miss P. von Morstein for help in locating it.

all thousands of times more – nothing can happen to you! – you're part of everything, and everything's part of you.[38] Nothing can happen to you!'

Es kann dir nix g'schehn! – the phrase was almost proverbial in Vienna,[39] so that its occurrence in Waismann's notes of the conversations that he and Schlick had with Wittgenstein in December 1929[40] is not an absolutely safe indication of a *terminus ante quem* for the experience. Nevertheless, the play is worth quoting to illustrate the sort of experience with which Wittgenstein felt some kinship. The reaction of the other character in the play is also interesting, and I have indicated (though without sufficient argument) that I would apply it to Wittgenstein, too.

Anton (*um zu verbergen, dass er ergriffen ist, derb*). *Du Sakra, du! Ja, was bist denn du nachher? Du bist ja kein Christ und kein Heid' und kein Türk?!* [Anton (gruffly, to hide his emotion). Damn it all! What *are* you when all's said and done? You're not a Christian, nor a pagan, nor a Muslim either!]

38 '*Du g'hörst zu dem all'n und dös all' g'hört zu dir.*' This is a typical expression of nature mysticism and involves two of the themes of the *Tractatus*: the world seen as a limited whole and the felt identity of the subject with the world.

39 Cf. Stefan Zweig 1943, p. 366.

40 '*Mir kann nichts geschehen*' – i.e., whatever may happen, it is of no importance (*Bedeutung*) for me.' *WVC*, p. 68 [We can now be fairly certain that the play in question had its effect on Wittgenstein when he was about 21 years old. See McGuinness 1988, p. 94.]

15

THE UNSAYABLE

A genetic account

By a genetic account of Wittgenstein's thought in this area I mean one that looks at the origin of his ideas, their causes, occasions, and progress. I can offer here only part of such an account. But even were it, which is almost impossible, complete, such an account would of course not be decisive as to the validity or value of those ideas – to think so would indeed be to commit the genetic fallacy. It should, however, enable us to identify those ideas better, to see what Wittgenstein was about when he expressed them, what he, at first at any rate, thought they signified. It will involve also looking at the context, the cultural and family surroundings, in which Wittgenstein came to them. This is not to be viewed as reductive in its tendency. The aim is to identify the thrust of Wittgenstein's thinking, after which it can be judged how well he conducted it and whether, perhaps, it throws up conclusions and insights other than those that he first expected, other even than those that he ever saw. In passing I hope we shall learn something about the intellectual enterprise that he was engaged on in later life also.[1] This, whatever it was, was an essential part of the hold he had on people, or some people. Like a character in an early Iris Murdoch novel he gave people the impression that they were seeing everything in a new and clearer light, and that for intellectual as well as for moral reasons.

I begin with what I might call a psychogenetic account, to be treated as a rough hypothesis: Wittgenstein had two sides corresponding to his mother and father, who stood in sharp contrast. Happy as their marriage was, says their daughter Hermine,[2]

> *so war es doch die Ehe einer ausgesprochen zum* Dulden *geborenen Frau*
> *mit einem ausgesprochen zum energischen* Handeln *geborenen Mann*

---

1 This has been one of the chief topics in a correspondence I have had with Professor G. Kreisel, from and in the course of which I have learnt much.

2 In her *Familienerinnerungen* (Hermine Wittgenstein 1944–9), here quoted and used *passim*.

(still it was the marriage of a woman distinctly born for suffering with a man distinctly born for energetic action.)

The mother, Ludwig himself said, had never brought a thought to completion – except at the piano. The father was a hard-headed businessman who despised professors and any learning not practical. He wrote in a scornful way about any vague economic and political aspirations. We can see parallels to this style in the letters of another son of his, Paul. I think there is even a likeness to the style of Frege, the same concreteness and hostility to *Pathos*. '*Heiliger Frege!*' ('Sainted Frege!') Wittgenstein wrote in the margin when he read Hilbert's remark about refusing to be driven from Cantor's paradise.[3]

Music was half his life (mused Wittgenstein in later years) but he had written nothing about it. There are whole areas that have to be dealt with by *Fingerspitzengefühl* (*finesse*) and it is silly to try to systematize them. '*Tovey, dieser Esel*' ('That ass Tovey!') was his comment on one of the judgements of that, as most think him, perceptive critic, one who was admired not only by Ludwig's brother Paul but even by their older cousin Joseph Joachim. Ludwig was sceptical also about the value of the work of the musical theorist Schenker (his nephew's teacher), thinking his remarks, when true, too obvious. There is much to be said, of course, on Ludwig's relationship with an intensely loving mother: there were elements in the whole female side of his family, their excessive *Liebenswürdigkeit*, for example – they could be *too* kind, *too* obliging, *too* hospitable – towards which he had very negative feelings, particularly evident during the period of his withdrawal from them into his village retreat when he was a schoolmaster. Still, in the longer term, he tried to accommodate this feminine side of himself (to use the terminology of that period) by putting it into a compartment of its own. (The parallels with Weininger's idea[4] of varying proportions of the two elements – MMMF or MMFF – curious how similar the notation is to Wittgenstein's own truth tables – will be clear.) Perhaps, at least at the time of the *Tractatus*, what went into that compartment was the unsayable. (Of course there was a 'feminine' side to his father too, which his children saw principally when he played the violin to his wife's accompaniment.)

The influence of Wittgenstein's father on his education was of a more straightforward kind. Karl's indifference to formal schooling led him to

---

3 The Hilbert remark on Cantor's paradise – or rather its being so often quoted – is an example of how needed the Wittgenstein therapy is. It is often the least considered remarks of the great that are repeated – perhaps '*Der liebe Gott würfelt nicht*' ('God does not throw dice') is one of them.

4 See Weininger 1906.

write that it didn't matter what Ludwig did at school in Linz or in his truancies from school. Let him *'faulenzen'*, amuse himself in Vienna: he would eventually enter an engineering works and learn what he really needed to. Note that this was not the wish that Ludwig would take over his father's business – Carl had long ago sold up his own enterprises: but no doubt he saw engineering as a natural career for a man, and for this mechanically gifted son in particular.

Meanwhile the curriculum at Linz was an exacting one. The school was not chosen at random, even if Hitler did go there. Ludwig no doubt learnt more from it than his sister thought. (She sees this in his father's case, but not in his own.) His plans for the future and the mode in which he executed them reflect his father's views. In school documents his choice of career is indicated as Physics or Engineering (*Maschinenbau*). These wishes are only apparently contradictory: he wanted to study under Boltzmann, and he also wanted to be an aviator (of course the original aviators were also aeroplane constructors). This latter interest was evident in his schooldays (a later letter of one of his schoolmasters asks whether he has kept up his interest in aeronautics). There is a slight intersection between these two interests, in that Boltzmann in 1894 gave a lecture predicting the superiority of the aeroplane over the airship. But Wittgenstein would have had to do some theoretical study anyway. Boltzmann's death at just that point meant that Wittgenstein did this at Berlin, but within a year or two he left for more practical work (on aviation) at Manchester. This was his father's pattern of rapidly learning all that he needed and then moving on to put it to use.

Wittgenstein in an often-cited diary passage from 1931[5] mentions that he was influenced by a number of thinkers, whom he gives apparently in chronological order of the influence exercised. The final list, for there were some afterthoughts, inserted above the line with much attention to order, was in fact: Boltzmann, Hertz, Schopenhauer, Frege, Russell, Kraus, Loos, Weininger, Spengler, Sraffa. The last two on chronological grounds alone can be left aside as subsequent influences, but there are traces of all the others in the *Tractatus* – Hertz for the whole picture theory, Schopenhauer for the attitude towards the world (where Wittgenstein attempts to accommodate both Schopenhauer's pessimism and Tolstoy's optimism), Frege and Russell for the treatment of logic and mathematics, Kraus for the refutation of positions from within the very language they are expressed in, Loos for a clear distinction between ornament and practical use (and hence for the idea that unnecessary units in a sign-language

5   *C&V*, p. 19.

mean nothing),[6] Weininger (in his 'Aphorismen') for a generally fatalistic attitude. Here I propose to discuss only some of these.[7]

The first influence was that of Boltzmann. I venture the hypothesis that Wittgenstein heard some of Boltzmann's popular lectures on physics in Vienna during the school vacations – or even during term, because there are some indications that he was rather cavalier (in the sense used by Baron Ochs) about school attendance. Boltzmann's 1903–6 lectures on 'Naturfilosofi', only recently published,[8] are full of attacks on attempts by philosophy to invade science. What Wittgenstein did not himself hear he could read in the *Neue Freie Presse (NFP)* or one of the other newspapers – so great was the interest this lecture series created and so superior to our own was the press of those days.[9]

Like Mach, who held the chair of Natural Philosophy before him, Boltzmann admitted, even claimed, to be no philosopher, but while Mach did so in a modest, almost self-denying manner, Boltzmann permitted himself a considerable measure of mockery and scorn. (It was his way and brought him much hostility, but is unlikely to have displeased the young Wittgenstein, if he was anything like his older self.) Thus we read (in the *NFP*, 27 October 1903).

Doch wenn das Sprichwort sagt, daß Gott mit einem Amte auch den notwendigen Verstand gibt, so sei das beim Ministerium nicht der Fall. … Er [Boltzmann] habe die Philosophen, hinter deren Wortschwall er den Gedanken meist vergeblich suchte, seit langem verachtet. … Man habe die Philosophie die Königin aller Wissenschaften genannt, und einmal hörte er sie auch eine gottgeweihte Jungfrau nennen, die aber, eben weil sie gottgeweiht ist, ewig unfruchtbar bleiben müsse. Hofrat Boltzmann… erklärte, daß man es ihm als Physiker, nicht verdenken dürfe, wenn er Dinge, die sich exakt physikalisch behandeln lassen, der Philosophie entzogen wissen wolle.[10]

But though the proverb says that God will provide along with an office the understanding required for its exercise, the same was not true of the Ministry. … He (Boltzmann) had long looked

---

6 *Tractatus* 5.47321.

7 For Schopenhauer and Weininger, see above my 'Solipsism' (Chapter 13 in the present volume), and also Gardiner 1963. Kraus and Loos are discussed in Engelmann 1967.

8 Fasol-Boltzman 1990.

9 Another period touch was the *NFP*'s remark that among the large audience there were (even!) many ladies. It is likely that among them was Wittgenstein's sister, Gretl, the later Mrs. Stonborough, who was to a large extent his first intellectual mentor and who had an informed interest in natural science.

10 The same thoughts, rationally softened, were reprinted in Boltzmann 1905 (English translation 1974, pp. 153ff.). Boltzmann's views at this period are illustrated and discussed at length in Blackmore 1995.

down on philosophers as such, having usually sought in vain for the thought behind their torrent of words. ... Philosophy had been called the queen of all the sciences and he had once also heard her called a virgin consecrated to God, who for that very reason was condemned to be for ever barren. Professor Boltzmann declared that no one should hold it against him if he, as a physicist, wished to take out of the hands of philosophy all matters that were susceptible of exact treatment by physics.

Boltzmann's lectures are, however, not only attacks on the invasions of philosophy into other areas. The subject itself is attacked from within, and the terms are just those echoed much later by Wittgenstein: Boltzmann's own instinctive definition of philosophy was as follows:

Das empfinde ich stets als einen drückenden Alp, das Gefühl, daß es eigentlich ein Rätsel ist, daß ich überhaupt lebe. Ebenso, daß die Welt ist; daß die Welt gerade so ist, wie sie ist. Die Wissenschaft, der es gelänge, dieses Rätsel zu lösen, schien mir die größte, die wahre Königin und dies nannte ich Philosophie. Ich gewann immer mehr an Naturerkenntnis, ich nahm die Darwinsche Lehre in mich auf; daraus sah ich, daß es eigentlich verfehlt ist zu fragen; daß es auf diese Frage keine Antwort gibt; daß die Frage ein Unsinn ist. So kommen wir wieder fast darauf zurück, daß die Philosophie eigentlich ein Unsinn ist.

It has always weighed on me like a nightmare – the feeling that it is actually a riddle that I am alive at all. Or that there is a world. Or that the world is just the way it is. The science that could succeed in solving this riddle would, I thought, be the real queen of the sciences. And this I called philosophy. I acquired more and more knowledge of nature, I made Darwin's theory my own, and it helped me to see that it is really a mistake to ask, that there is no answer to this question, that the question is nonsense. Thus it comes back practically to this, that philosophy is nonsense.

We find here an hostility to theory such as we have noted in Wittgenstein with regard to music, and which was indeed to character-ize him throughout his life. Looking, for the moment, at his later writings we can see that he was an opponent, as Kreisel puts it, of ISMS.[11] We can recognize various forms of this hostility to the general theory, to the a priori itself, for instance in Wittgenstein's insistence on the use of different methods in different areas – and sometimes in the same one.

11 Kreisel 1983.

Also (in total opposition to the tendency of his time and place) an objection to formalization extending over new areas – in linguistics, say, or in theory of music. We see him often bringing to bear some concrete observation, which explodes the constructions of the theorist, who often likes it when his results are counter-intuitive. Instances would be questions like, what do you actually do if a contradiction turns up? Try to doubt another's pain in a real case – and this means, what would it come, to do such a thing?

But such a rejection of theory is not itself a theory and does not amount to anything systematic, which others can work on or with. Kreisel draws the analogy of the complement of a set, which is not itself a set. Thus while Wittgenstein's destructive work may be meritorious – his rejection of traditional foundations for mathematics for example[12] – it might be objected that there is not necessarily any way of carrying it on. There may be only snippets of method – his attacks on *falsche Fragestellungen*, the error of asking the wrong questions, his turning up his nose at certain types of argument (Ryle's phrase in an obituary) and so on. Fragments of method – all amounting to something more like Aristotle's *Topics* than his *Analytics* and hence difficult to put together in a treatise (the *Topics* too has a rather artificial ordering). This is the criticism that a follower of Popper might bring and no doubt has brought against him. The picture of his life often given is that of one more impressive in conversation than in lectures and more in lectures than in the writings that later came to light, a spellbinder or charmer rather than a systematic thinker.

There might still be much to learn from him, from his awareness of the variety of so many subjects of discourse – mathematics, meaning, human motivation, the sort of behaviour that might be acceptable from this or that person. His writings after the *Tractatus* were an attempt to convey in a general way the effect of his conversation, which naturally was concerned with particular problems on particular occasions. Of course this is rather artificial – Sraffa's question: But has anyone ever actually made this or that confusion that you pillory? picks on this point. But is the artificiality a defect? A degree of simplification was inevitable: Wittgenstein could not be interested in learned controversy with its carefully guarded statements of position: he wanted to reproduce live discussion with all its crudity.[13] Plato's dialogues exhibit the same phenomenon – they are meant to be in an almost self-contradictory fashion an encour-

---

12 Kreisel (1998, p. 117) compares this to the attitude of Bourbaki.
13 'Say something crude, say what you want to say and then we shall get somewhere.' Gist of a remark to Oscar Wood at Wittgenstein's only known Oxford meeting, 1947. (Communication to the author by Philippa Foot.)

agement to one's own discussion. Wittgenstein aspired to convey, as surely Plato did convey, a variety of intellectual lessons.

However it is to misunderstand Wittgenstein to think that he pursued this discursive or divagatory path from ineptitude or out of perversity. He had reason to think that only in this way could the aims of philosophy be attained. Thus rather than leave the subject aside as Boltzmann did, or perhaps ought to have done (*que diable allait-il faire dans cette galère?*), Wittgenstein tried to show in a systematic way what those aims were and to what extent they were fulfillable. The upshot of this attempt was the *Tractatus* and it is significant that he wished it to be published alongside his later work. It showed why that later work had to be pursued in just the way it was pursued.

The path (a long one) towards the paradoxically systematic rejection of theory that was to be the *Tractatus* began with considerations to do with mathematics and logic. This was the form in which the passion for philosophy seized Wittgenstein, so his sister Hermine says. She dates this to his Berlin years (1906–8) 'or shortly after' (which would be in Manchester, 1908–11). He told friends that his interest progressed from the equations needed for the propeller that he was designing to the mathematics behind those equations, and this corresponds as we shall shortly see with the evidence of his letters. Mathematics and logic, which were an important locus of philosophical thinking at that period, entered naturally into Wittgenstein's life as an aspiring physicist or engineer.

Some thought about them may, however, also have been stimulated by Boltzmann's lectures already mentioned. After the introductory criticisms of philosophy as such – suggesting that the very title Natural Philosophy was a near absurdity – the lectures continue with a discussion of the various types of number. Boltzmann was by no means a realist as regards these. Mathematics being the language in which science was expressed, each new type of number was a device developed in order to deal with practical scientific needs. This was of a piece with Boltzmann's view of logic itself, whose laws were simply those which had been found useful in the course of evolution. As we shall see this differed in obvious ways from Wittgenstein's standpoint, yet had affinities with it.

We have three contemporary indications of the nature of Wittgenstein's interest in mathematics at this period. One is his annotation of a copy of Horace Lamb's handbook of *Hydrodynamics* that he bought in Berlin, a standard textbook at the time and indeed for long afterwards.[14] It seems to have been a private interest, for it is not easy to

14 Lamb 1906. The volume was discovered and recognized by Dr Peter Spelt of Imperial College and is described in Spelt and McGuinness 2001.

see any relevance to courses that he might have followed at this stage in his studies. His marginalia can briefly be characterized as an attempt to get the clearest possible statement at each point of what was presupposed and to avoid circularity in reasoning or definition. In some cases he is excessively rigorous, not appreciating that many equivalences are implicit in a formal theory of dynamics. It is as if he were questioning the very nature of mathematical theories.

The second indication is an anecdote again about Lamb (who was now his professor in Manchester) related in a letter to his sister Hermine.[15] Wittgenstein showed his work to the professor who said that he did not think the equations required were soluble with the means then available. It is an interesting and fundamental fact about mathematics that it will do many things for us, but it is not clear in advance which it can do easily and which it cannot do at all.[16] Some fundamental aspect of mathematics at any rate caught Wittgenstein's attention. Most probably someone at Manchester, perhaps the professor of philosophy, Samuel Alexander, who was beginning to be interested in such matters, told him of Frege and Frege's work led him to Russell. This corresponds to the order in which he mentions influences, though it is possible that he actually met Russell before meeting Frege. Another possibility is that he was first put in touch with P.E.B. Jourdain (1879–1919), the prolific historian and expositor of mathematics (who would also have led him to Frege and Russell). His first venture into the field on his own account, and the third indication I had in mind, was a communication to Jourdain, which alas is now lost but must have been prior to 20 April 1909, attempting to solve the paradox by which Russell had confuted Frege.[17]

These independent indications from various sources enable us to date his philosophical interest in mathematics and its origin. It began with his difficulties with the mathematics of Lamb (say in 1908) and culminated in his arrival at Cambridge in 1911, so well described by Russell, with Wittgenstein torn between an engineering and a philosophical vocation, exactly as his sister too describes.[18]

For a philosophical vocation, rather than a purely mathematical one, it turned out to be. Our concern is with the *Tractatus*, which, for all its disclaimers, is itself a theory, though one designed to end theory. It can be

---

15 *FB*, p. 22. The letter, dated 14 October 1908, is now lost. The edition relies on my own notes of it.

16 I take this point (if I have well understood it) from correspondence with Kreisel.

17 See McGuinness 1988, p. 74. Russell agreed with Jourdain that the solution did not work but seems to have forgotten the incident by 1911, when Wittgenstein came to Cambridge.

18 See McGuinness 1988, pp. 92 and 74 respectively.

viewed as the last theory of everything. In its own terms it would necessarily be the last because it is only by recognizing that its propositions are nonsense that we understand them, but it is also in fact the last in the logical tradition of philosophy to attempt to give a quite general account of the relations between language (not a particular language, but language as such) and the world. The chief aim of that theory is to dispel both theory and confusion (so far as these can be distinguished) by an extreme economy of ontological and of axiomatic assumptions. The vanishing of logical constants, of probability as an object, of classes:[19] these are examples of the former; while the denial that there exist fundamental laws of logic[20] is an example of the latter.

This 'theory', it will be remembered, is eventually presented largely as an account of the proposition as such, that is to say of the whole possibility of saying or thinking anything, which in turn must mirror exactly the possibilities of existence and truth. This key concept of proposition is explicated using the notion of picturing. That notion is largely borrowed or adapted from the work of Hertz, the second in Wittgenstein's list of influences. Hertz described systems of mechanics as pictures or models possessing the same multiplicity as the external objects and such that the necessary consequences (in thought) of the pictures are representations of the necessary consequences (*in rerum natura*) of the things represented.[21]

Wittgenstein's *Tractatus* is an attempt to apply this to language as a whole. His objects are parallel to the material points of Hertz – and like them are purely theoretical objects, assumed to exist only as required to represent the states of affairs we wish to represent but not or not necessarily identifiable by themselves. The possibilities of combination of names in sentences mirror exactly (and, we may say, necessarily) the possibilities of combination of objects in states of affairs. As Hertz dispenses with the notion of force, so Wittgenstein dispenses not only with the logical objects we have already mentioned but also with all connection between distinct states of affairs such as causality might seem to require.

We have no concrete indication of when Wittgenstein began to reflect on Hertz's work. Undoubtedly he will have known of Boltzmann's great respect for and large measure of agreement with that work. The influence of Hertz was perhaps longer and more persistent that that of

---

19 *Tractatus* 4.0312, 5.441 etc; 5.1511; and 6.031 respectively.
20 *Tractatus* 6.127.
21 Hertz 1894 (English translation 1956), Introduction. See also the section on Dynamical Models (p. 199, English translation p. 177), which Wittgenstein particularly refers to (*Tractatus* 4.04).

Boltzmann. The minutes of the Moral Sciences Club in Cambridge show how in 1939, when he made his first presentation after taking up his chair, and again in 1946, when he felt the need to defend his own conception of philosophy against Popper's attack, he made use of a favourite quotation from Hertz to suggest that philosophy might proceed not by giving an explicit answer to a question but by showing that the question itself was a muddled one.[22] Another long-term influence of, or at least similarity with, Hertz is a matter of some subtlety. Each man thought that his own chief merit lay not so much in originality as in the mode of presentation of things luminously obvious. The clarity of presentation is great in Frege also, but not the consciousness that this was the nub of the matter. The Preface to the *Tractatus* lays 'no claim to novelty in detail' but places the first element of the value (if any) of the work in that 'thoughts are expressed in it, and on this score the better the thoughts are expressed – the more the nail has been hit on the head – the greater will be its value'. Here Wittgenstein echoes Hertz's words, 'What I hope is new, and to this alone I attach value is the arrangement and collocation of the whole (*Anordnung und Zusammenstellung des Ganzen*) – the logical or philosophical aspect of the matter',[23] and the importance of just these elements is stressed in the draft of a preface that Wittgenstein wrote in 1938 for the work he then planned: 'the links between these remarks where the arrangement does not make them evident (*die Zusammenhänge der Bemerkungen, wo ihre Anordnung sie nicht erkennen läßt*), I shall clarify by means of a numbering system'.[24] (This promise was not exactly fulfilled.)

The notions of picturing and of the logical connection between pictures are no doubt derived from Hertz, but the problems that these notions enabled Wittgenstein to solve had a different origin. I have described elsewhere the successive preoccupations that he and Russell had in 1912–13.[25] Would that we were as well informed about his discussions with Frege! It became clear in the course of these years that a new general account of logic – Russell began to sketch one in 1912 – must in fact be left to Wittgenstein. *That* is why Russell said to Hermine Wittgenstein, 'We expect the next big step in logic to be taken by your brother'. Both 'Notes on Logic' and 'Notes dictated to Moore' are no doubt drafts (or perhaps to be read sequentially as *a* draft) of such an account. As a first step towards a solution of the

22 Professor Hugh Mellor kindly made it possible for me to consult the Minute Book. See also *CL*, p. 324. The quotation in question was also one considered as a motto for *PhI*. Allan Janik gives a good account of the influence of Hertz in Janik 1994.
23 Hertz *loc.cit.* Janik points out the importance of *rhetoric* for both Hertz and Wittgenstein.
24 In MS 117, p. 110. See the discussion in Baker and Hacker 1980, pp. 25ff.
25 McGuinness 1988, see in particular pp. 90ff. and 160ff.

foundations of logic he needed an account of the functioning of the most elementary proposition,[26] one which would both show it as the locus of contact between language and the world and place its bivalence beyond doubt. Some of the problems this raised can be seen in the chapter 'The Understanding of Propositions' in Russell's 1913 manuscript, posthumously published as *Theory of Knowledge*. We know from Russell's letters that precisely this chapter was criticized so severely by Wittgenstein that Russell abandoned the project of publishing the book as a whole.[27] That was the criticism of its account of judgement, which we find also in *Tractatus* 5.5422.

In 'Notes on Logic', however, there is also a criticism on the very point that concerns us here.

> Frege said 'propositions are names'; Russell said 'propositions correspond to complexes'. Both are false, and especially false is the statement 'propositions are names of complexes'. Facts cannot be named.[28]

In Russell's thought at this precise period propositions are not themselves entities: they are incomplete symbols, as he liked to say, that is to say there is reference to them only in statements, such as 'A judges that the proposition p is true'. When a proposition is true, the complex corresponding to it exists, when they are false there is no such complex. Wittgenstein had a general objection to this account, of which his criticism of Russell's theory of judgement is only a special case. Complexity as such is not a sufficient guide to what can be asserted or believed. A piece of nonsense might have complexity, as do also many things not capable as such of truth or falsity (the square root of –1, for example). In fact he came to distinguish between a complex (which following Russell might be called an incomplete symbol), which might enter into a fact, and a fact.

Wittgenstein's first reaction, as we see in the two sets of notes, was to say that a proposition's meaning was the fact that corresponded to it (and of course rendered it in some cases true, in others false).[29] So he thought until April 1914, but in the first wartime notes we find a quite different account and a notably different terminology.

---

26 Wittgenstein recognized this as early as the summer of 1912, when he wrote to Russell, 'I believe our problems can be traced down to the atomic propositions. This you will see if you try to explain how the Copula in such a proposition has meaning'. *CL*, p. 20 (see also pp. 17, 24).

27 Russell 1984, Part II, Chapter I. For Wittgenstein's criticisms see McGuinness 1988, pp. 173ff.

28 *NL*, p. 97 (p. 93 in earlier editions). The editions vary as to a *TLP* parallel, but in fact both 3.143 and 3.144 should be cited.

29 *NL*, p. 94 (in all editions), *NdM*, p. 111.

170

The background is the introduction of what is often called the 'Picture Theory', which is in reality a much wider theory (in the paradoxical sense of theory already indicated). Wittgenstein is conjuring up as the necessary counterpart of language a Hertzian model of a world of objects entering into relations which (given the simplicity of the model) cannot but either hold or not hold. It is here that the term *Sachverhalte* is introduced.[30] The idea that the objects (of thought or speech) can be indicated only in function of their combination with one another and that such combination constituted a state of affairs (*Sachverhalt*), which might hold (*bestehen*) or not was not an idea derived from Russell's work. Indeed when Wittgenstein tried to talk of these matters in English he was obliged to fall back on the notion of an atomic fact, which, being a fact, should perforce hold. The German terminology is more accurate in this respect. The thought owes something perhaps to Meinong's notion of the objects (*Objektive*) of judgement[31] but we need to find a terminology with which Wittgenstein might have been acquainted that is also closer to that he eventually used. The word *Sachverhalt* itself was adopted as a technical term in 1895 by Stumpf,[32] whom, conceivably but not very probably, Wittgenstein a few years later may have heard giving lectures in the University of Berlin when he himself was at the Technische Hochschule. But, as has long been recognized, there are more striking parallels to the vocabulary of the *Tractatus* in Adolf Reinach's essay on negative judgement which was first published in a *Festschrift* for Theodor Lipps in 1911.[33] That Wittgenstein might have had some interest in this book is an hypothesis but not an impossible one. Lipps, and indeed Stumpf may have been familiar to him from his interest in experimental psychology. We find him conducting experiments on musical hearing in Cambridge, probably continuing lines of thought suggested by T.H. Pear in Manchester.[34] (The *Festschrift*, however, is not primarily devoted to psychology.) Alternatively he may have read the account of Reinach's article given by Geyser in the *Archiv für die Gesamte Psychologie* for 1913.[35]

---

30 *Nb*, p. 5 (20 September 14), and *passim*. It is in the same context that Wittgenstein says, 'That a sentence (*Satz*) is a logical portrayal (*Abbild*) of its meaning is obvious to the uncaptive (*unbefangen* – 'unprejudiced' would be a better translation) eye'.

31 Meinong 1910, p. 101 explicitly rejects the use of the term *Sachverhalt* for this content of judgement and prefers *Objektiv*, because of the difficulty raised by negative and self-contradictory judgements. (Russell 1984, p. 108, identifies *Objektive* with his own 'propositions' and thus does not think them entities.)

32 Stumpf 1906 (report of a lecture delivered in 1905).

33 'Zur Theorie des negativen Urteils' in Pfaender 1911, also in Reinach 1989, English translation in Smith and Künne 1982, where see also the article 'Pieces of a Theory' by B. Smith and K. Mulligan.

34 See McGuinness 1988, pp. 125 ff.

35 See Geyser 1913 and Barry Smith's 'Annotated Bibliography' in Mulligan 1987: that volume also contains an intellectual biography and other useful articles on Reinach.

The fundamental idea common to Wittgenstein and Reinach is that language presupposes that objects (*Gegenstände*) enter into *Sachverhalte* which may or may not subsist. In any case these *Sachverhalte* belong to (indeed they constitute) the realm of the possible. When they do subsist they are also *Tatsachen* or facts and the relative judgements or propositions are true. It is simplest to apply the term *Sachverhalt* to the content of elementary propositions and use some other term (Wittgenstein chooses *Sachlage*) for the case where a complex 'state of affairs' (which we may call a 'situation') is in question. This terminology is used by Wittgenstein apparently to establish, but more truly to reflect, the essential bivalence of the system of propositions. Thought, assertion, truth all have purchase only when there is a suitable content. Julius Caesar cannot be asserted – a truism whose importance Frege saw. We need a *beurtheilbarer Inhalt*, a judgeable content (e.g. the thought-content that Brutus killed Caesar).[36] If we try to seize the essence of judgeability, *den Satzverband*, as Wittgenstein called it,[37] what holds a proposition together and makes it a proposition, we see that it is simply this quality of being either true or false (though, or and, not necessarily the one or necessarily the other); and this is what is meant by its presenting or asserting a *Sachverhalt*.

There is much rhetoric in this: a circular account is being given, neither objects and *Sachverhalte* on the one hand nor elementary propositions and names on the other are independently identifiable in practice. The account is presented as being the most satisfactory way of fitting in the features of propositions required for the construction of 'Logic' – i.e. what Wittgenstein and Russell thought to be such at the time. When an argument seems to be offered, as at *Tractatus* 2.0211–2, ('If the world had no substance [i.e. if there were no simple objects], then whether one proposition had sense would depend on whether another proposition was true. – In that case we could not sketch any picture of the world, true or false.') begs the question, because determinacy of sense, which for Wittgenstein means bivalence, is assumed.

The result reached, however, is far from being trivial. If Wittgenstein can establish that all the logical constants are implicit in the elementary propositions and that the general form of proposition so given is the 'one and only primitive sign in logic' (*TLP* 5.47, 5.472),[38] then he will have

---

36 '*Begriffsschrift*', p. 2 in Frege 1952. The example there used is a different one.
37 *Nb*, 20 September 1914, *TLP* 4.221.2.
38 This last point is equivalent to Wittgenstein's idea that one symbolic rule will suffice for recognizing all the logical propositions of the first eight chapters of *Principia Mathematica*, an idea formulated in November 1913 (*CL*, p. 52). There are two forms of such a rule: truth-tables and Wittgenstein's bracket notation (*TLP* 4.442 and 6.1203 respectively).

shown that the apparatus or symbolism that we have to employ, consciously or not, for affirming the simplest proposition is also adequate to establish any of the propositions of logic. Thus he will be well on his way[39] to providing the foundations required for the logic of *Principia Mathematica* precisely by showing that none are required. All this by formulating in a persuasive manner the conditions for any proposition whatsoever to be true-or-false.

Such is indeed the content of what I have elsewhere called the proto-*Prototractatus*,[40] the *Abhandlung* or treatise that Wittgenstein was writing in pencil on loose sheets in the autumn of 1915.[41] We have a version of it in the first 70 pages of the Bodleian manuscript of the *Prototractatus*. It ends (or ended before correction) with the three propositions:

6.2   *Die Ethik besteht nicht aus Sätzen*
6.3   *Alle Sätze sind gleichwertig*
7   *Wovon man nicht sprechen kann, darüber muß man schweigen.*[42]

It is even possible that these remarks were an afterthought inserted when the typescript was prepared (*ex hypothesi* in August-September 1916): those about ethics echo passages in the Notebook for July 1916. In that case the proto-*Prototractatus* would have ended with remarks to the effect that the propositions of logic say nothing.

With these three propositions or without, the *Abhandlung* will have been even more classically silent over what cannot be said than the *Tractatus* to which we are accustomed.[43] It will indeed be what Kreisel calls it, an ode to propositional logic,[44] a contribution to heroic philosophy like the works of Russell and Frege, giving an account of all that was thinkable not in terms of numbers or classes or concepts, but in terms of what could be said. Moreover it contrives to avoid being itself an a priori theory by saying that it is not a theory at all. All that is allowed – and

39 Of course many difficulties remained, of which some are touched on by Wittgenstein with a mixture of ingenuity and insouciance, but the plausibility of his approach at the time may be seen in the fact that F.P. Ramsey was still persuaded by it at the time of his contribution on mathematical logic to the *Encyclopaedia Britannica* (Ramsey 1926).
40 See 'Some pre-*Tractatus* manuscripts' (Chapter 23 in the present volume) for my account of the stages of composition of this manuscript.
41 See the letter to Russell of that date *CL*, pp. 103f.
42 6.2 'Ethics does not consist of propositions.' 6.3 'All propositions are of equal value.' 7 'What we cannot speak about we must pass over in silence.'
43 For some account of how Wittgenstein came under the influence of his Olmütz friends and their mentors (Kraus, Loos and Weininger) to add more remarks defining (still by negation) the sphere of the unsayable see above 'The idea of Jewishness' (Chapter 4 in the present volume).
44 Kreisel 1998, p. 116.

hence all that it does – is to show (Wittgenstein puts great emphasis on this word) what the logical features of reality are. Hence the importance for him of finding a formulation for logic in which it would be simply impossible to write down a nonsense: in later terms, one in which this could be excluded mechanically. If this could be done (as he wrongly, but not at the time hopelessly wrongly, thought), it would be clear that logic not only needed but was incapable of having a justification. As his book specifically shows nothing can be said in this area at all.

With this we have reached the turning-point, the *volta*, in Wittgenstein's early work (and Work). We have come round to a true understanding of the impossibility of philosophy of which Boltzmann spoke. Wittgenstein was led from engineering to mathematics, from mathematics to logic, from logic to language, and from language to the unsayable. In terms of Boltzmann's mockery of philosophy as a conse-crated virgin, we might say that while she has indeed no offspring, this very limitation is her gift to mankind. Wittgenstein puts this equally figu-ratively by saying that we must throw away the ladder of his propositions once we have climbed up it and less figuratively but still gnomically by saying that one who follows through his train of thoughts will see the world aright.[45] But only by following his thought or that of someone who might do the same work better is this possible: it is an *ignorantia*, yes, but a *docta ignorantia* that he propounds.

---

45 *TLP* 6.54. This itself is one of the remarks illustrative of the unsayable and its relevance to life which (I have argued in 'The idea of Jewishness') Wittgenstein was now induced to add to his original *Abhandlung* in response to the stimulation of his Olmütz friends (and to the influence of Kraus, Loos and Weininger). But the essential work was already done.

Part III

PHILOSOPHY REVISITED

16

WITTGENSTEIN AND THE
VIENNA CIRCLE

With the publication of the *Tractatus* Wittgenstein felt that he had made what contribution he could to philosophy. Perhaps it was for this reason, along with other, inner reasons connected with the defeat of Austria-Hungary in the war, that he retired into the Austrian countryside to teach at elementary schools. Frank Ramsey, the brilliant young logician at Cambridge, came to visit Wittgenstein and prevailed upon him to discuss philosophy. But a proper return to that vocation seemed out of the question: Wittgenstein wrote to Keynes:

> You ask in your letter whether you could do anything to make it possible for me to return to scientific work. The answer is, No: there is nothing to be done in that way, because I myself no longer have any strong inner drive towards that sort of activity. Everything that I really *had* to say I have said, and so the spring has run dry. That sounds queer, but it's how things are.
>
> (*CL*, p. 207)

The same thing happened in Vienna, where a handful of young mathematicians and philosophers under the leadership of Moritz Schlick had found in the *Tractatus* a fascinating and epigrammatic expression of the ideology they were themselves striving to formulate. This was the group that came to be known as the Vienna Circle. What mainly attracted them, it seems, was the ability of the *Tractatus* to account for the truth of the propositions of logic and mathematics, without allowing for any substantive science other than the natural sciences, as they were known. Some of them hoped that this insight would make it possible to apply the methods of natural science to the problems of humanity. They formed the left wing of the movement and were later to be hostile to the influence of Wittgenstein. He, as can be seen from the *Tractatus*, wished to reserve the realm of values as something completely outside the sphere of science. Other members of the movement such as Schlick himself were more sympathetic towards the mystical elements in the *Tractatus*; but all were anxious to hear from the man who had seen the true philosophical implication of the work of Frege and Russell. Schlick eventually managed to get in touch with Wittgenstein who was no longer a schoolmaster, and now was occupied in building a house in Vienna for his sister. Schlick wrote asking Wittgenstein to attend a meeting of the Vienna Circle, but Wittgenstein felt that a meeting with a number of people was impossible. He undertook to see Schlick alone. It would then become apparent, he said, whether he was at all capable of being of use to him. Accordingly Schlick was invited to lunch in order to discuss the matter afterwards. Wittgenstein told his friend Engelmann the next day 'Each of us thought the other must be mad', but Schlick's own impressions were evidently different. He went with the reverential attitude of a pilgrim and returned, so his wife said, in an ecstatic state.

After this first contact there were a number of meetings between Wittgenstein and members of the Vienna Circle. Feigl and Carnap have written about these and Waismann even made a number of written records of conversations between Schlick and Wittgenstein and himself. At first Wittgenstein insisted that he had said all he could say in the *Tractatus*. He was not even a very good interpreter of that work when they pressed him on details. But on one occasion the eminent Dutch mathematician Brouwer gave a lecture at Vienna and Waismann and Feigl managed to coax Wittgenstein to join them at it. Feigl reported:

> When afterwards Wittgenstein went to a cafe with us, a great event took place. Suddenly very volubly Wittgenstein began talking philosophy at great length. Perhaps this was the turning point, for ever since 1929, when he moved to Cambridge University, Wittgenstein was a philosopher again and began to exert a tremendous influence.

We have some record of the period immediately following this in Waismann's transcripts (*WVC*) and in the *Philosophical Remarks* and *Philosophical Grammar* of Wittgenstein himself, collections all now published. The chief interest of these for our purpose is that they enable us to see an attempt to hold together the essential standpoint of the *Tractatus* itself, some of the main theses associated with the Vienna Circle, and also some elements that are thought of as characteristic of the later philosophy of Wittgenstein. This later philosophy used to be contrasted sharply with Wittgenstein's earlier works but its continuity with them has now become clearer.

As an example of this I will discuss Wittgenstein's thesis that the sense of a proposition is the method of its verification. This was regarded in many quarters as the main slogan of the Vienna Circle, but by all accounts it originated in discussions with Wittgenstein. He frequently repeated it (and its corollary that difference in verification means differ-

ence in sense) in the *Philosophical Remarks* and in the conversations transcribed by Waismann. It is interesting that so many of the contexts in
which these ideas occur have to do with mathematics. The very opening
of the conversations with Schlick and Waismann shows this. A proof in
mathematics is not a means of getting to a proposition independent of,
and separate from, the proof. The proof is identical with the proposition
proved, and so on. Are there, or are there not, four consecutive 7's in the
decimal expansion of π? You cannot say there is an answer to this, unless
you have an effective way of determining which of these is the case. This,
of course, no one has. Themes such as these were central to Brouwer's
intuitionism, and though Wittgenstein was to reject the emphasis that
Brouwer put on the powers of the human mind, he clearly learnt much
that was valuable in other spheres from his reintroduction to the philosophy of mathematics in this particular way.

Wittgenstein in 1929 to 1931 did not regard himself as having given
up the Picture Theory, the idea that the notion of picturing could be used
to bring out the way in which a non-logical proposition had meaning.
Towards the beginning of the *Philosophical Remarks* he brings out what he
calls the pictorial character of propositions by suggesting that we think of
propositions as instructions to build models. In order to guide the
movements of my hand a set of instructions must have the multiplicity of
the activity it is desired to produce. This suggests a slight advance on the
account of propositions as pictures given in the *Tractatus*, especially in one
respect: the *Tractatus* does not say anything about our ability to follow
through all the ramifications of a proposition. Indeed, at 4.002, it
expressly says that the multiplicity may be entirely implicit:

> Man possesses the ability to construct languages capable of
> expressing every sense, without having any idea how each word
> has meaning or what its meaning is – just as people speak
> without knowing how the individual sounds are produced.

Perhaps the new point of view will become clearer if we look at another
way in which it manifests itself, both in the *Philosophical Remarks* and in
the conversations. In the *Remarks* he writes:

> The sense of a question is the method of answering it. What then
> is the sense of the question 'Do two men really mean the same
> thing by the words "white"?' Tell me *how* you look for something
> and I'll tell you what you're looking for.

This line of thought occurs repeatedly in both books. You can't look for
something without a method of looking for it. You can't ask a question
without knowing how to find out the answer. These ideas are not

altogether attractive. There is much to be said, in many areas, for asking vague questions, even at the risk of talking about nothing at all. Whether mathematics is such an area, I am more doubtful. Wittgenstein's applications of his principle in mathematics are both the most frequent and the most persuasive of his applications of it. But as a general principle and as applied in areas where (unlike mathematicians) we know that there are real things to be talked about, it seems rather restrictive.

However, our present topic does not require us to pass judgement on these thoughts, though objections to the verification principle are fairly easy to find. My purpose here is to point out that the new account of the sense of propositions in the years 1929 to 1931 was an extension or application of the account of the proposition as a picture. This new account included the verification principle in the forms already quoted but also included other elements which are normally associated with Wittgenstein's post-positivist period. A picture is readily enough conceived as showing how something should be done or constructed. Instructions, like a picture, must possess the multiplicity of the operation in question. This use of the notion of a picture became more and more prominent in Wittgenstein's thought. He says: 'I understand a proposition when I *apply* it. ... *The proposition is there so that we can operate with it*'. It hardly needs proving that this is a line of thought prominent in the *Philosophical Investigations*. Waismann indeed drew in conversation the conclusion which is often taken as one of the mottos of the *Philosophical Investigations*, 'The meaning of a word is the way it is applied'.

In many cases, the application we must make of the proposition is to treat it as a question. As such it will show us how to reach the answer yes or no. It is for this reason that Wittgenstein says that its sense is the method of its verification. This approach determines also the form in which he accepts the doctrine about sense. The utterance of a sentence is one step in a calculus, one operation: other human actions – the building of a boiler, for example – are further steps. Thus, naturally, Wittgenstein does not think of elementary propositions as verified by coherence alone: he insists that there can be a confrontation of a proposition with reality, a line later followed by Schlick.

The *Tractatus* was a theory about language in the abstract, about propositions, thoughts, and truth and falsity: in the later works Wittgenstein was to talk more and more about the concrete phenomena of language, about the uses to which we put language and the way in which our thoughts manifest themselves in an action. We can see the beginning of this development in the adoption by Wittgenstein of the thesis that the sense of a proposition was the method of its verification, and in his application of that thesis to mathematics. We can perhaps see also that he could not for long be at ease with the Vienna Circle in which logic and science were regarded not as two human activities among others, but as something invariant and unassailable against which all activities must be measured.

In most of his later writings Wittgenstein continued to assert that the sense of a mathematical proposition was not separable from the proof given of it. When two distinct proofs could be given for what was apparently the same proposition, we really had two distinct mathematical insights. It proved more difficult to accommodate this way of looking at things in an account of propositions outside mathematics. Wittgenstein saw that we could apparently have two different ways of verifying the same proposition. It is obvious enough that it has been raining when we can see the puddles in the street or when we remember the raindrops beating on the windows or when we hear a report from someone else to that effect. Are we therefore to say that we have three or more distinct propositions clothed in the same form of words, 'It has been raining'? At first Wittgenstein did incline towards this view. But later he came to think that he could regard the majority of our everyday statements as hypotheses: in the sense that they could be confirmed or disconfirmed by a considerable variety of sensory evidence. The statements that expressed this sensory evidence became the only true propositions. They alone were capable of complete verification. As for the hypotheses, we could only show them to be more or less probable. Wittgenstein illustrated this by saying that hypotheses were like a solid body and that observational propositions represented cross sections through that solid body. Just as the scattered points from which we make up and project a curve on a graph are an infinitesimal proportion of all the points on the graph so the propositions by which we check our hypotheses are a very small part of all that those hypotheses theoretically contain.

What became, in the light of this, of the idea that the sense of a proposition was its method of verification? Obviously enough the individual propositions (in the new sense given to that term by Wittgenstein) could be said to have their sense exhausted by the method of telling whether they were true or not – that method being simple confrontation of them with reality. But the more complicated hypotheses that he now spoke of had a large number of different methods, not indeed of verification, but of relative confirmation or disconfirmation. Moreover their significance did not lie solely in the relevant observational propositions but rather in the simplicity or beauty or convenience of the picture of the world that they gave us. They were recommended, it might be said, by their place in our picture of the world as a whole. It was a short step from this to the view, which everyone associates with the later Wittgenstein, that the significance of a proposition lay in the total difference that it made to our behaviour, to our common life. In time this became Wittgenstein's usual way of describing or finding out the meaning of any statement whatsoever and the old distinction between hypotheses and propositions vanished. The notion of a simple proposition which could be compared directly with reality and whose sense was identical with its method of verification fell away altogether. Certainly testing, questioning, confirming, or disconfirming remained important activities that could be carried out with any statement, but they were far from being the only ones. Even if there could be no checking or disconfirming, there might still be consequences for our lives in the acceptance of a proposition and these consequences would form the role of that proposition in our lives and that role was its meaning. Only when it had no such role would a proposition be like a cog attached to a machine by engaging with nothing. Wittgenstein thus retained from the period of the *Tractatus* the right to reject as nonsensical a range of philosophical propositions, but the precise criterion he used had become much more attuned to the variety of human needs and interests than the austere criterion of the *Tractatus*, or even of his positivist period.

From this sketch of the development of Wittgenstein's ideas on verification the difference between him and the Circle easily appears. The members of the Circle, even Schlick himself, took science and its validity as their starting point. They were also interested, as the example of Schlick in particular shows, in advances in science. Einstein and quantum physics changed their picture of the world and revealed new conceptual possibilities to them. (Thus they were glad to find in Einstein's remarks about length and the measurement of length an anticipation of the principle of verification.) Wittgenstein's case, however, was different. Advances in science passed over him almost without trace. He had learnt his physics, and still more important his conception of physics, from Hertz and Boltzmann. The task of physics was to give an adequate and inclusive picture of the world. The model of a system of point-masses in a minimum of purely mechanical relations appealed to the engineer in Wittgenstein. It gave him, indeed, not only his theory of physics but his theory of language in the *Tractatus*: Hertz is the only source quoted for it (though there is a well-attested indebtedness to Paul Ernst for the identification of certain misleading features in language). So construed, science is not the explanation of anything, nor does it give us the true nature of things. It is merely the exploitation of certain features of language for purposes of convenience.

The picture theory, therefore, arose in the context of science, in reflection on the work of Hertz. But Wittgenstein derives it, and ultimately the principle of verification, from general principles of language. Using that theory he wanted to show that science was only another form of description and hence (the conclusion is well known but not our immediate subject here) could not give us any deeper insight or the answer to any philosophical or ethical problems.

In following this line of thought Wittgenstein, with the compression that marked his exposition, particularly at the period of the *Tractatus*, left aside the technical problem of showing how in practice the principles and laws of science were related to elementary propositions. A few remarks to indicate the direction to be followed seemed to him enough. In a similar spirit he used to say to Russell before the First World War that the problem of constructing the whole of science on the basis of the sensibilia of a single person was not a particularly difficult one. The fact was that his preoccupations did not lie in that direction. Not problems of science but aesthetic and conceptual problems, he later said, were those that interested him. This, I think, led to misunderstandings, above all with Carnap, who thought that an idea was worth discussing only when it had been shown systematically to be applicable to the relevant subject matter (in this case science, but similar considerations applied to Wittgenstein's few reported thoughts on mathematics). It was a difference in style. Schlick was more sympathetic and prepared to marry his own awareness of contemporary cruces in physical theory to Wittgenstein's constant wrestling with central problems.

17

RELATIONS WITH AND
WITHIN THE CIRCLE

Is it a fact about us or a fact about Wittgenstein, that on many of the issues that arise in considering his life and work it seems difficult for us not to say too much either on one side or the other, not to patronize him or others, not to defend, not to take sides in disputes which risk being imaginary or anachronistic? I think here of, for example, his Jewishness, his relations with Russell, and in particular of my present theme; but other instances will easily occur to the reader. As already hinted, perhaps even my opening question is a *falsche Fragestellung*, not the right question to ask (as is certainly the case with some of the disputes). The problem really is our historical relation to Wittgenstein and to the issues raised: conceivably future or younger generations may be more easily able to say *wie es eigentlich gewesen ist*, how things actually were, though some subjects, and perhaps Wittgenstein is one, seem to put a particular strain on the historian's neutrality. It seems a truism, but it is not easy to accept, that lack of conformity and resistance to stereotypes has its awkward and unacceptable side as well as its exhilarating and liberating function. Useless, no doubt, to inquire how much a product of our own time, how *zeitgebunden,* this effect is.

Perhaps we should begin by asking why this awkwardness arises in the instant case. Is it that the impulse given to philosophy by the Circle and that given by Wittgenstein are still not exhausted, and we are unable to find a vantage point above the mêlée from which both can be seen to contribute to some grand pattern? Though here again there is a general predicament, this time in the history of philosophy. It is usual for a philosopher to have his devotees: there are (more or less consciously) Russellians, Popperians, Davidsonians, Kantians and so on. Every point that comes up the late-born adepts can absorb by saying that their prophet had this or that answer or the beginnings of it. This is possible because each philosopher's system (as it used to be called) defines what is a problem for him. To follow him is to accept that range of problems. And a range of problems is a way of life.

This would account however only for lack of mutual comprehension between those whose sympathies lie more with Wittgenstein and those whose lie with the Circle round Schlick; and such a lack no doubt exists. The tensions we have spoken of are more striking and arise from another element in the divergence between Wittgenstein and the Circle (and between him and Russell), namely from the fact that (in the case of each pair) the two seemed at one time so close: Wittgenstein the natural continuator of Russell, and the Circle the natural continuators of Wittgenstein. All the sentiments felt against the lost leader would be felt against him when he rejected or seemed to reject his own chosen allies. The rejection would be the more keenly resented in proportion as the identity of aim had seemed close and as the range of philosophical problems treated had indeed seemed emblematic of a way of life.

The fault, or the reason, lay in both cases on both sides. Russell had indeed wanted someone to complete and underpin his work still in the spirit of an enlightened, one might almost say an Enlightenment, mathematics. He was at first (and when it mattered) generous in accepting without a murmur not only the radical criticisms of his own position in the *Tractatus* but also Wittgenstein's refusal (in the event ignored) of his introduction to that book. With time, however, the new mysticism, the obscurantism as it seemed, of his former pupil shocked him: he did not (Ramsey thought) do justice to Wittgenstein's criticisms in the second edition of *Principia Mathematica*, and came to think of Wittgenstein as a wrecker merely. 'You would not later have appeared such a devil,' said the Marquise von O. in Kleist's story with that title, 'if you had not at first appeared as an angel.' Though note that it was not just Wittgenstein's much later philosophy that Russell distrusted: a reference in the introduction to the second edition of *Principles of Mathematics* (1937) describes Wittgenstein as holding that mathematics consists of tautologies, a misreading (though a common one) of the *Tractatus*, which Russell had to modify in subsequent impressions of *Principles* (e.g. in that of 1950), evidently because Wittgenstein had reacted with comic surprise when Russell repeated the remark at a Cambridge meeting.

Something of the same pattern we find in the reactions of the Schlick Circle. An amazing book, they thought, when Hahn and Schlick came across the *Tractatus* and Kurt Reidemeister expounded it for the Circle. It was greeted like Lohengrin in the opera: *Ein Wunder!* A miracle! It was not just what it said but the manner of its saying: Reidemeister's sister, not yet Marie Neurath, spoke for many of them when she said she would have been just as impressed if there had been a 'Not' placed before every sentence. Indeed Schlick made the same remark (it is one that Wittgenstein himself made about Weininger's *Sex and Character* [1906]). To be sure, some were at first put off by the dogmatism of the opening ontology, the Creation Myth as I have called it elsewhere:[1] they were mystified in a bad sense. So Menger, for instance – and Hahn himself confessed to the same response until he had heard the central sections explained by Reidemeister (a man of radiant intelligence and probably more patient in youth than I remember him in old age). Menger came to those sections only later, but then accepted wholeheartedly the importance of many theses in the book, though quaere whether he ever quite saw it as a whole.[2] (We shall return to this theme.)

Schlick especially, who, by no means to his discredit, had a well-developed capacity for reverence, went in awe of Wittgenstein as earlier of Einstein. The exquisite courtesy of his first and fruitless letter to the village schoolmaster was in his case perhaps no departure from normal manners, but when the meeting was at last arranged his wife Blanche was so struck by his attitude of a pilgrim that we can be sure more than politeness came into it.[3] Schlick never said (as some of his modern admirers do) that the idea of philosophy as clarification rather than dogma, and other favourite themes of Wittgenstein's, were already in his 1918 book. He, who could be ironical and sceptical, was no fool and surely did not characterize the *Tractatus* as the turning-point of philosophy for no reason. Something about the book held him captive, perhaps the combination of all the insights he and his circle already shared with the new ones they needed (chiefly those about logic), a combination, moreover, into a *Weltanschauung*, and one that had room for all the values that made him feel more at home in Vienna than in his birthplace, which was ('Sad, but true', he used to say) Berlin. And then the moral seriousness, the social assurance of Wittgenstein the man, the intensity of the intellectual and cultural life he led, deigning to appear every now and then in Mrs. Stonborough's salon, had their effect on Schlick, who was himself eminently *salonfähig*, he would be accepted everywhere. Wittgenstein's domestic setting in the late twenties was comparable to that of his youth, with changes only of epoch. Freud, the Bühlers, and the Vienna Philharmonic Quartet took the place of Brahms and Bruno Walter, Drobil of Krämer, and so on.

The aristocratic side of all this appealed to Schlick, who was already acquainted with Mrs. Stonborough (hence, of course, his meeting with Wittgenstein). Menger too belonged to those circles. Well connected, son of the leading Austrian economist (Crown Prince Rudolf's tutor) and, in virtue of other links, quite at home in the houses of the extended

1 McGuinness 1988, p. 199.
2 Much of this description of the reception of *Tractatus* in the Circle (when other sources are not mentioned or are obvious) is drawn from Menger 1994.
3 These events are described on pp. 13–15 of *WVC*.

Wittgenstein family, he embodied perhaps more than any of the Circle (and certainly more than Wittgenstein himself) the best aspirations of the bourgeoisie that owed their place to one of the learned professions, the *Bildungsbürgertum*.[4] Originality, yes, but above all the application of original ideas by a systematic mind, would – or alone had the potentiality to – transform the world. Literature, music, all the products of culture (Menger had a particular interest in graphic art and in the grammar of design) were as it were extras, *Zugaben* ('graces of fate' in Wittgenstein's phrase *'Gnade des Schicksals'*). Menger had no idea of a need for a fundamental change of view. His was like Russell's position, which has been described as that of one who thought that all the world's woes proceeded from man's irrationality, and therefore proposed the solution – that men should become rational. Perhaps Schlick, by contrast, felt less at home in the world than Menger. He had (as his writings on the sense of life and even his book on ethics show) aspirations. Menger's book on ethics[5] is in comparison (and deliberately) dispassionate, a study of the logical relations between cohesive groups of persons with a more or less uniform value-set for each group. Only at the end does Menger mention that he personally would prefer the sort of higher-order system making for mutual tolerance. (It is hardly a coincidence that the book was written in Austria in the winter of 1933–4, when social cohesion finally broke down there and Hitler was just established in Germany.)

I have mentioned that Schlick accepted the *Tractatus* as a whole (and here we can include the thought of Wittgenstein in the early 1930s, not yet seen as very different). He wished (I am not sure one can say that he tried) to do justice to all elements in it. Menger's attitude[6] will perhaps serve as a contrast. He records how a cousin of Wittgenstein's asked him, 'Is there really any merit in saying "Whereof one cannot speak, thereof one must be silent"?' – a question very typical of the family reaction to any inquiry about standards: for them (as for Wittgenstein himself, only in a different way) the requirement of decent behaviour was a *Selbstverständlichkeit*, went without saying. Menger was able to explain that this was a sentence of great importance for philosophy. But Menger's reaction still was that of one who treated Wittgenstein's final sentence (and the remark 'Whatever can be said at all can be said clearly') as maxims, starting-points, *Sebstverständlichkeiten* almost, whereas viewed in the context of the book the last sentence is a point of arrival. No doubt

---

4 Many of Wittgenstein's attitudes (his frequent changes of occupation, for instance) are indicative of a background (much though he fought against it) based on *Besitz* or property, a subtly different sector of the bourgeoisie.
5 Menger 1974.
6 Still drawn from Menger's memoirs.

Wittgenstein's aphoristic style seems to license one to treat every proposition as standing on its own, but it is not meant to have that effect and,
in general, the way of the florilegium is (though a very common one) no
way to read philosophy. Slogans do not matter, as the *Tractatus* now para-
digmatically, now paradoxically, teaches. Menger saw very clearly and
welcomed many elements in *Tractatus* that were, or were thought, new: in
his reckoning these were the stress on a critique of language, the clarification of the role of logic (that great gap in the empiricism of Mill and
Mach), and the definition of and emphasis on tautologies. He does justice
too to other subtle but fundamental points of originality in Wittgenstein's
discussion of logic. Sad to relate, he indulges in the rather pointless
historical exercise of pointing out that Mauthner too had thought philosophy a critique of language, that Peirce had independently discovered
truth-tables and Post tautologies, and so on. To this sort of thing one
wants to say first 'Yes and no' – the others did not say exactly the same
things as Wittgenstein (Mauthner certainly not) – and then 'So what?':
the interest of Wittgenstein, we need not speak of his merit, is to have put
these and many other ideas together at the time that he did and, above
all, in the way that he did. And to have done it with the purpose of giving
a certain direction to philosophy, not, as it happens, similar to that of any
of the parallel figures mentioned by Menger. If you treat Wittgenstein's
work as a quarry for stones to use in your own building, then of course
you will ask what on earth this or that angle, which does not fit your
needs, is doing there. Wittgenstein's ontology emerges in a particular
way from his account of symbolism; and his mysticism (I mean his attitude towards the unsayable), far from being an excrescence on his work,
is the essence of it.

I say all of this not to belabour Menger as an historian – he was both
an agreeable companion and a most formidable opponent, whom I
should not wish to dismiss now that he cannot answer. But we have to see
his account for what it was: a contemporary's view (even if mostly
composed towards the end of his life) and, for that very reason, of particular interest to us. Like the central members of the Circle (his own adhe-
sion to which, by the way, was far from absolute) Menger looked to
Wittgenstein for a contribution to a continuing purification of philosophy, which he wished to see moving in the direction of a typically mathematical presentation based on the careful introduction of terms and
rigorous proofs with a view to answering the sort of question that arises
in a mathematician's universe.[7] There is a paradox here: Menger used to
say that a mathematician is to be judged not by what new results he has

---

7 Frege's reaction to the *Tractatus*, now known from his letters to Wittgenstein, is not
dissimilar, see McGuinness 1989, pp. 19ff.

produced but by what new subjects he has created, of the type (though he did not say this) of his own dimension theory. Yet he found it difficult to see that Wittgenstein intended to create a new subject based on the supposition, right or wrong, that philosophy in the old sense was over. As we shall have occasion to see once again, there were features both of Wittgenstein's style of presentation and of the reasoning he used which (for good reasons) tended to obscure the divergence of his aims from those which even his well-wishers ascribed to him.

It is a similar story – that of strong admiration mingled with some bewilderment – as regards the other members of the Schlick Circle who have left us, or who gave me, accounts of their first contact with Wittgenstein. As early as 1927 Schlick brought Wittgenstein into contact with Waismann and Carnap. The latter, who had belonged to the youth movement of *Junges Deutschland*, was immediately taken with the informality of Wittgenstein's appearance, a man with no tie, who straight away sat down on the floor to discuss something that interested him. '*Sehr interessanter, origineller, sympathischer Mensch*' ('a very interesting original and attractived person'), he noted in his diary, adding, to sum it all up, '*Künstlernatur*', a man of artistic temperament: in all languages this is not quite as flattering as it seems and means something like, 'has to be handled with care'.[8] (Feigl used the same description talking to me decades later.) But at first they liked the idea of a *Künstlernatur*. Wittgenstein was *heftig*, 'vehement' – I think this must be the right reading of the shorthand – on various occasions, against Esperanto (a fad of Carnap's), occultism, or the popularization of science. There would be discussions of intuitionism, identity, or the like – sometimes Wittgenstein insisted on conducting them in English, perhaps because he was planning a reply to Ramsey (a letter which Carnap actually typed for him).[9] Wittgenstein would read to them from Wilhelm Busch or (in Feigl's time) Rabindranath Tagore. For these readings Wittgenstein turned his back to the company, 'because he did not want to see their expressions as he read'.[10] All of this at meetings where Schlick and Waismann were also present and sometimes Feigl

---

8 My account of Carnap's early acquaintance with Wittgenstein draws on Carnap's personal communications to me (see also his 'Autobiography' in Carnap 1963) and on diaries (in part, as here, extracts from diaries) and letters preserved in the University of Pittsburgh Library and in the Vienna Circle Archive of the Royal Dutch Academy in Amsterdam. I am very grateful to these institutions for permission to publish these extracts and to Dr. Richard Nollan of Pittsburgh for transcriptions from Carnap's shorthand and other help. (The Vienna Circle Archive is now in the Rijksarchief in Noordholland in Haarlem.)

9 Printed in *WVC*, pp. 189–91.

10 Feigl's account of Wittgenstein's word, given to me (like the rest of the Feigl material here) in a series of personal communications.

also.[11] In 1928 Carnap (who had been away for the winter) did not see Wittgenstein again – if this was because of a rift he did not later recall one – but Waismann and Feigl (and no doubt Schlick) did see Wittgenstein; as did Feigl's fiancée, Maria known as *'die Kasperle'*, with whom he even wished a more exclusive friendship. At Menger's suggestion Feigl and Waismann brought Wittgenstein to the Brouwer lecture of March 1928[12] – and were rewarded by more vigorous philosophical discussion than usual. This was Wittgenstein's first, perhaps also his last, meeting with the Circle assembled in strength, and Hahn, who greeted him, had not seen him before. (Perhaps, incidentally to our main theme, all these circumstances give some idea of how dependent Wittgenstein was on personal rather than institutional relations.) Wittgenstein, of course, knew about intuitionism long before, as his conversations with Carnap showed: Ramsey actually regarded him as himself having been a 'moderate intuitionist', evidently on the basis of conversations in 1923–5,[13] and he was also labelled a half-intuitionist by Oskar Becker.[14]

True enough, after leaving for Cambridge at the beginning of 1929, Wittgenstein seems to have had Vienna discussions only with Schlick and Waismann, who then carried the word to the Circle as a whole (*WVC* is the record, perhaps only of some of these discussions) but Wittgenstein wrote from Cambridge greeting *'die Tafelrunde'* ('the company', a surprisingly convivial word for Wittgenstein) so I suppose he remained on friendly terms with a larger group. All memorialists agree that he never attended the regular meetings of the Circle.

It is worthwhile giving some detail of these contacts before 1929 because they have not been much recorded. What we know about them illustrates too (as do the publications of the members at this time) the degree of identity of interest between Wittgenstein and the Circle and at the same time the divergence of approach. Carnap thought that Wittgenstein rapidly and intuitively took up a position and only subsequently considered how to support it. As Feigl saw it, Carnap had a machine-like mind while Wittgenstein, more intuitive (that word again), objected to the request for intermediate steps and thought Carnap unable to get from A to B. (Moore, we know, incurred a similar criticism.)

11 In August 1927 Schlick writes about small Monday evening meetings (which he hoped to see resumed in November), *WVC*, p. 16.
12 Wittgenstein seems to have attended the first of two lectures, that on 'Mathematik, Wissenschaft und Sprache', subsequently printed in *Monatshefte für Mathematik und Physik*, 39 (1929), 153–64.
13 So Ramsey, speaking of the past, in a letter to E. Fraenkel of 26 January 1928, of which we have the draft.
14 Becker 1927, p. 286–7, but this may be on the basis of the *Tractatus* alone.

Still, Wittgenstein talked to them about 'their' topics – some we have listed, another was probability, a special interest of Feigl's and Waismann's – but he also spoke about themes of his own and in his own way, harking back to the more general lessons of *Tractatus*. He told Feigl, for example, that it was necessary to get rid of metaphysics in order to make room for *den Ernst des Lebens*, the seriousness of life. Deep commitment was required, not rational justification, and whoever had the former (Feigl later thought this meant, whoever had a strong superego) would not worry his head about the existence of the world or the ultimate substance of it. Nor indeed were the problems internal to natural science of real importance, *Kümmert euch nicht um den Lärm im Haus der Wissenschafter*! ('Don't concern yourself about the noise in the scientists' house!' – as if it were 'the neighbours'). And there were comments also, as we see later in the Waismann notes,[15] on more topical matters: he told Feigl of the shock that he had felt as an Austrian at the end of the First World War (then not yet First unless one were very pessimistic) and the distaste he had felt for the Mephistophelean attitude in such matters, the cynicism and sarcasm, of the Jews and half-Jews.[16] (This is one of the straws in the wind showing that his admiration for Karl Kraus was seriously qualified after the war.) The friendship with Feigl went so far that Wittgenstein dined with Feigl's parents: not a great success, Feigl felt, this dinner in the large house of an industrialist: too much like home, we may suppose.

I have not spoken in detail of Waismann. By 1929 he was already developing Wittgenstein's ideas on probability and had undertaken to produce the volume *Logik, Sprache, Philosophie* as a kind of summa wittgensteiniana.[17] He became almost too identified with Wittgenstein for our purposes here and his future relations with Wittgenstein, ultimately a sad story on both sides, are an instance of the difficulties of personal relationship to which these two were perhaps more sensitive than it is comfortable for men to be. My theme here is how the same difficulty was felt by Wittgenstein, and (perhaps more surprisingly) evoked by him in others, in less intimate relationships.

Waismann apart, our intention has been to show that the ideas of Wittgenstein fitted and at the same time did not fit into the pattern of the

---

15 *WVC*, p. 142 has remarks, anything but those of a bien pensant, on America and Russia.

16 That the Wittgensteins had Jewish blood was of course no secret in Vienna: Neurath, we shall see, refers to it, and Menger too, though, for what it was worth, he thought the style of the family more like that of rich non-Jews among his acquaintance.

17 The book appeared posthumously, as *Principles of Linguistic Philosophy*, 1965, an editor's title, chosen to suit the taste of a later epoch. The original title and a certain amount of earlier waismanno-wittgensteinian material are restored in the German edition, 1976.

Schlick Circle. Their articles and books, starting with Carnap's *Aufbau*,[18] testify to the influence of his ideas – on the general approach more than in the development of details – and they were generally (we shall have to refer to one exception) generous enough in acknowledging their indebtedness, as, notably, in their *Sendbrief* or 'Epistle to the Learned World', *Wissenschaftliche Weltauffassung*.[19] He did not approve of this publication, but that is another matter: our concern here is with their recognition of indebtedness to him.

We are arrived at the point where the contradictions in the Schlick Circle's reception of Wittgenstein can be summed up: in a brilliant book he set them on the secure path of a programme of clarification, both in the sense of ridding the edifice of science (in the wide acceptation of the term) of much lumber and also in that of rendering intelligible and ordered the structure that remained. For this, he in part provided them with the tools but much more certainly he gave them the final orientation that they needed. This is, remember, a point about reception. Even if you think (as I do not) that they might have better obtained their orientation elsewhere or that they themselves already possessed the nub of it, they then did not see the matter so. But at the same time, they gave Wittgenstein a special status. There was a sense of a further or a wider vision on his part. He could be an arbiter of taste, of judgement, of conduct even. At any rate he was a guarantee that they were still in touch with the world of values and of culture (when they are paired this seems the correct order) which they earnestly hoped not to sacrifice on the altar of modernity. He represented their old gods and personified the variety of their city itself. In so far as they were a Vienna Circle (as which they trod the world stage) and not the Schlick Circle (as they more commonly styled themselves) or the Ernst Mach Verein (a legal entity), he was Vienna – or, like his own building in the Kundmanngasse,[20] a modern house of perfect taste in that baroque city, a bridge between past and future.

And yet, there was an underlying reaction like that of Harvard to Russell:[21]

---

18 Carnap 1967.
19 Wienerkreis 1929: The Vienna Circle itself ('Der Wiener Kreis') is given as author. Translation ('The Scientific Conception of the World') in O. Neurath 1973, pp. 299–318.
20 Interesting that Carnap was enormously impressed when another member of the Circle took him to see the house (as Rudolf Haller kindly told me from his reading of the Carnap Diaries).
21 Expressed in T.S. Eliot's 'Mr. Apollinax', which I may be forgiven for quoting yet again.

'He is a charming man.' – 'But after all what did he mean?
… He must be unbalanced.'

One member whom I have not yet mentioned would constantly quote to the others the dubious propositions of the *Tractatus*:

The sense of the world must lie outside the world.
Not how the world is the mystical but that it is.
There is indeed the inexpressible. This evinces itself; it is the mystical.

(6.41, 6.44, 6.522)

We can still imagine how these would have sounded in Neurath's mouth – the Argus of the Circle, Menger calls him (it is Menger's report, and indeed translation, that I follow above), but other classical parallels might be Cleon or Thersites. Neurath was at least consistent. He never fell under Wittgenstein's spell. He recognized Wittgenstein's contributions, to be sure, as we can see from his 1931 article on 'Physicalism',[22] which opens with a handsome statement of the indebtedness of the new movement of 'Logical Empiricism' to Wittgenstein and the *Tractatus*, but he could not read *die Angelsätze des Traktats*, its cardinal propositions, without *Erschütterung*, without being shocked, and regrets that Schlick 'is probably not aware of the degree of metaphysics that there still is, as far as one can see, even in the new Wittgenstein' (*wahrscheinlich sich nicht über das Mass von Metaphysik im reinen ist, das, wie es scheint, selbst im erneuerten Wittgenstein steckt*).[23]

And there are many such remarks in his correspondence. The clear-sightedness is that of the politician. Wittgenstein was not a joiner, he would not adapt himself to the demands of party, he would not subscribe to a programme. As we know, Neurath's was almost as much a political as a philosophical programme: *hinc illae lacrimae*, hence too perhaps some of the party spirit that is still with us. There was matter for regret here:

'What a nice life (Neurath says) Wittgenstein could have among us, as one of us. He'd be so spoilt. No? Instead of which he is the God and Waismann is his unhappy prophet.'
'Wie nett könnte Wittgenstein unter uns leben, wie einer von uns. Er wäre so verwöhnt werden. Gel? Statt dessen ist der der Gott und Waismann sein armer Prophet'.[24]

---

22 Neurath 1931, pp. 297–303, see Neurath 1983, pp. 52–7.
23 Letter to Carnap of 27 July 1932. Neurath's letters are in the Carnap Collection at the University of Pittsburgh Library, to which I am once again indebted for permission to quote.
24 Letter to Carnap of 20 August 1932.

and he goes on to other mockery such as one finds in a personal letter and from which a certain low pleasure, not to our purpose here, may be derived. The same letter, an expression of solidarity with Carnap in the priority dispute to which we shall shortly refer, shows how Neurath reacted to that atmosphere of superiority about Wittgenstein, which had its fascination for some of the Schlick Circle. Wittgenstein cites no one himself but cannot take it in the long run – 'aristocratic' natures are like that, *'was alles durch die jüdische Abkunft noch einen besonderen Schmelz erhält'* ('to which a special gloss is added by his Jewish origin').

The letter as a whole is reminiscent of some modern critics who say that Wittgenstein 'ought to have been' more receptive of (e.g.) his Jewishness, which is the same as to say he 'ought to have been' a different person. (There is a similar controversy about Pasternak.) Here Neurath toys with the idea that Wittgenstein might have been a good party man, an idle thought, because Wittgenstein wanted to use the sort of discussions that he and the Circle were involved in for the attainment of a different sort of result.

Neurath however took the coincidence in themes treated (partial only, as we shall see) as evidence that the 'other party' (Wittgenstein, Waismann, and quaere Schlick) were coming round *quasi ab ipsa veritate coacti* (as if the truth itself were compelling them) to the correct view. Waismann's production of a book by constant reformulation of *rätselhafte Thesen*, puzzling theses, continually brought to birth by Wittgenstein was indeed a curious method of producing a book:

> But everything has to be different for members of a sect. The important thing is that their sectarian doctrine is coming closer and closer to the true doctrine that we now profess.
> *Aber bei Sektierern ist alles anders. Die Hauptsache ist, dass ihre Sektenlehre sich der wahren Lehre, wie wir sie jetzt vertreten, immer mehr annähert.*[25]

So the Wittgensteinians were a sect and the Circle (with a prophet or without?) was the true church. In time the heresy deepened and the minority became in Neurath's vocabulary *'die Ich-Gruppe'* (*'Schlick ist ganz verwittgensteinert'* etc. – 'the Ego Group', 'Schlick is totally Wittgensteinified'): this was after Wittgenstein's interest turned to philosophical psychology, a most interesting shift of focus, but treated as defection by Neurath, whose own strongly a priori treatment of psychology was only a few years off.

25 Letter to Carnap of 20 May 1932.

Our task (I said or implied at the beginning) is not to take sides, but here we can see that Neurath took a side and perhaps Wittgenstein too, since he so clearly refused to enter into the Circle as a group. Between these too at least there was no love lost.

In a sense Neurath and Wittgenstein understood one another. Each knew that the other had totally different aspirations. But with Carnap, with his 'Prussian' background, it was a different story. He expected things to be done in a certain way: the way from A to B must be shown not just indicated, while if anyone suggested a connection between A and Z, that was empty talk. This, I think, was the reason why, at the Königsberg Congress, he dismissed Waismann's account of Wittgenstein's views on mathematics saying (who decided to print this remark in *Erkennntis*, I wonder?)[26] that Wittgenstein's ideas, though important, were not yet available *in einer spruchreifen Form*, were not developed to a point at which they could be discussed. The remark must contain some feeling of exclusion from the discussions in Vienna, though Carnap never admitted to such a feeling (perhaps not even to himself). It is in a way contradictory: how could the ideas be important (or be known to be important) if not yet ready for discussion? But it well illustrates Carnap's ability to grasp something only when it had passed through slow mills of discussion and elaboration (there is no denying his power in these respects).

A similar story must be told also as regards Carnap's 1932 article on physicalism.[27] Wittgenstein felt that this drew on his ideas without due acknowledgement and made this known to Carnap through Schlick. I shall not discuss the topic itself in detail but, asssuming the facts of the affair roughly known,[28] will propose some aids to understanding. Carnap, it seems to me, was temperamentally unable to see that physicalism was contained in the *Tractatus*. The identity of fact-stating language with science is affirmed there but not worked out, and the truth, the option rather, that all facts are susceptible of physicalist expression, though clear enough, might be termed implicit only.[29] (The same option is mentioned in *Der logische Aufbau*). But it is significant that

---

26 *Erkenntnis* 2, 1931, pp. 138ff.
27 Carnap 1932, translated by Max Black and revised by Carnap as *The Unity of Science*, 1934.
28 See Hintikka 1989.
29 The whole of the *Tractatus* is a demonstration that all fact-stating language falls under Hertz's description of mechanics; but see especially 4.1's and 6.3's. The implication of 'physicalism' (Wittgenstein protested at the term, perhaps simply because it was an 'ism') is perhaps clearest in 6.3751: the logic of colour statements can be seen from the form they take in physics. There were other points, notably concerning hypotheses and ostensive definition, where Wittgenstein also felt Carnap should have acknowledged indebtedness: these account for *WVC*, pp. 209–11.

Carnap was also unable to see that physicalism was contained in Neurath's *Scientia* article of 1931,[30] and so, in Neurath's view, did not make proper acknowledgement of that either.

> *Ich habe meinen Standpunkt prägnant zum Ausdruck gebracht, nicht nur als Anregung.*
> ('I gave succinct expression to my point of view. It was not just a suggestion.')

So Neurath protested, fearing that all Schlick's readers would know Carnap and Wittgenstein, while his article would be ignored. Carnap ought now to make it clear that Neurath's article was written first.[31]

Trouble in Paradise! Some amusement may be derived from the fact that Carnap in a short space received similar complaints from both Wittgenstein and Neurath, while the latter was prepared to mock Wittgenstein for his *Plagiatsorgen* (his worries over plagiarism) and his aristocratic (or non-aristocratic) attitude towards them. But it is amusement mixed with rue: 'Who but must laugh if such a man there be?' says Pope in the better version of these lines, 'Who would not weep if Atticus were he?'

These three were condemned to feel strongly (for clearly Carnap too was affronted) because they were hopelessly at odds. Wittgenstein had given the impulse (his was the *Anregung*, stimulus or suggestion), Neurath proclaimed the importance of the thing, Carnap saw the relation to the ideas of Duhem and Poincaré and began to work out the details (perhaps this is even truer of his *Logical Syntax of Language*,[32] where the idea of the formal mode also seemed to Wittgenstein a mere borrowing, insensitively applied). Each of the three was convinced that his was the really important task: differences in way of life come out.

When we look at the whole relationship with the Circle from Wittgenstein's side, we see a situation developing inevitably, but of some complexity from the start. On the one hand he originally thought that the essential task of *Tractatus* had been performed.[33] The ground rules for talking (or not talking) about language and the world, about logic, and about natural science had been sketched. There was still something needed to deal with mathematics, but that apart he wanted to move on to new areas, and in particular that of psychology (hence the *Ich-Gruppe*). Mathematics and, in a wide sense, psychology are the most obvious themes of his first writings after his return to philosophy, whether in his

---

30 See note 22 above.
31 Letter to Carnap of 8 February 1932.
32 Carnap 1937, first published as *Logische Syntax der Sprache*.
33 See for example his remarks to Waismann in *WVC*, pp. 183–4.

large numbered notebooks or in extracts from them such as the collection now styled *Philosophische Bemerkungen*.[34] Thus he was bound to be at odds with those in the Circle who wanted to exploit the findings (as it were) of *Tractatus*. The work of clarification, for Wittgenstein, had been done by showing that it could be done – hence his remark to Feigl.[35] Instead of tidying up the clearing, he went back into the wood: here one thinks particularly of his criticism of Schlick's ethics[36] and of his later work on Frazer. All this was the reverse of what they looked for from him. He had seemed (to revert to an allusion above) to come from *Glanz und Wonne*, but in fact he would have led them back to *Nacht und Leiden*.

Still, for him, as for the others, there was a positive side in their interaction. He needed discussion – at first he needed it to bring him out from the circle of the family, where his intellectual gifts were either over- or undervalued, where, certainly he had nothing to stimulate his thoughts. For it is an important feature of Wittgenstein that, while he turned his back on philosophy, he needed its type of argument and its problems in order to do so. (But perhaps he always found the facial expressions of the others hard to take.) He discussed all his life, or until near the end. At first he got some of his themes by suggestion or countersuggestion from Ramsey, from the Circle, from Sraffa; later he gave his little circle laws and dominated the discussion at the Moral Sciences Club in Cambridge (this too shocked Russell).

Inevitable that this should lead to problems about publication. Wittgenstein was constantly changing his position and could not quite arrive at the point he wanted to reach. Perhaps there were theoretical reasons for this: the aim was always to stimulate a new way of thinking, and so, by the kind of bind that occurs in various forms in his life, his task could never be complete, never reside in a written book. Plato describes this dilemma in his *Phaedrus* (itself, be it noted, a dialogue rather than a treatise, and one deliberately infused with a sense of unreality) and Plato indeed by describing the dilemma in some measure resolves it. Perhaps Wittgenstein's marvellous but frustrating bequeathal of so many not quite complete alternative books is his solution.

But to return to his pupils, his hearers, the readers of his hand-outs, or those with second-hand knowledge of what he was doing (and hence

34 This was shown to Trinity College, Cambridge, as evidence of work in progress but Wittgenstein also made such extracts as a stage in his work on the themes he was thinking about. One such (probably no. 211 in von Wright 1982) was shown to Waismann in 1931 (*WVC*, p. 166).

35 '*Kümmert Euch nicht* (etc)' above.

36 e.g. the deeper interpretation according to which 'The good is good because God commands it', see *WVC*, p. 115.

once again to the members of the Schlick Circle also), many of these were bound to feel frustrated. If they had learnt anything, it was hard not to make use of it; yet since Wittgenstein had not got to the end of the lesson, they would be doubly at fault. It was difficult not to seem to be diverting his waters (still in spate) to turn a private mill or irrigate some bordering field. If they published, they used his ideas before him (and deprived him of the credit for them), and since they published prematurely (if for no other reason) they were bound to get his ideas wrong. Contorted attempts to avoid these pitfalls are alas more numerous than successful ones – though the latter exist.

Needless to dwell on the point that there are parallels in his personal life (indeed it is difficult to divide his personal from his public life). There too the life lived in common with Wittgenstein, as a friend or in a group of friends, was demanding. No half measures were permitted, no failures in sympathy or even taste were glossed over. Yet what else, he might ask – we remember his remark, 'Of course I want to be perfect!' – was life for?

And perhaps something of this nature is especially true of philosophy. What point is there in doing it except to get something exactly right? At least this is what a man of genius (which Wittgenstein clearly in some sense was) must say, and in his case it fits with other features of his life: the rigour that required the raising of a ceiling by centimetres or the filing down of radiators by a millimetre; and the security and wealth that made such demands possible. So he must strive for an absolute originality, and any watering down of his work or use of it for the purposes of a school must be anathema. Yet since he started from a range of problems shared with others, they were likely to want to make use of him.

It is the problem of the paradigm-changer, to use Kuhn's model:[37] a problem both for the changer himself and for the normal scientist. Not just from vanity, but so as not to be misunderstood, he does not want to be treated as a contributor merely, and yet their style (though they value his originality) is to recognize contributions. Only fairly recently has philosophy functioned like a natural science: certainly that was the aspiration of many members of the Schlick Circle, and this perhaps makes Wittgenstein's predicament seem odder than it is. The loneliness of a philosopher of originality is not more unusual than such philosophers themselves. Schopenhauer and Nietzsche are only the most obvious examples, but very few of the great (it is chastening to think) learnt much from their contemporaries or juniors. What is perhaps peculiar to

37 Kuhn 1962.

Wittgenstein and made it difficult for him to be at ease with his closest followers (or for them to be so with him) is an aspect of his acute self-consciousness, namely that he always wants to take one step further, as if to have reached a standpoint would mean to have stopped doing philosophy. Waismann noted this in his attempt to write a compendium,[38] and as a general hypothesis it perhaps best explains how the Schlick Circle did get something from Wittgenstein but could not do so without, to a large extent, breaking with him.

And he? Did he still feel against philosophers that *ressentiment* which had led him to give up philosophy (so at least Schlick told Menger in 1927[39] though we must doubt some of the story)? The French word was used and Menger rightly stresses that it is stronger than some uses of the English: *'souvenir d'une injure, avec désir de s'en venger'*. Perhaps Wittgenstein did feel, with his customary intensity, that mathematicians should have learnt more from his work[40] – certainly there are signs of this in Ramsey's letters to him – but the reasons that he himself gave, earlier on, for not continuing with philosophical work were expressed to Keynes in quite other terms:

> You ask in your letter whether you could do anything to make it possible for me to return to scientific work. The answer is, No: there is nothing to be done in that way, because I myself no longer have any strong inner drive towards that sort of activity. Everything that I really *had* to say I have said, and so the spring has run dry. That sounds queer, but it's how things are.
>
> (*CL*, p. 207)

> *Nein, in dieser Sache lässt sich nichts machen; denn ich habe selbst keinen starken inneren Trieb zu solcher [einer wissenschaftlichen] Beschäftigung. Alles was ich wirklich sagen musste, habe ich gesagt und damit ist die Quelle vertrocknet.*[41]

---

38 Waismann to Schlick, quoted in *WVC*, p. 28: 'Er hat ja die wunderbare Gabe, die Dinge immer wieder wie zum erstenmal zu sehen. Aber es zeigt sich doch, meine ich, wie schwer eine gemeinsame Arbeit ist, da er eben immer wieder der Eingebung des Augenblicks folgt und das niederreisst, was er vorher entworfen hat.' (He has the marvellous gift of always seeing everything as if for the first time. But I think it's obvious how difficult any collaboration is, since he always follows the inspiration of the moment and demolishes what he has previously planned.)

39 Menger 1982, p. 88: in his memoirs Menger specifies this as *ressentiment* against mathematicians.

40 Later M.H.A. Newman was told that he (no doubt not alone among mathematicians) ought to have been strangled at birth.

41 Letter to Keynes of 4 July 1924. *CL*, pp. 205–7.

Not his talks earlier with Ramsey, nor his visit to England in 1925, but his contact with the Schlick Circle brought an end to this intellectual drought. No doubt, there were many personal reasons also, as for its setting in, so for its ceasing (we have indicated one above), but this outward stimulus was also needed. If at times the stimulus was felt as a provocation, it certainly did not lead him to turn his back on philosophy but on the contrary to try to bring something to fruition. And always thereafter his occasional decisions to give up philosophy[42] were in fact nullified by his first wanting to finish some work, which (in some ways fortunately) he never did.

---

42 One such expression of velleity (without apparent objective motive) during the 'Physikalismus' correspondence with Schlick may have added currency to the *ressentiment* account.

18

PROBABILITY

Perhaps the greatest difference between Schlick and Neurath was in their estimation of Wittgenstein. Was he the chief inspirer – almost the only begetter – of scientific philosophy in its new form? Or was he at heart a reactionary, who would preserve all the rights of metaphysics, provided it was his own metaphysics? A general answer will not be attempted here, but both attitudes may have overlooked the extent to which Wittgenstein was not a completed revelation but a questing philosopher, not a book but a man. His difficulties in working with others in the way Neurath wanted to work obscured the fact that while his main preoccupation may have been a whole philosophy of philosophy itself, he was also, and indeed as a necessary feature of this preoccupation, concerned with individual problems of philosophy, and in part with just those that – and in much the way that – they preoccupied the 'ordinary' members of the Vienna Circle. This could perhaps be shown for meaning and verification, as may emerge from other items in this collection. But here my subject is one broached in the *Tractatus*, left unresolved in the *Allgemeine Erkenntnislehre*, and then carried further in conversations with Schlick and Waismann, and finally in Wittgenstein's own manuscripts of the early 1930s, selections from which now from time to time get published, all of which are however available in the Bergen/Oxford edition.

Wittgenstein rediscovered – unprompted, so it seems – the logical definition of probability sketched by Bolzano. His formulation of it, mediated by Waismann, is the ancestor of Carnap's early account and other modern logicist accounts of the notion. The essential feature is that probability is defined in terms of logical relations already assumed as known. There is no further logical object or relation to be described and introduced: Wittgenstein's account of inference is enough also to account for probability. This of course was the reason for including a discussion of it in the *Tractatus*.

It will be remembered that Wittgenstein there defines the probability that r gives to s as the proportion of truth-grounds of r that are at the same time truth-grounds of s. Von Wright[1] points out that Wittgenstein could instead have taken the notion of the probability *simpliciter* of a proposition as fundamental, being the proportion of the truth-possibilities of a proposition that are also truth-grounds of it – thus, p and q being distinct elementary propositions, p v q has the probability *simpliciter* of 3/4. The probability that r gives to s will then be the probability simpliciter of $r.s$ divided by the probability *simpliciter* of r. Thus, p and q being elementary, p v q gives to p the probability of 2/4/3/4, quite in agreement with the circumstance that two of the three truth-grounds of p v q are also truth-grounds of p.

The case on which Wittgenstein concentrates is the probability given to s by the totality of our knowledge, call it R. Von Wright claims that if we assume R to consist of a finite set of logically independent propositions each of which is either known to be true or known to be false, and if s is neither known to be true nor known to be false, then the probability of s given R cannot be other than 1/2. This is, in fact, not completely accurate. It holds, of course, if s is elementary but if s is a truth-function of elementary propositions, its probability *simpliciter* may be other than 1/2, its probability given R may be other than its probability *simpliciter*, and its probability given R may be other than ½.[2] As an obvious consequence, variations in the bulk of our knowledge can lead to variations in the probability of s, even if we assume the bulk of our knowledge to consist of a finite set of logically independent propositions each known to be true or known to be false. Thus if p and q are elementary and neither they nor their negations occur in R, then R gives p v q the probability 3/4 (equal to its probability *simpliciter*), whereas if $R' = R{\sim}q$ then R' gives to p v q the probability 1/2.

Von Wright, then, is making the tacit assumption that s is elementary and no doubt does so because it seems that the probability of a given molecular proposition can be determined only by calculation from the probability values of its elementary propositions. But perhaps the typical situation, when a probability estimate is being made, is that the analysis of the proposition in question into elementary propositions is itself not clear. It will not be possible to explore this suggestion here.

What von Wright wished to show with the help of this assumption was that Wittgenstein *had* to suppose the bulk of our knowledge to contain, alongside elementary propositions and their negations, disjunctions of elementary propositions and negations thereof, such disjunctions being known to be true without the truth of any of their disjuncts being known.

1 Von Wright 1969. The bulk of the present paper was written for a review of von Wright's philosophy.
2 Von Wright has since accommodated this point in his exposition.

Such a supposition is undoubtedly implicit in Wittgenstein's discussion of probability, even if not theoretically necessary in quite the way von Wright suggests. The supposition is not altogether unproblematic for Wittgenstein; von Wright hints as much but does not attempt a more general interpretation of the *Tractatus* than is necessary for his immediate purpose.

The difficulty arises from the doctrine expressed in the 5.1's of the *Tractatus* (which discuss probability as a special case of inference), that the events of the future cannot be inferred from those of the present and that no future action (and by parity of reasoning no future event) can be known in advance. If I can *know* a disjunction such as ~p v q, there seems to be no theoretical reason why p should not describe an event known to have occurred and q a future event known in consequence.

Still, as von Wright points out, Wittgenstein does appear to allow some knowledge of disjunctions, consequences, it seems, of 'the laws of nature assumed as hypotheses'. We need not force him to say that these actually are known, since he explicitly calls them hypothetical: everything proceeds *as if* they were known. Thus suppose that P is a description of all the forces acting on a material particle at a given time and that the laws of mechanics allow us to predict the exact position of the particle at a certain later time, i.e. yield an ungeneralized proposition of the form $P \rightarrow q$, then on the basis of this piece of knowledge and these laws assumed hypothetically, we may say that q is certain, or that we know that q, or that P together with the laws of mechanics gives q the probability 1.[3] This is the limiting case of probability, Wittgenstein says, for of course it is an ideal – we never know all the forces acting on a body, nor do we know all about the laws of mechanics. If a man falls from an aeroplane, it is overwhelmingly probable that he will kill himself, but not certain. If a partition between two gases is removed, it is overwhelmingly probable that they will mix, but not certain. (The example is deliberately drawn from the works of Boltzmann,[4] an early influence on Wittgenstein.)

If we now consider a typical case of a judgement of probability – say that a die is as likely to fall with an even as with an odd number uppermost – we assume hypothetically that the laws of mechanics will govern the path of the die from its first shaking to its final rest. These laws we roughly know, but we are aware that in their application to the path of

---

3 This accords, I think, with Miss Anscombe's interpretation of *Tractatus* 4.464 and 5.525: 'The certainty of a situation is expressed not by a proposition but by an expression's being a tautology etc.' It is not the tautology itself that is 'known' or 'certain', (see 5.1362), but one or more propositions can make another certain or enable us to know it, and this is expressed by a tautology. See Anscombe 1959, pp. 155ff.
4 See, for example, Boltzmann 1905, p. 36 (1974, p. 17).

the die they will be modified by special respects in which the material used differs from the rigid bodies of theory, as for example the nature of the surfaces of the die, the dice-box, and the table. These special respects are tantamount to a further set of laws to which these particular objects are subject. Also we do not know the initial position of the die, the configuration of the shaking to which it is subjected, the impetus with which it is cast, all of which (together with the general and special laws assumed hypothetically) would be enough to determine the face that would fall uppermost. If we could know all these things (in the sense of knowledge which includes hypothesis), we should be certain of the result. As it is, we know only certain very general features of the relevant laws – for example that they are indifferent to which number is initially uppermost. Whichever number that may be, there are an equal number of paths to any of the six possible results. Naturally, on a particular occasion the shaking, the cast, the frictional properties of the substances in use etc. make it scientifically necessary that a certain result should in fact eventuate. But here again there are an equal number of possibilities for each alternative, and there is nothing in the antecedents to favour one result. The shakings that lead to a six would not form a recognizable group, reproducible because subject to muscular control, even if all other factors could be held constant. (I am aware, of course, that these are substantial claims.) In short, and in Wittgenstein's own terms,

> What I am aware of in probability propositions are certain general properties of the ungeneralized propositions of natural science, as for example their symmetry in certain respects and their asymmetry in others, etc.[5]

The ungeneralized propositions referred to here correspond to the various paths I have mentioned above, and we know that the ungeneralized propositions are symmetrical in this case, or in other words that the possible paths are equally divided, because of our knowledge, all incomplete as it is, of the laws of nature:

> I cannot say before drawing whether I shall get a white ball or a black one, since I do not know the laws of nature accurately enough for that. But this much I do know: that if there are equally many black and white balls, then the number of black balls drawn will approach the number of white as drawing continues. My knowledge of the laws of nature is accurate enough for that.

---

5 This passage and the one quoted immediately below are taken from *Nb* for 8 and 9.11.14.

The example is different, but the principle the same, and it seems legitimate in this case to use the *Notebooks* to interpret the *Tractatus*: they explain in what way the probability proposition can be regarded as a sort of excerpt from other propositions (*Tractatus* 5.156). Max Black implies the same interpretation when he says[6] that we are strongly inclined to believe we can 'see' that the propositions describing the various drawings from Wittgenstein's urn have the same logical form.

How can this inclination be supported by sound argument?, Black asks. Have we not here 'the ancient puzzle of how to choose "equiprobable alternatives" or "equally likely cases" in disguise'? Black's doubts are fundamental ones, because (as von Wright points out) the distinguishing feature of the logical definition of probability is that the requirement of equipossibility is *not* worked into the distinction of truth-possibilities. If we had to be able to assign equal possibility to a number of cases in order to reach any judgement of probability, then such judgements would involve a logical constant over and above those involved in tautological inference, and Wittgenstein's main problem would not have been solved.

Black seems to ask too much here. There is bound to be some assumption about the world in any concrete assignment of probability. Wittgenstein locates this assumption not in any direct judgement of likelihood but in the nature of the demands that we make of any framework for describing the world. If we made no demands, and hence had no general assumptions about the course that events would follow, then we should be able to assign to a proposition only a probability corresponding to the number of lines in its truth-table that verified it: probability would simply be the measure of intrinsic nearness to tautology or remoteness from contradiction. But it seems that this is an impossible supposition: we are bound to try to view the world and to describe it economically by the use of some network or other. (The metaphor is developed by Wittgenstein in the propositions 6.3 ff. etc of the *Tractatus*.) The employment of one network rather than another is equivalent to the assumption that the laws of nature (to be assumed as hypotheses) will have one form and not another. Thus for example we might assume that there were causal laws (6.32–6.321), or we might make the yet more restrictive assumption that all phenomena were somehow to be brought under the laws of mechanics (6.343). It is also possible to allow for different forms of laws in different areas (corresponding in the metaphor to a network made up of a mixture of triangles and hexagons – 6.342), but for our present purposes we can ignore that. To apply this general view of science to our present case: as long as we are resolved to assume that the

6 Black 1964, p. 257.

movement of a die is governed by the laws of mechanics, for so long will there be from any arbitrary initial position, no more and no fewer paths by which six could be reached than any other single number, always granted that the die is true (in the sense of symmetrically constructed) and that the properties of the various surfaces are likewise indifferent. Here we know something about the laws of nature involved, namely that they are indifferent to what result will ensue. We are not, therefore, advocating a Principle of Indifference based on ignorance. *Pace* Black, Wittgenstein does not have to meet 'the devastating battery of objections directed by Keynes and others against it'.[7]

We do not, therefore, need a specific assumption of equipossibility: equipossibility (or some other assignment of initial probabilities) is given us in practice by the sort of laws we assume to hold in the relevant area (say in dice playing). We cannot then ask, But *are* these alternatives equally possible?, since 'equally possible' means the same as 'being neither favoured nor frowned on by any law of a type known or conjectured by us, such laws being adequate (all circumstances being given) to account for any particular result'. We can indeed ask, Are the laws known or conjectured by us adequate?, and that will have to be answered by the three tests of a picture of the world mentioned by Hertz: Is it logically admissible? Is it true to the facts? Is it serviceable?[8]

Questions of this sort can be seen to arise when the observed frequencies disagree with the predicted probability. It is, of course, not altogether easy to determine when this has happened. At 5.154 Wittgenstein imagines an experiment concerning the probability of drawing balls from an urn. This is envisaged as successful, but had there been divergence from the expected probability, it is clear that some circumstance (some individual fact or some law) to account for that would have to be supposed to exist. To avoid some complications arising from the diminishing number of balls in the urn, let us take our example of the die. At what point do we say that the frequency of 6's diverges sufficiently from the norm for us to alter either our estimate of this die or our calculations about dice in general? Obviously we can and must tolerate some divergence from a frequency of one six in every six throws, but there is no definite answer how much. It depends on our purposes and our convenience. If we

---

7 A prominent objector, much cited by Keynes, was J. von Kries. It is quite possible that his work was known to Wittgenstein either through conversation with Keynes or through reading of Boltzmann. But von Wright's conjecture that the notion of *Spielraum* was drawn from von Kries is out of place, since Wittgenstein does not in fact use this notion in connection with probability, that application being made by Waismann.

8 Hertz 1956, pp. 1–3: for an account of the parallels between Hertz and Wittgenstein see Griffin 1964, pp. 99–108.

wanted a die to produce the equivalent of a set of random numbers, we might reject out of hand one that produced 10 or 15 consecutive 6's in favour of another. A manufacturer of dice for the same purpose, on the other hand, might be very reluctant to accept such a run as proof of false- ness, if for example the die were by all obvious tests a true one. It depends too on the alternatives available: is it just this die that is biased towards 6's? or any die thrown by this person? or finally is it to be supposed that all dice are so biased? The last possibility demands such changes in our conception of nature that it will scarcely be entertained. It is much more attractive, as long as the complications do not themselves become unattractive, to assume that there is something peculiar about this die or this thrower.

In these and similar ways, the experiment, if it reveals a divergence, will leave us with 'the choice between attributing the frequency observed to chance and to some further law to be assumed'. Von Wright – for it is his words I am citing here – regards this as a valuable insight of Wittgenstein's. He argues, however, that it makes Wittgenstein's defini- tion superfluous as a method for computing probability-values. If an unknown law can readily be conjectured in order that the calculated probability may match the observed frequency, then we are in fact not using the laws of nature to calculate the probability but are moving directly to it from the observation of a frequency.[9]

Now it is true that the observation of actual frequencies is the only way in which current experience can affect our acceptance of a probability judgement, and for that reason it seems to correspond to the verifica- tion or falsification of that judgement. There was thus a strong tempta- tion in the early thirties to explain the meaning of probability judgements in terms of such observation. To some extent Wittgenstein was affected by this temptation.[10] But is it clear that this forces us to abandon the definition of probability given in the *Tractatus*? It seems rather, as von Wright points out (1969 p. 273), that the definition helps to show that it is not legitimate to make any inference about probability from the mere fact of an observed frequency. The proposition concern- ing the future whose probability we wish to assess will in general be independent of those propositions descriptive of the past that come into a report of observed frequency. To affect its probability, therefore, we need to add to the bulk of our knowledge some hypothesis inspired, perhaps, by an observed frequency, but not identical with a statement of that observed frequency.

9 Von Wright 1969, pp. 275–6.
10 I will not discuss here the shift from the logical to the epistemological pole in Wittgenstein's thinking which von Wright describes convincingly.

Von Wright, to whom this is perfectly clear, suggests that what the observation on frequencies can inspire is precisely an hypothesis about probability values. The definition will then become otiose in the following way: it purports to define the probability of a proposition as the ratio of the truth-grounds of the bulk of our knowledge that are also truth-grounds of the proposition in question. If this is to be an adequate definition, the bulk of our knowledge cannot itself include probability statements; but in practice that is precisely what the operative part of the bulk of our knowledge will consist of.

Now in a trivial sense any laws or hypotheses from which a statement of probability can be inferred will themselves be laws of probability or 'probability hypotheses'. This appears to be the sense of a passage quoted by von Wright from *Philosophical Remarks*:

> The laws of probability, i.e. those on which the calculation [of probability] is *based*, are hypothetical assumptions, which are subsequently dissected by calculation and, in altered form, confirmed – or refuted – by experience.[11]

Obviously this is no objection to a logical theory of probability, for the point of such a theory is that there will be no more content in a judgement of probability than there is in the hypotheses on which it is based.

Von Wright's doubts have their origin elsewhere: he notes that Wittgenstein, who initially supposed that probability was calculated by considering the laws of nature and how they applied to the proposition in question, also or eventually held that the resulting statement of probability was to be checked by means of statistical observation with a view to possible revision of the laws of nature assumed. This leads von Wright to ask, in effect: Is it perhaps not the laws that determine the probability but rather the observed frequency that dictates what laws are to be assumed? To be sure, von Wright puts this by saying that 'it is no longer the measures of the sets of truth-grounds which *determine* the probabilities [but] the hypothetically assumed probabilities which now determine (hypothetically) the measures of the ranges',[12] but this way of putting it, though rhetorically effective, corresponds to nothing real. Logically speaking, a ratio of measures (in the present paper: a truth-ground ratio) is *identical with* the probability conferred on one proposition by another. In the order of discovery, von Wright would not suggest that an assumption of probability itself comes first. His point is that the calculation of probability starts

---

11 *PhR*, p. 290, quoted in von Wright 1969, l.c.
12 The notion of measure introduced by Waismann is not essential to the argument of the present paper.

from an observed frequency, not as Wittgenstein suggests from a set of laws of nature.

A superficial answer to von Wright would be to say that while the observed frequency does indeed inspire the hypotheses from which probability is calculated, nonetheless, as he himself points out, something more than a statement of observed frequency is needed to yield a statement of the probability form. The least advance on an observed frequency that will serve for this purpose is a statistical hypothesis, the elevation of the observed frequency into a law. The probability statement will then run: The circumstances known to us, including the statistical laws that experience recommends, give to such and such an event the probability p. Wittgenstein's hypothetical laws of nature have been replaced by statistical laws, likewise hypothetical, the experimental testing and the inspiration of probability statements have been assimilated to one another, and the calculation of further probabilities from those so assigned can proceed according to classical methods.

This suggestion amounts to treating a statement of relative frequency as the only, or the chief relevant, law of nature from which initial probabilities are calculated. Von Wright[13] is justly reluctant to adopt this method of harmonizing the various statements of Wittgenstein about probability. There are difficulties of principle about the suggestion – so that if Wittgenstein did adopt it, his views would be open to criticism and, so far forth, would not work. And there are exegetical difficulties – that is to say the suggestion is hard to reconcile even with the surface meaning of what Wittgenstein says. The difficulty of principle arises because (if there is any continuity with the *Tractatus* in the writings of the 1930s) Wittgenstein's aim is to exhibit probability statements as a way of showing a certain relation between the logical forms of statements that are themselves unproblematic – or relatively so. Typically, as we have seen, this will be between a prediction and a set of observation statements and laws of nature. Now a law of nature will be a general hypothetical or disjunction with clear implications for observation. A statement of relative frequency, however, in the sense of a statistical law, can have no such simple relation to observation. We could proceed to observe any frequency whatsoever and still maintain that our hypothetical statistical law was not refuted, since the statistical law contains no stipulation of the time within which the observed frequency has to approach the predicted one. In other words, statistical laws behave, as regards verification and falsification, exactly like judgements of probability. When we enounce a statistical law

---

13 See the reported discussion after his paper (von Wright 1969, p. 281), where he describes the use of the term 'laws' for statistical laws as a piece of mystification.

we are not saying what *will* happen within a specified time but what it is *reasonable to expect* to happen. It is of no use to introduce that notion to explain what probability is, since it itself is what requires explanation. Or, to put it in terms of the problematic of the *Tractatus*, a probability value will be part of the content of our hypotheses, so that probability will not be explicable as a certain pattern of other logical relations but will be a primitive notion. (*This* is why von Wright says – and regards it as an objection to Wittgenstein – that what observation inspires is precisely an hypothesis about probability values. The objection is an important one, even though the passage from *Philosophical Remarks* by which he supports it has a different *portée*, as explained above.)[14]

This difficulty of principle can be put in another and more acute form. It is not for nothing that Wittgenstein in the *Tractatus* wants to exhibit probability as a form of logical relationship between propositions. The alternative is to suppose that there is such a thing as probability *in rerum natura*. But just as there is no causal nexus (*Tractatus* 5.136) so there is no *tendency* in things, no tendency, say, to fall out a certain way in 57.8 per cent of all cases on average. One way of becoming clear about this is to see that nothing will count as evidence that there is such a tendency. From an observed frequency, we can indeed predict inductively that the same frequency will prevail over the next *n* cases. But we are never in a position to say within any show of reason that the observed frequencies entitle us to disregard a particular run and call it chance. By parity of reasoning we must adjust our inductive prediction with every one of those *n* cases. This is why Wittgenstein says:

> If we draw inferences from the relative frequency of an event about its relative frequency in the future, we can do so, of course, only in accordance with the frequency actually observed so far, and not in accordance with a frequency obtained from the observed one by some process for calculating probabilities.[15]

If frequency is what we rely on, we are at the mercy of frequency, and we can never arrive at a statement that will allow for a temporary divergence from the 'real' probability.

Probability is essentially something from which the course of events can diverge: and they clearly cannot diverge from their own actual course. Is there then such a thing as probability? According to Wittgenstein, there is – only not as a feature of the world, but as a feature of our system of

14 See footnote 10 above and text.
15 *PhG*, p. 234 (= *PhR*, p. 292).

description. It is not a tendency in things that enables us to disregard a particular run – for that would involve the arbitrary preference of a shorter statistical series to a longer one – but a picture of the world to which we are independently committed. The world-picture is subject to revision in the light of experience, including the statistical results in question, but it does not have to fluctuate with every trough and crest in the series. The concept of probability, as we have it, exists because there is a tension between the a priori expectation and the frequencies we can observe.

These two elements – the a priori and the a posteriori – make their appearance in the last paragraphs of the section on probability in *Philosophical Remarks*:

> What does it mean to determine that two possibilities have the same probability?
> Does it not mean, first, that neither of the two possibilities is preferred by the laws of nature known to us and, second, that the relative frequencies of the two events approximate to one another in certain circumstances?[16]

No matter that the formulation is crude: the presence of the two elements is clear enough – and it is naturally enough a central feature of Waismann's 1929 paper, which professedly and actually developed Wittgenstein's ideas.[17] In his conversations with Schlick and Waismann Wittgenstein discusses the procedure of postulating further causes to make the relative probability agree with the probability a priori and insists that 'the further circumstances that we introduce ought not to have the character of assumptions invented *ad hoc*'.[18]

In practice this last demand means that we do not speak of an above-chance probability, for example of a clairvoyant's being right about the pips on a card unless we are prepared to suppose that in certain physical conditions the number or the gestalt of the pips has some effect (perhaps an ambiguous effect) on her. Some half-way plausible story must be envisaged if there is to be an assertion of probability at all. It should be noted that this is not a recommendation of Wittgenstein's about how to talk or what sorts of demands one ought to make before introducing the word probability. It would indeed be reasonable to make such a recommendation about what sort of predictions to rely on. The point here, however, is

16 *PhR*, p. 297.
17 See Waismann 1930, reprinted in Waismann 1973. English translation in Waismann 1978.
18 *WVC*, p. 95 (conversation of 5 January 1930).

a logical one: a statement can be a statement of probability only if it has some independent basis in our picture of the world, some anchorage which makes it resistant for the time being to the fluctuations of frequency.

The criterion is a vague one: clearly it prevents us from saying, immediately we observe a relative frequency, 'The world must be such that this frequency holds', since as already observed we could then have no reason not to alter the probability the moment a variation in the proposed frequency appeared. But how much of a story and how well supported a one is demanded? Vagueness here is in one respect no disadvantage. Obviously assignments of initial probabilities in different areas can be variously supported and can differ in degree of reliability. There are however some areas where our information is a mixture of statistical data and reasonable expectations and in these it is not easy to see how Wittgenstein's criterion applies or whether (in consequence) we can properly speak of probability at all. The prime example here (it is his own) is mortality statistics, as used by insurance companies. The a priori probability available to us is of slender importance: we know something about the usual causes of death. Assuming no reason for them to increase in virulence, we suppose that there are changes in the human body as it gets older which increase the number of ways in which each of these agencies can produce death (more briefly put, resistance to each cause of death decreases with age). But whether these agencies will increase in virulence in a particular period, for reasons of famine, pestilence, or war, we often cannot say. This suggests a fairly simple age-pyramid – or different ones for men and for women, since the aging process is obviously different in the two sexes. But there are very general considerations: and there is very little reason to expect a particular height for the pyramid or a particular direction of difference in longevity between men and women. We can imagine physiological theories that would allow a shape other than pyramidal – say theories allowing for a climacteric. It is possible to accommodate our theories to the statistics, and this may indeed prove a fruitful source of ideas for research into cellular structure or other phenomena associated with aging. But just by themselves, and if they have no purpose except to fit the statistics, such theories are (as in the present paper) the merest vapourings. They would not alter by a tittle the odds that a person knowing the statistics would be prepared to accept.

It seems then (and practice agrees with this) that in these cases it is simply the observed frequency that determines the assignments of a probability value. In the conversation referred to above Wittgenstein drew the conclusion 'Here it is a matter of probability *a posteriori*. There is no connection with probability [sc. with probability proper]'.[19]

19 To this remark Waismann appended a mark of interrogation. Much of this conversation may have been intended as criticism of Waismann's paper, which was delivered in 1929.

An insurance company, according to this view, obtains the 'probability' that a 40-year old man will live to be 60 purely by induction from the number known to have survived for so long (Wittgenstein does not specify over what period). This is a prophecy of what will happen 'over the next ten or seventy years' and is straightforwardly verified or falsified by the way things actually turn out.

Very little, I believe, speaks against the above account as an interpretation of Wittgenstein. It is the general tendency of his remarks in the three sources from the early 1930s (*Philosophical Remarks*, *Philosophical Grammar*, *Wittgenstein and the Vienna Circle*) though a little obscured by an allusion (not followed up) which appears to make the gambler parallel to the insurance company.[20]

More doubt will be felt about the truth of the account. It is a bold claim that no amount of statistical evidence can alone provide a basis for judgements of probability. It is a nice distinction which allows that we have inductive grounds for expecting k per cent of men now aged 40 to die in the next twenty years but refuses to admit that such a man has a probability $= 100-k/100$ of living to be 60. Both claim and distinction, however, rest on an insight and a conviction which have (like Wittgenstein's whole doctrine of probability on von Wright's account) both a logical and an epistemological aspect. The epistemological point is that no more can be drawn from statistical data than they contain: you cannot combine two statistical probabilities to obtain a third without some grounds for assuming independence in respect of the relevant properties, but these grounds will either consist in an a priori theory (contrary to hypothesis) or rest on a further statistical observation, which would of itself serve to establish the third statistical probability. The logical point is a deeper one, and explains some of the obliquity with which the epistemological point has been expressed: a statement of probability must place a proposition against a background taken for granted and say of the proposition, not indeed that it is true, but that it is a reasonable expectation (up to a certain degree). In order to utter a statement of probability, therefore, we must posit some such background; and the word 'posit' is chosen because the background is fixed and the expected frequency (in cases of recurring phenomena) is derived from it. If the background were to alter immediately with the observed frequency, then there would be in effect an immediate inference from observed to expected frequency and the calculation of probability would indeed be an idle step in the inference.

---

20 *PhG*, pp. 23–5. On my interpretation of Wittgenstein, the gambler, in contrast with the insurance company, is guided by a priori probabilities. Perhaps there are different kinds of gambler.

It will not be argued here that Wittgenstein was successful either in excluding purely statistical reasoning from the realm of probability or in showing that reasoning about probability was only apparently statistical. Either task is difficult and this perhaps accounts both for the indecisiveness of Wittgenstein's pronouncements in the early 1930s and for his not returning to the precise subject in his later work.[21] The purpose of this paper is to suggest that the logical definition of probability advanced by Wittgenstein was on the one hand an ingenious answer to a relatively isolated problem, but also rested on a fundamental insight or tenet of Wittgenstein's. The insight I have in mind remained with him in some form or other throughout his philosophic life. At the time of the *Tractatus* it is to be seen in his view of the most general propositions of science as a network that, once elected, determines our description of the world. The network imports necessary propositions and inferences which logic alone would not suffice to produce. At the end of his life, in *On Certainty*, it reappears in his notion of a world-picture, which embodies the way of life of a community: such a world-picture too, like the network of the *Tractatus*, issues in certainties that are not those of logic.[22]

It follows also, I think, even though Wittgenstein's 'solution' of this problem was certainly not the last word on it, that he had it in him to be a philosopher both in Schlick's and in Neurath's understanding of that word. In which role he was (let alone, would have been) greater, it is hard to say.

---

21 The probability mentioned in *PhI* §§ 482 and 484 is the probability of an hypothesis, and so, according to Wittgenstein, something totally distinct from that in question in the present discussion.

22 Some parallels between *On Certainty* and the *Tractatus* are drawn in Chapter 21 of the present collection.

19

PHILOSOPHY OF LANGUAGE AND PHILOSOPHY OF MIND

The concentration of philosophy upon language is not a phenomenon confined to the analytic philosophy of the Anglo-Saxon world, but it is very marked in that world. So much so that the main part of philosophy now is the philosophy of language, so called. In some ways this is natural enough. Philosophy must above all be a criticism of thought, of culture, of all the sciences. At present it conducts that criticism by studying their language. Being a critical activity, it must also be self-critical: this is a tradition going back to the ancients and grounded in the fact that philosophy is an ultimate activity – there is nothing further to be a critique of it. Thus at present and in that environment, the self-criticism of philosophy takes the form of philosophy of language.

It will become apparent that in my opinion there is a false emphasis, or false exclusiveness here.

The idea of a philosophy of language can be traced back to Herder, if not beyond. The whole tendency made itself felt in writings such as those of Mauthner and circles of language-fanciers (the first practitioners of linguistics) in various countries around the turn of the century. This was also the period of artificial languages, and of projects of world-citizenship of Volapuk and Ido, of Zamenhof and Count Koudenhove Kallergi. In our tradition, however, the original work professing to treat philosophy as a critique of language was Wittgenstein's *Tractatus Logico-Philosophicus*. The need for this work arose from the difficulty then justly felt of explaining the interrelationship of logic and mathematics on the one hand and natural science on the other.

While the *Tractatus* did propound a new analysis of logico-mathematical 'propositions' and also propositions of natural science, this did not exhaust its aim. It was intended also to exclude from these two realms both metaphysical statements and reflections about human life, religion, or aesthetics. Metaphysical statements were nonsensical. They were attempts to *say* what could only be shown. They tried to express in normal fact-stating propositions the nature of reality or of language. For this the *Tractatus* left no room at all. For ethics and religion, which equally could not be expressed in factual propositions, there was the alternative of letting these things be shown. The inexpressible might have – indeed must have – an important influence on our life, but its nature would be distorted and it itself misunderstood if the attempt were made to clothe it in fact-stating, i.e. pseudo-scientific, propositions.

The Vienna Circle of the 1920s and 1930s – the first heirs of the *Tractatus* – accepted gladly its rejection of metaphysics; they were happy to consider philosophy as devoted to improving the diagnosis of the special position of logic and mathematics and to analysing the various propositions and principles of natural science. They differed from Wittgenstein (while thinking they were following him) in supposing that the idea was that ethics and religion should be replaced by scientific disciplines treating the same subject matter. In this they were missing what Wittgenstein described as the main point of his book.

But I will spend no longer on their praise – or what they thought to be praise – of his book. I will only remind the reader that their attitudes determined a considerable part of analytic philosophy for the next fifty years – especially in America, where the influence of the Vienna Circle was greatest.

I turn, instead, to the criticism that they made of the *Tractatus*. I have referred to its paradoxical character, and it was this that they (not very surprisingly) failed to appreciate fully. The paradox was that while denying the possibility of metaphysics, and of all description of the relations between language and the world, it itself consisted of a lengthy description of those relations. I will illustrate this later, pointing out that Wittgenstein himself resolves or attempts to resolve the paradox by saying that the book is properly understood only by one who on reading rejects its propositions as nonsensical.

This was too much for Neurath and some other members of the Vienna Circle, who treated the propositions of the book as straightforward attempts to say something, and therefore *condemned* them as void of sense. They also rejected all references to the inexpressible or unsayable as likewise metaphysical. Here again they were not taking Wittgenstein's attitude seriously. They supposed that anything said about these areas must be of a fact-stating or else of an analytic character. They could not accept that Wittgenstein was trying to *show* that in these areas there could be no fact-stating discourse.

Now: the position of the *Tractatus* is a very difficult and paradoxical one; so one can share the frustration of Neurath and the others. At the same time it is possible – I think it is even likely – that they were missing something about the nature not only of ethics and religion but also of philosophy by itself. The questions of philosophy cannot be settled by a few definitions, leaving us free to get on with the development of ingenious logical formalizations. No. Philosophy must be (so Wittgenstein thought) a way of working through, of seeing through, a number of illusions induced by the very nature of language and thought, so that in the end we see the world properly. This means that as a result of philosophy we are enabled to carry out all our other activities – science, yes, but also ethics, poetry, life itself – in the right spirit. At the time of the *Tractatus* Wittgenstein hoped to do this at one blow – or rather he thought that just one book would be his contribution to it. *If* you could understand his book, you would have a method of dealing with the language-generated illusions that hinder our thought. Later he came to see that the human mind was always throwing up illusions of a philosophical kind. The work of demystification was never done. This is implicit in the *Tractatus* itself. Even from that book it follows that there *is* no final and adequate description of man and his place in the world. However, the book seems to be so successful in exhibiting the nature of logic and mathematics on the one hand and natural science on the other, that it might be thought to provide a model for dealing with all sorts of philosophical illusion. Now it was realized in the 1920s and 1930s that many problems remained inside mathematics and science (problems, I mean, precisely about their nature and foundations – if that word is not itself one of the philosophical illusions). Moreover, Wittgenstein himself began to see that there were many more uses of language than he had reviewed in the *Tractatus*. That work is based on the idea that description is the central function of language. There is in the *Tractatus* a brief review of propositions that seem to sin against the principle that every proposition should either be a picture or should be a truth-function of picture-like propositions (and hence itself also a picture in a sense). It seems to be assumed that all the other functions of language – to express a wish, to give an order and obey one, to tell a story, to relate a dream, to congratulate, etc., etc., are somehow definable in terms of description (i.e. of picturing). Wittgenstein points out how implausible this is at the beginning of his *Philosophical Investigations*.

But most of all Wittgenstein later began to see that he had to deal with the wrong impression that he had given in the *Tractatus* by seeming to talk of the nature of reality and the features of it that made us capable of talking about it. The criticism of metaphysics was a valid one in so far as he had not guarded himself against misunderstanding on this point. It may even be that he began to believe himself that his earlier work *was* a metaphysical one. If so, I think he was misinterpreting his own earlier self. But at all events he had failed to provide the method of dealing with all philosophical problems, which he had aspired to give.

The *Tractatus*, we have seen, seemed to provide a charter, a justification, for the pursuit of philosophy of logic and philosophy of science – difficult but unproblematic subjects, which could be tackled as technical questions if the natural sciences were studied. Many people breathed a sigh of relief when it seemed possible to rescue philosophy from the vague vapourings of two thousand years (but particularly those of the nineteenth century). A scientific philosophy was then pursued and in many places still is today. Some apprehension is felt because the foundations of mathematics and the principles of scientific thought are not quite so easy to work out as was hoped. But essentially work goes ahead on partial problems; no doubts are felt about the whole programme. This is the position of those who feel that philosophy of logic and philosophy of science more or less exhaust the subject, leaving at any rate no room for old-fashioned general philosophy.

On the other hand, there is a tendency, perhaps particularly evident in England, to regard questions of general philosophy as not yet settled. Several factors were operative here. On the one hand there was the long-standing empiricist tradition in England. This made the new philosophy from Vienna acceptable as a variant of the tradition that ran from Bacon and Locke through Hume and Mill down to Russell. But this was not a philosophy that automatically gave pride of place to natural science. Russell of course did so. He argued that if naive realism is true, science must be true; and further – if science is true naive realism is false: naive realism must therefore be false. And in general Russell is prepared to bring results and procedures from natural science in as a test for any proposed philosophical theory. But the normal English empiricist reacted, like Russell, against the English idealism (the English form of Hegelianism) of the late nineteenth and early twentieth centuries, but did so much more from a standpoint of phenomenalism. What was certain came through the senses: science must be justified in the light of that. These welcomed Wittgenstein's theory of meaning, which could easily be adapted to fit their prejudices, although it was probably designed to be neutral between physicalist and phenomenalist bases.

Now while Wittgenstein was no more of a friend to those who began with the prejudice that the senses spoke to us in accents of truth than he was to those who thought that natural science was the only or the main instrument of progress, he did share something with the English philosophers among whom he lived. They thought that philosophy should not confine itself to the procedures and the language of natural science, but should also take into account, indeed take its starting point from, the language of everyday life. With this attitude they were much more likely to agree with Wittgenstein's insistence on looking at *all* the features of the use of words, not just their role in an artificial calculus. Also they were open to Wittgenstein's lesson that there was very much more to the use of language than the utterance of observation reports and the development of hypotheses with regard to observations reports. These 'ordinary language' philosophers were also at one with the later Wittgenstein on another point. They thought that much more was to be gained by the piecemeal solution of apparent difficulties than by the attempt to develop a theory that would deal with all philosophical issues at one blow.

Wittgenstein's own method was not to concentrate on ordinary language but to consider imaginary languages and to work out what would happen in them. Sometimes this led to the perception of the absurdity of a philosophical thesis. As he said, his aim was to lead from concealed absurdity to open absurdity. At other times the idea was to reveal unrecognized assumptions or prejudices of our own language or way of life. The imagined language, then, would correspond to another equally possible one. It was rather in this spirit that Samuel Butler wrote his book *Erewhon* (i.e. 'Nowhere') describing a country where crime was treated as a disease and disease as a crime. If someone stole something, people rushed round with sympathy and remedies. If he had a headache he had to conceal it at all costs or suffer the severest censure. And so on: thus in that country banks were a sort of temple and monetary transactions had a religious nature. I think this was based on the fact that the Bank of England looked like an ancient temple and I believe that the same is true today of the World Bank. Wittgenstein's interest in alternative life forms comes at various levels. He constantly uses examples such as that of the tribe that counts '1 2 3 4 5 many' and discusses how they would carry out operations like addition and subtraction (there are various possibilities). Akin to this is the man who when asked to add 2 (or to continue the series '0 2 4 6 8 ...') continues as we do up to 100 and then goes on '104 108 112 ...' Others are, for example, the tribe that never *shows* its grief. And he also discusses as real life examples forms of life based on magic and ritual. He was a great reader of Frazer, the Fellow of Trinity, who wrote *The Golden Bough*, an analysis of so-called 'primitive' ways of thought. The interest for Wittgenstein was that these 'beliefs' (contrary to Frazer's practice) were *not* to be treated as failed scientific beliefs. Primitive man was quite capable of cause-effect reasoning but he also had room for something else in his life. And this will make clear to us that we also have room in our lives for much that is quite remote from cause-effect reasoning or means-end behaviour. Wittgenstein reminds us of the enormous number of rituals we carry out. Our ways of greeting. The way we express our anger – striking (in his case) a walking stick against the ground or a tree. We don't think, Wittgenstein says, that the tree has harmed us, or that we are getting somewhere by striking it: we simply give vent to our anger.

There are many other examples. They show us partly what is wrong with one-sided analyses of our ways of thinking. But they also serve to reveal something positive about our way of thinking. Do not be too impressed by Wittgenstein's hostility to science. He was an engineer and thought that engineering had an exact and defined contribution to make to our lives. What he objected to was the presence of science (or rather of a minority of scientists) to be the arbiters of what was to count as knowledge or thinking. Engineering and technology in his day were not at the degree of development that they are today. Everyone believes that computers, based partly on a theory devised at Cambridge by his pupil and friend Turing, have changed our lives.

One imagines that this would not have pleased Wittgenstein – or would have seemed to him one more example of our modern lack of culture; but it is not a problem he actually had to face. He was opposed, then, not to science, but to an inflation of science beyond its proper role – though I must also say that he thought it better for an individual's life that he should be a doctor or an engineer than a scientist.

It is important to read Wittgenstein's works, the *Investigations* in particular, with an eye for his use of irony and paradox, which we have seen to be important in understanding the *Tractatus*. So also with this topic of the philosophy of language. It may be (I think this is in part the argument of Baker and Hacker (1980) in their interesting commentary on *Philosophical Investigations*) that the refusal to give a philosophy of language is itself a philosophy of language. For Wittgenstein is rather frustrating to the reader who seeks definite theses. He insists that there is no such thing as the essence of language, yet he himself constantly talks about language in general, as opposed to individual languages (*langue*, as it were, rather than *parole*). He won't let us say what language is, what it must be, nor will he allow us to talk about the world or thought as a whole. Yet he is doing so himself. Is this simply in order to show us the futility of the operation (as seems to be the case in the *Tractatus*) or are there lessons we are meant to draw which can be expressed in a more positive way?

Certainly there is the lesson, though not a very positive one, that language misleads us. But what language? In the *Tractatus* he thought that only our everyday language was misleading. It was possible to have an ideal language that mirrored reality accurately. When he returned to philosophy ten years later he at first hoped for a primary or phenomenological language which would exactly match our basic experiences. This brings us to the discussion of our main topic today: is there perhaps some artificial language which will not lead us into error and (worse still) senselessness; or is natural language after all the best we have and in order as it stands? This is the same question in a way as that after the essence of language, because the essence is supposed to be that hidden core, expressible only in an artificial language, a core that is at the centre of our thinking and talking.

The rejection of essence and the rejection of artificial language (for that is what we find) occur for many reasons, but come to the same thing, which leads to the supposition that the reasons also come to the same thing. Many of them are implicit in the appeal to the model of family resemblance: there are countless things that we can do with language, countless different forms of sentence, countless different forms of linguistic activity. This is not because our languages happen to be very complex: he is not talking about English or German, but about language as such (this is the paradox that I mentioned, for he is not supposed to do so). No, the fact is that the possibilities of language are in a way limitless because they are identical with those of life itself. This is an insight expressed in so many words in the *Tractatus* but implicit (and, it could be argued, explicit) in the *Investigations* also: it is behind his idea that to imagine a language is to imagine a form of life. The phrase is now so familiar that we agree to it without seeing all its implications. It is not simply that language expresses itself in life, adding as it were colour and vivacity to what would otherwise be dull and prosaic. No: language, once it is there, becomes the form of life that is lived. Wittgenstein denies that language can be viewed as or explained as a tool for doing something specifiable without reference to language.

Language is not something used inside life to achieve certain ends, but is rather a dimension within which life is lived. Ours is a linguistic life in that the association with the involvement of linguistic expression conditions all our actions and reactions. Here for linguistic one might read conscious: it will at once be accepted (I hope) if instead of the above I say that consciousness is not a tool, not an extra in life: consciousness is life. Is life ... for us. And language is life for us. Not so for the animals. We understand now Wittgenstein's riddle: If a lion could speak, we could not understand him. The lion's is not a life lived through language: he has not got anything to *say*. Certainly the lion wants something and stalks its prey, but if it *could* say what it wanted and what it was doing, then what it wanted and what it was doing would not be what they now are. To put the same point conversely, the wants and intentions of a lion cannot be expressed linguistically.

Wittgenstein's paradox might also be put like this: if the lion *could* say what it wanted, that would not count as a linguistic communication. For any linguistic communication a shared life is necessary. That requirement, incidentally, explains why and to what extent we are able to talk to animals. There is communication with them, which works perfectly. In a sense, there is nothing that we fail to get over to them. There is no way in which the animal could take in, could be said to or thought to take in, the extra messages that we might, in fantasy, like to convey to them. We can indeed develop new relations with animals – some even live with them and mimic them (ape them, so to speak) – and a discovery of communication between them that we were not aware of has become commonplace. But it is ridiculous to suppose that the animal might one day be *given* language, might open its mouth and say 'What I was thinking all the time you were training me was ...'. This means that what is going on in the animal's mind is *just what we see*: a set of reactions to training, or to a joint life with its keeper, or to an experimental situation, which may be fumbling and hesitant, or sensitive and ready. And in most cases it will be a development, not an exploration.

An artificial language, and by parity of reasoning any definition of language, is to be condemned, because it is an attempt to set and meet a specification – to limit what language can do and what we can do with language. A language-*game*, on the other hand, is an illustration of how natural language works and thus goes in quite the opposite direction to an artificial language.

In the construction of a language-game we think of a number of operations and see how they would be carried out *in life*. We are seeing what would be the *natural consequences* of adopting the practices in question. Our construction of the language-game depends on possible human forms of life. It is the common human way of acting – *die gemeinsame menschliche Handlungsweise* – that controls and is in turn illuminated by Wittgenstein's method. This method, as we find it in *Philosophical Investigations*, should be contrasted with the study of the logical features that must be possessed by reality if it is to be capable of being depicted by a system of representation. Frege's third world is a systematic representation of such features and only in so far as he attempts to give us that, is he a philosopher of language. He is actually studying not language, but the logical framework of reality, to which (according to him) language gives us some clues.

In the *Tractatus* Wittgenstein appears to follow Frege's lead and to argue from the nature of the picture to that of the pictured. As I have said, he reverses or corrects this impression in the conclusion of the work itself as well as in his later writings.

Thus in both his earlier and his later writings a reconstruction of language is attempted in order to show that *any* attempt to define its structure runs into all the difficulties of circularity.

The main lesson we have so far extracted from Wittgenstein's rejection of artificial language is that a philosophy of language is impossible. But we have also seen that language is a human activity and that places limits upon possible languages. This is akin to what Wittgenstein says about myths and rituals. Practically anything can be made into a ritual, but only something *practical*. It is true that we can invent rituals, and yet ritual is not purely arbitrary. It always answers to some need or possibility in human life.

The same considerations which prove that there can be no a priori limitation of what language is like and what it can do, also allow us to see that the limits of language can be *shown* (as opposed, of course, to *stated*). Many examples of this can be found in Wittgenstein's work. He tries to show us the place of intention and meaning in human life. He rejects, in this same context, the notion of an inner object, precisely because to such a conception there corresponds *no* form of life, *no* mode of interaction between men. Similar thoughts occur in his discussions of mathematics, where the point is not that everything is arbitrary but that the admissibility of any mathematical procedure depends on the ability of mathematicians to live with it: the test is whether mathematical life can go on.

I hope it would be possible to develop the philosophy of mind implicit in these remarks: I have indicated it only. It is not my view that for Wittgenstein the inner must be replaced by the outer – the form of behaviourism attributed to him by Professor von Savigny. Rather what Wittgenstein wants to do is to make clear the place of the inner *in* the outer. What we *can* utter and share and convey certainly exists and is there to be seen: what we cannot does not and is not. Note here that what can be uttered, shared, and conveyed is as such something created by language. Thus we can say that language creates the inner world and by doing so it *intentionalizes the outer world of man's practices*. It is enough to think of a few of those practices: getting married, making a vow, conferring an honour, betraying, flattering, loving, – patterns of behaviour, yes, but patterns of intentional behaviour. And nearly all our practices are intentionalized in this way: the exceptions are few and mostly frightening: they occur in situations of panic and famine. *War* is, or often has been, intentionalized or institutionalized. Eating is so, or was until recently: think of all the ritual of meals. Nowadays, it is true, the habit of 'grazing' has grown up: people walk around in the street eating. The Greeks were *ashamed* to be seen eating, as anecdotes about Diogenes show.

Thus the study of the philosophy of language becomes the study of the inner side, the significance, of all our practices. It *is* therefore the study or the philosophy of mind. Its aim will not be to give us an analysis, say, of the inner in terms of the outer – there should be no reductionism in it – but to bring out the complex nature of this or that utterance or intention or practice (and these three are one).

20

FREUD AND WITTGENSTEIN

Wittgenstein's remarks about Freud amount to no systematic or reasoned criticism of psychoanalysis. Their origin alone explains this. They occur in the course of notes made by Rhees on conversations, or else are scattered through Wittgenstein's own notebooks at points where he was talking about some general topic – symbolism or myth or science – which also has connections with Freud. (The latter, now printed in *Culture and Value* (*C&V*), are more fully authentic and more strikingly expressed and I draw slightly more on them, but readers of *Lectures and Conversations on Aesthetics* (*LCA*) will not find the picture essentially changed.)

Wittgenstein told Rhees that he first read Freud sometime after 1919. In 1940 he still regarded himself as a disciple or follower of Freud, a claim that has been found surprising, but which I hope to make more plausible. His reading seems to have been in the interpretative works from before the First World War: he quotes the *Psychopathology of Everyday Life* and (above all) the *Interpretation of Dreams*. But he will have known a good deal more simply by osmosis. A small example is that *Studies in Hysteria* was to be found in the libraries of his family and he seems to have formed some idea as to its contents, as appears from the following entry in a 1939 notebook:

> I believe that my originality (if that is the right word) is an originality belonging to the soil rather than to the seed. (Perhaps I have no seed of my own.) Sow a seed in my soil and it will grow differently than it would in any other soil.
>
> Freud's originality too was like this, I think. I have always believed – without knowing why – that the real germ of psychoanalysis came from Breuer, not Freud. Of course Breuer's seed-grain can only have been quite tiny. ['may have been quite minute' is also a possible translation and, I think, more probable.]
> (*C&V*, p. 36; passage dated 1939–40)

As is well known, Freud freely acknowledged that much of his work consisted in a development of 'the great discoveries' of Breuer: particularly was this true of the view of psychoanalysis as an interpretative art, which was the aspect that most interested Wittgenstein. Earlier in the 1930s Wittgenstein had already used the relation of Freud to Breuer as a parallel for his own situation: he thought it was characteristic of a Jewish thinker to be merely reproductive; his own task has been not to discover a new way of thinking but to clarify those given him by others. He then wonders whether it is right to say that Freud was inspired by Breuer, just as he, Wittgenstein, was inspired by Boltzmann, Hertz, Schopenhauer, Frege, Russell, Kraus, Loos, Weininger, Spengler, Sraffa. (It will be noted that some of those who inspired Wittgenstein were, like Breuer, Jews.) I believe (though this can only be speculation) that Breuer interested Wittgenstein because Breuer himself renounced the pursuit or exploration of the insights won together with Freud. There were dangers in this new art. Wittgenstein points to those dangers in his conversations with Rhees and also in another remark of 1939–40:

> In a way having oneself psychoanalysed is like eating from the tree of knowledge. The knowledge acquired sets us (new) ethical problems; but contributes nothing to their solution.
>
> (*C&V*, p. 34)

Wittgenstein was indeed acquainted with the practice of analysis: he had lived, it is enough to say, through the 1920s in or near Vienna. Friends and relations had looked to it as a way out of their personal problems: Wittgenstein was inclined to think that the chief good it would do them would reside in the shame they were bound to feel at all the things they would have to reveal to their analyst. He himself had to undergo a psychological examination for legal reasons: we know nothing of its outcome or his reaction, except the resentment he felt at the loss of privacy, always characteristic of him and likely to be increased by the compulsory nature of this examination. His sister, on the other hand, was analysed by Freud and largely from speculative curiosity. She and Wittgenstein would exchange dream reports and give interpretations of each other's dreams. It was a kind of playing with the mind that they both found attractive. In a somewhat similar spirit they both had themselves hypnotized – at widely remote times and for different purposes. Wittgenstein's purpose was to see whether hypnosis, which made man capable of lifting great weights, would make him capable of the super-human efforts of concentration needed to solve the problems of the foundations of mathematics. As for hypnosis, both brother and sister proved impossible to hypnotize during the session but fell into a deep trance the moment it was over. How common such counter-suggestibility is I do not know. The fascination with dreams and the freedom of interpretation assumed are important for understanding Wittgenstein's attitude towards Freud. More even than a work of art, a piece of music, or a work of literature, a dream seemed to call out for interpretation. Its meaning was not there all at once but would appear only in the course of further discussion. The understanding of a dream was a particularly good example of the truth that the understanding of anything might well be a process extended in time; thus even in speech and even in philosophy you may discover what I mean before I do. This theme was to appear often in Wittgenstein's philosophy. Another that he often dwelt on and which was well illustrated by the interpretation of dreams (and the Freudian method in particular) was the complicated way in which the human mind made pictures of facts – in this case so complicated that the picture given hardly deserves the name, as he says in a manuscript of 1944 (*C&V*, p. 44).

This sketch of the background of Wittgenstein's interest in Freud will help, I hope, to prepare us for the main point in Freud that gets discussed: namely the criteria of dream interpretation. Freud was, Wittgenstein thought, very clever at interpretation: *'geistreich'* – the word contains a hint of criticism, and it is a fairly common criticism of himself by Wittgenstein that he was too attached to this quality. Freud then was clever enough to produce interpretations which, in part because of their ingenuity, were attractive. Did Wittgenstein want us to regard them as embodying pseudo-explanations? Not exactly, as I think can best be shown by considering the following passage:

> In a Freudian analysis the dream is, so to speak, decomposed. It completely loses its original meaning. One could imagine the dream as something performed on the stage, whose action was sometimes rather incomprehensible but in part quite comprehensible, at least in our eyes: now, one might imagine, the action of the play is torn into small parts and each part is given a quite new meaning. Or one could imagine a large piece of paper with a picture drawn on it: the picture is now pleated up in such a way that pieces which were quite unrelated in the original picture are now visually adjacent and a new picture (meaningful or meaningless) results: this new picture would be the dream as dreamed, while the original picture would correspond to the latent dream content.
>
> Now, I could imagine someone who saw the unfolded picture exclaiming, 'Yes, that is the solution, that is what I dreamt, but without the gaps and distortions'. In that case the solution would be constituted as such by the dreamer's recognition of it and by nothing else. It is just as when you are writing something and looking for a word and suddenly say *'That's* it, *that's* what I wanted to say': your recognition of the word stamps it as the

word that you were looking for and have now found. (Here is a case where you really could say, rather in the way Russell speaks about wishing, that you only know what you have been looking for when you have found it.)

What is intriguing about a dream is not its causal connection with events in my life etc. but rather that it functions as part (indeed a very lifelike part) of a story the remainder of which is in the dark. (One wants to ask, 'Where did this figure suddenly come from, and what happened to it?') Indeed, even when someone subsequently shows me that the original story wasn't a proper story at all but was really based on a quite different story, so that I am inclined to exclaim, in disillusion, 'Oh, is that what it was!', even then the impression remains that I have been robbed of something. To be sure, as the paper unfolds the original picture disintegrates – the man that I saw was taken from *there*, his words from *here*, the surroundings of the dream from a third place, but the dream-story has its peculiar charm, like a painting that attracts and inspires us.

Of course one might say that we view the dream in an inspired way, that it is we who are inspired. Because when we relate our dream to someone else, generally the imagery doesn't inspire him. The dream affects us like an idea pregnant with possible developments.

(*C&V*, pp. 68–9; passage dated 1948; my own translation)

Wittgenstein's fondness for analogies will be seen from the passage. It was in the invention of analogies that he thought he came nearest to originality, according to the passages on originality that I have partly quoted. Some of his analogies – pictures, games, etc. – have proved useful tools for thinking. But the analogy of the pleated paper in this case is one that Wittgenstein means us to view with suspicion. Sometimes we feel like saying 'So that's what it was!' but it is only our now feeling this that makes it (if the word is appropriate) true. Wittgenstein is suggesting that there is not really a full and coherent picture or story there all the time. What is there at the earlier stage is an idea capable of development. The latent content is created by the development, which might have taken a quite other course with equal validity, for it is evident what answer to the question about the criteria for the interpretation of dreams is implicit in our passage. Acknowledgement, acceptance, or recognition is the sort of criterion envisaged. I say *the sort of* criterion because (as the conversations with Rhees make clear) Wittgenstein thinks Freud sometimes talks as if the right interpretation might be clearer to the doctor than to the patient, or as if the right interpretation were the one whose acceptance by the patient would lead to the most favourable outcome to treatment. Much thought has been devoted to this matter and I will not pronounce on it here, though it seems plausible to say with Wittgenstein that in practice a blend of these criteria is employed. What is important for the question about criteria is not how exactly these things are worked out in the therapeutic situation, but that they are worked out there. The right interpretation is one that works, that is to say one that contributes most to the activity being jointly conducted by the doctor and patient. Generally that will mean one which the dreamer either embraces or rejects, not one to which he is indifferent. The correct interpretation – or rather, as we must say, *a* correct interpretation – will be one that says something to the patient.

This brings us to the other theme of the passage quoted from Wittgenstein. In any such interpretation there is something lost, namely and precisely the richness and indeterminate character of the original dream. The dreamer must be prepared to sacrifice this if he is to take part in the joint activity with the analyst already mentioned. Not only must he be prepared to accept interpretations of his dream, but also to accept as correct only those interpretations that relate his dream to figures and wishes from his past. In doing so he is (in Wittgenstein's terms) accepting a mythology propounded by Freud. Wittgenstein gave one or two examples in his conversations with Rhees to show the attractiveness of this mythology:

> The attractiveness of the suggestion, for instance, that all anxiety is a repetition of the anxiety of the birth trauma, is just the attractiveness of a mythology. 'It is all the outcome of something that happened long ago.' Almost like referring to a totem.
>
> Much the same could be said of the notion of an '*Urszene*'. This often has the attractiveness of giving a sort of tragic pattern to one's life. It is all the repetition of the same pattern which was settled long ago. Like a tragic figure carrying out the decrees under which the fates had placed him at birth. Many people have at some period, serious trouble in their lives – so serious as to lead to thoughts of suicide. This is likely to appear to one as something nasty, as a situation which is too foul to be a subject of a tragedy. And it may then be an immense relief if it can be shown that one's life has the pattern rather of a tragedy – the tragic working-out and repetition of a pattern which was determined by the primal scene.
>
> (*LCA*, p. 51)

We shall see that it is by no means a condemnation of Freud's thought to call it a mythology. A myth to function as such must say something to human beings, and Freud's is a powerful mythology. What the mythological character of the thought does rule out is its forming a science. The test of a science used by Wittgenstein is its dependence on experiment to establish causal laws, and he points to the absence of experimental evidence in psychoanalytical explanations. He does not spend long on this point, discussions of which I can assume to be familiar to readers. Therapeutic success, if it can be identified, is not experimental evidence of the required kind. It establishes only that the result of the therapy is acceptable to society or to the patient— it testifies only to, it consists in, the effectiveness or the welcome nature of the mythology, of the stories told. It has itself nothing to do with their truth. There can of course be small areas in which an apparently scientific method can be applied – if for example (and it is an example given by Wittgenstein) one formed the hypothesis, on the basis of dream reports, that the dreamer can be brought to recall such and such memories. This hypothesis might or might not be verified. What would success in such prediction show? It shows in the first place the effectiveness of the technique in leading from one avowal to another; but even if the memories so reached were always veridical, there would be no proof of the psychodynamic apparatus invoked to account for the route from the original event to the dream report. We should just have the fact that a certain dream report (or set of dream reports) could be read as the expression of certain memories, without any means of explaining how this came about. If a great degree of success with all sorts of subjects were achieved in respect of dream and memories, the result would be very striking, though, I think, no more a justification for a causal hypothesis than a similar hypothetical success in astrology. In practice, however, success of this kind is achieved only with patients already thinking in ways favourable to the analytic process. In their case a communication conveyed in the oblique way typical of that process bears witness only to the wholeheartedness of their participation in it. They have enabled the analyst to understand them before they understood themselves.

The contrast between a psychoanalytic explanation and a scientific one can be made clearer by taking an example not actually used by Wittgenstein – that of slips or errors in the transmission of texts. Here there has grown up in the course of centuries of critical work on transmission a modest science that embodies the most frequent forms of corruption in a set of principles. There is for instance the error of trivialization – the familiar word is substituted for the unusual but correct one; or *le saut du même au même* – the eye of the copyist (or his memory when he recites to himself a passage he is in the course of copying) jumps either forward or back from one occurrence of a word or word-element to another, thus resulting either in an omission or a repetition. Countless instances of these errors can be found, and most slips discussed by Freud in the *Psychopathology of Everyday Life* can be explained on such principles without great difficulty. This has been shown by Sebastiano Timpanaro in his book *The Freudian Slip* (1976), on which I draw heavily. (It would also be possible, no doubt, to embody such principles in a study of attention in general by the methods of experimental psychology, but in practice the empirical evidence available in the special field of the transmission of texts, together with some fairly elementary commonsense reflections, suffices.)

What good then does Freud's account of the origin of these slips (as they occur, say, in memories or quotations) do? It attempts to show why just these errors (and not all the others that would also be possible according to the principles) occurred. But we are not entitled to suppose that there has to be a reason why just these errors occurred, just as we cannot demand a cause for every coincidence. The scribe's liability to certain types of error is activated in a particular case by the state of the weather, the fact that he is tired, and so on. If you insist that inquiry must go until a reason of Freud's sort has been found for every slip, you are expressing a determination to find that sort of explanation and to be content with it and with no other. What appears to be a healthy scepticism and hostility to chance as a factor in human affairs is in reality a blind prejudice in favour of one kind of account. This can be seen from the fact that, even if we conceive it as a causal explanation, the Freudian explanation of slips must also leave room for chance: it cannot hope to explain why just these Freudian slips and no others were made. Like every other form of explanation it must say, 'Well, conditions just happened to favour these particular slips'.

The plausibility of the explanations given by Freud, the reconstructions made in the course of them and so on, do not show that a whole area of causation has been laid bare here. In line with our previous remarks drawn from Wittgenstein these factors show rather that a process of free association and judicious questioning by the analyst will nearly always lead to matters of central concern to the subject.

Here, starting from the supposed scientific character of the explanation given, we arrive instead at an insight into its mythological nature. Everything has an explanation, everything is significant: this is not the expression of a scientific attitude but of a primitive one. A chance conjuncture tells us something – birds flying a certain area of sky from the right or from the left tell us who will win a forthcoming battle. The position of the stars at the moment of a man's birth is not accidentally connected with his fortunes. Divination and astrology are for most of us defunct practices, but we can understand what their function was in many ways. The need to see a meaning in everything, the need to have some *ratio decidendi* in obscure but important questions, the need to have some account or other of why things happen to a man, some rationalization of it. It may be that any reflection on the human condition, such as astrology must involve, will reveal something to us. Or it may help one to have an account of what one is likely to do, so as to guide one in life, rather as Wallenstein is thought to have lived out as if on purpose the remarkably accurate prediction made by Kepler. Astrology, witchcraft, and magic may favour and encourage certain forms of life; they may be necessary for certain people. And usually we can understand their need even if we do not feel it.

Wittgenstein wrote more than once during the 1930s about magic and ritual, principally in connection with his reading of Frazer's *Golden Bough*. This was part of the ethnological or anthropological way of looking at things that came to him from the economist Sraffa and that he regarded as one of the most fruitful lessons of those years. (The bulk of the remarks are collected in two slightly different collections by Rhees, *BüF* and *RoF* in our bibliography.) It is important to understand Wittgenstein's attitude towards this pervasive phenomenon. Religious and magical ways of thinking and acting do not rest on false scientific beliefs (nor on true ones either). They are not given up or changed simply when some matter of fact is pointed out to those concerned. Moreover, our lives too and our thinking, not merely those of primitive peoples, have much ritual in them and much mythology (it is there indeed that philosophy has its origin, according to Wittgenstein). Its essence may be seen clearly enough in small things such as kissing the picture of the beloved or striking some inanimate object when angry.

> When I am furious about something, I sometimes hit the ground or a tree with my stick, and the like. But I certainly don't think that the ground is to blame or that this hitting can help at all. 'I give vent to my anger.' And that is what all rites are like. Such actions could be called instinctive actions. – And a historical explanation, e.g. that in the past I or my ancestors used to believe that it helped to strike the ground is humbug, because it is a superfluous assumption that explains nothing. The important thing is the similarity with an act of punishing, but nothing more than similarity is to be found.
>
> Once such a phenomenon has been brought into a relation with an instinct we ourselves possess, that alone is the desired solution, i.e. the solution that resolves this particular difficulty. Any further research into the history of my instincts would follow quite different paths.
>
> (*BüF*, p. 244; omitted in *RoF*)

Similarly, understanding the ritual of a primitive people involves bringing in an inclination we ourselves feel. And this is nearly always possible: it is as if we have already in our minds the principle underlying the whole diversity of primitive usages. 'The inner nature' of a ritual, 'the inner life of thought and feeling' that accompanies it, is something familiar to us. We feel that we could invent primitive usages and that it would be a mere accident if they were nowhere found in reality. (This is quite consistent with the point he also makes that festivals such as Beltane are not free inventions of man.)

This brings us back to Freud and to Wittgenstein's view of his achievement. Freud invented, on that view, a way of thinking and talking and a life associated with it, which corresponded with something universal in the human spirit (and which therefore easily fitted many pre-existing myths). So far as the statements made in the exposition of this way of thinking were taken as scientific, Freud or his followers fell into error, the same sort of error that is made when magic is analysed scientifically. (This parallel, I must point out, is my contribution.) But if this error was not made – what then? First, something illuminating had been done by the very demonstration of the possibility of this way of thinking. Second, if it were adopted and followed in a consequential manner, a certain impoverishment of our mental life – a shrinking, if one may so term it, to a single one of the many possibilities of development – would ensue. Third, a man might still learn a lot about himself by adopting it, that is, by undergoing analysis, but he would at the same time have to resist the strength of the mythology – to see it, I suppose this means, as only one of the ways of thinking about these matters. On a small scale this would amount to seeing that dreams and slips may not *all* serve a single purpose or follow a single pattern. I compare this with the savage, who, as Wittgenstein says, 'to all appearance sticks pins in his enemy's picture in order to kill him, but also builds his hut with real wood and cuts himself an arrow skilfully and not in effigy'. (*BüF*, p. 237; *RoF*, p. 4; the present translation, however, is my own.)

The above is not intended as a casting-up of accounts on Freud, which it would be ridiculous to attempt on the basis of a few scattered insights, interesting though I find them, in Wittgenstein. It will serve though to introduce the question why and with what justice Wittgenstein regarded himself as a follower of Freud's. Discussion of the point may throw light on both thinkers.

For a while after the Second World War it was fashionable to refer to Wittgenstein's work as 'therapeutic positivism' (B. Farrell, M. Lazerowitz). The noun is certainly unfortunate: the original positivists wanted all thinking to follow the pattern of natural science, whereas even in his first work Wittgenstein's aim was to show that large areas of human concern were not accessible to science. When he returned to philosophy in the 1930s, his *bête noire* was the attempt, say, of Jeans and Eddington to reach a world-view through science. He thought of his own work (as appears from the preface composed in 1930 and now printed with his *Philosophical*

Remarks) as written in a spirit quite different from that of the age: the spirit of the age was one of confidence in progress and in science (it is interesting that the motto to his *Philosophical Investigations,* chosen probably round 1945, is also expressive of distrust in progress). His aim was a profounder understanding rather than any progress. All the moral and social problems that we faced were not even touched by science. Not that there was anything wrong with science, only with its status in our culture. We needed a change in culture. Here, in his anti-positivism, Wittgenstein was indebted both to Freud and Sraffa, to Freud for the vision of how a problem could (though with great difficulty) be taken up by the roots and put into a quite new way of thinking, to Sraffa for the idea of a way of thinking as reflecting the character of a culture. (I speak of where he actually got these ideas from – he could no doubt have learnt more from Freud if he had read more than the pre-First World War works.)

Though his work was thus no positivism, there were grounds for calling it therapeutic. He himself was a little annoyed by the idea. 'When you think of the investigation of philosophical problems as a form of psychoanalysis, you think like a physician – "We'll soon put that right!"' (reported conversation with R. Rhees). Perhaps some who made the comparison did think of the 'dissolution' of philosophical problems (compare the decomposition of the dream of which Wittgenstein spoke) as proceeding rapidly – whereas Wittgenstein thought that the source of philosophical problems was so deeply rooted in our thinking that any advance would be very slow. The advance that he thought possible was to be made by the individual, and here Wittgenstein himself drew the analogy with psychoanalysis: the individual was to be the judge of success, that is, relative to himself. The philosopher is plagued by a problem. Some expression disturbs him, seems to demand to be used in a certain way which he cannot quite allow (we shall see an example shortly). He has to find a context in which the disturbing expression is at home. When its full context is shown, it is no longer problematic. This is where a lesson learnt from Freud that we have already mentioned comes in: the idea that the meaning is not there all at once but is something that appears in the course of discussion, so that understanding is a process extended in time.

The philosopher is one with a susceptibility to certain so-called problems that are really the result of a muddle. He has a temptation to overcome:

> A philosopher has temptations that an ordinary person does not have. We *could* say he knows better what the word means than the others do. But actually philosophers generally know *less*. Because ordinary people have no temptations to misunderstand language.
> (Notes taken in Wittgenstein's lectures of summer term, 1936,
> by Rush Rhees)

233

Slightly earlier he thought that the difficulty was a resistance in the will. An heroic effort was required if metaphysics was to be given up, a revolution in our thinking, not only in the sense that we needed to turn round and look in the opposite direction (one of the hardest things in the world to do) but a revolution in the other sense, something like the Russian revolution. Wittgenstein thought that nothing was to be hoped for from Western culture: it was a thing of the past, its energy had been spent by about 1850: the only hope lay in Russia where everything had been destroyed. And a similar complete departure from former ways of thinking was required in philosophy too. He criticized his friend Ramsey for being a bourgeois thinker, not prepared for this complete renunciation. He himself felt that he was writing for a future race, for people who would think in a totally different way. Here his kinship with Nietzsche is very evident.

What we have to break loose from in the first place is metaphysics, a bewitchment by language and its forms, which lead us to make statements which have all the form of empirical or factual statements, but which we know to be not statements of fact at all. Such are the statements of Wittgenstein's own first book, in which he talks about the form of the world and the way it is mirrored in language, as if such entities existed and stood in relations to one another just like those of solid, everyday objects. We have the idea as we read the book that it contains the results of a super-science, which gives us the most general laws. Of course that book does end with the insight that its own propositions are nonsensical, but it is a testimony to the attractiveness of a certain picture. We feel that language is a system that is there to be talked about, whereas we cannot describe language or thought by one formula, but can only exhibit the sorts of thing we can do with it in practice. Another example (quoted by Rhees below from Wittgenstein's discussion of language and ritual) concerns the phrase 'I meant him' – the process of meaning or intending:

> I say, 'Please come here', and beckon to him. I meant A and not B. I did mean him; there is no doubt about that. And yet it seems to be clear that unless I want to fabricate something there was no connection between me (or my speaking) and him other than, say, my glance and the like. This 'meaning him' construed as a connection is like a myth. And a very powerful myth. Because whatever sort of connection I imagine, none of them does what I want. No connection that I can imagine will be adequate, and consequently it seems that meaning must be a specific connection quite incomparable with all other forms of connection.
>
> (MS 116, 275)

If we look at the surface of our language it seems to demand a simple referent for all such words – as if 'meaning him' were like 'hitting him'. And we even rather enjoy that way of thinking about it, as Cantor enjoyed talking about the set of all real numbers – and imagining it written down in a certain order. We feel that by giving a name to something, or by performing operations on a set, we have mastered it, have got beyond our inability to grasp it as something simple, to see it. We obtain by these means, in our own estimation, an angel's knowledge, and this pleases us. But of course we *ought not* to do this. As Wittgenstein said about philosophy in a conversation reported by R. Rhees: 'I am not trying to get you to believe something you don't believe but to do something you won't do'. What the philosopher ought to do is to draw attention to the great multiplicity of things that are normally done, practices of the group, which make it possible for me to 'mean him'. That philosopher's question should be: '*When* do we say that one person means another?' not, '*How* is it done?', because the latter contains another surrender to the mythology implicit in our speech-forms. ('Well it is after all a process … it must either be going on or not.') This is not a mistake about the facts of the case. 'Meaning' is indeed a process, or at least a process-word, but it is a mistake to be obsessed with this feature of our language, which is of little importance, a philosophical mistake, which can have the aim merely of feeding our vanity but can also help us to avoid thinking clearly in important matters.

So Wittgenstein wants to avoid the mythology implicit in our first reflections on language. He wants to substitute a form of reflection that avoids it – though perhaps at the risk of introducing a new mythology of its own, that of 'use' as something present all at once, for example. He wants to see through the surface grammar of a word to its depth grammar. This (it seems to me) is what made it natural for him to call himself a pupil or follower of Freud, for he had in Freud an example of how a new and deeper but often less flattering interpretation could be substituted for the apparent meaning and at the same time of how a mythology could captivate. He accepted and rejected Freud in equal measure, perhaps healthily.

21

ON CERTAINTY

Comments on a paper by G.H. von Wright

Professor von Wright's contribution to the Helsinki *Entretiens* on theory of knowledge (von Wright 1972b) was a particularly lucid presentation of the main ideas of a difficult work of Wittgenstein's when it was as yet unfamiliar. He advanced interesting suggestions regarding the application and scope of those ideas. If I dwell first on some parallels (to which he has drawn attention) with Wittgenstein's earlier work, the *Tractatus*, I hope it will become apparent that this is not wholly due to my own preoccupations but has an important bearing on the subject of the *Entretiens*.

Looking at the *Tractatus*, then, in the light of such an interest, we can see that a distinction is there drawn between, on the one hand, what is shown, namely logic, meaning, and the form of the world, and, on the other, what can be said, namely that certain states of affairs hold, that certain facts are indeed facts, that the world has a certain content. The former realm belongs to what von Wright has called our *Vor-Wissen* or pre-knowledge and thus Wittgenstein says that it must be known to anyone who can talk or think at all. The latter realm is that in which our normal concepts of knowledge, belief, and other propositional attitudes operate. As is well known, Wittgenstein thinks that this body of *Vor-Wissen* cannot be expressed in propositions at all. As we might say – *das Vor-Wissen ist kein Wissen*, pre-knowledge is not knowledge. In so far as the *Tractatus* does not merely *show* the form of the world but attempts to describe it, it stands self-condemned as a typical work of philosophy.

A few corollaries of this view deserve mention. Even the propositions of logic are not properly said to be known. Wittgenstein does, it is true, sometimes refer to them as propositions, though often with misgivings, but in one interesting passage *(Tractatus* 5.1362) he says that '*A* knows that *p*' is itself a tautology when *p* is a tautology. It is certainly not true that everyone knows all the propositions of logic in any ordinary sense of the word 'know': I believe that Wittgenstein's thought is that to know a tautology is not to know anything. A second and more questionable corollary is that the propositions of logic, like pseudo-propositions which purport to state what can only be shown, are not properly called true.

Certainly, if we had to call them either true or false, we should elect to call them true, for a reason given by Ramsey: added to other true propositions they will at any rate not yield false conclusions, whereas contradictions will or may. But it remains the case that this use of the word true is an extension of the basic use, which applies to propositions that happen to be true; and in making the extension we must be very careful not to carry over more of the notions normally connected with truth than we are strictly entitled to.

It is easy to see that a lot of this applies to the later body of ideas described by von Wright. The realm of *Vor-Wissen*, whatever exactly it contains, will be closely associated with the notion of meaning. Again and again in *On Certainty* Wittgenstein points out that if anyone expressed doubts about what is certain, he would provoke the question whether he knew what he was saying, whether he knew what his words meant. These certainties, moreover, are not things we are properly said to know: that word has a different use and application. (I think I can take this as established in von Wright's exposition.) When we have said, as Wittgenstein suggests we must say, that these are things that must be known before I can even make a mistake, we have taken them out of the realm of knowledge proper. I have sometimes thought of saying that we could call them knowledge only by erecting a notion of intuitive knowledge, to be contrasted with ordinary or discursive knowledge, and perhaps it will later be possible to judge whether there is anything in this suggestion. Finally it is interesting that works of epistemology and perhaps works of philosophy in general often contain attempts to describe or outline the content of our *Vor-Wissen* and to indicate in some systematic way how our ordinary knowledge is connected with it. Now, just as Wittgenstein in his earlier work condemns such attempts as a misunderstanding of the nature of propositions, of language, and of thought, which can only show this *Vor-Wissen*, not formulate it, so his later work differs from most of what we are accustomed to regard as philosophy: it does not contain theses (such as that there is an external world or that the will is free or whatever) and the defence of those theses, but amasses facts and possibilities the consideration of which is meant to free the reader from the temptation to assert these theses or to deny them or even to consider them at all. One who does philosophy in the ordinary way can still derive much from Wittgenstein's writings but will inevitably be irritated by the author's refusal to do what I may call normal philosophy (with an allusion to the work of Kuhn's mentioned by von Wright [Kuhn 1962]). Perhaps some *détente* might be possible if Wittgenstein's recognition – I think I may call it discovery – of the special status of *Vor-Wissen* proved to be reconcilable with something like the methods of normal philosophy. Perhaps this suggestion was contained in von Wright's closing remarks: at any rate I shall return to it.

I have so far ignored the most surprising new element in *On Certainty*, namely that Wittgenstein there includes in our *Vor-Wissen* some things which on any other view would be contingent truths. Part of what von Wright (following Wittgenstein) has well called our *Weltbild* (world-picture) are a large number of certainties which are not facts or truths or true propositions to be placed alongside other facts or truths and compared with them to determine their degree of acceptability but form part of the framework within which we assess supposed facts and truths. This new element is surprising only because it is at variance with an unacknowledged and powerful prejudice in recent theories of knowledge, a prejudice from which possibly Descartes was free. Professor Williams (in von Wright 1972a, where the present piece originally appeared) with a rather different approach has also drawn our attention to it. It is the prejudice which consists in supposing that when we search for certainty in life, we are essentially considering a set of propositions and must first find a subset of those which on grounds internal to them as propositions can be seen to be certain. But once we turn away from the idea that we are trying to produce a set of self-guaranteeing propositions, no one has any difficulty in seeing that we are often wrong about matters which are decidable a priori, and after the discussion of Moore and Wittgenstein that von Wright gives us I will venture to say that no one will deny that there are many certainties which neither admit of question nor belong to the realm of the a priori on any useful definition of that term.

Not of course that Wittgenstein is simply making the point that among propositions that come up for question there are those that are a priori decidable and those that are decidable only a posteriori and that among both classes there may be those that are known, those that are doubted, those that are falsely believed, and so on. This is indeed true but it is by no means the whole of the truth. There are also the certainties – that twelve twelves are one hundred and forty four, that I have two hands, that (when it is so) I am now standing in a lecture-room in a country foreign to me, and perhaps even that the Battle of Hastings was fought in 1066. I agree with von Wright's view, if I understand it correctly, that these are not well called propositions. In the normal way they would be uttered only in teaching arithmetic or a language or the basis of some subject or other. They are not things put forward which we acknowledge but things which all our actions in a certain area show that we take for granted. I question slightly, therefore, von Wright's remark that they have 'a peculiar logical role'. This seems to suggest that they are a third class of propositions alongside the a priori and the a posteriori, in reality however (and perhaps the word role does after all indicate this) they have not an intrinsic logical character but a special relation to us which Wittgenstein often describes in terms of the way of life, the fundamental decisions, the *faith* of a community. Now, to go back to our original point, these certainties give us the framework both of a priori and of a posteriori knowledge.

All of this is not *quite* new as far as the *Tractatus* is concerned, because Wittgenstein there points out that the *scientist* approaches nature with a framework, actually he says network, of principles which he will not *allow* to be upset. This network is not a set of a priori propositions but it shares a characteristic which Wittgenstein (wrongly, as I believe) supposed to belong to all a priori propositions, that of belonging to the *Vor-Wissen* at any rate of a certain set of men. This network fulfils the role that Kuhn in his account of the history of science assigns to a paradigm, and Wittgenstein insists as Kuhn allows, that different paradigms, different networks are possible. In his book on the *Tractatus* Professor Stenius made the very interesting suggestion that the possibility of different frameworks held not only for science but for all our language: the world on this view, admits of different analyses into facts and hence can be conceived as having different *forms*. Various alternative bodies of *Vor-Wissen* are possible. It is irrelevant for our present purposes that I do not believe that this is a possible exegesis of the *Tractatus:* the main point is that it certainly holds of *On Certainty,* and the question I want to ask is, what follows for Wittgenstein's own position from the fact that different bodies of *Vor-Wissen,* different sets of certainties are possible for different communities and groups? We can think of various examples, many mentioned by Wittgenstein – a Newtonian paradigm opposed to an Aristotelian one, a religious opposed to a non-religious, a magical as opposed to whatever we have now among educated people.

Now it by no means follows that we are not in fact certain of all the things we have discussed. We are certain of them in that they are part of our way of life. On the other hand Wittgenstein is not especially wedded to our way of life; other peoples might be just as certain of their different *Vor-Wissen*. Wittgenstein does not, as has sometimes been said, worship the common man: he simply says that no man can give up or change his *Vor-Wissen* on rational grounds: what is required is a conversion.

So his philosophy, true to its programme, 'leaves everything as it is': we see that certain things are part of our *Vor-Wissen* and we also see that we can in the nature of things have no justification for their being so. But now is not his just *one* paradigm of philosophy – one paradigm among others? Wouldn't it be possible for philosophy to consist in the attempt to convert others to a different framework – or to acquire a different framework oneself? Something like this was what Descartes was doing and his work is rightly seen as a turning point in the history of philosophy, because he tried to formulate and to impose a new paradigm, which was emerging in his time. He *was* wedded to this paradigm and his reflection, which he wished others to follow, showed him more and more things which, thinking and living as he did, he could not give up. In this way he developed a paradigm which (I give here an impression, being no real historian of ideas) had important consequences for moral, religious, and intellectual life. Call it a faith, if you like, or an ideology, or even, as I have suggested, a body of intuitive knowledge. This, surely, to return to Kuhn's terminology, was a piece of extraordinary philosophy, not like either magic or science, but like the attempt to convert oneself and others from magic to science or from one scientific paradigm to a new one. The activity of normal philosophy would of course not be so revolutionary as this, but neither would it be the working out or the application of our normal paradigms, because that is our normal non-philosophic activity. It will not be a far cry from Wittgenstein, or I think from the truth, to suggest that normal philosophy is the further recommending of an established paradigm and occurs particularly in cases in which we have more than one paradigm applied to a certain area, or, in other terms, where different language-games overlap. If this is true most of Wittgenstein's own practice will not be normal philosophy at all, though it will be a valuable preparation for it (supposing the activity itself to be valuable), because his practice for the most part consists in pointing out the confusion of language-games and not in recommending which is to prevail. So it does leave things as they are, for better or for worse.

Part IV

PHILOLOGICA

22

BERTRAND RUSSELL AND
THE 'NOTES ON LOGIC'

The volume of Wittgenstein's writings entitled *Notebooks 1914–16*[1] contains as Appendix A one version of Wittgenstein's so-called 'Notes on Logic'. In the first edition (all printings down to 1979), which will be referred to throughout this paper, this is the version first printed in the *Journal of Philosophy*, liv, no. 9 (1957), 230–245 with a note by Harry T. Costello explaining that he copied it from a manuscript dated September 1913 brought to Harvard by Russell in the spring of 1914. This 'manuscript' and the copy made of it by Costello are at present lost, but two earlier stages of the work still exist in the Bertrand Russell Archive of McMaster University. The *second* of these is a pair of typescripts, one foliated 1–8 and entitled 'Summary', the other foliated 1–25 and containing the following headings: '*First MS*' on f.1, '*Second MS*' on f.4, '*3rd MS*' on f.8, and '*4th. MS*' on f.17. (Other features of these typescripts will be described later.) These typescripts are evidently those shown by Russell to Mr. D. Shwayder in the early 1950s, at which time copies made from them enjoyed a certain circulation.

The Costello version is obviously a rearrangement under chapter headings of the Shwayder version. Some doublets are dropped, a sentence is added to compensate for a change of context, the English is improved, and some references to 'you' or 'I' (*sic*) are changed into references to 'Russell'. A thorough analysis of these changes was made by Mr. J.P. Griffin in the late 1950s[2] and the editors of *Notebooks*, Professor von Wright and Miss Anscombe,[3] accepted his contention, based essentially on internal evidence, that the rearrangement was Wittgenstein's own work. For this reason, and because the Costello version seemed to them

---

1 Actually the notebook entries which form the bulk of the volume contain some entries from 1917.
2 I am much indebted to Professor Griffin (as he now is) for access to his notes.
3 The editors' first thoughts had been that the Costello version was not Wittgenstein's own work: see their remarks in *Journal of Philosophy*, liv, no. 15 (1957), p. 484.

an improvement, they adopted it for their volume, correcting only what they call 'copyists' errors'.

The aim of the present paper is to examine the genesis of this work and in particular the part played by Russell in it. It will be suggested that the rearrangement can hardly have been Wittgenstein's own; and from this it follows that for purposes of studying Wittgenstein's thought the second version cannot be an improvement. Some corrections of the text will also be possible. It will become obvious that the conclusions reached rest for the most part on external evidence and documents which were not available to Mr. Griffin or the editors of *Notebooks 1914–1916*.[4]

The *first* stage of the material contained in 'Notes on Logic', filed by Russell under the title " 'Wittgenstein on Logic' 1913', consists of two parts. First a typescript of seven sheets with manuscript corrections by Russell and Wittgenstein and the title *'Summary'* in Russell's hand; second a manuscript of twenty-three sheets in Russell's hand entitled 'Wittgenstein' on f.1 and bearing the sub-headings *'First MS.'* (f.1), *'2nd MS.'* (f.4), *'3rd MS'* (f.7), and *'4th MS'* (f.16).

The *Summary*, which is evidently from the same machine as the second-stage typescripts mentioned above, bears all the marks of a typescript made from dictation or from a stenogram ('judge is' for 'judges', 'has' for 'is', 'error' for 'arrow', 'x for y' for 'xRy', etc.). Many mishearings or misreadings have been corrected by Russell, some by Wittgenstein; and in some cases Wittgenstein has corrected Russell's conjectures. Wittgenstein also added some explanations and comments. Two square-bracketed passages occur and function as footnotes: the earlier of these '[NB. *ab* means the same as WF, which means true-false]' has a marginal note in Russell's hand '[Note by B. R.]'. This seems to indicate that Russell intervened in the dictation or at some stage in the transcription and perhaps the second square-bracketed comment '[Components are forms and constituents]' is also by Russell. Costello omits the former note but the editors of *Notebooks* include a similar note of their own on p. 97. The substance of Russell's second comment is included by Costello and occurs in *Notebooks*, p. 106, l.27.

The genesis of this *Summary* is fairly clear from Russell's correspondence. After a summer in Austria Wittgenstein was in Norway and wrote to Russell on 20 September 1913:

---

4 Here is the place to record my great debt to Mr. Kenneth Blackwell of the Bertrand Russell Archive who has readily given me access to all sorts of material. He himself has noticed many of the facts that I draw attention to, though I have not yet been able to persuade him to accept all my conjectures.

Types are not yet solved but I have had all sorts of ideas which seem to me very fundamental. Now the feeling that I shall have to die before being able to publish them is growing stronger and stronger in me every day and my greatest wish would therefore be to communicate everything I have done so far to you, *as soon as possible* ... I want to ask you to let me meet you *as soon as possible* and give me time enough to give you a survey of the whole field of what I have done up to now and if possible to let me make notes for you *in your presence*.

A meeting was arranged for 4 October but it is evident from a letter of Russell's to Lucy Donnelly[5] that more than one meeting took place. After mentioning Wittgenstein's 'bursting in like a whirlwind' he goes on

Now Wittgenstein, during August and September, had done work on logic, still rather in the rough, but as good, in my opinion, as any work that ever has been done in logic by anyone. But his artistic conscience prevents him from writing anything until he has got it perfect, and I am persuaded he will commit suicide in February. What was I to do? He told me his ideas, but they were so subtle that I kept on forgetting them. I begged him to write them out, and he tried, but after much groaning said it was absolutely impossible. At last I made him talk in the presence of a shorthand writer, and so secured some record of his ideas. This business took up the whole of my time and thought for about a week.

Such a letter is not intended as an exact calendar, but it may be conjectured that Wittgenstein first saw Russell on 4 October (Russell has a note to this effect on the Wittgenstein letter quoted above) and went on seeing him until 11 or 12 October. Shortly after this Wittgenstein left for Norway and on 17 October (misdated '17.9' by Wittgenstein) wrote from the ship, evidently already in Norway, 'Hope you have got typewritten business all right'. This probably means not that Wittgenstein had sent Russell a typescript but that he hopes Russell has already had made the typewritten version of what Wittgenstein dictated. At any rate it will be evident shortly that Wittgenstein only later received the typescript of the *Summary* from Russell and returned it to him with comments.

But first Wittgenstein's letter of 29 October must be considered.[6] In a postscript he asks Russell, 'Did you get the copy of my manuscript?' It

---

5 Printed in part in *Russell* 2 (summer 1971), p. 6. The letter is dated 19 October 1913.
6 Excerpts are printed in *Nb*, p. 122. The full texts of the Wittgenstein letters quoted here are, of course, now available in *CL*.

seems inconceivable that Wittgenstein should so refer to the *Summary*, which is a typescript made from his dictation, so it seems probable that he is talking about one or more of the manuscripts referred to in Russell's twenty-three-sheet manuscript described above. It is anyway natural to assume that these manuscripts did reach Russell after his letter to Miss Donnelly, in which he said that Wittgenstein had been unable to write anything or leave him any record of his ideas except the dictation.

The first clear reference to our *Summary* comes in Wittgenstein's next extant letter to Russell, which Russell dated '[October–November 1913]'. This is printed in *Nb* p. 123 and begins 'Thanks for your letter and the typed stuff! I will begin by answering your questions as well as I can'.

There follow the answers to nine questions and in Wittgenstein's next extant letter (dated 'November 1913' by Russell) he reminds Russell of the questions, which were originally put in a letter of 25 October.

The first six questions seem to fit our *Summary* and the influence of the answers can be seen in its present state. Thus, for example, Wittgenstein says 'Whether *ab*-functions and your truth-functions are the same cannot yet be decided' and Russell, presumably later, added the words '[Note by B. R.]' to the note '[NB. *ab* means the same as WF which means true-false]'. Again Wittgenstein refers to a 'misprint' – 'polarity' for 'bi-polarity' – and Russell has corrected it in the *Summary*.[7]

The sixth answer ('Explanation in the typed stuff') is not a piece of rudeness but evidently a reference to one of Wittgenstein's written explanations and expansions in our *Summary*.

Of the remaining questions number seven quotes a passage in German which corresponds to 'Neither the sense nor the meaning of a proposition is a thing. These words are incomplete symbols', words which occur on f.13 of Russell's manuscript. The answers to eight and nine refer Russell to 'the manuscript'. It does not require an Oedipus to conclude that the manuscript in question was the German original of at least part of Russell's twenty-three-page manuscript. The passage quoted occurs in the so-called '3rd MS', which also contains what may be 'the exact *ab*-indefinable' referred to by Wittgenstein (that given on *Nb*, p. 102, ll.31ff;) but 'general indefinables' (the subject of question nine) are discussed under that name only in the '2nd MS' and '4th MS.'

Russell's manuscript is quite evidently a translation, and probably by Russell: the English is much superior to that of the *Summary* and the written text contains improvements upon first thoughts: 'denote' corrected to 'designate'; 'simple propositions' to 'atomic propositions' (by 14 October 1914 Wittgenstein called these '*Elementarsätze*' but in *Principia*

---

7   The occurrence is that printed in *Nb*, p. 94, 1.17.

Mathematica an elementary proposition means one not containing apparent variables); 'A comparison' to 'An analogy for the theory of truth' (*Tractatus* 4.063 '*Ein Bild*'); 'the point on which the analogy depends' to 'in which the analogy fails' (*Tractatus* 4.063 '*Der Punkt, an dem das Gleichnis hinkt*'), and one or two others. Where we know or can conjecture the original German, the translation is excellent.[8] The manuscript distinguishes square from round brackets, the latter being evidently Wittgenstein's brackets while the former seem to enclose Russell's additions to the text. Thus, for example, on f.16, after 'If we formed all possible atomic propositions, the world will be completely described if we declared the truth or falsehood of each', there is added '[I doubt this]' (The Costello version (= *Nb* p. 98, l.3) is a clumsy paraphrase of the two remarks). Clearly Russell is expressing a doubt about Wittgenstein's view: and we do indeed find the *view* expressed later in *Tractatus* 4.26 and the *doubt* in *Our Knowledge of the External World* (Russell 1914b), p. 53 and n.

The genesis of the second stage of the material we are considering is easier to describe. The *Summary* was typed out again on the same machine, incorporating Russell's corrections and Wittgenstein's corrections and additions. Wittgenstein's '*You* – for instance imagine every fact as a spatial complex' is changed to '*Russell* – for instance imagines'. Spelling is corrected. One misreading of Wittgenstein's hand is introduced and will be given in a list of textual points later. The distinction between square and round brackets is retained.

The Russell manuscript is also copied, with considerable accuracy, in a separately foliated typescript from the same machine. There are some marginal numbers and question marks and corrections, all apparently in Russell's hand, which will be described later.

Included with these typescripts in the Bertrand Russell Archive are:

(i)   a sheet bearing the following in Russell's hand:

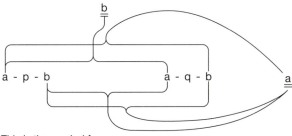

This is the symbol for ~p v ~q

8   A small instance is the surely correct rendering 'The plain man' for 'Der Unbefangene', which in *Nb* (p. 5 and *passim*) is rendered 'The uncaptive (spirit &c.)'.

(ii) a list of section headings in Russell's hand corresponding to those in the Costello version;

(iii) a sheet with some diagrams involving points A, B and C irregularly placed, whose significance is hard to conjecture.

Sheet (ii) will be discussed later. Sheet (i) must have been written after Wittgenstein had explained this notation to Russell in a letter of November or December 1913, Russell having previously not understood it (*Nb* p. 126). Russell adapts the example there given to the logical indefinable of the original third MS.

The whole of this second stage is covered by a sheet containing in (it seems) Russell's hand of a later date: 'Notes on Logic by Ludwig Wittgenstein September 1913'.

The sequence of events may now be summarized.

20 September	Wittgenstein requests an interview
4 October	First interview
11? October	Last interview, dictation of 'Summary'
Before 29 October	Typing of Summary, corrections by Russell, despatch to Wittgenstein in Norway
16 October	Arrival of Wittgenstein in Norway
Between 16 and 25 October	Despatch of manuscript from Norway to Russell
Between 29 October and some time in November	*Summary* arrives in Norway together with questions about 'the manuscript'
?late October or November	Translation of manuscripts by Russell, typing of second stage of 'Notes on Logic', (presumably) return of German originals to Wittgenstein

Detailed discussion of the structure of this version of 'Notes on Logic' is not so necessary now that it is printed, but the following may be said. First: the *Summary* was intended as a summary of all Wittgenstein's work up to that time but was taken by Russell to represent chiefly work done during August and September. On examination it proves also to be primarily, though not exclusively, a summary of ideas contained in the four manuscripts. Usually the formulation in the *Summary* suffers not only from the difficulty for Wittgenstein of dictating in English but also from lack of context. Thus the *Summary* includes the gist of the last three lines of the paragraph in the 3rd MS as an analogy for the theory of truth (= *Nb*, p. 95, ll.16–32) but not the argument, and the *Summary*, followed here by the Costello version, places the remark, 'however, for instance, 'not p' may be explained, the question 'what is negated' must have a meaning', after the statement that a proposition itself must occur in the statement that it is judged (*Nb*, p. 96, l.18) whereas the 3rd MS places it more intelligibly after the statement that within logical functions whole propositions must occur (= *Nb*, p. 96, ll.39–43, after which the remark we are discussing occurs in the MS). The Costello version does not always omit one of a pair of doublets, but when it does so it generally omits the version from the *Summary*.

However, the *Summary* also contains formulations not in the manuscripts that Russell translated, as for instance the anticipation of *Tractatus* 5.522:

> What is essential in a correct apparent-variable notation is this:
> (1) it must mention a type of propositions; (2) it must show which components of a proposition of this type are constants.
> (Cf. *Nb*, p. 106, ll.25ff.)

It is tempting to suppose that Wittgenstein read out this remark from a volume of his *Tagebuch*[9] and perhaps most of the *Summary* consists of such impromptu translation.

Second: the four manuscripts contain a number of formulations which, in the German original, must have taken, almost precisely, a form that we find again in the *Tractatus*. This can be verified by examining the parallels signalized by the editors of *Nb*. These are by no means all the parallels that exist, but it happens that they are practically all MS passages and not *Summary* passages. The exceptions are the parallels to 5.5422 and 5.2341 on p. 97, to 5.43 on p. 100, and to 3.332 on p. 106. The difference between the *Summary* and the manuscripts in this respect can be illustrated from *Nb*, p. 106, ll.4–13. The first sentence here is a *Summary* passage (with editorial additions) and seems to be an abbreviation of the sentences that follow, which come from the 3rd MS and are a much more exact parallel to *Tractatus* 3.315.

> *Summary* (original text). In a proposition convert all its indefinables into variables; there then remains a class of propositions which is not all propositions but a type.
> *3rd MS* If we change a constituent a of a proposition $\phi(a)$ into a variable, then there is a class
> $$\hat{p}\,\{(\exists x).\,(\phi x) = p\}.$$

---

9   The 1914–17 Notebooks are such *Tagebücher*. He refers to them also in a letter of November 1913: 'I am convinced I shall never publish anything in my lifetime. But after my death you must see to the printing of the volume of my journal [*Tagebuch*] with the whole story in it' (translation) (*CL*, pp. 58, 61).

This class in general still depends upon what, by an *arbitrary convention*, we mean by 'φ (x)' But if we change into variables all those symbols whose significance was arbitrarily determined, there is still such a class. But this is not now dependent upon any convention, but only upon the nature of the symbol 'φ (x)'. It corresponds to a logical type.

Tractatus 3.315 (translation adapted). If we change a constituent of a proposition into a variable, then there is a class of propositions all of which are values of the resultant variable proposition. This class in general still depends upon what by an arbitrary convention we mean by parts of the original proposition. But if we change into variables all those symbols whose significance was arbitrarily determined, there is still such a class. But this is not now dependent upon any convention, but only upon the nature of the proposition. It corresponds to a logical type.

A natural conclusion is that parts of the *Summary* were read out from, and most, if not all, of the German manuscript material was copied from, manuscripts which later served Wittgenstein as a quarry for the aphorisms of the *Tractatus*. We have Paul Engelmann's testimony that these comprised seven office-books or ledgers,[10] no doubt volumes of what Wittgenstein called his *Tagebuch*. It may be conjectured that at least one of these dated from 1913.

The four manuscripts were evidently extracts from different parts of the *Tagebuch* and differ slightly in terminology and standpoint. In the first MS there is no mention of WF-functions or *ab*-functions. The second MS speaks of TF- or WF-schemata and suggests only tentatively that logical constants may be non-existent. The third MS speaks of ab-functions, written $^{a}_{b}p$, and the fourth writes them *a-p-b*. The third and fourth MSS are both more emphatic about the non-existence of logical objects. (All the general remarks printed in the 'Preliminary' section of the Costello version are from the fourth MS.) The *Summary* incidentally uses all three ways of speaking of truth-functions, but in his manuscript additions Wittgenstein uses the form *a-p-b*. The change from calling the poles of the proposition 'W' and 'F' (reasonably enough altered to 'T' and 'F' sometimes by Russell, sometimes by the editors of *Nb*) to calling them '*a*' and '*b*' seemed important to Wittgenstein. The story of Wittgenstein's visit told by Whitehead (himself the subject of many anecdotes) rings true in this respect: Wittgenstein was shown in and after a period of silence said explosively 'A proposition has two poles. It is *apb*'

10 Cf. G.H. von Wright's 'Historical Introduction' in *PT*, p. 4. (Now see also Chapter 23 in the present collection.)

but when asked what a and b were, answered in a voice of thunder 'a and b are indefinable'.[11] He seems to have thought that a certain bipolarity, sense, or directionality was essential to propositions: they not only indicated two possibilities (p and $\sim p$, as we should say) but preferred one of the two. This feature explained truth and falsity and was more fundamental than either. Hence his doubt about the equation of WF-functions with ab-functions and hence his attempt in the 'Notes dictated to Moore' (April 1914) to explain how asymmetry between the a-pole and the b-pole is introduced.[12]

The Journal passages from which the manuscripts were taken (if these conjectures are accepted) were presumably written during August and September. At the end of August when Wittgenstein came to England he told Pinsent (according to Pinsent's diary) that he had discovered a new system which seemed to clear up everything, although it upset a lot of Russell's work on the fundamental concepts of logic. And on 29 August Pinsent writes 'It seems that both Russell and old Whitehead are most enthusiastic about his recent work in Logic. It is probable that the first Volume of the '*Principia*' will have to be rewritten and Wittgenstein may write himself the first eleven chapters'.[13] The diary also records the intensity of Wittgenstein's work and his frequent disappointments during their holiday in Norway in September. The sequel we have seen.

The most important clues to the effect of this work of Wittgenstein's on Russell are the marginalia in the second-stage typescript, taken together with the headings on the attached sheet numbered (ii) above. It must be emphasized that these were written in *after* Wittgenstein's departure for Norway and must therefore be entirely Russell's own work. They consist of a projected set of headings and an allocation of the paragraphs of the typescript to a heading judged appropriate. Two paragraphs are cancelled through and one is marked 'o.', for 'omit', but the other omitted paragraphs are all given a heading-number, under which, generally, their doublet occurs in the Costello version.

With the aid of these marginal numbers it is possible to construct the Costello version out of the second-stage typescript by cutting out the paragraphs, putting them in seven piles, arranging each pile in the

---

11 Russell 1967, vol. II, p. 101. David Pinsent recorded in his diary that Wittgenstein planned to stay a night or two with the Whiteheads at Marlborough between 26 and 30 August 1913. This is probably the occasion to which the anecdote refers.

12 See *Nb*, p. 112, ll.27ff. Since this method appeals to the fact that a certain symbol is a tautology and not a contradiction it seems to invoke the notion of truth. Perhaps this is why Wittgenstein in the *Tractatus*, and already in the *NdM*, seems to think that a proposition is given sense by being either-true-or-false.

13 Pinsent 1990, p. 90.

desired order by shuffling (and in many cases by subdividing individual paragraphs), throwing away unwanted doublets, pasting the remaining slips on new sheets, and then writing in manuscript additions or corrections to improve the style and the continuity.[14] This process is merely laborious when it is a matter of matching an existing Costello version but originally, when each step involved an exercise of judgement, it must have cost someone a great deal of work and study.

The question is, whom? Hardly Wittgenstein. He did not see Russell between October 1913 and the end of the war: Russell's references to a meeting at 'the beginning of 1914' (e.g. on p. 99 of Russell 1967, vol. II) can easily be shown to be a mistake, for Wittgenstein in fact made the decision there referred to (to go to Norway) much earlier, as Russell's letter to Lucy Donnelly, quoted above, shows; and his letters to Russell show that he planned to, and in fact did, go to Vienna for Christmas 1913[15] and return straight to Norway. His letters to Moore and Moore's diary also seem to exclude a visit to Cambridge early in 1914. The division into sections is Russell's and it is not to be supposed that he then sent the material to Wittgenstein for final rearrangement. The polishing and in some cases enfeebling of the text is hardly Wittgenstein's: he would not have changed 'If a word creates a world so that in it the principles of logic are true, it thereby creates a world in which the whole of mathematics holds ...' to 'If there were a world created etc.' (*Nb*, p. 96, ll.6ff.).[16] On the other hand he would have changed the content in the light of the new ideas that he had had since returning to Norway. His ideas about identity, for example, or the derivation of the whole of logic from one primitive proposition (see his letter of 29–30 October in *Nb*, p. 122) and the associated notion of tautology (see his November letter, *ibid*, p. 125) would have prevented him from leaving unexpanded the remark that it is impossible to dispense with propositions in which the same argument occurs in different positions (*Nb*, p. 104, l.31) and the remark that Frege's or Russell's laws of deduction are not primitive propositions (*ibid*., p. 100, l.32).

It seems then that Russell, who began the reorganization of the material, must have completed it himself. Wittgenstein's logical theories deeply impressed him. Thus Moore's diaries of this period (October 1913–February 1914) mention a number of conversations about those theories between Moore and Russell, Moore and G.H. Hardy, and Russell and Hardy. On 28 February 1914, when Moore was planning to visit

---

14 This was presumably done with a duplicate of the typescript that we still possess.
15 He seems to have visited Frege on the way to Vienna.
16 Tractatus, 5.123 has 'If a god creates a world etc.': 'word' may be a misreading (*'Wort'* for *'Gott'*) or miswriting (affected by 'world' which follows) of Russell's, but is quite probably a reference to the Word of God through which all things came into being.

Wittgenstein in Norway,[17] he went to Russell 'to hear about Wittgenstein's theories' and, significantly, he 'read Wittgenstein' – surely some version of what we know as 'Notes on Logic'. One indication of this is that the 'Notes dictated to Moore' in April 1914 can refer to the *ab*-notation as something already familiar. It is not at present known which version Moore read but it seems likely that it was the Costello version, for the following reasons. First, Russell sailed for America on 7 March and presumably had with him, already prepared, the 'manuscript' that Costello copied. Second, Moore returned to Cambridge on 17 April. On 27 April in Hall he met Fletcher, congratulated him (W.M. Fletcher [Sc.D. 1914, Secretary of the Medical Research Council 1914] an experienced administrator and a distinguished physiologist was Wittgenstein's tutor), and 'asked about Wittgenstein'. On the next day he wrote to Wittgenstein 'about Dissertation'. We have Wittgenstein's angry reply to this letter, which caused a breach between him and Moore. It reads, in part:

> When I wrote Logik [sic] I didn't consult the Regulations, and therefore I think it would only be fair if you gave me my degree without consulting them so much either. As to a Preface and Notes, I think my examiners will easily see how much I have cribbed from Bosanquet.

The context is easily reconstructed: Wittgenstein was an Advanced Student (in 1913–14 renamed Research Student) and could obtain a BA for a dissertation embodying the results of his research. The regulations went on to say:

> The applicant shall state, generally in a preface to his dissertation and specifically in notes, the sources from which his information is derived, the extent to which he has availed himself of the work of others, and the portions of the dissertation which he claims as original.

Moore had shown Fletcher, or described to him, a dissertation of Wittgenstein's called *Logic* that lacked Preface and Notes of the required kind, and Fletcher had pronounced it inadequate. (Wittgenstein would also have had to complete six terms of residence before actually receiving the degree, which would have cost him a term or two more.) Clearly only the Costello version of 'Notes on Logic' would have constituted even an

---

17 He did so from 24 March to 13 April. I am very grateful to Mrs. Dorothy Moore for permission to use the diaries and to Mr. Paul Levy for actual access to them.

inadequate dissertation, so it is natural to suppose that it was this version that Moore read. Indeed we must suppose that he had a copy and, if this is so, he may have taken it to Norway and Wittgenstein may have seen it then if not earlier. But for all this, and although Wittgenstein may have approved the project of using it as a dissertation, the external and internal evidence seems to exclude his actually having compiled it. Moore's diary for the period of the Norway visit does not mention any revision of 'Notes on Logic' but does, of course, mention the 'Notes dictated to Moore' (*NdM*), and it may be that these, rather than or together with some version of 'Notes on Logic' were to form the proposed dissertation. They too are actually entitled 'Logic'.

Russell's motive in compiling 'Notes on Logic' was not only to help Wittgenstein towards a degree. He was also anxious to understand, to digest, and to pass on to others those logical theories that 'persuaded [him] that what wanted doing in logic was too difficult for [him]'.[18] True, what affected Russell most was Wittgenstein's criticism of what he had written about theory of knowledge, but if we look at those parts of Russell's 1913 manuscript on *Epistemology* (sic) which he left unpublished,[19] we find a number of ideas that are implicitly criticized in 'Notes on Logic' – the conception of facts as complexes (cf. *Nb*, p. 93, l. 30, p. 96, l. 34), the belief that there were logical objects with which we were acquainted (cf. *Nb*, p. 93, l. 33, p. 99, l. 19, p. 100, l. 41), the conception of 'understanding' (and hence of 'judging') as a relation between a person and the several components of the proposition understood (or judged) (cf. *Nb*, p. 96, l. 14, p. 97, l. 27, p. 101, l. 9, p. 103, l. 27), and the conception of truth and falsity as properties of propositions (cf. *Nb*, p. 95, l. 30). Also the 'Notes on Logic' carefully explain the difference between a name and a form or general indefinable (cf. *Nb*, pp. 98f., p. 100, l. 25), whereas *Epistemology* tends to speak simply of constituents and (by Wittgenstein's standards) to neglect the differences between them. Finally it is surely significant that the third and most logical section of *Epistemology*, 'Molecular Propositional Thought', seems not to have been written at all,[20] so that the book never got as far as the subject of knowledge, which would have come fourth in Russell's original plan.

18 Letter to Lady Ottoline Morrell (written in 1916 but looking back to 1913–14) printed in Russell 1967, vol. II, p. 57.

19 Now in the Bertrand Russell Archive. The first six chapters (missing from the manuscript) were published in the *Monist* between January 1914 and April 1915, though obviously with some changes. Later the whole was published as *Theory of Knowledge* (Russell 1984).

20 These were my first impressions of the Russell manuscript, confirmed by supplementary information from Mr. Kenneth Blackwell, but see now [2001] Professor E.R. Eames's study of the relevant material in Russell 1984.

If the above account is correct in essentials the Costello version of 'Notes on Logic' is Russell's compilation, and for the most part his translation, from Wittgenstein's notes. Its faults are that it often incorporates, in a puzzling manner, both a full and an abbreviated statement of the same point and, perhaps more important, that it places points in an order and a context which, however rational, is not one that ever occurred to their original author. In *Zettel* this was perhaps unavoidable (the slips in their original date and order, where known, would have produced a rather disconnected text; besides in some cases, now probably unidentifiable, Wittgenstein arranged the slips in bundles), but in 'Notes on Logic' we have an earlier and more authentic stage, in which the order seems random, perhaps, but was to some extent chosen by Wittgenstein. The Costello version certainly shows us how Russell viewed the material: the typescripts and manuscripts in the Russell Archive give us clues to Wittgenstein's development. They would be a better choice for a printed version.

Appendix on the text

For those who have the Costello version, it may be useful to indicate a few points where the material discussed above suggests that the text there printed misrepresents Wittgenstein's (and sometimes even Russell's) intentions. (References are to *Nb*: '*a/b*' should be read as '*a* should be *b*'; S = the first stage of the *Summary*, R = Russell's manuscript, T = Russell's second-stage typescripts).

p. 93	l. 3	NOTES ON LOGIC/LOGIC (Wittgenstein's letter to Moore).
	l. 4	*September 1913/August to November 1913* (argument above).
p. 94	l. 2	necessarily/[necessarily] RT (a footnote is needed to say that square-bracketed passages are supplied by Russell).
	ll. 8–9	(constituent = particular, component = particular or relation, etc.) – this is meaningless here and appears to be a misplaced editorial note of Russell's.
p. 95	l. 28	I can indicate a point of the paper which is white and black – RT have 'what is white and black' with a query in the margin of T, presumably a mistranslation (owing to homoioteleuton) of '*Wir können auf einen Punkt des Papiers zeigen auch ohne zu wissen, was weiss und schwarz ist*' ('without knowing what black and white are') as in *Tractatus* 4.063. 'which is black and white' is meaningless.
p. 96	ll. 20–22	'A judges (that) p'/'A judges p' ST (*bis*) – cf. also the doublet on p. 97, ll. 11ff.
p. 97	l. 9	functions with sense (*ab*-functions)/*ab*-functions RT – the editorial expansion of Russell's is unnecessary if harmless. The *Nb* footnote, '*ab*' = 'WF' = 'True-False', is at least questionable, *v.s.*

p. 97   l. 17   the *ab*-notation (later explained)/the *ab*-notation RT – if anywhere this editorial addition of Russell's should be made in the passage just discussed. At *this* point, incidentally, RT have a diagram:

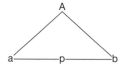

p. 98   l. 3   (the textual point here – Russell's doubt about Wittgenstein – is sufficiently covered by the *Nb* footnote, *v.s.*)

p. 98   l. 6   If there were a world created/If a word creates a world etc. – *v.s.*

p. 98   l. 12   A name cannot only/A name can not only RT.

p. 98   l. 13   Propositions, which are symbols having reference to facts/Propositions [which are symbols having reference to facts] RT.

p. 98   l. 27   We do want to know that our names have meaning and our propositions sense/We want to know the meaning of names and the sense of propositions RT – Russell's editing here may have reversed the sense of the original: the earlier version should at least be mentioned.

p. 98   l. 32   The form of a proposition may be symbolized in the following way/The form of a proposition symbolizes in the following way RT – an unfortunate improvement by Russell. The doublet in the *Summary*, omitted in the Costello version, reads 'The form of a proposition has meaning in the following way …'.

p. 99   l. 25   logical types (forms)/logical types RT.

p. 99   l. 32   Every statement about complexes/Every statement about apparent complexes RT – the translation may be clumsy but the idea is that a statement can only *seem* to be about a complex (cf. p. 99, l. 37, the *Summary* doublet).

ibid.   can be resolved into the logical sum – this occurs in R and is therefore probably an archetypal error for 'product'.

p. 101   l. 26   a TF (or *ab*) scheme/a TF scheme ST.

p. 101   l. 34   *ab*(TF)-functions/*ab*-functions ST.

p. 101   l. 39   [This is quite arbitrary …] – a footnote in Wittgenstein's hand in S. This should not have square brackets.

ibid.   fixed on which order the poles have to stand in/fixed on which sides the poles have to stand S, misread by R.

p. 102 l. 10   (cf. Sheffer's work) – not in ST, presumably a note by Russell.

p. 103 l. 25   a relation of questioning to the facts – T queries this in the margin.

p. 104 ll. 12–16 This paragraph is marked 'IV' in 1 and clearly ought to go there, like or instead of its *Summary* doublet (= p. 103, ll. 7–9).

p. 104 l. 17   Alternate indefinability/alternative indefinability RT.

p. 105 ll. 32–3   it comes to seem as if logic dealt with things which have been deprived of all properties except complexity/it comes to seem as if logic dealt with things which have been deprived of all properties except thing-hood, and with propositions deprived of all properties except complexity RT.

p. 106 l. 6   which does not include all propositions, but does include an entire type/which is not all propositions but a type ST.

p. 106 l. 27   components (forms and constituents)/components [forms and constituents] ST.

While the above was printing I learnt from Dr. Griffin that Russell in a letter of 1958 said that he had only one memory about 'Notes on Logic', namely that they were dictated to a German male stenographer who, when Wittgenstein said, 'A is the same letter as A', remarked, 'Well that is true anyway'. (Wittgenstein's remark occurs in the third MS.)

I further heard from M. Kenneth Blackwell, who has been examining Russell's letters to Lady Ottoline Morrell, now in the library of the University of Texas, that these show: (a) that Wittgenstein 'spent Tuesday [7 October 1913] at Birmingham dictating extracts from his notebook to a German short hand writer'; (b) that on Thursday, 9 October, P.E.B. Jourdain's secretary was to come to take down, presumably in English, Russell's conversation with Wittgenstein; (c) that in February 1914 Russell was busy 'translating, classifying, and copying' the notes Wittgenstein had left him in October.

It will be fairly obvious how far this additional information confirms and corrects my conjectures. It also shows the degree of certainty possible in inquiries of this kind. I owe a renewed debt of gratitude to Dr. Griffin and Mr. Blackwell.

Note added in 2001: It is evident, even from the endnote above, that at least one of Wittgenstein's 'manuscripts' mentioned above was dictated to a stenographer (and then probably typed or transcribed) in England. This need not change my account in essentials.

I am now inclined, however, to believe that the actual composition of the Costello version was probably due to Costello himself, working on the basis of Russell's indications of the sections to which each remark was to be assigned and of the titles of those sections. This is much more likely than that Russell himself (a man who had never tied up a parcel in his life) undertook the work of marquetry that I have described. Many of the mistakes also cannot plausibly attributed to Russell, though on other points we know that he (so Wittgenstein thought) misunderstood the points at issue. On this new hypothesis the manuscript from which Costello 'copied' the Notes may have been the very manuscript now at McMaster with Russell's marginal numbering.

A third consideration I should like to advance is to question whether the Costello version is in principle an inferior one. I do this with reluctance since the editors of *Notebooks 1914–16* were persuaded by my arguments above and substituted the original version for the Costello one in a second edition (1979). Some rearrangement such as Russell envisaged is a great help in reading the Notes, even though there are a number of errors and infelicities in the actual execution. (These could probably be covered by discreet footnotes or simply corrected.) This is to touch on a perpetual problem for editors of Wittgenstein.

More important than these afterthoughts is to indicate that the texts of the summary, of Russell's translation and of the Russell typescript are now available in the Oxford/Bergen edition of Wittgenstein's works, where they can also be viewed in facsimile, while all of these, together with the Costello version are discussed in the second volume of Michael Biggs's *Editing Wittgenstein's 'Notes on Logic'*, in a series of Working Papers from Bergen. In volume 1 he takes issue with a number of the assertions in my paper above, but largely on matters of detail which do not, I think, alter the general picture I gave of the inchoate character of the original, the genesis of the Costello version or the type of errors that entered in.

23

SOME PRE-*TRACTATUS*
MANUSCRIPTS

There has recently come to light a list of manuscripts and typescripts, with instructions for their disposal, which suggests a number of hypotheses concerning the composition of Wittgenstein's only printed work. The list, and a subsequent letter, were made available to me by Frau Charlotte Eder of Vienna and have now found a home in the Brenner-Archiv of Innsbruck University thanks to the generosity of Herrn Dipl. Ing. Otto Vest-Rusan of Vienna and of the Wittgenstein family, and can now be consulted either in the Brenner-Archive or in the manuscript section of the Austrian National Library.[1]

The list is written out in the hand of Wittgenstein's sister Hermine and dated January 1917. It runs as follows:

1) Buch gross Kanzlei bei Trenkler   Handschriftlich
existiert auch
Maschin. in Olmütz corrig.

2) 2 Bücher Quart bei Trenkler

3) 1 Buch Quart   (Ein Teil davon existiert schon im Maschinengeschriebenen Heft) nur handschriftlich

4) Buch Octav   wörtlich jeder Satz in der Reihen-folge ohne jede Korrectur

5) Buch gross Kanzlei enthält die Umarbeitung
von 1) und 2) zur Veröffentlichung.

---

1   I am grateful to Frau Eder, as also to Dr. Walther Methlagl and Dr. Allan Janik, both of Innsbruck, for information about, and discussion of, the recent find of papers relating to Wittgenstein.

Russell erhält 3) 4) u 5) u 1) u 2) in Maschinschrift
und die goldene Uhr

Pinsent erhält 1 in Manuskript

Maschinenschrift bie Trenkler zu zerstören.

An explanation will serve also as an English translation. Five items are listed. 1) and 2) are respectively a 'large Chancery'[2] volume and two quarto volumes. All these are manuscripts, as is indicated in a side-note, which adds that the material also exists at Olmütz in typescript and corrected. 3) and 4) are respectively a single quarto and a single octavo volume. A side-note to these two jointly states that the material exists only in manuscript. Against item 3), however, there is a further side-note (presumably an afterthought) stating that part of it was already included in the fascicule of typescript (we shall discuss later which). Item 4) also has a second side-note, stating that it contains 'literally every proposition in order without any corrections'. Item 5) is another 'large Chancery' volume, containing the revision of items 1 and 2 and is for publication. Items 3, 4 and 5, are to be sent to Russell, along with the typescript of items 1 and 2 and the gold clock. Pinsent is to have 1 in manuscript, while the typescript in Trenkler's possession is to be destroyed.

We have here, fairly plainly, a copy of instructions for the disposal of his literary effects in case of his death given to his sister by Wittgenstein on the occasion of his return to the front (an officer now) in January 1917. The letter from his sister already referred to bears this out. It is dated 7 June 1917 and (lightly adapted to print) runs as follows:

Ich wollte heute Deine Verfügungen hinsichtlich Deiner Schriften auf ein besseres Papier abschreiben und sie meinem Testament anfügen. Dabei bin ich aber draufgekommen, dass sie vielleicht doch nicht *ganz* deutlich sind, und ich schicke sie Dir, nachdem ich sie abgeschrieben habe, mit folgenden Fragen:

Erstens schreibst Du, '1.) und 2.) existiert auch maschinenschriftlich in Olmütz corrigiert.' Das ist offenbar nicht identisch mit Nr. 5.) da Russell Beides bekommen soll. Bitte nenne das also Nr. 6.) und schreibe das Format dazu.

Zweitens schreibst Du bei 3.), 'ein Teil davon existiert schon im maschinengeschriebenen Heft'. Auch dabei möchte ich die Nummer wissen, wohl Nr. 6.)?

---

2 'gross' and 'Kanzlei' here mean the same, I think, rather than forming a technical expression equivalent to the English 'double Chancery'.

Drittens: ist 5.) handschriftlich oder maschinschriftlich?
Die Maschinenschrift bei Trenkler könnte man noch Nr. 7
nennen, damit man alles numeriert hat.

Du wirst Dich vielleicht über meine Fragen wundern, aber ich
finde solche Verfügungen können nicht klar genug sein.

(In the course of making a fair copy of his instructions to be attached to
her own will, she comes across some points that are not quite clear. The
typescript at Olmütz cannot be identical with item 5, otherwise Russell
need not be sent both: should it be numbered 6? and what is the paper
size? In which typescript is part of item 3 to be found? Is this item 6? And
should the typescript Trenkler has be numbered 7? Such dispositions can
never be too clear.)

These, his own instructions, are to be found in a collection of letters *to*
Wittgenstein, because they were sent back to him for clarification. His
sister had not got the volumes or fascicules by her, otherwise she could
have checked some points herself. We may assume that in addition to the
five numbered items (all manuscript material) there were indeed two
typescripts, of which one, which in January had been in Olmütz, was to
be preferred. The other remained in Vienna with some of Wittgenstein's
earlier notebooks.

Trenkler was the Wittgenstein family's man of business at this time,
working no doubt from the Kanzlei Wittgenstein, the office for family
business, in the Alleegasse. Books or typescripts not listed as with
Trenkler or in Olmütz were presumably taken with him by Wittgenstein.

We now proceed to a tentative identification of the documents referred
to. Item 1 was probably Wittgenstein's Norwegian notebook shown to
Moore in April 1914, containing material which we know in part from
Notes on Logic (translated by Russell in autumn 1913) and from *Notes
dictated to Moore* (translated by Wittgenstein for or perhaps with Moore)
and a few allusions in letters. The material in the two sets of notes is laid
under contribution – verbally cited, it seems certain, though we have not
the German[3] – in the 'Prototractatus' and in the *Tractatus* itself. It must
have been represented in the notebook at Wittgenstein's disposal during
the war and indeed, when he writes to Russell in December 1914, he
specifically mentions a plan of sending the volume seen by Moore in
April.[4] A pre-war volume is also likely to have been the one chosen as a
memento for David Pinsent, the Cambridge friend with whom

---

3 Compare for example *TLP* 3.315 with *NL*, p. 101 [4], 3.322 with p. 97 [2], 3.344 with
  NdM, p. 117 [5].
4 *Briefe*, 1980, p. 66.

Wittgenstein had spent his holidays and, in effect, had discovered Norway.

The next item will have comprised the first two of the wartime note-books we still possess (MSS 101 and 102). These actually contain instruc-tions that they are to be sent to Bertrand Russell at Trinity (little did Wittgenstein know how the war would affect Russell's relations with that college!), but we may suppose those instructions to have been given before any typescript had been made from the volumes. It need not be supposed that a further volume intervened between that shown to Moore and the first of the wartime notebooks. Some time after Moore's visit, probably in May 1914, Wittgenstein wrote to Russell[5] that he was exhausted and could not work; and when he wrote again in December 1914[6] he talked of arranging to send Russell only a single pre-war volume (that already mentioned) together with one that he had written during the war (our MS 101, obviously): thus no significant intervening manu-script will have existed. The second wartime notebook was composed after the December letter to Russell and continued until June 1915, by which time Wittgenstein was attached to a workshop train in Galicia. The next evidence we have of Wittgenstein's writing at this time is a letter to Russell of 22 October 1915 in which Wittgenstein says that he has worked well in the last months and is engaged in summarizing everything and writing it down in the form of a treatise.[7] If Wittgenstein dies, Russell will be sent the latest version, written in pencil on loose sheets. This last we do not have preserved, nor does Wittgenstein refer to it in January 1917. Perhaps the material in it was absorbed into one of the typescripts made later, and it itself discarded. The composition of this summary may account for the gap about this time in the series of notebooks, whether those preserved or those that may be presumed to have existed. For it seems likely that item 3 in the 1917 list is in fact the third of the wartime notebooks we still have preserved, MS 103, which runs from April 1916 to January 1917.[8]

This results from various considerations. The weightiest, perhaps, is that MS 103 certainly existed when Wittgenstein drew up this list, yet no other item in the list can represent it: it is not itself a summary nor a setting of propositions in order, and, conversely, it is itself drawn upon for the *Tractatus* (immediately, of course, for the 'Prototractatus', which

---

5 *ibid.*, p. 56.

6 *Loc. cit.* in note 4.

7 'Ich bin jetzt dabei das Ganze zusammenzufassen und in Form einer Abhandlung niederzuschreiben.' *Briefe*, 1980, p. 74.

8 The editors nonetheless entitled their volume *Notebooks 1914–1916*, perhaps from a distaste for pedantry, since the 1917 remarks are few in number.

we shall discuss shortly). Secondly, if there had been a notebook in immediate continuation of MS 102, it too would have been included in the revision and summary represented by the typescript or typescripts (Hermine Wittgenstein's 6 and 7) and by the manuscript item 5. Instead we find that only part of item 3 is so included – surely because item 3 was, up to the date of the list itself, still in the course of composition (as is indeed true of MS 103). On this hypothesis, Wittgenstein's philosophical work from June 1915 to March 1916, when MS 103 begins, will have consisted in preparing his treatise – the summary already mentioned of MSS 101 and 102 and the missing Norway notebook, a summary written first on loose sheets and then in a notebook. From either or both of these a typescript was made. It is natural to suppose that Wittgenstein's item 5 was this notebook and that at any rate the earlier of the two typescripts (presumably that which remained at Vienna with Trenkler) was made from it, probably in September 1916, the date of Wittgenstein's first home leave.[9]

I suppose that work on the manuscript treatise ceased in March 1916 when Wittgenstein, in complicated circumstances,[10] left the comparative safety of the workshop train for the front. A comrade describes how Wittgenstein then packed what was necessary and gave everything else away. It is natural to suppose that all previous notebooks and the summary or summaries of them were sent back to Vienna at this point (to Trenkler, no doubt) and that Wittgenstein left for the front and there opened a new notebook. The code entries in MS 103 do indeed begin at the end of March 1916, though there are no philosophical entries until 15 April.

This was the summer of the Brusilov offensive and I have described elsewhere the hardships that Wittgenstein endured and the strong ethical, one can say religious, tone that even his philosophical notes (in this very notebook) now took. In September (as we have seen) he went on leave to Vienna. At this point he must have arranged for the preparation of a typescript, probably by dictating to a typist, whether from his notebooks (MSS 101, 102, and now 103 partly filled) or from those together with manuscript summaries (items 4 and 5 in the list we are considering and perhaps a loose-leaf predecessor).[11] In fact, as will

9 A citation preserved in the *Kriegsarchiv* has Wittgenstein 'in the field' until 2 September.
10 Described in McGuinness 1988, pp. 237ff.
11 Dictation to a typist was a method of composition often used by Wittgenstein and in 1953 (see next note) Paul Engelmann wrote to Professor F.A. von Hayek (letter of 12 June 1953) of his recollection, *'Vor seinem Abgang an die italienische Front hat [Wittgenstein] sein Manuskript in Wien in die Maschine diktiert.'* ('He dictated his manuscript to a typist in Vienna before leaving for the Italian front.' If the Italian front is really meant, this must be a reference to 1918 – and probably to the composition of the final typescripts of the *Tractatus* – but the method used earlier will have been the same.)

appear, I think it likely that two typescripts were made. Item 4, the small (octavo) volume referred to, was probably a transcript made in order to facilitate the production of the typescripts. It cannot be plausibly identified with any known manuscripts and perhaps its not surviving is due to the fact that, containing none of the necessary corrections, it became actually misleading.

After his autumn leave in 1916 Wittgenstein went to the Officers' Training School in Olmütz, where he remained until shortly before Christmas. There he seems to have had several notebooks with him. Engelmann recalls having seen 'large office-books bound in black and green cloth of the kind used in Austria as ledgers', from seven of which (subsequently destroyed) Wittgenstein extracted the *Tractatus*.[12]

Certainly he had with him MS 103, since many of its entries date from that period. And almost certainly at least one typescript, since, when he went to Vienna for Christmas, he left in Olmütz a typescript which, given the conditions of life at the time, is unlikely to have been produced there. What he very probably did do while in Olmütz was to introduce corrections into the typescript, thus superseding its sister in Vienna.[13]

We shall now attempt to identify more precisely the large-format notebook which is item 5 in the list. In my view this can be none other than MS 104, which in its present state contains the whole of the 'Prototractatus' and another eighteen pages of drafts or corrections intended for the final 'Ahbandlung', but which was then not written up to anything like that extent. It would not naturally be described as a ledger but it is distinctly larger than the wartime notebooks, and, as it happens, is bound in black and green. The first 70 or so pages do indeed contain a summary of the first two wartime notebooks and the pre-war notes, that is to say, a set of propositions or remarks largely based on those notes and so numbered as to form a treatise when read in the order indicated. Typically, some of the best remarks are picked out, a numbered framework is set up first, and a large number of other remarks, of the nature sometimes of additions to the framework, sometimes of infilling, are added. Naturally, intermediate stages, such as the loose-leaf summary mentioned by Wittgenstein, may also have been drawn upon, but in the case of quotations from the notebooks it is

---

12 Letters quoted in G.H. von Wright's 'Historical introduction' to *PT*, 1971, pp. 4, 8. For various reasons (not least their incompatibility with the list we are discussing) I believe that factual details given by Engelmann should be treated with reserve (as indeed he himself recommended).

13 A typescript made in Vienna at Christmas would not have been ripe for destruction in January and it is hard to see when a window for the production of a typescript will have opened before the autumn of 1916.

scarcely necessary to postulate the existence of such stages. In a sense the seal is set on this work when on p. 71 (of Wittgenstein's pagination) the following two propositions are written in:

6.3 Alle Satze sind gleichwertig.
7   Wovon man nicht sprechen kann, darüber muss man schweigen.[14]

These complete the scheme of propositions written on p. 3 and are followed by a line in the MS, as may be seen in the facsimile given in *Prototractatus*, 1971. Though such lines admit of various interpretations, we may very naturally take this one to mark a provisional closing-point – that of the proto-'Prototractatus', as it were.[15] For reasons which will appear I believe that the similar line on p. 78 of the manuscript represents the end of a first revision. It is some confirmation of these hypotheses that the few pre-p. 71 (or indeed pre-p. 79) numbers which presuppose post-p. 71 (or post-p. 78) numbers show some sign or other of having undergone revision.[16] Such reasoning is rather exclusive of a possible objection than itself demonstrative: in this manuscript there is an almost universal tendency for the numbers that come later to presuppose those that come earlier, and not conversely. That is only what one might expect if Wittgenstein first chose nodal propositions and then grouped others round them. Nonetheless, down to p. 71 there is a natural progression, the 6's being filled in last, and it is legitimate to seek an explanation of the difference between that progression and the general revision and introduction of new material that takes place from pp. 79 to 103. (pp. 71 to 78 inclusive I propose to deal with shortly.)

These notes constituted the first *Abhandlung* or Treatise so described by Wittgenstein. It will have consisted for the most part of an account of the nature of propositions as such (the principal problem for Wittgenstein at the beginning of the war) and will have ended up with an account, rather brief even by Wittgenstein's standards, of the nature of logic. (We shall see shortly what additions were needed to make this into the

---

14 6.3 (subsequently altered to 6.4) 'All propositions are of equal value.'
  7 'What we cannot speak about we must pass over in silence.'
15 A mark added later, presumably. The many changes in numbering leave several possibilities open, but most probably the original numbering of the former of these propositions as 6.3 was due to the presence of a deleted 6.2 which can just be seen at the head of p. 71: it seems to have read: *Die Ethik besteht nicht aus Sätzen* (Ethics does not consist of propositions).
16 This may be indirect. Thus the insertion of 4.4302 from p. 79 has not led a change on p. 46 to produce 4.4303 (which always had that number) but to the demotion, on the same page, of *4.4302 to produce what is now 4.43011. 5.314 from p. 87 seems to have been fitted in by an analogous method.

'Prototractatus' and *Tractatus* as we know them, and roughly the order in which these came to be made.) There seems to have been a stage in the composition of this early *Abhandlung,* indicated by the line towards the foot of p. 70, when it ended with one of the propositions from the context of 6.13 Die Logik ist keine Lehre sondern ein Spiegelbild der Welt.[17]

But it probably fairly soon occurred to Wittgenstein that he could close very effectively with the two brief sentences quoted above (as *6.3 and 7). So composed the *Abhandlung* would have been even more classically silent over what could not be said than in its present form.

My hypothesis thus is that the *Abhandlung* that Wittgenstein was writing out in October 1915 is preserved for us in the first 70 pages of 'Prototractatus', which thus will probably have been written out between that date and Wittgenstein's departure for the front in March 1916,[18] and will be physically identical with item 5 in the list drawn up in January 1917 (though further pages may have been filled by then). This need not be exactly right, but it must be significant that no passages drawn from the 1916–1917 notebook occur before p. 76 in the 'Prototractatus',[19] whereas the earlier notebooks are, prior to that point, drawn on promiscuously, without special regard for temporal order. Clearly it is part of my present surmise that this *Abhandlung* (MS 104, pp. 1–71) was used in the preparation of at least one typescript in September of 1916. It is even probable that at this point Wittgenstein included in the typescript the propositions of pp. 71–8 (which contain five or so quotations from MS 103, but none from entries later than 19 September) – though conceivably these were only inserted in a second, slightly later typescript. The existence in January 1917 of at least one typescript including pp. 71–8 (together with the fact that there were later entries in MS 103 [= item 3]) would account for the statement that the typescript covered that item only in part. As for content, these pages (pp. 71–8) will have added to the *Abhandlung* the whole discussion of science,[20] the defence of extensionality, and hence the account of propositions of the form 'A believes p',[21] and will have expanded slightly (though not to its full later extent) the discussion of ethics and the

---

17 'Logic is not a body of doctrine but a mirror-image of the world.' I mention the possibility of the original *Abhandlung's* ending here because of the slightly odd fact about proposition 7 that I report later.

18 This will also account for the absence of *Notebook* material between 22.6.15 and 15.4.16: Wittgenstein was engaged on a different task.

19 *Nb*, pp. 84 and 90 indicate parallels with *TLP* 5.136 and 5.523 (= *PT* 5.0441 and 5.322) respectively, but these latter will be found to be rather parallels with, than actual quotations from, the notebooks.

20 Numbered 6.3 in the final version of 'Prototractatus' as also in the *Tractatus*.

21 *PT* 6.001ff, 71 *TLP* 5.54ff.

problem of life.[22] Dealing with these new themes Wittgenstein draws on MS 101, on the volume shown to Moore, and on his own recent notebook (MS 103) respectively.

At or towards the end of September Wittgenstein went to Olmütz, evidently taking his volumes with him,[23] and taking or having sent after him a typescript. The Olmütz months were a period of intense discussion during which Wittgenstein continued to make entries in his notebook and perhaps also to fill in further, in effect to modify, the *Abhandlung* itself (MS 104, *ex hypothesi*). Perhaps this (or other reasons) led him to make manuscript alterations in the typescript and possibly to attach manuscript pages to it. This may be how it came to supersede the typescript left in Vienna (if indeed it did not from the start contain more than the other). When he went home at Christmas Wittgenstein left this typescript (I conjecture) in the hands of his friend and Engelmann's, Heinrich Groag.[24] Groag recollected the loan of an *Abhandlung* numbered as the *Tractatus* is but remembered it as handwritten. I think the list we are discussing rules out the existence of a further entire manuscript at this date, but I have indicated how there may have been a typescript with handwritten parts. (Wittgenstein himself later[25] asks for the return, regardless of postal risks, of 'my manuscripts', but nothing will have turned on exact terminology in that request.)

This typescript may have been needed by Wittgenstein for the further work on the *Abhandlung* that clearly continued. That is not the theme of the present article, but for completeness, and to indicate what elements were missing in the early *Abhandlung* that we have attempted to reconstruct, the following may be said. The final version of 'Prototractatus' was reached by the addition of pp. 79–102. These give the impression (much more than pp. 71–8, already discussed) of being a general revision of the *Abhandlung*, but they too introduce some whole new blocks of material, such as the discussion of mathematics (the 6.2s) and that of solipsism. Death, ethics, and psychology are all introduced or given more space, and, in the course of this, not only is MS 103 drawn on heavily but passages are also extracted from earlier notebooks (or, of course, from intermediate documents, though there seems to be no necessity to postulate their existence). Roughly the extracts from MS 103 predominate in

---

22 6.4ff. and 6.5ff, both *PT* and *TLP.*

23 Engelmann's letters quoted above in note 11.

24 I have long believed I was wrong in inducing Professor von Wright (loc. cit.) to date this loan a year later. The turn of the year 1917/18 does not agree with my recollection (though it does with my notes) of what Dr. Groag said, and would hardly have been possible given the military service of the two men.

25 Undated letter to Engelmann, *Briefe*, p. 79.

pp. 80–90, while pp. 90–100 contain more material that is either original or drawn from elsewhere. In particular there are considerable additions to the difficult discussion of the application of logic (PT 5.34ff, *TLP* 5.55ff.) for which few earlier parallels can be found. There may have been a 1917 notebook discussing these matters, or, of course, MS 104 may itself be that discussion.

This work may lie anywhere between January 1917 and July 1918. An examination of Wittgenstein's writing during that period as close as that we have attempted so far is not in place in the present inquiry (and our sources of information seem to be fewer). It should perhaps be mentioned that the letter of inquiry written by Hermine Wittgenstein in June 1917 contains in Wittgenstein's hand a version of proposition 7 (PT and *TLP*): *Worüber man nicht reden kann, darüber muss man schweigen.*[26]

It is hard to think that Wittgenstein reached p. 71 in MS 104 as late as this, so I am inclined to explain the jotting as a tentative rewording of a crucial proposition, seeking on the one hand more obvious symmetry *(worüber/darüber)*[27] and on the other more contrast (*reden* more opposed to *schweigen* than *sprechen* is). Stylistically my own feeling is that the new version runs the risk of seeming overemphatic.

Work on 'Prototractatus' came to an end in July 1918 when Wittgenstein came on leave (evidently after health difficulties) and prepared a *Korrektur* – a version revised and renumbered so as to resemble closely our *Tractatus*. These corrections are not written into MS 104 but presumably into one of the typescripts, since, when new material was needed, it was written into MS 104 (it fills the pages following p. 103 and is not printed in *Prototractatus,* 1970). Moreover that new material presupposes a typescript that uses the same rather inadequate devices as the final *Tractatus* typescripts (which we do possess) to represent logical notation.[28] With the exception of two propositions[29] the new material (pp. 103–121 of MS 104) does not draw on previous material that we know of. There are additions to every part of the previous *Abhandlung* (i.e. to the ultimate 'Prototractatus') but particularly to the theory of names and objects, to that of sense and reference, and to the account of

---

26 'What we cannot talk about, we must pass over in silence.' As in *PT* and *TLP* only with the substitution of 'worüber' for 'wovon' and 'reden' for 'sprechen'.

27 Compare here the Ogden/Ramsey translation 'Whereof one cannot speak, thereof one must be silent.'

28 These devices are imitated in the Ostwald printing of the *Logisch-philosophische Abhandlung* ('LPA') and (subsequent to that printing) were manually corrected in the Engelmann TS (202 in the catalogue given in von Wright 1982). It is a curious fact that Wittgenstein did not accommodate himself to the typist *before* p. 103. Perhaps only from then on would the material have to be typed from manuscript rather than dictation.

29 3.322 *cf. NL*, p. 97 [2]; 5.503 cf. *Nb* 13.7.16 [3].

inference and probability. In particular the notion of operation (5.2s[30] and 5.3s) is much further developed than in 'Prototractatus'. All these additional remarks appear in MS 104 in exactly the form they take in the surviving typescripts of *Tractatus*, which, though based on other sources too, must have drawn on this manuscript at a late if not final stage,[31] so that we may safely say that we have here the final stage in the composition of that work.

The support of hypotheses and the exhibiting of convergent probabilities has required much detail and many of the results to which they lead may justly be thought no more than tentative. Yet the general conclusion (*pace* Professor von Wright)[32] that it is not necessary, and even an error, to suppose the loss of many of the notebooks from which the *Tractatus* was composed may be regarded as highly probable. So too, perhaps, may the division of the 'Prototractatus' into stages roughly like those described, and, above all, the possibility of using that manuscript to elucidate the order in which Wittgenstein introduced into his final *Tractatus*, his only printed work, as I have called it, things new and old.

---

30 An intermediate version of these remarks occurs in the second part of PT, pp. 108f.

31 The Engelmann TS 202 and the recently rediscovered Gmunden TS 204 are largely identical though 202 contains more manuscript corrections and, as said, was used for the first printing. The Vienna TS 203, curiously enough, is the latest of the three, the typist has incorporated the small manuscript corrections inserted in the other two, but it contains no typed change of substance and practically no manuscript *additions*, and thus is of little philological interest.

32 Obviously many new facts have come to light since he wrote.

24

MANUSCRIPTS AND WORKS
IN THE 1930S

Two collections of Wittgenstein papers, one described and one discovered in recent years, throw light on his methods of work and particularly on the genesis of the first version of the book he was planning in 1936–1939, which it will be convenient to refer to by the name 'Philosophische Bemerkungen [1938]'. We do not have a full version of this projected small volume but it can be constructed with some approximation from the typescripts 220/239 and 221 (von Wright's numeration,[1] which will be followed throughout). It includes more than what Baker and Hacker[2] call 'Proto-Philosophical Investigations' (PPI) as will be shown in due course.

The former of the two collections is catalogued in a sheaf among the papers relative to her brother, papers that Hermine Wittgenstein preserved but which were for a long time lost. They are now for the most part in the Austrian National Library (there are copies in the Brenner Archive of Innsbruck University).[3] I here transcribe and translate two of the relevant documents:

> Fragment of a letter from L.W. to Hermine Wittgenstein:
> [one or more pages missing]
> *dergl. Nicht, daß ich das glaube aber man muß sich erkundigen. Besteht entschiedene Unsicherheit, so würde ich meine M.SS. erst nach Cambridge nehmen, wenn ich selbst das nächste Mal von Wien nach Cambridge gehe. Aber lieber wäre es mir, wenn sie jetzt geschickt werden könnten. Wenn Du*

---

1 von Wright 1982, pp. 35ff. This was the first of a number of publications in which he admirably confronts the necessity of placing publications from the *Nachlass* in the context of Wittgenstein's life and the physical history of the papers. A great difficulty, which he and those he consulted felt at the time, was to individuate the items. Different copies of a typescript often have very diverse manuscript additions. This is perhaps true of 220 and 239, the latter of which was not even known at the time of the first production of the catalogue. A third copy of the same typescript must have existed, *quaere* what number ought to be assigned to it (for the catalogue allows for items that have been lost)?
2 Baker and Hacker 1980, p. 10.
3 See also *FB*, p. 160 f.

sie nun schicken läßt, so laß, bitte eine kleine aber starke Kiste für sie anfertigen, vielleicht mit Scharnieren & Vorhängeschloß, wenn das geht & bei der Versendung keine Schwierigkeiten macht. Meine M.S.S. werden nämlich bis auf weiteres für niemand, außer mir & noch einem, in der Bibliothek zugänglich sein. – Ferner: Diese Manuskripte sind die folgenden: Neun numerierte Bände handgeschrieben & zwei Pakete Maschingeschriebenes In Deiner Verwahrung befindet sich außerdem noch ein M.S. in Papier eingemacht & ich glaube versiegelt dieses bitte ich Dich nicht mitzu schicken. Sollte noch irgend eine Unklarheit sein, so, bitte, laß mich's wissen.

Die Adresse, an die die M.S.S. zu schicken sind ist:
The Librarian
Trinity College, Cambridge
England
Ist keine Zeit mehr dem Max den Krug zukommen zu lassen (wenn es nichts mit der Briefwaage ist), so werde ich ihm jetzt bloß Blumen schenken & den Krug ein ander mal.

Ich bin ziemlich beschäftigt und es geht mir gut. Bitte grüß alle Freunde!!
Dein Bruder/Ludwig

Translation:
[one or more pages missing]
... the like. Not that I believe it, but one had better find out. If there is a definite risk, I would take my manuscripts to Cambridge only when I myself next travel from Vienna to Cambridge. But I should prefer it if they could be sent now. If you have them sent now, please have a small (but strong) box made for them, perhaps with hinges and a padlock, if that can be managed (and does not create any difficulties in the sending). The thing is that in the library my manuscripts will, until further notice, be accessible to nobody but myself and one other person. –

Further: the manuscripts in question are the following: nine numbered volumes in manuscript plus two packets of typescript. Besides these there is also in your keeping a manuscript wrapped in paper and (I think) sealed: please do not send this one with the others. If any obscurity remains, please let me know.

The address to which the manuscripts should be sent is:

The Librarian, Trinity College, Cambridge, England

If there is no longer the time to get the jug to Max (if nothing can be done with the postal scales), then I will just give him a present of flowers for now and the jug another time.

I am fairly busy and things are going well. Please give messages to all friends.

Your brother,
Ludwig

Notes on the letter:

Max. L.W.'s (and H.W.'s) brother-in-law Max Salzer. He was born on 3 March 1868, so this letter was probably written shortly before his seventieth birthday.

ein M.S. in Papier eingemacht/a manuscript wrapped in paper. Probably of a personal character which, significantly, he did *not* want sent to Cambridge.

alle Freunde/all friends. This expression (instead of naming the friends) became typical of the family correspondence during the Anschluß, of which Wittgenstein surely had some presentiment. The letter carefully dissimulates the anxiety about affairs in Austria that he expressed openly in a letter to Ludwig Hänsel on 22 February 1938 (probably of even date with the present letter).

(Hermine Wittgenstein's) List of MSS and TSS

[This exists both in manuscript – apparently in her own hand – and in typescript, with insignificant variations (e.g. *'getippt'* (MS) for *'maschingeschrieben'* (TS)). There is also a manuscript version, in a different hand (possibly Friedrich Waismann's) but also on the writing paper of the Argentinierstrasse house. This version was among Wittgenstein's papers in Cambridge. In the typescript all items are 'ticked' manually, except for *'Inhaltsverzeichnis'* ('Table of contents') and *'1 Paket ohne Aufschrift'* ('1 parcel unlabelled').]

Verzeichnis der Manuskripte (handschriftlich)

I.	Band	Philosophische Bemerkungen	
II.	''	''	''
IV.	''	''	''
V.	''	Bemerkungen	
VI.	''	Philosophische Bemerkungen	
VII.	''	Bemerkungen zur Philosophie	
VIII.	''	''	'' philosophischen Grammatik
IX.	''	Philosophische Grammatik	
X.	''	''	''

Nr.1 ? (ohne Titel)
Philosophische Betrachtungen
Nr.5 (ohne Titel)
Logisch-philosophische Abhandlung
'Inhaltsverzeichnis' (beigeschlossen ein Teil des Verzeichnisses maschingeschrieben; ferner 24 Seiten maschingeschrieben)

Maschingeschriebene Manuskripte:

---

1 Paket mit der Aufschrift 'Alte Durchschläge'
1 ''   ''   ''   ''   'Neue Durchschläge'
1 '' ohne Aufschrift, anscheinend nach Materien geordnete
  Durchschläge.

Translation:
List of Manuscripts (handwritten)

Vol. I	Philosophical Remarks	
'' II	do.	do.
'' IV	do.	do.
'' V	Remarks	
'' VI	Philosophical Remarks	
'' VII	Remarks on Philosophy	
'' VIII	Remarks on Philosophical Grammar	
'' IX	Philosophical Grammar	
'' X	do.	do.

No. 1 ? (no title)
Philosophical Observations
No. 5 (no title)
Tractatus Logico-philosophicus
'Table of contents' (attached is part of the table of contents in typescript;
together with 24 pages of typescript)

Typed Manuscripts:

---

1 parcel with label 'Old Carbon-copies'
1 do. do. do. 'New Carbon-copies'
1 do. without label, apparently carbons arranged by subject.

All of these were evidently once contained in an envelope on which is written in Hermine Wittgenstein's hand:

> Ludwig Herbst/Verzeichnis von Wittgenstein's Ludwigs Manuscripten und Durchschlägen von Dr Waismann aufgestellt/25 Sept 1936

> (Ludwig Autumn/Catalogue of Ludwig's Manuscripts and Carbon-copies compiled by Dr Waismann/25 Sept 1936)

In fact we know from a letter to Wittgenstein from his sister Margaret Stonborough dated 26 September 1936[4] that, after the death of Schlick,

---

4 *FB*, p. 152.

Wittgenstein had been concerned about the whereabouts of at least one of his manuscripts and that a check by Waismann had established that there were in fact none missing. A card with ticks against the various titles seems to be the record of Waismann's investigation and gives some more details of the material, which are not essential to the present discussion.

This letter and list are curiously parallel to a similar pair during the First World War, which I have discussed elsewhere.[5] Not all the items mentioned can now be identified, but Volumes I to X (less III) are clearly nos. 105–14 (less 107). These, sometimes referred to as *MS-Bände*, are the part of the series of large bound notebooks in which Wittgenstein wrote out his thoughts in semi-final form, usually in order later to dictate a selection from them. Some general and personal observations are fairly frequently included, sometimes in code. The Anschluß and the years that followed had the effect that the instructions in Wittgenstein's letter were never carried out, and so these volumes remained in Austria throughout the war, as did volume III/no. 107, whose omission from the list is perhaps illusory, since in fact it bears the title 'Philosophische Betrachtungen' ('Philosophical Observations') and so is probably the item with that title lower down in the list.

After Wittgenstein's death all these became the property of his family, since by explicit provision his English will did not apply to property in Austria, with regard to which he consequently died intestate. They came to light between 1952 and 1967 and are now held in part by the Austrian National Library and in part by Trinity College Library in Cambridge, except for the only known manuscript with the title 'Logisch-philosophische Abhandlung' which is that discovered by von Wright in Vienna in 1965, now in the Bodleian Library at Oxford: no doubt it is the manuscript with that title mentioned above. The bulk of this last has been published under the title *Prototractatus* (*PT*, Routledge 1971, 1996). I can offer no firm hypothesis as to the identity of the remaining manuscripts, except that the three typescripts mentioned are surely those discovered by Mr. and Mrs. John Stonborough in Gmunden in the 1970s, which I myself conveyed to Rush Rhees for deposit in Trinity College Library. They belong to the period of putting together von Wright's no. 213, which is rather confusingly referred to as the Big Typescript, since there are three exemplars of it and anterior to it there was yet another typescript which is bigger. What is usually meant is the latest revision of the material of which we have earlier versions here.

The items listed, or those identifiable, were probably regarded as having their natural home in Vienna[6] and to some extent had already

---

5 McGuinness 1989, pp. 33–4, also reprinted in the present volume, see Chapter 23 above.
6 A slight confirmation of this supposition is that the other numbered series of notebooks from the same period bear the inscription 'C [for Cambridge] 1–8' (Mss 145–52).

served their purpose, in that their content was incorporated in a published work (the *Tractatus*) or had been digested into typescripts that he could take to Norway or to Cambridge and these typescripts in turn had been further digested. But they, and the *Ms-Bände* in particular, were his copy of record, which he now wished to put in a place of safety. This account indicates his pattern of work down to 1936 – writing in Cambridge and on the family estate, the Hochreit, followed by dictation in Vienna (or occasionally also on the Hochreit). We shall see another example of this shortly. In the present case we can certainly exclude any further use of these manuscripts for Wittgenstein's later compositions, since it turned out that he no longer had access to them. Thus to cite them as 'sources' for *Philosophical Investigations* would be only mediately true.

The pattern of work changed in 1935, when Wittgenstein did not go back to the Hochreit for the summer but travelled instead to Russia with the idea, never realized, of starting a new life there. In the summer of 1936 he was again absent from the Hochreit since he went to Norway, still with the idea of first finishing his book and then leaving philosophy. His Trinity Fellowship had already run out. Of the progress of his work in Norway we shall speak shortly, but at this point only say that in the winter of 1937 he no longer felt able to face the solitude and darkness of Norway and that after spending Christmas with his family in Vienna he returned to the British Isles.

At this point it is instructive to consider the other collection of Wittgenstein's papers, which came to light only in 1995, namely that entrusted to Rudolf Koder by Mrs Stonborough, and released after the death of Koder's widow. These have been described in an article by Professor Johannes Koder[7] and so I can here list, and that summarily, only those that throw some light on my inquiry. These are:

1 A manuscript of the 'Lecture on Ethics' (*LE*), no doubt the missing no. 139b in von Wright's numeration (originally dated, erroneously, to 1929). This was evidently the manuscript promised to Mrs Stonborough in 1931.[8] It is a duplicate of 139a, containing fewer corrections and second thoughts, so perhaps is the final version used for the delivery of the lecture.

2 A manuscript of 'Philosophische Untersuchungen', labelled by Wittgenstein as having been begun in Norway in 1936 and containing the dedication 'Gretl von Ludwig/zu Weihnachten 1936/ein schlechtes Geschenk' ('To Gretl from Ludwig/for Christmas 1936/a poor

---

7 In Koder 1993.
8 Letter of November 1931, not printed in *FB*.

present').[9] It is clearly the manuscript with that title which von Wright saw in 1952 but could not find again in 1965 and to which he provisionally assigned the number 142. It will be commented on below.

3 A 'Tagebuch' containing remarks of a personal nature dating in part from 1930–1 (in Cambridge), in part from 1936–7 (in Norway).[10]

4 A typescript of 'Logisch-philosophische Abhandlung', basically identical with the Engelmann typescript in the Bodleian Library, Oxford (von Wright no. 202), but with fewer manuscript corrections. (It also exhibits a couple of other peculiarities.) This may be the typescript that von Wright saw in 1952 and called the Gmunden typescript (no. 204), despite the fact that it has not got attached to it a typescript of Russell's introduction, as was the case, in von Wright's recollection, at Gmunden. It has some association interest since it was certainly the copy sent to Frege and probably also the copy fruitlessly sent first to Ficker then to Reclam with a view to publication.[11]

5 Miscellaneous pieces of paper including two pages, each torn out of a large school exercise book and containing a dream-description by Wittgenstein (no doubt dating from the first half of the 1920s when he was a schoolmaster).[12]

One is bound to speculate why, sometime between 1952, when von Wright saw some of them, and 1958, when Mrs Stonborough died, just these items were entrusted to Koder and not any of the other manuscripts (such as those in the first group we considered) that were in her possession. Perhaps more than one factor was at work. On the one hand items 3 and 5 were highly private documents, and Mrs Stonborough, as she explained to F.A. von Hayek in May 1953,[13] was strongly opposed to any investigation into the life rather than the work of her brother. 'Eine biographische Skizze in

---

9 Mrs Stonborough wrote to her brother from Vienna in December 1936 looking forward to seeing him at Christmas and to receiving a manuscript as a present: *FB*, p. 154.

10 This has been edited by Dr Ilse Somavilla and published as *Denkbewegungen (Db)*.

11 It has, supplied in manuscript, the missing page that Frege asked for at the beginning of 1919 (*FB*, pp. 53ff.) The hand is that of Wittgenstein's companion in captivity Ludwig Hänsel who must have copied the 'Engelmann' typescript then at Cassino. Curiously enough this 'Koder' typescript is the one originally given to Engelmann. It was he who sent it to Frege (and was blamed for losing p. 10) and then later sent it to Ficker, with the warning that it was not the *Druckmanuskript* ('copy for the printer' is meant: this note is in Engelmann's hand). Later Wittgenstein must have given Engelmann MS 203, which was the *Druckmanuskript* for the Ostwald printing and contains also (a copy of) the corrections for the Kegan Paul printing.

12 Similar dream descriptions seem to have been available to W.W. Bartley III when he wrote his *Wittgenstein* (Bartley 1973). His interpretations are necessarily fanciful, as, no doubt, were those of Wittgenstein and his sister.

13 In a letter shown to the present writer by Hayek.

der von seiner Kindheit, von Familien Geschichte, Elternhaus oder Milieu die Rede ist hätte er zornig und entsetzt abgewehrt.' (He would have rejected with scorn and anger a biographical sketch with talk about his childhood, family history, his home or milieu.) Now that he was dead regard for his outlook on life demanded of his friends and family 'ein ernstes Schweigen' (a respectful silence): 'I feel very deeply about that', – she added in English. It is consentaneous with this attitude that she wanted to put the documents we are considering into the hands of someone she trusted to share her views. Members of her own family might have other ideas and the practice of confiding more in friends than in relations was one she shared with her brother Ludwig, who often entrusted delicate tasks or information to Hänsel or indeed Koder. In a related matter and at much the same time, Mrs Stonborough went further, for she burnt all her brother's letters and pointedly told one of her sons that she had done so.

The other items were keepsakes of particular emotional value, the most immediate contact with his work that her brother could give her. Moreover they had been specifically given to her whereas (we must suppose) she did not regard other manuscripts or typescripts as her property even if they were deposited in one of her houses.

Of the items above the second throws by far the most light on Wittgenstein's philosophical work and its development, particularly when studied in combination with contemporary typescripts, especially 220 and its pendant 239, and letters to and from Wittgenstein. It contains in manuscript essentially the same material that we now have in the first 189 sections of *Philosophical Investigations*. I use italics to refer to published works and roman between quotation marks to refer to manuscript titles or to works that were projected by the author. We cannot assume that he was constantly guided towards the texts now published, as Aeneas was towards Italy.

In 142, then, there is a note by the author's hand that the composition of these 'Philosophische Untersuchungen' was begun at the beginning of ('Angefangen anfangs') November 1936. At this date Wittgenstein was in Norway. Von Wright conjectures that it was ended in December 1936, but it is a little difficult to imagine that these 157 much revised pages were composed in so short a time and in fact some of the material clearly dates from 1937 on the evidence of dated entries in a notebook Ms 157b in which Wittgenstein assembled material for entry in 142.[14] The corresponding part of *Philosophical Investigations* consists in large part of passages for which von Wright himself can find no earlier manuscript source, so that 142 was not the product simply of copying from material

14 A reference I owe to Dr.Pichler (the entry is from February).

composed earlier than 1936. I give below what, I think, are convincing external reasons to date the manuscript's closure to December 1937.

Mrs Stonborough did indeed write to her brother from Vienna in December 1936[15] looking forward to seeing him at Christmas and to receiving a manuscript as a present. This may have been the manuscript intended though it will hardly have been very far advanced at that point. But whatever manuscript was then intended, the handing over of this one had to wait for the next Christmas. It is here that typescript 220 may enlighten us. It is so similar in content to 142 that we can suppose Wittgenstein to have dictated the one from the other, as was his wont, seeking greater intelligibility and deciding between alternatives. He also altered the numbering of the remarks or groups of remarks. (A different set of alterations appears in 239, which is in part a carbon copy, in part the top-copy, of 220.)

When did this dictation take place and where? Another letter from Mrs Stonborough to her brother before Christmas the next year[16] suggests an answer. She asks whether he will once again dictate, mentioning how she had enjoyed it before and the hot soup that went along with it. Further Wittgenstein's pocket diaries for the academic years 1936–7 and 1937–8 respectively show a large number of sessions with 'Gretl' (as Mrs Stonborough was known in the family) in May and again in December 1937, the two occasions later than Christmas 1936 when Wittgenstein was back in Vienna from Norway. In passing we may note that Wittgenstein often found it a valuable stimulus to have the right person with him when he dictated. In 1913 it was Russell, in the 1930s he dictated to particular pupils: when there was a cooling in his relations with Miss Ambrose, dictation had to stop, because with Skinner alone he felt unable to go on.

In the typescript 220, which we suppose to be the result of this dictation, we can trace three distinct stages. Three different machines were used, though machines and stages are not coterminous. The opening, in fact a revised opening, is typed on pages i–iii, on a smaller paper size and with a typewriter not provided with the umlaut sign, presumably an English machine. Pages 2–45 and 46–65 are typed on two distinct machines, but since there is no break of sense between them I assume that the change of typewriter was due to some trivial technical or clerical difficulty. Together these 64 pages correspond to pp. 2–76 of the manuscript, whereas the revised opening mentioned above is given precisely on pp. 77–8 of the manuscript. Pages 66–137 of the typescript, taken from the remainder of the manuscript, are again typed with the first of the 'German' machines. The 'English' machine must have been in Cambridge, since it was once

---

15 *FB*, p. 154.
16 *FB*, p. 159.

again used to produce the preface that Wittgenstein dictated (from one or more previous drafts) in August 1938. (The above hypotheses can be verified, or so I judge, by viewing the images of the typescripts in the Bergen electronic edition of Wittgenstein's papers.)[17]

It is natural to suppose therefore that Wittgenstein dictated pp. *1 (the missing original opening) and 2–65 of the typescript in May, took the manuscript and typescript with him to Cambridge, where he was in June and July, and only then wrote the new opening on p. 77–8 of 142 (otherwise he could have had it re-typed in Vienna) and produced 220 pp. i–iii. The original introduction (p.*1) must have contained a considerably shorter version of the first two or three sections, since they there fitted on half a page, but this can be accounted for by the fact that both the quotation from St. Augustine and the opening two paragraphs are considerably shorter in the opening, superseded pages of 142.

It was at latest during the summer that Wittgenstein completed the manuscript as we have it. I say this because once back in Norway, from August 1937, he was engaged on the continuation of it which he later dictated into typescript 221/239. It is a slight puzzle that he at no point inserted this material into 142 itself. Possibly he did not have that manuscript with him but had for some reason sent it back to Vienna in May. In any case, on my hypothesis, it was the second part precisely of 142 (pp. 78, 91–167 of the manuscript, pp. 66–137 of the typescript) that he dictated in Vienna in December. In October he had thought of arranging future dictation in England, sending his companion Skinner to their friends the Pascals[18] to find a typist, but this project seems to have been fruitless.[19] It shows incidentally that Wittgenstein had as yet no regular typist in Cambridge and confirms the production of the first half of 220 in Vienna (and the end, as we have seen, was typed on the same machine and hence also in Vienna).

After the dictation he left the manuscript in the hands of his sister and took the typescript away with him to the British Isles. I say 'the typescript' but there were at least two exemplars, 220 and, as we have seen, the typescript discovered later and given the von Wright number 239 (which number, no doubt, is meant to reflect the date of some of the corrections in it): its peculiarities do not concern us, except that it has undergone a renumbering distinct from that of 226 and that Rhees's

---

17 *Nl* on CD-Rom. The relevant facsimiles are to be found on Image Disc 1.

18 Roy Pascal was a university lecturer in German, previously in Cambridge, then in Birmingham; his wife Fania was Wittgenstein's (and Skinner's) Russian teacher.

19 This letter of Skinner's (14 October 1937) I have been able to consult by courtesy of the Brenner Archiv of Innsbruck University and Dr. Monika Seekircher in particular. The same applies to letters subsequently quoted unless otherwise indicated.

translation of part of the material (226) presupposes some but not all of the corrections present in it (but not in 220).[20]

I pause in the sequence of events to say that Dr Schulte[21] believes that the dictation from 142 was begun in December 1936 and was complete by May 1937. This does indeed fit the fact, mentioned above, that from August 1937 on Wittgenstein was engaged on subsequent work and (apparently) did not have with him the manuscript 142, but it raises biographical (and codicological) difficulties. Over Christmas of 1936 our sources mention no dictation and Wittgenstein was passionately involved in another and painful matter: that of his confessions. The same is true of the January days that he spent in Cambridge (except that he was there further disabled for some time by flu). In neither place had he the leisure, or I imagine, the taste for dictation. In any case some of the dictation (and if some all) must have been done in Vienna. All in May, therefore? Possibly, but in that case what dictation was it that took place in December 1937?[22] Not that of 221, the material for which was not complete, and which in any case was not produced on either of the Vienna machines.

To return to the beginning of 1938: Wittgenstein's next actions were rather unpredictable. At some point in January 1938, that is to say immediately, he sought permission to deposit his papers in Trinity College Library.[23] He seems to have decided that it was impossible for him to complete or even to continue his book and this was the understanding of the Trinity authorities at the time. It is a paradox rather typical of its author that the book (220/239) breaks off just when he is discussing the continuation of a series. (Of course there was further material present in his papers, which he had been working on until November and these he seems to have thought might be useful in the future.) It is also typical that he did not announce this important decision to anyone that we know of – typical in that other important moves, such as returning to Cambridge in 1929 or remaining in Norway in 1913, equally came as a surprise to his friends.

As in many of his decisions, or perhaps of human decisions generally, it is difficult to isolate one factor as determinant. That he felt unable to stay on in Norway is clear from his occasional diary entries, and in a letter to Pattisson in the autumn[24] he had announced a return to Cambridge or

---

20 Dr Pichler and Dr Schulte have independently pointed this out to me.
21 In correspondence, but his grounds for his views will no doubt be given in the edition of *PhI* in German that he is preparing.
22 As in other instances I discount the hypothesis of a lost typescript: Ockham's law is the best guide in this field too.
23 *CL*, p. 288.
24 Not more precisely datable.

Dublin. In itself that would not have prevented him from working on philosophy – in Ireland if Cambridge again proved unsuitable. He had savings, which could have supported him for a year or more. The main factor must have been dissatisfaction with the progress of his thoughts or at least the effectiveness of his writing, which we know he thought inferior to that of his teaching in person. The greatest philosophical interest perhaps attaches to the question whether there was a particular difficulty arising at this point in the argument. I should mention here the hypothesis of Baker and Hacker in their admirable discussion of the preface to *Philosophical Investigations*[25] that the reason he abandoned hope of publication at about this time was the difficulty of grafting on to 220/221 (which they call 'PPI' – Proto-Philosophical Investigations) his reflections on rule following, necessity and possibility. This seems improbable given that the natural continuation of the 142 material was already written out in his *Ms-Bände* and, as we shall see, he had little initial difficulty in continuing when he decided to do so.[26]

I do not want to rehearse here all the ways in which the events of 1938 affected Wittgenstein. In the whole course of his life, for reasons of birth as well as of character, he had enjoyed freedom of choice. It may even be doubted whether this was entirely a good thing for him: perhaps (to adapt a perceptive remark of his about a protégée) 'his freedom was his curse'. At this point, however, the fate of Austria was to make a continuation of university life the only sensible option for him. Against his will, or his professed will, he found that he had best stay in England, that he ought to apply for naturalization and that some sort of post would help him to obtain it. Thus he found himself once again involved in teaching and discussions in Cambridge: the move away from philosophy had not taken place. Later in the year the prospect, never previously envisaged, of succeeding to Moore's chair opened up. It was imperative for him to have such a post. The University had already given notice that it could not continue for a further year the small payments it made for his lectures, which gave him a slender title of employment in Britain. In this context to finish and publish his book must have seemed highly desirable and we find him showing it to Keynes and Moore when he applied for the chair. But he had already given other reasons for changing his mind about its opportuneness: for we find him writing to Rush Rhees on 13 July 1938:

---

25 *op. cit.* p. 23.

26 Baker and Hacker (1980) say we can see the strains (arising from this grafting) in *PhI* §189ff., but that is to adopt the 'Aeneid' view of the genesis of the book. The 'strains' may well arise because §189 is not here followed by its original planned continuation, which we should look for in TS 221.

The gist of it is that I am thinking of publishing something before long after all so as to end the constant misunderstandings and misinterpretations. I very much want to talk the business over with you. Please forgive my fickleness or, at any rate, suspend your judgement until you've had another talk with me.

A month later we have his preface (225, typed on the same machine as 220, i–iii) in which he says (in a passage still used, with slight variations, in the 1945 preface printed in *Philosophical Investigations*):

> Up to a short time ago I had really given up the idea of publishing *[these remarks]* in my lifetime. *But the idea has been revived* mainly by the fact that I *have been* obliged to learn that *the results of my work*, which I had communicated *orally, in lectures and discussions*, more or less mangled or watered down, were in circulation. – This stung my vanity *and continually threatened to rob me of peace of mind, unless I put the matter to rest (at least as far as I myself was concerned) by a publication of those results. And such seemed in other respects the most desirable course.*

I here follow the translation published in *Philosophical Investigations*, except where the 1938 text and context require a change, which I then print in italics. And what was that context? The whole series of events that I have related above suggests that it was at the beginning of 1938 that Wittgenstein gave up the plan of publishing, and thus in the course of that year that he changed his mind in favour of publishing. A change indeed is signalled in the letter to Rhees just quoted, but I think we can be more precise about the source of Wittgenstein's fears about misrepresentation of his work by others. We must look for some new element in the year 1938, since earlier fears or resentment (say about Braithwaite or Ambrose or Wisdom) had not sufficed to hold him to his design of publication.

The element peculiar to the year 1938 can perhaps be found in the presence in Cambridge of Waismann, who had arrived as a visitor, though virtually a refugee. He was soon actually to become such, as a result of the German annexation of Austria. We know that this was a year in which the relations between him and Wittgenstein changed for the worse in a way that was painful for both. Waismann had with him the text of his long projected survey of 'our philosophy', as he thought of it (meaning that professed by Wittgenstein, Schlick and himself), and was arranging for its publication in German as well as for its translation into English. Some material from it he also used for his Cambridge lectures. Precisely in July, the month of the letter to Rhees, the Joint Session of the Aristotelian Society and the Mind Association was held at Oxford. The occasion was the most public one in the English, or even British, philosophical year: at the corresponding event in 1929 Wittgenstein had, with some reluctance, sung his own cavatina. This year Waismann contributed to the discussion of 'Is Psychology relevant to Logic?' with a piece that was heavily dependent on Wittgenstein's thought.

It is idle to discuss the rights and wrongs of the disagreement: the two men were moving on totally different planes, each with an attitude and a justification totally intelligible to himself and unintelligible to the other. Wittgenstein saw Waismann, the first to be invited to work with him, as now the chief invader and spoiler of his ideas. We can infer this from the attitude of Wittgenstein's pupils, as when James Taylor, who had been closely associated with Wittgenstein in that year, wrote from Berkeley (24 September 1938) describing his own teaching:

> Thanks to you I'm clearer about some things than these people [his colleagues] have had a chance to be. I don't use things you've said, as Waismann, say, does, or Schlick did sometimes, directly; and if I do use a phrase or an example or an idea of yours, which I try to do as seldom as possible, I mention that it is yours.

No matter that Waismann of course saw things from a different point of view: this is how they were seen by Wittgenstein, so that, along with external circumstances, Waismann's book, which in the event was not to appear until both men were dead, may have played a part in the genesis of Wittgenstein's: one nail driving out another.

But what book was it that Wittgenstein now planned? Was it to consist simply of the content of 220/239 and was it to be called 'Philosophische Untersuchungen'? Neither of these things seems to be the case. He spoke to Taylor (for example) of publishing a small volume, but 220/239 would not have reached even to that. Moreover he took seriously his own confession that what he wrote could never be more than remarks, *Bemerkungen,* and 'Philosophische Bemerkungen/Philosophical Remarks' was the title proposed to Cambridge University Press. For details of the publishing history I refer to von Wright,[27] though I am surprised that he is surprised at the change of title. After all the work did not have to be called 'Philosophical Investigations'. Perhaps the composition of 142 and the subsequent work on what became 221 was now seen by Wittgenstein as a sort of compromise, an attempt to produce a summary account of his thoughts since his revisions of larger existing typescripts were running into sand.

A small volume would indeed have been produced by putting together 220/239 (or a corrected copy of it) with 221 (ditto), and the two typescripts

---

27 *Op. cit.* pp. 112–136.

are paginated consecutively (though as we have seen 221 was not produced on the same machine as any part of 220). If that were not enough we should take into account the fact that shortly after approaching the Press, and having given 239 to Rhees for translation, Wittgenstein spent much time with typists, as his pocket diary shows: 23 hours in all between 1 and 7 November 1938. We also have in a letter of roughly this date a reference to a visit to Miss Pate's office, the legendary university typing office where Frank Ramsey had once dictated a translation of the *Tractatus*. The typing may have been organized through that office, if not executed there.

We can take it as established that the bulk of 221 was typed at this period, with a view to making up the book Wittgenstein was to publish. Probably few people still believe that the contents of 220/239 alone were to constitute that book but all can see that it is inconceivable that Wittgenstein would have started on an independent typing project at just that time. The bulk of the material used (though reordered) could have been drawn from manuscripts that Wittgenstein had had with him in Norway.[28]

The book was evidently still on course for publication when Wittgenstein sent the preface to Taylor in February 1939, and in September 1939 he meant to complete it: indeed it must have been substantially complete since he wanted to send a copy to von Wright in Finland.[29] The risk of loss at such a period unfortunately prevented its despatch; else we might still have a corrected copy today and not merely the first draft (220/239 and 221) plus some reorderings of the latter, whose date and authority is dubious.[30]

I will not pursue further the fortunes of the projected book. I comment merely on some implications of the fact that it was projected in this form. It is true that Wittgenstein was later dissatisfied with this compilation and began to rewrite and rearrange it, particularly, as we have seen, the second part. We must take into account what Waismann discovered, that Wittgenstein was rarely content with his own work when he returned to it. There is a certain parallel in Schumann, who sometimes cancelled some of his best passages, three or four songs, for example, from *Dichterliebe*. In Wittgenstein's case the tendency is perhaps due to the indeterminate literary form of his writings after the *Tractatus*. Nothing has to be where it is, so anything can be moved to a better place. We have already suggested that there are disadvantages in freedom. The

---

28 Dr Schulte tells me that it is largely drawn from 117 and 118, without extensive revision or even rearrangement.

29 In letters of 24 February 1939 and 13 September 1939 respectively.

30 No doubt Dr Schulte's forthcoming edition will throw light on these.

final result may nonetheless attain (or in parts attain) a certain harmony, as Baker and Hacker, I believe, show.

At all events these typescripts do not – or, since it is so paginated, we may say this typescript does not – belong to the category of those that he commissioned simply in order to facilitate overview, revision and rearrangement of material. That category certainly exists and we find him avowing such a purpose in a letter to von Wright of 6 November 1947:

> I'm dictating some of the stuff which I wrote during the last 2–3 years. It's mostly bad but I've got to have it in a handy form, i.e. typewritten, because it may possibly give rise to better thoughts when I read it.

An example would be what I once called 'Extrakt der Manuskriptbücher' (211), which can be contrasted with the clean version of 213, the so-called 'Big Typescript', which was a projected work like 220–1.[31] Other working typescripts are probably the two sets 'Bemerkungen I' and 'Bemerkungen II' (228 and 230), whereas 227 (now Part I of *Philosophische Untersuchungen*) was surely a projected work, though quaere whether a complete one. One might even say that the early 'Notes on Logic' was a working document, whereas its rearrangement by Russell (or Costello on Russell's behalf) was a projected work: that is to say a form of publication was envisaged, if only that of distribution to Russell's class at Harvard. 'Notes dictated to Moore' was perhaps also a projected work, in that Wittgenstein may have hoped that (perhaps together with 'Notes on Logic') it would serve as his BA thesis. *Philosophische Bemerkungen* is a hybrid case: he put it in very limited circulation, showing it to Russell, Moore and Littlewood when he had to produce some evidence for a fellowship, but it can never have been thought to be the final phase of anything. It even begins, as is well known, with a reference back to something that was earlier in the *MS-Bände*, its source, but is mentioned only later in this set of extracts.

Perhaps the most valid approach to the mass of material that Wittgenstein left to his literary executors and to us would be to concentrate on the projected works (wherever these are available) and to regard the working papers as a guide to them. Notebook entries, a yet earlier phase, are still more obviously to be treated as background material. In particular the recording of alternatives or of alterations, *pentimenti*, so to speak, is of interest chiefly when there are particular difficulties of understanding (this is rare) or questions about the order in which his ideas

---

31 For the concept of a 'work' of Wittgenstein's I am indebted to discussions with Dr. Schulte.

came to Wittgenstein. In this respect it is significant that much of the work of dictation from 142 into 220 consisted in choosing between a number of alternatives. It was related of Plato in antiquity that he had re-written the first sentence of his *Republic* many times and indeed died with the tablet containing the final version in his hands. Wittgenstein seems to have polished the opening of the work we are considering with almost equal assiduity.[32] His aim must have been to confront the reader not with choices that would delay and fragment his reading, but much rather with the most natural and smooth expression of the author's thought. The dictation finished, Wittgenstein could leave the manuscript with his sister and we can leave the rejected alternatives to supplementary volumes.

For these reasons the short projected work we have described deserves attention, and fortunately modern methods allow it to be reconstructed and read very easily from the Bergen electronic edition already referred to. 'Philosophische Bemerkungen (1938)', as we have proposed to call it may serve as a corrective to a perhaps excessive emphasis in *Philosophische Untersuchungen* on problems connected with psychology. The book projected in 1945 seems to have been what is now called Part I, and that it should be so called is in a way right, for Wittgenstein thought of it as a first volume only. A second volume would clearly have contained the more mathematical discussions (though there is not a very clear distinc-tion of topic). It is interesting that the package containing a surviving copy of typescript 227 (from which the text of 'Part I' is taken: the actual *Druckmanuskript* is lost) is labelled 'Philosophie der Psychologie'. The title 'Philosophical Investigations'[33] was always meant to cover the mathemat-ical material as well. More important for Wittgenstein than either subject matter was the philosophical method he had developed. In the work that forms the hypothesis of the present paper he endeavours to present this more nakedly. The fascinations and distractions of the Private Language Argument form an important part of his message but are not at its root.

---

32 See, à propos, Pichler 1997.

33 The titles 'Philosophical Investigations', 'Remarks', 'Grammar', etc. such as we now have are slightly absurd, since any of these names might be attached to any of the works concerned. Ideally dates might instead be attached to a uniform title. 'Remarks on the Foundations of Mathematics' has some authority as a title (*PhI* pt II, p. 232, which however gives more support to 'Investigation(s) etc.'). It leaves me uneasy, since Wittgenstein did not believe that mathematics had foundations and, as pointed out in the text above, Wittgenstein did not consider these investigations distinct from his other philosophical ones. 'On Certainty' and 'Remarks on Colour' can of course be justified (though why 'Remarks' in the one case and not in the other?). The title 'Zettel' seems to suggest some-thing unique to Wittgenstein or at any rate unknown to the English-speaking world: 'Cuttings', 'Slips', or 'Fragments' would be a more explanatory title.

BIBLIOGRAPHY

Anscombe, G.E.M., *An Introduction to Wittgenstein's Tractatus*, Hutchinson, London 1959.

Anscombe, G.E.M. and Geach, P.T., *Three Philosophers*, Blackwell, Oxford 1961.

Anscombe, G.E.M., Rhees, R. and von Wright, G.H., 'A Note on Costello's Version of the *Notes on Logic*' in *Journal of Philosophy*, 54: 1957.

Anzengruber, Ludwig, *Die Kreuzelschreiber*, Gotta, Stuttgart 1910.

Baker, Gordon, and Hacker P.M.S. (eds), *Wittgenstein, Understanding and Meaning*, Blackwell, Oxford 1980.

Bartley III, W.W., *Wittgenstein*, Lippincott, New York 1973.

Becker, Oskar, 'Mathematische Existenz' in *Jahrbuch für Philosophie und phänomenologische Forschung*, 1927.

Berlin, Isaiah, *Tra filosofia e storia delle idee*, S. Lukes (ed.), Ponte alle Grazie, Florence 1992.

Bettelheim, Samuel (ed.), unsigned article, 'Aus der Geschichte der Juden in Waldeck', *Judaica* 5–6, 1935.

Bezzel, Chris (*et al.*), *Wittgenstein: Biographie, Philosophie, Praxis*, vol. 1 (catalogue of an exhibition) Wiener Secession, Vienna, 1989.

Biggs, Michael, *Editing Wittgenstein's 'Notes on Logic'*, 2 vols, Working Papers from the Wittgenstein Archives at the University of Bergen, Bergen 1996.

Black, Max, *A Companion to Wittgenstein's Tractatus*, Cambridge University Press, Cambridge 1964.

Blackmore, John, *Ludwig Boltzmann, His Later Life and Philosophy*, 2 vols, Kluwer, Dordrecht 1995.

Boltzmann, Ludwig, *Populäre Schriften*, Barth, Leipzig 1905, English translation *Theoretical Physics and Philosophical Problems*, Vienna Circle Collection, Reidel, Dordrecht 1974.

Bolz, Robert, notice of German translation of McGuinness 1988, in *Philosophische Rundschau*, Tübingen 1992.

Brouwer, L.E.J., 'Mathematik, Wissenschaft und Sprache', in *Monatshefte für Mathematik und Physik* 39, 1929.

Butler, Samuel, *Erewhon, or Over the Range*, H.P. Breuer and D.F. Howard (eds), Associated University Presses, London 1981.

Carnap, Rudolph, *Der Logische Aufbau der Welt*, Weltkreis Verlag, Berlin 1928.

—— 'Die physikalische Sprache als Universalsprache der Wissenschaft', in *Erkenntnis 2*, 1932.

—— *The Unity of Science*, English translation by Max Black of Carnap 1932, Kegan Paul, London 1934.

—— *The Logical Syntax of Language*, Kegan Paul, London 1937.

—— *The Philosophy of Rudolph Carnap*, P.A. Schilpp (ed.), Open Court, London 1963.

—— *The Logical Structure of the World*, English translation by R.A. George of Carnap 1928, Routledge and Kegan Paul, London 1967.

Dummett, Michael, *Frege, Philosophy of Language*, Duckworth, London 1973.

Engelmann, Paul, *Letters from Ludwig Wittgenstein with a Memoir*, Blackwell, Oxford 1967.

—— *Ludwig Wittgenstein. Briefe und Begegnungen*, Oldenbourg, Vienna and Munich 1970.

Ernst, Paul, 'Nachwort' in vol. 3 of J. and W. Grimm's *Kinder- und Hausmärchen*, Georg Müller, Leipzig 1910.

Fasol-Boltzman, I.M. (ed.) *Ludwig Boltzmann: Principien der Naturfilosofi*, Springer, New York 1990.

Flitch, J.E.C., *Angelus Silesius*, Allen and Unwin, London 1932.

Frege, Gottlob, *Translations from the Philosophical Writings*, P.T. Geach and M. Black (eds), Blackwell, Oxford 1952.

—— *Grundgesetze der Arithmetik*, Georg Olms, Heidelberg 1962.

Freud, Sigmund, *Psychopathology of Everyday Life*, Penguin, Harmondsworth 1975, Blackwell, Oxford, 1952.

—— *Interpretation of Dreams*, Penguin, Harmondsworth 1976.

Freud S. and Breuer J., *Studies on Hysteria*, Hogarth Press, London 1955.

Gabriel, Gottfried, 'Wittgenstein, Weininger und das Wiener Moderne' in *Zwischen Logik und Literatur*, Metzler, Stuttgart 1991.

—— 'Solipsismus' in *Historisches Wörterbuch der Philosophie*, vol. 9, Wissenschaftliche Buchgesellschaft, Darmstadt 1998.

Gardiner, Patrick L., *Schopenhauer*, Penguin, Harmondsworth 1963.

Garver, Newton, *This Complicated Form of Life*, Open Court, Chicago 1994.

Geyser, Josef, 'Beiträge zur logischen und psychologischen Analyse des Urteils' in *Archiv für die gesamte Psychologie* 26: 1913.

Gombrich, Ernst, 'The Visual Arts in Vienna circa 1900 and Reflections on the Jewish Catastrophe', a lecture in *Occasions 1*, Austrian Cultural Institute, London 1997.

Griffin, J.P., *Wittgenstein's Logical Atomism*, Oxford University Press, Oxford 1964.

Hacker, Peter, *Insight and Illusion*, Clarendon Press, Oxford 1972.

—— see also Baker.

Heller, Erich, 'Ludwig Wittgenstein, Unphilosophical Notes' in *Encounter* 72, 1959.

Hertz, Heinrich R., *Die Prinzipien der Mechanik*, in *Gesammelte Werke*, vol. 3, P.E.A. Lenard (ed.), Barth, Leipzig 1894.

—— *Principles of Mechanics*, P.E.A. Lenard (ed.), Macmillan, London 1899 (later edition: Dover, New York, 1956).

Hintikka Jaakko, 'On Wittgenstein's Solipsism' in *Mind* 67: 1958.

—— 'Ludwig's Appletree' in *Traditionen und Perspektiven der analytischen Philosophie. Festschrift für R. Haller,* W.L. Gombocz, H. Rutte and W. Sauer (eds), Hölder Pichler Tempsky, Vienna 1989.

Huxley, Aldous, *The Doors of Perception*, Chatto and Windus, London 1954.

Ishiguro, Hidè, 'Use and Reference of Names' in *Studies in the Philosophy of Wittgenstein*, P. Winch (ed.), Routledge & Kegan Paul, London 1969.

James, William, *The Varieties of Religious Experience*, Longmans, Green and Co., London 1902.

Janik, Allan, 'How did Hertz influence Wittgenstein's Philosophical Development?', in *Grazer Philosophische Studien*, 49: 1994/95.

Jefferies, John Richard, *The Story of my Heart*, Eyre and Spottiswood, London 1949.

Kienzler, Wolfgang, *Wittgensteins Wende zu seiner Spätphilosophie, Eine historische und systematische Darstellung*, Suhrkamp, Frankfurt 1997.

Koder, Johannes, 'Verzeichnis der Schriften Ludwig Wittgensteins im Nachlaß Rudolf und Elisabeth Koder', in *Mitteilungen aus dem Brenner-Archiv* Nr. 12: 1993.

Kreisel, Georg, 'Einige Erläuterungen zu Wittgensteins Kummer mit Hilbert und Gödel' in *Epistemology and Philosophy of Science*, Proceedings of the Seventh International Wittgenstein Symposium, Weingartner and Czermak (eds) 1983.

—— 'Second thoughts around some of Gödel's writings' in *Synthese* 114: 1998.

Kuhn, Thomas S., *The Structure of Scientific Revolutions*, University of Chicago Press, Chicago and London 1962.

Lamb, Horace, *Hydrodynamics*, 3rd edn, Cambridge University Press, Cambridge 1906 (German translation: *Lehrbuch der Hydrodynamik*, Teubner, Leipzig and Berlin 1907).

Laqueur, Walter, (discussion of Viktor Klemperer) 'Ich will Zeugnis ablegen bis zum Letzten Tag' in *Holocaust and Genocide Studies*, Winter 1996.

Leitner, Bernhard, *The Architecture of Ludwig Wittgenstein*, Halifax, London 1973.

Lurie, Yuval, 'The Jew as Parable' in *Iyyun* 37, 1988.

Mach, Ernst, *Knowledge and Error*, B. McGuinness (ed.), transl. P. Foulkes, Vienna Circle Collection, Reidel, Dordrecht 1976.

—— *Principles of the Theory of Heat*, Vienna Circle Collection, Reidel, Dordrecht 1986.

Malcolm, Norman, *Ludwig Wittgenstein, a Memoir*, Oxford University Press, London 1958.

—— see also von Wright.

Mann, Golo, *Geschichte und Geschichten*, S. Fischer, Frankfurt a. M. 1962.

McGuinness, B. and Spelt, P.D.M. 'Marginalia in Wittgenstein's Copy of Lamb's Hydrodynamics', in *Wittgenstein Studien* 2, 2001, pp. 131–148.

McGuinness, Brian, *Wittgenstein, A Life*, vol. 1, Young Ludwig 1889–1921, Duckworth and University of California Press, London 1988.

Medding, W., *Korbach: die Geschichte einer deutschen Stadt*, Stadt Korbach, Korbach 1951.

Meinong, Alexius, *Ueber Annahmen*, 2nd edition, Barth, Leipzig 1910.

Menger, Karl, *Morality Decision and Social Organization*, Vienna Circle Collection, Reidel, Dordrecht 1974 (first published in German as *Moral, Wille und Weltgestaltung*, Springer, Vienna 1934).

—— 'Memories of Moritz Schlick' in *Rationality and Science*, E. Gadol (ed.), Springer Verlag, Vienna 1982.

—— *Reminiscences of the Vienna Circle*, B. McGuinness, L. Golland and A. Sklar (eds), Kluwer, Dordrecht and Boston 1994.

Moore, G.E., 'The Nature of Judgement' in *Mind* 1899.

Mulligan, Kevin (ed.), *Speech Act and Sachverhalt*, Nijhoff, Dordrecht 1987.

Neurath, Otto, 'Physikalismus' in *Scientia*, 50: 1931.

—— *Empiricism and Sociology*, Vienna Circle Collection, Reidel, Dordrecht 1973.

—— *Philosophical Papers 1913–1946*, Vienna Circle Collection, Reidel, Dordrecht 1983.

Ogden, Charles K. and Richards, I.A., *The Meaning of Meaning*, Kegan Paul, London 1923.

Pears, David, *The False Prison,* vol. I, Clarendon Press, Oxford 1987.

Pichler, Alois, *Wittgensteins Philosophische Untersuchungen: Zur Textgenese von PU 1–4*. Bergen: Working Papers from the Wittgenstein Archives at the University of Bergen 14, 1997.

Pinsent, David H., *A portrait of Wittgenstein as a young man: from the diary of David Hume Pinsent, 1912–1914*, G.H. von Wright (ed.), Basil Blackwell, Oxford 1990.

Pfaender, Alexander (ed.) *Münchener philosophische Abhandlungen*, Barth, Leipzig 1911.

Ramsey, Frank, article 'Mathematics: Mathematical Logic' in *Encyclopaedia Britannica*, New Volume 2, 13th edn (3 vols), Encyclopaedia Britannica Company Ltd, London 1926.

—— *The Foundations of Mathematics*, R.B. Braithwaite (ed.), Kegan Paul, London 1931.

Reinach, Adolf, *Sämtliche Werke*, vol. 1, Philosophia, Munich 1989.

Rhees, Rush, 'Some Developments in Wittgenstein's View of Ethics' in *Philosophical Review* LXXIV, 1965.

—— *Discussions of Wittgenstein*, Routledge & Kegan Paul, London 1970.

—— *Ludwig Wittgenstein: Personal Recollections* (revised edition), Oxford University Press, Oxford 1984.

Rieckmann, Jens, 'Zwischen Bewußtsein und Verdrängung/Hofmannsthals jüdisches Erbe' in *Deutsche Vierteljahresschrift 67*, 1993.

Rosen, Charles, *Critical Entertainments*, Harvard University Press, London 2000.

Russell, Bertrand, 'Meinong's Theory of Complexes and Assumptions' in *Mind* 1904.

—— 'On Denoting' in *Mind* 1905.

—— *The Problems of Philosophy*, William & Norgate, London 1912.

—— 'Mysticism and Logic' in *Hibbert Journal* 12: 1914a (also in *Mysticism and Logic and Other Essays*).

—— *Our Knowledge of the External World*, Open Court, Chicago 1914b.

—— 'On the Nature of Acquaintance' in *Monist*, 1914c.

—— 'On the Experience of Time' in *Monist*, 1915.

—— *Mysticism and Logic and Other Essays*, Longmans Green, London 1918.

—— *Principles of Mathematics*, Cambridge University Press, Cambridge 1903, 2nd edition 1937, reprinted 1950.

—— 'Ludwig Wittgenstein' in *Mind 60,* 1951.

—— *Logic and Knowledge: Essays 1901–1950*, R.C. Marsh (ed.), Allen & Unwin, London 1956.

—— *The Autobiography of Bertrand Russell*, Allen & Unwin, London 1967.

—— *Essays in Analysis*, D. Lackey (ed.) Allen & Unwin, London 1973.

—— *Theory of Knowledge, The 1913 Manuscript*, M. Eames and R. Blackwell (eds), Allen & Unwin, London 1984.

Russell B. and Whitehead A.N., *Principia Mathematica*, 3 vols, Cambridge University Press, Cambridge 1913 (2nd edn 1927) (= *Principia Mathematica*).

Savigny, Eike von, *Wittgensteins 'Philosophische Untersuchungen'* Band I, Klosterman, Frankfurt 1988.

Schlick, Moritz, *Allgemeine Erkenntnislehre*, Springer, Berlin 1918 (2nd edn 1925, English translation of 2nd edn: *General Theory of Knowledge*, Springer, Vienna and New York 1974).

Schopenhauer, Arthur, *The World as Will and Idea*, R.B. Haldane and J. Kemp (eds) Trubner, London 1833.

—— 'On Suicide' in *Essays from the Parerga and Paralipomena* (ed. T. Bailey Saunders), Allen & Unwin, London 1951.

Schneider, Ursula, *Paul Engelmann: Architektur, Judentum, Wiener Moderne*, Folio Verlag, Vienna 1999.

Sjögren, Marguerite, *Granny et son temps*, privately printed, Neufchatel 1982.

Sjögren, Cecilia, 'Die Familie' in *Wittgenstein: Biographie, Philosophie, Praxis*, Wiener Secession, Vienna 1989.

Smith, Barry and Künne W. (eds), *Parts and Moments*, Philosophia, Munich 1982.

Stern, J.P., 'Vorwort' in *Wittgenstein: Biographie, Philosophie, Praxis*, Wiener Secession, Vienna 1989.

Stenius, Erik, *Wittgenstein's Tractatus, A Critical Exposition of its Main Lines of Thought*, Blackwell, Oxford 1960.

Stumpf, Carl, 'Erscheinung und psychische Funktionen', in *Abhandlungen der königlichen preussischen Akademie der Wissenschaften* (Berlin) phil-hist Kl. IV 1906.

Timpanaro, Sebastiano, *The Freudian Slip*, NLB, London 1976.

Tolstoy, Lev, *A Confession*, World's Classics edn, London 1940.

—— 'Hadji Murád' in *Iván Ilých and Hadji Murád*, World's Classics edn, London 1935.

—— *Anna Karenina*, World's Classics edn, London 1949.

Toury, Jakob, 'Die Juden im Vormärz' in *Bulletin of the Leo Baeck Institute*, 8, 1965.

—— *Der Eintritt der Juden in das Bürgertum*, Diaspora Research Institute, Tel Aviv 1972.

Tugendhat, Ernst, 'The Meaning of Bedeutung in Frege' in *Analysis* 30, 1970.

Urmson, James O. (ed.), *Concise Encyclopaedia of Western Philosophy and Philosophers*, Hutchinson, London 1960.

von Wright, G.H., 'Wittgenstein's View on Probability' in *Revue Internationale de Philosophie* 23: 1969.

—— (ed.) *Problems in the Theory of Knowledge*, Nijhoff, The Hague 1972 (=1972a).

—— 'Wittgenstein on Certainty' in von Wright 1972a, 47–60 (= 1972b).

—— 'Epistemic Reasoning and the Logic of Epistemic Reasoning' in R. Chisholm, *Logic and Philosophy*, Nijhoff, The Hague 1980.

—— *Wittgenstein*, Blackwell, Oxford 1982.

—— and N. Malcolm (eds) *Wittgensteinian Themes: Essays 1978–1989*, Cornell University Press, Ithaca 1995.

von Wright, G.H., and Malcolm, N., 'Biographical Sketch' in *Ludwig Wittgenstein a Memoir*, Oxford University Press, London 1958.

Waismann, Friedrich, 'Logische Analyse des Wahrscheinlichkeitsbegriffs' in *Erkenntnis* 1: 1930–31, also in *Philosophical Papers*.

—— *Was ist logische Analyse*, (ed. Reitzig) Athenäum, Frankfurt 1973.

—— *Philosophical Papers*, Reidel, Dordrecht 1978.

—— *The Principles of Linguistic Philosophy*, 1st edn., R. Harré (ed.), 2nd edn, G.P. Baker and R. Harré (eds), Macmillan, London 1965, 1997 (in German *Logik, Sprache, Philosophie*, G.P. Baker, B. McGuinness and J. Schulte (eds), Reclam, Stuttgart 1976).

Watson, William H., *On Understanding Physics,* Cambridge University Press, Cambridge 1938.

Weininger, Otto, *Sex and Character*, William Heinemann, London 1906.

—— *Ueber die letzten Dinge*, M. Rappaport (ed.), Braumüller, Vienna und Leipzig 1907.

Wiener Kreis, *Wissenschaftliche Weltauffassung*, Artur Wolf Verlag, Vienna 1929, also in Neurath 1973.

Wijdeveld, Paul, *Ludwig Wittgenstein: Architect*, Thames and Hudson, London and New York 1994.

Williams, Bernard A.O., 'Knowledge and Reasons' in *Problems in the Theory of Knowledge*, G.H. von Wright (ed.), Nijhoff, The Hague 1972.

Wittgenstein, Hermine, *Familienerinnerungen* (typescript circulated privately), Vienna 1944–9.

Wittgenstein, Ludwig

Manuscripts and typescripts are referred to under the numbers given in 'The Wittgenstein Papers' in von Wright 1982.

—— *Briefe, Briefwechsel mit B. Russell etc.*, B. McGuinness and G.H. von Wright (eds), (Band 4 of *Wittgenstein: Schriften*) Suhrkamp, Frankfurt 1980 (= *Briefe*).

—— *Cambridge Letters*, B. McGuinness and G.H. von Wright (eds), Blackwell, Oxford and New York 1995 (= *CL*).

—— *Culture and Value* (G.H. von Wright (ed.), transl. P. Winch: German text in *Vermischte Bemerkungen*, Neubearbeitung, Frankfurt 1994), Oxford, 1980 (= *C&V*).

—— *Denkbewegungen, Tagebücher 1930–32*, I. Somavilla (ed.), Haymon Verlag, Innsbruck 1997 (= *Db*).

—— *Familienbriefe*, B. McGuinness, M.C. Ascher and O. Pfersmann (eds), Hölder-Pichler-Tempsky, Vienna 1996 (= *FB*).

—— *Lectures and Conversations on Aesthetics*, Blackwell, Oxford 1966 (= *LCA*).

—— 'Logical Form' in *Proceedings of the Aristotelian Society,* supp. vol. 9, 1929 also in *PhO* (= *LF*).

—— *Logisch-philosophische Abhandlung/Tractatus Logico-philosophicus* Kritische Edition, B. McGuinness and J. Schulte (eds), Suhrkamp, Frankfurt 1989 (= *LPA*).

—— 'Logisch-philosophische Abhandlung' in *Annalen der Naturphilosophie*, Ostwald 1921 (= 'LPA').

—— *Ludwig Wittgenstein–Ludwig Hänsel: Eine Freundschaft*, I. Somavilla *et al.* (eds), Haymon Verlag, Innsbruck 1994 (= *LH*).

—— *Ludwig Wittgenstein and the Vienna Circle*, Conversations transcribed by F. Waismann, Blackwell, Oxford 1979 (in German: *Ludwig Wittgenstein und der Wiener Kreis*), Blackwell, Oxford 1967 (also Band 3 of *Wittgenstein: Schriften*, Suhrkamp, Frankfurt a. M. 1967) (= *WVC*).

—— *Notebooks 1914–16* (actually 1914–17), G.H. von Wright and G.E.M. Anscombe (eds), Blackwell, Oxford 1st edn 1959, 2nd edn 1979 (= *Nb*): references are to the 1st edn, pagination of *NL* varies, of *NdM* add 1 for the 2nd edn.

—— 'Notes dictated to G.E. Moore in Norway', 1914, printed in *Nb* (= *NdM*).

—— 'Notes on Logic' (translated by B. Russell in autumn 1913, with a note by H.T. Costello) in *Journal of Philosophy* liv, no. 9, 1957, also in *Nb* (= *NL*).

—— *On Certainty*, G.H. von Wright and G.E.M. Anscombe (eds), Blackwell, Oxford 1969 (= *OC*).

—— *Philosophical Grammar*, A. Kenny and R. Rhees (eds), Blackwell, Oxford 1974 (*Philosophische Grammatik*, Suhrkamp, Frankfurt 1984) (= *PhG*).

—— *Philosophical Investigations*, transl. G.E.M. Anscombe, Blackwell, Oxford 1953 (*Philosophische Untersuchungen: Werkausgabe*, Band I, Suhrkamp, Frankfurt 1984) (= *PhI*).

—— *Philosophical Occasions*, J.C. Klagge and A. Nordmann (eds), Hackett, Indianapolis 1993 (= *PhO*).

—— *Philosophical Remarks*, R. Rhees, R. Hargreaves and R. White (eds), Blackwell, Oxford 1975 (*Philosophische Bemerkungen*, Suhrkamp, Frankfurt 1984) (= *PhR*).

—— *Prototractatus*, B. McGuinness, T. Nyberg and G.H. von Wright (eds), Routledge, London 1971, 2nd edn 1996 (= *PT*).

—— *Remarks on Frazer's* Golden Bough, R. Rhees (ed.), Brynmill, Retford 1979 (= *RoF*), earlier and fuller collection 'Bemerkungen über Frazers *The Golden Bough*', *Synthese* 17 (1967) 234–253 (= *BüF*).

—— *Tractatus Logico-Philosophicus*, Kegan Paul, London 1922, 2nd edn 1933; new translation 1959, 2nd edn 1974; German only in LPA (Italian translation by G.C. Colombo, S.J. Fratelli Bocca Milano, 1954) (= *TLP* or *Tractatus*).

—— 'Wittgenstein's Lecture on Ethics' in *Philosophical Review*, LXXIV 1965, also in *PhO* (= *LE*).

—— *Wittgenstein's Nachlass*, Oxford 1998, on CD-Rom (= *Nl*).

Zaehner, Robert C., *Mysticism, Sacred and Profane*, Clarendon Press, Oxford 1957.

Zemach, Eddy M., 'Wittgenstein's Philosophy of the Mystical' in *Review of Metaphysics* 18: 38–57, 1964.

Zweig, Max, *Lebenserinnerungen*, Bleicher, Gerlingen 1992.

Zweig, Stefan, *The World of Yesterday*, Cassell Co., London 1943.

—— *Die Welt von Gestern*, Fischer, Berlin 1955.

INDEX OF NAMES

Note: Italic type indicates a citation that appears only in the footnotes